SOUTHERNERS
A Journalist's Odyssey

SOUTHERNERS

A Journalist's Odyssey
by Marshall Frady

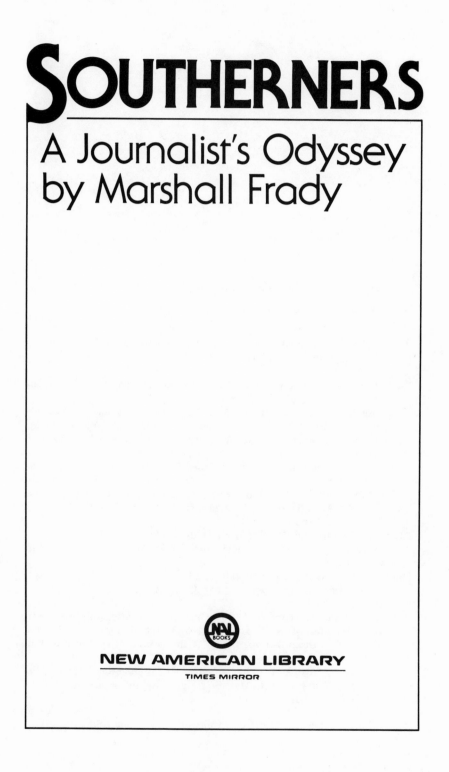

NEW AMERICAN LIBRARY

TIMES MIRROR

"The Judgment of Jesse Hill Ford," from *Life*, October 29, 1971, "The Continuing Trial of Jesse Hill Ford," © Marshall Frady

"What Happened That Summer to Warren Fortson," from *Atlanta Magazine*, July, 1969, "The Propitious Prime of Warren Fortson," © Marshall Frady

"A Meeting of Strangers in Americus," from *Life*, February 12, 1971, "Small Victories in Americus, © Marshall Frady

"An Alabama Marriage," from *New Times*, March 8, 1974, "Tassy and Johnny Are Lovers . . . and the South Will Never Be the Same Again," © Marshall Frady

"A Question of Plastics in Beaufort County," from *Harper's*, May, 1970, "The View from Hilton Head." © Marshall Frady

"Tracking Sin in the New South," from *Esquire*, December, 1975, "The Private Eye," © Marshall Frady

"The Technician from Plains," from *New Times*, February 20, 1976, "The Democrats: In Search of a Hero," © Marshall Frady; and from *The New York Review of Books*, May 18, 1978, "Why He's Not the Best," © Marshall Frady

"Travels with Brother Will," from *Life*, June 16, 1972, "Fighter for Forgotten Men," © Marshall Frady

Introduction to "The South Domesticated" from *Newsweek*, July 28, 1975, "My Turn," © Marshall Frady

 NAL BOOKS TRADEMARK REG. U.S. PAT. OFF. AND FOREIGN COUNTRIES
REGISTERED TRADEMARK—MARCA REGISTRADA
HECHO EN CRAWFORDSVILLE, INDIANA, U.S.A.

SIGNET, SIGNET CLASSICS, MENTOR, PLUME, MERIDIAN and NAL BOOKS are published by The New American Library, Inc., 1633 Broadway, New York, New York 10019

Designed by Julian Hamer

Library of Congress Cataloging in Publication Data

Frady, Marshall.
    Southerners, a journalist's odyssey.

    1. Southern States—Civilization—Addresses, essays,
lectures.   2. Southern States—Biography—Addresses,
essays, lectures.   3. Politicians—Southern States—
Biography—Addresses, essays, lectures.   4. Southern
States—Politics and government—1951–   —Addresses,
essays, lectures.   5. Southern States—race relations—
Addresses, essays, lectures.   I. Title.
F216.2.F7   975   80-18756
ISBN 0-453-00387-7 (pbk.)

First Printing, September, 1980

1 2 3 4 5 6 7 8 9

PRINTED IN THE UNITED STATES OF AMERICA

This book is dedicated, with gratitude and love,
to my mother, Jean Bolton Frady,
and to my father, J. Yates Frady

Contents

THE SOUTH DOMESTICATED 279

Introduction

As a magazine journalist and a Southerner myself, I have been writing about, and out of, the South—this peculiar dream-province of the Republic—with some regularity since 1965. That was the way this book took form—through a series of sojourns beyond the boom of headlines into particular and individual episodes of trouble and glory and farce. Thereby it has wound up not so much an academic and systematic assessment of Southern society as a sequence of tales which happen to be true. For the most part it proceeds from those already familiar insights from such classic commentators as W. J. Cash, James McBride Dabbs, and C. Vann Woodward, who have approximated the truth of the Southern experience probably as closely as we can ever comprehend the real shape and pitch of the mysteries in which we live. This book, however, is also an illustrated log of a fourteen-year passage through the actual play of those mysteries of the human heart and human community in the South—its glees and furies, its personalities both gentle and savage, its weathers and ceremonies and ghosts.

About seventy years after the Civil War, a popular suspicion began to emerge that the South still remained incorrigibly unlike the rest of the United States in some elemental and darkly meaningful way. This suspicion provided, at the least, a spectacular literary strike, which over the years has been as exhaustively prospected as the Sweetheart Lode—and even now the strip-mining is still going on. Central to this notion of the South's singularity has been a vision of the white Southerner as something like the lost and haunted Ishmael of American history, and no one proved fonder of this proposition than certain cultivated circles of white Southerners themselves. Much of this vision was made up, no doubt, of that slightly haggard romanticism indigenous to the region. But it was no less a reality for that: however illusionary by all exterior perspectives, romanticism nevertheless largely determined and directed the course of affairs in the South, both private and public. It was taken, and acted on, as the reality of things, and so by that measurement constituted the effective reality. This sense of comprising some spiritual order of the outcast and benighted— a kind of perversely, left-handedly chosen people—was all the more beguiling to Southerners because the rest of the nation seemed so ready to collaborate in the conceit.

But no matter how tatty a commonplace it became, the final truth is that the South *did* long constitute something like another country within the map of the United States. It amounted to something like America's Ireland, or America's Sicily. For the last decade or two, as the South has industriously undertaken to alchemize itself into a replica of Pasadena, its old simple passionate definitions of life have begun to wane and diffuse into the pleasant monotone coma of the rest of corporate American suburbia. But by lucky accident, like others of my colleagues during the Civil Rights movement in the Sixties, I happened to be writing about the South at one of those climactic moments of truth when everything—past and present, inward and outward—suddenly glares into a resolution larger and more urgent than its ordinary aspect. This book does not purport, of course, to give that immense experience its tongue. It is simply a recollection, in a succession of journalistic acts, of what happened to some people in the South during that time. But as a distinct society—one could almost say another civilization, issued out of its own separate past and mythology—the South was passing then through a saga that was, all at once, a re-experience of and judgment on that past which had created it. Indeed, while this is principally a book about white Southerners, that necessarily means it is also, to a profound degree, about black Southerners, who have always abided at the uneasy secret center of the white Southerner's heart. Because, in myriad and unwitting ways, the white Southerner became, and remains, the creature of the black man he hauled through violence and abasement into his midst.

A Personal Preliminary

QUESTIONS OF SEEMLINESS ASIDE, there is perhaps a central fallacy in the exercise of any writer explaining himself as a way of introducing his work. Any novel, or historical chronicle, or collection of stories or poems, always ought to be larger and more interesting than the writer himself. Perhaps more importantly, it should be hoped that the person of the writer—the hand that did the transcribing—will remain more or less invisible through the movement of a story. The teller is simply not that important. What he tells is.

Nevertheless, for whatever accesssory illuminations it may afford, and with an advisory to the good reader that it is only after these several pages that the true business begins, I furnish this personal preface.

I grew up not only a Southern Baptist, but a Southern Baptist minister's son, in the small cities and towns of my father's nomadic pastorates over the inland South—the plainer, pre-shopping-center South of roadside gas pumps and rusted RC Cola signs and flat little main streets, where a rigorous religiousness was simply one of the natural elements, like heat or lightning, of the surroundings. I became familiar quite early with all the clashings and smoke and wonder of those fearsome sagas of iniquity and judgment in the caverns of the Scriptures, and with the smell of soap and Juicy Fruit gum at Wednesday-night prayer meetings, with radio gospel boomers and successions of tent evangelists through the autumns, with the awful splendors of Sin and the voluptuous throes of Repentance.

In that religious atmosphere, the Old Testament and the Crucifixion always seemed to count for more than the New Testament and the Resurrection. Religion in the South was principally a romance about the Cross—a dire melodrama of thorns and betrayal and midnight anguish, with nothing in the life of Jesus mattering quite so much as his suffering and his death. The Southern Jesus was an almost Pre-Raphaelite figure of pale languishing melancholy, with a tender, grave, bearded face much like those thin faces of young Confederate officers that stare, doomed, out of ghostly tintypes. And nowhere was this Southern Christ so passionately defined as in those old heavy-hauling hymns that most Southerners had sung, at least once in their youth, at some summer night's revival in a bug-swarmed tent on the ragged outskirts of town: *What can wash away my sins? Nothing but the blood of Jesus. . . . Oh! precious is the flow that makes me white as snow. . . . In agony and blood, He fixed his languid eyes on me. . . . O Jesus, Lord! how can it be that Thou shouldst give Thy life for me, to bear the cross and agony in that dread hour on Calvary. . . . Oh, how I love Jesus! Oh, how I love Jeees-SUSSS! . . .*

My father always remained somewhat elusive about his own youth. I caught only occasional glimpses of a honky-tonk flashiness, hints of freight trains and lonesome hitchhiking wanderings with a sparse wad of dollar bills sewn by his mother into the hip pocket of his long underwear, night-time jobs in bowling alleys in Delaware and a short course in electronics in Chicago, mysterious brushes with death on snowy nights along forsaken roadways. But this is a part of him that always seemed like some untamed twin brother of his, long-ago lost and almost forgotten. An emotional motif that has always been especially throat-clogging to the Southern Baptist sensibility is that of the Prodigal Son, and he eventually surrendered himself to it: he would become a preacher. He was a small, wiry youth, quick and dark and vigorous with bright-black rippling hair, somewhat volatile, his rather outsized nose lent a permanent angle by a fracas once, and he met my mother while energetically leading the singing at a revival in North Augusta, South Carolina. On the whole, his divine calling did not much subdue him: while a ministerial student at Furman University he paid a local press to print a collection of verse he had written, and then peddled the pamphlets, titled *Twilight Thoughts*, on street corners and in office buildings around town.

But the other people among whom I was reared—other ministers, and the congregations of my father's successive pastorates—seemed oddly like displaced persons in life. Sober, sturdily wholesome and earnest, they were simply not a secular kind. Most earthly diversions they regarded as incidental distractions in their passage through this world to a better land, the only land that counted. Their own festivities were confined for the most part to church picnics and spaghetti suppers, all utterly innocent of alcohol or ribaldry. Even so, they were an extraordinarily conscience-stricken people. When the Southern Baptists gathered in general convention each year, they would engage in spectacular public feats of conscience-wrestling, all of which, no matter how vapid the outcome, involved some of the most magnificent exercises of oratory still to be heard in the age, declamations and soliloquies luxurious with irony, wryness, urgency, indignation. Even their bewilderment was uttered on a scale of grandeur.

Early on I realized I was at the center of a peculiarly fierce and unflagging, if gentle, acquisitiveness. When I was about four, there was a woman in our church whom I shall call Miss Giddings—a thirtyish, rather amply apportioned, but militantly austere spinster and erstwhile missionary, with a face as sunless and glossy as a boiled onion, whose only occupation seemed to be to appear at virtually every event at the church, carrying her Bible with a certain manful and easy authority. She was, I suppose, a kind of misplaced Calvinist nun. She conducted Bible lessons for children with flannel-board figures in the basement of the church one day each week, and as I was leaving one of these classes late one afternoon, I suddenly heard her oxfords clopping after me, with a subdued but determined briskness, down the dim corridor—I knew immediately that I was being pursued. She knelt beside me, her arm fastened around my shoulders. "You know, you're old enough now to start thinking about letting Jesus come into your heart. Wouldn't you like to accept Jesus, right now, here with me, as your personal saviour?" What I felt was a profound and bewildered aversion to this abrupt assault of violent intimacy. It ended, at best, inconclusively, with her offering a brief report to the Almighty while I remained captured in her arm, the silent and humiliated object of this consultation between the two of them. From then on, I avoided Miss Giddings with an elaborate cunning.

Eventually, of course, I did succumb. It was during the high flush of a revival meeting, when Judgment Day (that instant thunderclap of trumpets in a yellow evening sky announcing it is all over with, Jesus and the heavenly host suddenly spilling earthward to apply the Great Period to time) and Heaven (an everlasting sunlit Sabbath morning) and especially Hell (a vast night-canyon of flames and wails and gnashing teeth) became quite palpable realities. No more than the next party did I wish to sizzle for all eternity. I was baptized in the copper-plated tank set behind the pulpit, my father waiting for me in the water in a white robe pulled over waist-high rubber duck-hunting boots.

Whatever the waxings and wanings of my state of grace, through the first sixteen years of my life there was always church: an unalleviated metronomic repetition of Sunday school and preaching each Sunday morning and Bible class and preaching again that night, along with Wednesday-night prayer meetings, seasonal week-long revivals, and Vacation Bible School, which, with paper hats and wan devotionals and punch and cookies, maddeningly deferred for a whole bright week of June one's liberation into the delicious barefoot days of summer. When I was six, we moved to Augusta, Georgia, a mildly raffish little river city, where we abided for the next ten years. The church there—Second Baptist, a sooty brick bulwark of originless architecture, set on a corner in a sullen downtown neighborhood of once-genteel gingerbread houses huddling among oil storage tanks and ice plants and lumberyards— became like a second home, its eccentric inner arrangements of spaces and passageways in time as familiar to me as my own person: eternally dusky and stale corridors with heavy black ceiling fans like those in tropical hotels, barren Sunday-school rooms tinged with some aged whiff of dust and a dull chill on wet winter mornings, small gas heaters uttering rims of brimming flame along their grills with a soft constant muttering. What I remember more than anything else is the sensation of being recurrently pent there for long static ruthlessly abstracted hours of piety and propriety and the commemoration of a wholly inscrutable theology, for which one had been arbitrarily extracted out of the easy barbarities of boyhood, out of wind and earth and leaves. . . . Sometimes, during the Sunday-evening preaching service, I would suddenly feel a strange extra distance removed from everything around me: my father's figure in the pulpit, the congregation gathered before him, the lights overhead, all dwindled to a remote and unreachable miniaturization, as if viewed from the wrong end of binoculars. Arrested in the hiatus of those hours at church every week, I found one naturally developed a condition of detachment, and turned to explorations of an interior universe of one's private imagination and a ceaseless conjuration of grand private expectations. Years later, I was to come on a line in Enid Bagnold's autobiography with a pang of rich recognition: "I rested my teeth on the wood of the pew in front of me as I knelt and prayed: *God, make me famous.*"

At the same time, this gradual process of distancing happened to evolve within a highly charged field of emotional electricity. One's true spiritual baptism took place in those nighttime revivals reeling with contrition and exultation, dread and glory, with the old juggernaut hymns of the Invitation surging slowly and tremendously in the grim glare of shadeless light bulbs: *Almost persuaded now to believe. Almost persuaded, Christ to receive. . . . Seems now some soul to say, Go, Spirit, go thy way, some more convenient day. . . . Sad, sad, that bitter wail: Almost—but lost!* There was something about those Invitation hymns at the climax of the preaching that left one forever after with a special understanding of the nature of doom. In all, the kinetics of guilt and penitence and redemption inevitably became a part of one's sense of life. What was at work those nights, in fact, was a terrific moral engagement that approached, in sweep and energy and purity, the heroic: in those services was joined again the immemorial struggle against the wiles and sweet entrancements of this earth, a furious striving against the clinging clay.

But such a perfervid alertness to the perils of earthly beguilements also tended, back-handedly, to powerfully enhance their glamour. When I was a bit older, I would sit in a back pew with a precociously plush girl, the two of us leafing through a hymnal and pausing to shyly smile at such titles as "Fall Fresh on Me," "Nothing Between," "Breathe on Me" . . . I spent the entire week of one revival sitting with this same girl in a pew along a far wall, both of us singing at full-lung those billowing hymns while, beneath our mutually crossed arms, our fingers mingled deliciously.

Even so, it was a manner of life that fixed in one a sense of final apartness from the general world around. On Sunday, ball games and most other excitements were forbidden, and while other children in my neighborhood attended movies with a casually gluttonous regularity, I was restricted to one a month —and that only after my parents had assured themselves it was a seemly story seemly told. Since then, I have understood Thomas Wolfe's remark about the English being able to write about food with such opulent lustiness because their own fare is so frugal and sodden. Down the street from us in Augusta lived a friend of mine whose home seemed as alien and exotic to me as the bower of some Persian sultan: there were always glittering bottles of whiskey on the kitchen counter and obscure erotic novels on the living room shelves with illustrations drawn in the coyly naughty style of the Twenties, and I heard of unbridled Saturday-night parties there. Whenever I entered that house, if just for a drink of water on a hot afternoon, I felt myself in the presence of some illicit mystery.

Gradually then, the simple joys and hopes and diversions of the people close around me were already beginning to seem strangely crimped, drab, and inadequate. I began to regard with a vague nausea the very physical trappings of that way of life: the varnished wooden-slat chairs and milky blackboards in those sallow Sunday-school rooms, the radiators clinking under the dusty window ledges through Wednesday-night prayer meetings. Then, by some curious happenstance, during a Christian Training class in a bare room one bleary Sunday evening, I discovered an old copy of *The New Yorker* —how it had managed to filter in to that unlikely cranny I still can't conceive—which contained a review of the play, *Picnic*. It was like a secret pulsation from another cosmos: I had become acquainted in the sixth grade with the circumspect passions of Longfellow, Whittier, and Lowell, but beyond that, the literature I had grown up with consisted almost exclusively of the cheerful rhymed sentiments on the back of the church bulletins, sermon anthologies, and a couple of Lloyd Douglas' costume pageant like *The Robe* and *The Big Fisherman*. Finally, one raining spring afternoon, I came across, in a *Reader's Digest* collection of condensed novels, Steinbeck's *East of Eden*; when I had finished it, I fancied I had passed through a momentous portal.

Approaching thirteen now, I had already begun essaying, however fitfully and only half-knowingly, to smuggle myself out of everything I had known before. One medium of that process was pinball machines—those battered and cigarette-scorched contraptions, since doomed by law, that paid nickles for extra games won. For the better part of a year it was as if I were hung in a single changeless pose, arms spread to grip the edges of the machine, in a tense lean toward the illuminated scoring board—illustrated, like a simple rude talisman of the essential sensuality of gambling, with comic-strip visions of glad bubbling girls in bathing suits on some palmed beach under a tropical moon, these nymphs of luck posed in arrested blithe frolic around the windows of numbers. These machines were found in a murky hind-region around Augusta of cinder-block roadhouses and old gas stations and pool halls, places like clandestine depots beyond which lay the more ancient territories of human experience, and at the least, one tended to come by certain epiphanies in such locations. Once, while I was playing pinball in a roadhouse across the river, the door to a back room opened—and there was a glimpse, no longer than the glimmer of a few frames of film, of smoke gauzing under a lightshade and a flicker of white dice across a green expanse of felt, around which was stirring a dense eddy of brilliantly plumaged people. Among them was a tall rangy woman in a violet gown who, holding a drink, was poised slightly off-tilt with her mouth open in avid laughter, a chunky balding man beside her with his small dainty hand spread against her flank. It wasn't until the door had shut again that I realized she was one of my grammar school teachers—up until that instant only a memory of a gangling figure in glum sagging woolens usually smudged in eraser dust, who lived, unmated, in a shuttered ante-bellum house with several sour female collies and an unmown yard.

All this while, I was ransacking through a helter-skelter assortment of books—Mencken, Mickey Spillane, Françoise Sagan, Tarkington, Dickens, Sinclair Lewis. I had also begun to engage in fulminous, interminable, room-stalking arguments with my father about Faith, Reason, Truth—which he bore, for the most part, with an equanimity that impresses me now as Job-like. When I was sixteen, we moved from Augusta to the small South Carolina mill city of Anderson, and there I began accompanying a few friends to the house of an attorney's wife, a Radcliffe graduate, something of a strayed but ebullient Auntie Mame in bangles and baggy blue jeans who conducted a salon of sorts for incipient intellectuals from the local high school. I swiftly discovered I had not reached the last magnitude of sophistication quite yet; those were, in a way, feline and cruel afternoons, a running living-room tournament of flank attacks and mutual razor-snickings, with me holding a glass of watery ginger ale on my knee and feeling utterly lugubrious and impaled as they pattered of Schopenhauer, Salinger, Yeats, Joyce while Carl Orff's *Carmina Burana* pealed from another room.

Then, shortly after reading *For Whom the Bell Tolls*, I came across a brief mention in *Time* of a swashbuckling little pack of guerrillas holed up in Cuba's Sierra Maestra Mountains—an apotheosis was at hand, at last! Here, incredibly, was the same lyric scenario transpiring just ninety miles off my own shores. I was still sixteen, but I took a year out of high school and made three tries, three all-night Trailways bus rides down the length of Florida, to deliver myself into those far mountains of trans-figuration. It was only on the third run that I finally made it to Cuba—but wound up stalled in Havana, where, with only a re-turn ticket and some seventeen dollars, I spent a week accosting puzzled and edgy Habaneros with an offer to exchange the crumpled and funky linen suit I had worn on the bus ride down for a bicycle, on which I figured I could pedal the 750 miles on to Oriente Province. I never made it to the poetry going on up in those mythic mountains. However, Havana in Batista's day —a labyrinth of uproarious streets breathing a hot and roasted sweetness, where at twilight there would noiselessly and magi-cally appear numberless women ranked in the doorways, heavy-hipped, with a bright and almost violent sensualness—was a not unwoozying carnival for a sixteen-year-old fugitive from a South Carolina mill town suddenly to find himself in. When I returned for the last time to Anderson, getting off the bus in a fresh evening with a cool smoke of autumn in the air, it was with satisfaction enough of having been transcendentally transformed.

At last, sitting on a back pew during prayer meeting one listless Wednesday evening, with the service proceeding around me only a toneless and unmeaning hum, I abruptly stood and walked out—walked back through the quiet night streets to our house, where I stood for a long while in the stillness of the dim-lit kitchen, my heart shouting. I felt the most wild-winging exaltation of release—the last dry thread had been snipped, I was loose now in the limitless air. I was Alone. . . .

What I did not recognize at the time, though, was that this

final deliberate gesture of repudiation that night was itself a flourish born directly out of the very moral sentimentality of what I had repudiated. Then, some years later, while rocking my infant daughter to sleep on a winter night in Iowa, I suddenly found I was singing to her those old swooping hymns— one after another, they came welling forth again, whole and unforgotten and, amazingly, still overwhelming. That was when it first occurred to me that, despite everything, it was possible I had never really said goodbye—and never would. In time, I also came to a suspicion that, no matter what sophistications he may later imagine he has acquired and however intensely he may become involved in the wider affairs of the world, anyone bred a Southern Baptist will always have a sense of still being on the outside looking in: he can never completely overcome a certain wonder and titillation at being a part of large secular matters.

Then, not many years ago I drove past that corner in Augusta where Second Baptist Church had bulked so bleakly in my life through ten years that seemed more like a geological epoch, and discovered there, with a wholly startling blow of despair and dislocation, only a razed lot. That intimately familiar dingy edifice with its odd interior plottings of alcoves and passageways, which I had presumed would remain forever because its structure and shapes abided as a primary setting of my past and therefore as a part of who I was, had all vanished into the very air.

The strange shock of dispossession this visited on me acted, in a way, to confirm forever that, in walking out of that prayer meeting service a long time ago, I had not really left anything. There was, actually, no leaving it ever. For anyone assiduously raised a Southern Baptist, it will always be there. Most of all, he can never spirit himself beyond that sweltering, heaving, gaslit moral dramaturgy of guilt and redemption, of struggle and suffering and grace. It will continue to haunt him, to lurk in his life and work like the distant steaming of a robust and unabashed calliope.

II

The writing began—as I suppose it usually does—with those first excitements about what I was reading, and then wanting to see if I could make those excitements happen myself. The earliest try was Edgar Rice Burroughs, and then I wanted to do what Steinbeck did: so move the heart. And then—it was like turning to find oneself looking full into the face of the sun—it was Faulkner. Faulkner is an experience that a lot of Southern boys spend the rest of their lives trying to recover from.

But it was while I was working one summer in the Atlanta bureau of *Newsweek*—still a raw young provincial just graduated from Furman University, lobbed abruptly into the tumults and mighty theater of the Movement in the South, the Damascus Road event in more lives than mine—that I began to suspect, with all the rumors going around then about the novel and journalism having begun to keep house together, that perhaps my own errant star was to be that of a forestalled, unbegotten novelist left with journalism to do it all in. . . . Later on, other, somewhat more august speculations occurred to me: that we had come into a new age—after the age of faith and the age of romance, we were living now in the age of the journalistic reality. And through technology's electronic communalization of mankind, people were now so closely and continuously involved in the actual—*real* ordeals, *real* adventures, *real* heroes and heels and buffoons—that man's understanding and observance of his own tragedy and comedy might, after verse and the theater and the parlor literature of private fancy, simply be taking a new form (which, for that matter, was very close to its oldest, original form): bringing to narrations of the figures and passions of our time all the perceptual and dramatic senses of the poet or playwright.

All of this was hardly in my head, however, when I left *Newsweek* to do a book on Alabama's George Wallace— though Wallace did seem to me a curious instance of life imitating art imitating life. Not only were the parallels with Robert Penn Warren's variation on Huey Long, Willie Stark, uncanny and myriad, but it also seemed that Flem Snopes had a lot to do with Wallace. I then found, when I moved on into Wallace's life, that there was indeed much novelistic business there—only all of it was true. In that sense, I was not the one really writing it; Wallace's life wrote it, and his kinfolks and his cronies and the weathers and looks of the land. It was simply a matter—as it became with all the stories that followed—of going for an ultra-recognition of what was there.

But I also discovered something else: for that sort of total telling, exactly what you must do is move into someone else's life. Wholly without premeditation, in an almost automatic suspension of your own persuasions and sensibilities, you enter into an identification with your principals, perhaps not unlike that an actor reaches with a character, so complete that you almost *become* them, become who and what you'll later be writing about. To offer a somewhat high-faluting metaphor: it is not incomparable to Ulysses binding himself to the masthead with his ears unsealed so he could hear the sirens, know the sounds of their singing to his spirit. In the case of Wallace, it was akin to passing through a kind of debauchery in order to withdraw afterward and describe what it was like. But the same thing was to happen over the following years with most of the others—Wilbur Mills, Julian Bond, Lester Maddox, Mendel Rivers, Jesse Hill Ford: you actually *experience* them, experience their situation, to an extent that you come to feel you know them better than your own family, better even than you know yourself.

But after these personal absorptions in a character and his moment, you arrive at a point where it is time to detach again —to withdraw to that remove only from which can it all be fully apprehended and fully told. No matter how intense your empathy with your subjects while you were with them, it is when you sit down at the typewriter that the real understand-ings take shape, the moment of truth arrives. In fact, it's as if it's only then, in the recounting of it, that the whole experience actually happens. And your only loyalties at that point are to the important meanings in the story.

Therein, however, awaits the troll under the bridge. It's a process that necessarily involves something finally very like betrayal—to your subjects, afterward, quite indistinguishable from betrayal: the icy shock of such a disinterested detach-ment after what had seemed such a close affinity. In fact, there is probably a natural underground kinship between all true writers and double agents. Over a period of time, however, this recurrent sequence of deep empathy and then disengagement followed by accusations of betrayal began to take a certain toll. An uneasiness would overhaul me upon moving into a new story. I imagined I could spy, in approaching a new character, the accumulated shades of all those past aggrieved ones glaring over his shoulder like so many Banquo's ghosts.

Where I reached something of a climactic despair over this

was in the piece, about midway in this volume, on Jesse Hill Ford, the respected white Southern novelist who by ghastly mishap had shot to death a black man parked in his driveway one night. From the beginning I entertained a definite queasiness about the idea of one writer, even if a journalist, writing about another writer: something implicit in it of inverted mirror-gazing. That queasiness was soon complicated when it seemed, on my first visit, that Ford could only come off as grotesquely flip about what had happened. If writers are afforded precious little of a society of relationships in which they can enjoy the luxury of behaving as gentlemen, at least one decency still to be answered to was that scruple of Hemingway's—that writers are already embattled by enough enemies and adversity without visiting additional grief on each other. To write about Ford, as he initially appeared to be acquitting himself in his winter of tribulation, seemed an ultimate kind of betrayal. (As it turned out, though, Ford himself came to pronounce a blessing on the enterprise—there was something in him that *wanted* it written about, as he confessed, "just so it's written well.")

In time there developed other disquiets. After laboring for so long as a kind of broker or magpie collector of other people's passions and struggles, you begin to feel you are receding further and further out of any real life yourself. You seldom experience its charges directly and personally any longer, becoming instead someone made up of assorted secondhand momentoes of other people's realities. Attendant to this is the little difficulty that you tend to start confusing yourself with the public station of those you're writing about, assuming— and this was particularly a problem with a figure like Mendel Rivers—something of their consequence and celebrity. You begin to act like them with waiters and stewardesses, you take extravagant umbrage at slights to your magically acquired importance now. This occasions a lot of rowdy scenes and misunderstandings with desk clerks and doormen.

But most of all, there is the unmapped ethical territory that comes along with this sort of total journalism. Not *can* but *should* you even try writing about real persons as intimately, as deeply in the round, as, say, Lewis wrote about George Babbitt or Arthur Miller wrote about Willy Loman? If not, then this experiment you're working in, this ventured synthesis of journalism with the novelistic, is going to be something considerably less than it aspires to be. But there is the quite serious question of those very real people who happen to be attached to your principals: their spouses, their children. Do you disregard the effects on them?

Again and again, you repair to what it's all supposed to be for, this continuing expense to whatever small reserves of honor you still possess exacted by other people's outrage and embarrassment and accusations of duplicity. You keep returning to that original impulse: to move people, with true accounts, as you have been moved in reading, with the courage or folly or gentleness that is there in the story. And if, as in the best stories it always does, that should result in quickening again the reader's nerves and wit and sense of life, of the strange and sweet and varied fugue of human experience, then perhaps that is a value in itself at least equal to the gentlemanly values.

Despite all that, on more stories than Ford's I arrived at the conclusion that I had been working long enough in this questionable literary deviation, this odd unchurched coupling between the novel and journalism—that over a fourteen-year digression into this as-yet uncertain, cross-conceived genre, which had brought along with it such a baggage of wearying and unanswerable moral frets, I simply didn't have any more of those cycles of rapport and withdrawal left in me, that not very far down the road lay perfect schizophrenia, and it was at last time to move on to that first agenda of writing novels. . . .

But curiosities, fascinations kept intervening: real tales, real characters—like Lyndon Johnson, like a detective in Atlanta—kept interrupting.

Besides, there is this about journalism, about being propelled about from one story to the next: it may be good for a writer to be constrained once in a while beyond his own calculations of what he feels like doing; that way, he can keep getting surprised now and then. Because when a writer confines his work to his own designs and inclinations, chances are he's going to stop getting surprises, and winds up just emptying out the old surprises of his life over and over again. If I may be allowed to invoke, after Ulysses, one more slightly ponderous voyaging metaphor, perhaps it is good to be goaded or lured into going out of sight of familiar shores occasionally, to go on out to waters and depths where you've never fished before: whether you come back with something or not, whether or not you snag something that you then can't bring in with the frail little skiff of your talent and will and understanding, still, nothing else is worth it. There's still nothing finer, more worth breath, than that trying.

Finally, I remain in the South, as I once explained to an inquiry from my editor at *Harper's*, Willie Morris, because I've never been too sure that it is benign for a writer to spend any great length of time in the company of New York's estate of appraisers from afar and traffickers in reactions and responses. Because maybe you start after awhile writing from those secondary vibrations, instead of from the primary pulses and shocks you can't afford to lose. Perhaps writers ought to be scattered out over the land: one here and another way over there, ideally separated no less than a hundred miles from each other, more or less lost in the life of the country, not special esthetic creatures apart from most men but only another suburbanite, another townsman, another farmer, who just have this secret eccentricity of an obsession to write, to scribble. That way you're always writing out of what you're living in, there can be that energy and immediacy and very flash of life in your work. All the while, covertly, you're actually a kind of undercover agent, stranded out in the cold and sending dispatches from those far brawlings of life to Dickens, Twain, Gogol, Balzac, Cervantes, and all those others you got to know a long time ago, telling them what's going on now—*Let me tell you what these people did. Let me tell you what this character is like and what he did and what happened to him. . . .*

THE SOUTH
TRIBAL

WHILE THE REST of American history has been most notable
for an eager and nimble application to the possibilities of the
moment, it remained the peculiarity of the South that it always
seemed somehow vaguely adrift and lost in time. It was as if it
had been overly memoried: the shades of other ages, not only
of its own grave, gray, tragic Crusade but of even remoter
periods such as Arthurian England, lingered over its sun-
stricken stretches like multiple overlays of nostalgia—as if it
were a region hung in some old abiding implosion of history.
The first ransacking swarm of Anglo-Saxons left behind them
over the land, among the ghosts of its vanished Indians, a litter
of placid villages named out of yet another past: Canaan,
Bethany, Zion, Hebron, Moab—the primeval geographies of the
Old Testament reinvoked, four thousand years later, among red
hills and gullies and broomsage fields on the other side of the
globe. At the same time, vagrant filtrations from another an-
tiquity eddied over the South's interior, with communities
named Carthage and Troy and Corinth, and planters and bar-
risters out in the obscure reaches of Alabama and South Carolina sitting on their back galleries the whole of a long hot
Sunday afternoon, surrounded by a locust-stitching emptiness
of loblolly pines and limitlessly level cottonland, reading Tacitus
and Livy in the original tongue.

This habitual intercourse with the past no doubt partly accounted for that sense of the South as somehow older than the
calendar counted—older, in a way, than Philadelphia or Boston or even Plymouth Rock. To the rest of the country, it
often seemed as alien as Syria or Afghanistan—an insular territory of cave beliefs and shotgun violences and scruffy hills
where, after dark, solitary horned cows wandered the mild dust
of back roads under a calm mottled moon. It was as if, finally,

3

the South belonged to a time before the Western hemisphere was even suspected—was, at the instant of its emergence, already as profoundly old as Mesopotamia or Ur. And in a sense, it was.

For one thing, for over two and a half centuries, well before and well beyond the Civil War, the South was, with slavery and then its sequel, absorbed in an interior, collective experience wholly outside the general American sensibility of innocence and rationality and optimism—an experience belonging in fact to an older and direr script about the human situation. While the epic of the West was a physical experience as immense and furious as the South's, providing the United States with its only approximation of a true national romance, still it was principally an exterior happening, a simple, single-minded exertion outward against exterior circumstances of earth and weather and anonymous adversaries. But unlike the Western adventure, the South's experience was both an exterior and an interior happening. The convulsions of slavery and then the war and the hundred years that followed were matched by an equally turbulent inner conflict: it was an outer violence that simultaneously exploded inward upon a whole people's spirit and vision. In embarking on the kind of folk war it did over a century ago—pitching into it so much of pride and risk, however inflationary and illusory that headlong investment may have been to the actual circumstances that occasioned it—the South could not really afford to lose. But it did, in full measure to the extravagance of its commitment, cataclysmically. And it was in trying then to abide that insupportable defeat— insupportable because of the arrogance that had preceded it, and the even more implacable irreconcilability that followed it, the incapacity to forget—that the personality of the South was completed. In a nation that began as a foundling and waif of history and that still, after some three hundred years, had not concluded who it was and what it was for, the South—dwelling in an ancient memory of itself, with an extra sense, an inner ear, for the long melancholy music of time—became the one region of the country with its own active interior mythos, its own native tragic legend of blood and fire and guilt. Most critically, guilt.

Along with this, and perhaps as important, while the rest of the nation was massively mutating into metropolises and fac-

tories and brokerage houses, the South lingered on as a civilization of villages—indeed, a kind of tribal society, still belonging
more to the earth than to machines or systems, living closer to
the skin and the simple heats of mortality. It answered to a
tribal sense of community made up not so much of documents
or ideas, but of the old blood values of common earth and
common weather, common adversities and celebrations, common memory. The Southerner always tended to believe with
his blood rather than his intellect.

In no way has this been more eloquently evident than in the
politics of the South. It is no accident that it has been even
more rife with spectacular politicians than with writers—the
two virtuosities that have constituted perhaps the South's most
memorable offerings to the American fancy. The rowdy energies of its tribal order of life peculiarly rendered it the most lusty
political clime in the country. So let us begin with that.

Folk Politics

The House of Long

EVEN INTO THE Sixties, there was much about the sun-glowered lower reaches of Dixie strangely evocative of Cairo or Marrakesh—so much obsessive coffee drinking in such muffling heat, a general drowsiness of hanging half-dazed in historical ennui, purple twilights heavy with jasmine, and a rather rococo gallantry and sentimentalism, a compulsion to replace brute reality with endless Scheherazadean unscrollings of rhetoric. The difference, of course, was that the South's lush landscapes had mostly been populated by a haphazard spill of bony, misery-bitten Celts and Anglo-Saxons out of the wintry wastes of Scotland and Ulster, bringing over with them a fierce flinty rectitude out of those sleety desolations. It was always an uneasy and incomplete and violently awry grafting, those chill Calvinists mixed into brutal sun-glare and a sensuous swimming of wisteria, into summers touched with a faint moldering sweetness of carnality.

That may be one of the reasons why there always seemed a special blustery flourish taken on by American politics in its farther Southern drifts, a gaudy theatricality not altogether dissimilar to the kind of political opera common in those palmy Latin republics a short distance below, rather than the sober regulations and protocols devised in Philadelphia. There were regularly such scenarios as the time in Georgia in 1947 when young Herman Talmadge, after his roostery and scarlet-suspendered daddy Eugene expired of throat cancer before he could assume the governorship again, seized the capitol building by simple tribal right of primogeniture with his daddy's country-cured viziers one drizzling winter twilight. It took all

The New York Review of Books, February 26, 1970
The London Sunday Times, December 7, 1975

the siege machinery of the courts to dislodge him finally, whereupon he ran for the succession by popular anointment in the next campaign and reclaimed his father's totem-stick of power by general acclamation.

In the folk politics of the South up until the late Sixties—with ideologies and cerebrations never counting as much, no matter how commendable, as those older loyalties of blood and common past—there developed a free-for-all play of personalities in a one-party (Democratic) government that was as total as that in any Persian Gulf sheikdom, blithely undistracted by any organizational disciplines imposed by party competition. Instead, there tended to be a politics of tribal leaders—in Louisiana, many still refer to Huey Long by his first name, as if they are still living personally in his presence—and the power was frequently passed on down through the generations of what could only be called dynasties of tribal chieftains, like cigar-brandishing, ice-cream-suited Houses of Atreus: the apple-faced Byrds of Virginia; and the House of Talmadge in Georgia, with Ole 'Gene, the raucous grandsire, taking Herman as a small boy out into the back country to begin practicing his stump rhetoric before long rows of cotton.

But the most swashbuckling and durable and profuse of all those dynasties has been the Longs of Louisiana. Their dominion in one way or another, as Congressmen, governors, and Senators, has spanned now almost half a century of their state's life. They constitute a classic fable of tribal power in the South.

For two or three generations, the Longs were no more than a modestly enterprising family of landowners and bankers and lawyers in the piney outback of north-central Louisiana, members of that frayed-cuff lesser gentry hung in a social limbo between the truly destitute and genuinely patrician. Unpedigreed, vanishing into oblivion when traced any further back than the Revolution, they had ambled from Maryland to Ohio and then down to Mississippi, and first materialized in the shabby hill country of north Louisiana's Winn Parish on an icy brilliant Christmas Eve day in 1859—a bulking blond man named John Long, with a wife beside him hidden in a sunbonnet, driving oxen and a wagon lumbering under a teeming load of children. In time, other members of the clan filtered out of vague distances and pasts to collect there with them. The bedraggled countryside around was inhabited by an equally bedraggled Anglo-Saxon yeomanry having only some thousand slaves among them and never notably given, through the subsequent years of bombast around them, to those florid Southern-cavalier sentimentalisms cultivated by the plantation squire-archy farther down in the moss-wreathed deltas. John Long himself owned no slaves and abstained from the war because, as family apocrypha later styled it, "he had a hernia."

His son, Huey's father, in time assumed the muddy lots of cattle and hogs that made up the patriarchal holdings and gradually amplified them into a respectable-enough estate for those bleak parts, including fruit orchards and blooded horses. Before long he possessed himself also of a slight and delicately crafted orphan girl of fifteen named Caledonia, a somewhat more finely tuned creature than her boisterous husband ("You always knew two blocks before you got there that he was there"), whom, according to some reports, he had toted home from the church on the back of a mule.

It was with their second son, Huey, that abruptly, like a combustion out of nowhere, the Longs swarmed forth over the offices of power in Louisiana, appropriating the whole state with the quick ferocious rampancy of kudzu. Huey himself, the most extraordinary of the litter, was to come stunningly close to managing the same thing with the entire country before he was done. In appearance, they were by and large a homely and unprepossessing lot—Huey a potty figure, his younger brother Earl with dingy cottony hair over a face like a rumpled paper bag. Among themselves, they were a compulsively fractious clan, always fiercely wary of each other. In T. Harry Williams' monumental 1969 biography, *Huey Long*, he quotes Huey as having muttered once of his brother, "You have to watch Earl. If you live long enough, he'll double-cross you." (And he did, at least once.) Huey vigorously advertised it about that "this state's full of sapsucker, hillbilly, and Cajun relatives of mine, and there ain't enough dignity in the bunch of 'em to keep a chigger still long enough to brush his hair." For his part, while he was governor, he refused to admit any of them into the mansion, including his father, who by then had fallen on tenuous circumstances and was being passed about by miscellaneous relatives. Inevitably, as Earl, trotting along close after Huey's progress, began to mull the stirrings in his own flanks for the musky delicious bitch of power, there ensued rousing dogfights between the two of them. Finally striking out on his own for the lieutenant governorship, Earl staged his campaign as a running statewide family rhubarb, proclaiming that he had always had to rescue his brother, "that big-bellied coward," in schoolyard fights. His brothers and sisters lent Earl their vociferous support. Huey simply rejoined, according to Williams, "I will be a better brother to them than they are to me."

Taken altogether, though, their careers compose a dynastic pageant holding portents that, if America has as yet any unmined lode for a truly native tragicomic literature, it likely lies in such sagas of tribal power as that of the House of Long.

I
"Shut Up, You Sonsabitches! This Is the Kingfish Talking!"

In any democracy, even so approximate and sporadic a democracy as America's, the great politicians are also like the great common denominators of mankind—the rudimentary incarnations of a species of chronically contentious and conspiratorial social creatures, inexhaustibly acquisitive and garrulous. So that, if any extraterrestrial intelligence were to make an expedition to the planet to take back with it a consummate specimen of the form of life here called human beings, it would likely make off back to the stars with some democratic politician contained in a hermetic chamber exactly duplicating the tawdry hotel room in Kansas City or Boston from which he had been plucked, kept alive with a smog of cigar smoke and sodden hamburger steaks and little pools of raw warm bourbon in bathroom glasses, with a ceaselessly shrilling telephone nearby to maintain a psychic sparking of reported political power shortages and brokerings, along with occasional vagrant easy turnings of anonymous female flesh.

Huey Long himself was as immediately and plainly mortal as a bunion. In fact, to a number of discriminating souls in his day, he amounted to an unspeakable vulgarity—people of social and political gentility frequently could not even bring themselves to utter his name, referring to him, as if briefly lifting something vile between two fingertips, as merely "that man." A Louisiana judge during Long's governorship sputtered once in desperation that the man had "a malformed and diseased mind," and when Long was in the United States Senate, Roosevelt's Secretary of the Interior, Harold Ickes, delivered the memorable epithet that the gentleman from Louisiana suffered from "halitosis of the intellect."

A dumpy figure, plain and pudgy as a potato, Huey had an Emmett Kelly face under a kinky scribbling of damp rusty hair, with a nose like a radish bulb and an oddly straight mouth like the hinged slot of a ventriloquist's dummy. His garb, even after he reached the Senate, ran toward white suits with pink neckties and orange handkerchiefs, fawn and lavender silk shirts, and brown shoes trimmed in white—he resembled a walking dish of fruit ambrosia. At the same time, he was the sort of chap who would get into fracases in the men's rooms of nightclubs.

Even so, he also seemed awesomely larger than the life around him—at once, somehow, both mundane and Promethean. And his career was made up of all the engines of epic drama—there is power, hubris, farce, blood, and smoke in the tale, nightmare and, finally, great mystery. There seemed, from the first, something oddly preternatural, almost extra-mortal about him—as if he had received with his conception some extra pulse of extravagant aliveness, an image of his species taken with an extra instant of definition.

In the first months of his existence, in the scrappy little dirt-laned lumbermill town of Winnfield, he would spill himself down the front steps of his house, crawl to the fence gate, pull himself up to scrabble open the latch, and then crawl on out and situate himself by the side of the street to gaze raptly for hours on end, still blank of language, at all the large barging creatures of his own kind passing before him. From the first, he had a voracious curiosity about his surroundings. By the time he was nine months old, he had managed the trick of walking and promptly commenced to scurry on out everywhere around him: once, when the first freight train ever glimpsed in those parts came clanging into Winnfield and paused there, momentous and looming, he scuttled under one of the box cars for a meticulous perusal of its underside, the entire length of the train having to be held, coughing and steaming, until a family member was fetched to retrieve him.

Then, as soon as he was into his teens—a spindly youth, toothy, bulb-eyed, always bagged in clothes too large for him— he began making weekend expeditions to a neighboring town to consort with certain schoolmarms there, scandalizing his family and his own townfolk. He seemed propelled by a constant pell-mell urgency, like the frantic flurrying of those moths that have to get it all done from sunrise to sundown, as if in some dim desperation over the finite envelope of time and place in which he found himself caught. Meanwhile, collections of people anywhere always inordinately excited him—he was utterly a creature of public places, the din and clatter of the street-corner, the marketplace, the town square. When a circus parade came surging once through the dust-hazed main street of Winnfield, Huey, who was then twelve, spurted from the crowd and esctatically began flinging stones at the elephants— "He would do anything to attract even unfavorable attention," one witness recalled to Williams. Later, during the frequent melees and uproars that accompanied his political emergence, he would gleefully leap atop a chair and wallop away at his chest, bellowing, "Blame it all on me! Me! Huey Long!"

While fascinated by his fellow humans in crowds, though, he displayed a strange queasiness at personal contacts with individuals; it was as if he were infatuated with mankind in general, but disconcerted and vaguely repelled by it in the particular. "Many who knew him," Williams reports, "have said he had the limpest handshake they ever felt." Even his appetite for women turned out to be, at best, fitful. Williams cites one incident when "on a train trip Huey was invited to the car of a man he met and . . . later he attacked his host's daughter. When his companions reproached him, he said, 'You gotta try, don't you?'" He purportedly maintained a desultory liaison with his secretary. But on the whole, it seems he had about the sexual attention span of a hamster—quick, scuffling, distracted and fleeting. He had, as well, only an incidental sense of family. Huey met his wife, Rose, a small neat dark-eyed girl who was a stenographer for an insurance agency, at a cake-baking contest during his early days as a traveling salesman. After a somewhat erratic courtship of two and a half years (he once retrieved the ring he had given her because, he notified her, he'd come across another girl he might marry instead, later returning the ring to Rose with the explanation that the girl hadn't looked the same when he saw her again), they were finally married by a conscripted Baptist minister in the Gayosa Hotel in Memphis. After that, he simply did not seem to notice her to any great extent. Upon his election as governor, she lingered only briefly in the mansion with him, shortly returning to her hometown of Shreveport with their three children (including Russell, later to be a United States Senator himself), and Huey dwelt thereafter mostly in hotels.

What it all came down to was the fact that, as Williams puts it, "Huey was oppressed by time." The normal constraints of man's lot seemed to fill him with a kind of hectic frenzy; he generally slept only four hours out of every twenty-four, and he was possessed of a savage unflagging energy which swatted him along at a subdued gallop, feet flinging out to each side in an odd splayed gait. That, above all else, became the demon, the harpy of his life—the temporality in which he was confined. Even during his salesman days—in which he served a peculiarly appropriate political novitiate as a traveling drummer of lard substitutes, Never Fail lamp-kerosene cans, and Black Draught laxative from the Chattanooga Medicine Company—he was eagerly dispatching an endless series of letters out of the void of his anonymity to Senators in Washington because "I want to let 'em know I'm here,"—notifications that he was impending. His wife was later to remember that, even that early, "he was measuring it all. . . . It almost gave you the cold chills."

Huey had the good luck to have occurred in a state with a gusto for politics comparable to the indefatigable scrimmaging of the old Chinese warlords. In Louisiana, as Williams explains, "politicians were and are much like feudal barons. They operate as rulers of geographical principalities or personal followings, independently, calculatingly, and sometimes irresponsibly and petulantly. Two barons may seem to be friends and allies, and then suddenly, because one or the other senses an advantage to be gained or is seized by a whim, they break and become enemies. . . . The objective [is] to win, and in no other state [are] the devices employed to win—strategems, deals, oratory—so studied and admired by the populace." Candidates accordingly would stampede into a race with absolutely no expectation of showing at the finish, in it simply for personal sport—like a country-fair steeplechase open to all comers. In fact, Louisiana eventually contrived to distribute its various political heats throughout the calendar so as to provide itself with a political season running all year long, year after year, on into eternity.

But before Huey—which, in the life of Louisiana, has come to mean something like before the wheel—much of that lustiness was largely illusory. Like many other deep Southern states, most notably South Carolina, Louisiana was presided over by a combine of assorted financial interests with a tidy and grim insularity. It really amounted more or less to an industrial colony, with a common order of life not all that remote from, say, ninth-century Europe. Its board of directors included not only such native eminences as the sugar growers, the lumber industry, and railroads and gas and electrical companies, along with the New Orleans electoral machine and the larger metropolitan papers, but also migrant industrial conglomerates like, most formidably, Standard Oil. All in all, it was a government of excellent pince-nez gentlemen, and there prevailed the same conventional mirage that more recently attended the events of Watergate: sober men of circumstance are, whatever may be their occasional indiscretions, essentially honorable. As Williams puts it, "Huey's opponents were gentlemen, and . . . cultured, gentle people do not do evil or corrupt things—therefore, the Louisiana conservatives could not have done anything immoral. Huey, on the other hand, was not a gentleman. He was a crass popular leader. . . ."

Indeed, to the sensibilities of those respectable overseers of the state, Huey Long amounted to a squalid imp of the perverse. He did not have about him the style of decency. Brazen, clangorous, almost berserkly avid in his first political assertions, he didn't "associate with nice people," as one Louisiana patrician dismissed him. As for the clan from which he issued, as someone else put it, "they [were] not even house-broke." In truth, Huey himself, in his plungings about the state, was given, whenever pausing in cafes or hotel dining rooms, to helping himself casually from the plates of those around him while steadily yammering on, absently plucking up a pork chop here, a biscuit there, a potato here. One of his admirers later reflected uncertainly, "In some ways, he didn't act like a human being. He would reach over and take your meal and eat it." As Louisiana's elect of power, then, regarded Huey bawlingly bearing down on them out of the scrub hills of the back country—at twenty-two still runtish and goggle-eyed, accosting a legislative committee with demands for a modification of restrictions on injury and death claims by workers; winning election to the state's utility regulatory board, which he promptly converted into a podium for a sustained one-man donnybrook with the telephone company and Standard Oil; finally offering for governor in 1924 and only barely missing— he afforded them all about the same aghast dismay of the Roman gentility beholding Alaric hauling down on them out of the wolf-winds of the north.

But to the jacquerie of Louisiana, Huey rapidly became a folk hero—a squat, obstreperous, garish avenging angel who had abruptly flurried forth out of their midst. The truth was, of course, that Huey's own origins were not nearly so abject as those of his congregation—he having grown up, like most great popular tribunes, in the inconclusive and restless suspensions of a middle social latitude, in a household respectable enough while still outside what passed for the local aristocracy, but distinguished by the fact that they ventured periodically into reading things beyond mail-order catalogues. For his part, Huey as a small boy had been consumed by a biography of Napoleon, along with a world history that consisted of rather heavy-heaving narratives of similarly histrionic personalities. (Huey himself would wind up later being called "The Napoleon of the Pine Stumps" and "The Caesar of the Bayous.") In fact, however incidental his certified schooling, he had actually become, somewhere on his own, prodigiously read— haphazardly and, in a certain sense, almost monstrously literate. One New Orleans newspaper referred to him incredulously as "the polysyllabic Huey." But it was not lost on him that, whatever might have been his own inclinations, he would always be stranded outside the pale of those muted and lattice-shuttered chambers with potted ferns and burnished brass lamps from which Louisiana's traditional custodial community had always decorously governed the state. It was not all that unmeasured a passion, then, that impelled him to cast his destiny with the desperate and dispossessed of Louisiana.

They had never really had anyone before. And it was as if

Huey had long sensed their eagerness, had been relishing their jubilation when at last they would discover him. When he presented himself to them, then, it became a shivaree of mutual exultation in each other. On one early stump tour, Huey squalled to a gathering of dirt farmers, "How many of you wear cotton socks?" and to a thicket of upraised hands, he hitched up his own pants leg to show a cotton sock, then yelled again, "How many of you have holes in your socks?" and, to another wide flourish of hands, snatched off his shoe to reveal his big toe waggling through his sock, with a detonation of whoops and applause around him.

"It was weird to watch the people," one of Huey's old cronies recalled, "they would reach out and touch him as he passed." It was, actually, a phenomenon of cultural politics that was beyond principles and precepts, in a way even beyond class ideology—a mass passion born out of a particular folk style and sense of life, which is much, for that matter, of what all politics comes to anyway. (As more recently, and in quite a different way, the distinction was often lost in the grand angers of the New Left between what was authentically political and what was really a kind of cultural aversion: those young psychedelic guerrillas of the Sixties not so much political creatures as heirs and partisans of the cultural sensibilities of Rimbaud and Genet and William Burroughs, undertaking to politicize D. H. Lawrence's Apache sun-vision, affronted by the bourgeoisie as much for their tastes and the tacky banality of how they lived as for their political inclinations.) In any event, the identification between Huey and the lowly of Louisiana was immediate and personal; Huey moved like them, guffawed like them, angered like them, looked like them, dressed with a nickelodeon fluorescence that was their own style of fanciness and importance.

But if the communion between Huey and the multitudes approached the mystic, to Louisiana's corporate boyars, it was terrible and foreboding. When the unmentionable had suddenly become the inevitable and Huey was at last waiting to be inaugurated governor, this coalition of gentlemen briefly thought they might be able to assimilate him. It was soon obvious that was hopelesss. From then on they fell into solemn rumblings about the approach of Russian Communism, with an editorial headline in one Shreveport paper trumpeting, "Louisi-

ana Must Not Let Bolshevism In." Indeed, Long's political impulses were, by almost any measure at that time in Louisiana,
revolutionary, if not apocalyptic. He was, like George Wallace
decades after him, a twentieth-century rearticulation of the old
Populist evangelism that had rampaged over the South back
during those gaunt years between the end of the Civil War and
the turn of the century—a kind of spontaneous Jacobin popular
offensive out of the countryside, made up of a smoldering economic discontent and a pentecostal egalitarianism, fired by a
rural Protestant vigor. It ranged itself against the proprietorial
interests of Wall Street and those various merchants, bankers,
railroad potentates, textile lords, and petty capitalists of the
Gilded Age, all of whom tended to regard the movement, not
without some legitimacy, as an ominous insurgency. Populism
was probably doomed from the beginning because it finally
answered, in the face of a wholesale industrialization of American society, to agrarian values and nostalgias—in particular, to
the old Jeffersonian dream of a democracy of small farmers. In
a sense, it was the last great struggle in America of the country
against the city. But it long continued to work volatile effects
in the political course of the South.

Long, for his part, had a rare indifference to the fustian romance of the Confederacy perpetuated by the more polite
circles of power in Louisiana: "Unlike other Southern politicians of his time," says Williams, "[he] did not oratorically
employ and exploit . . . audiences of rural poor with the magnificent irrelevancy of how their grandpappies had charged up the
slope of Gettysburg. . . . [He] talked about crucial economic
issues of the present." And when he was at last elected governor in 1928, his tenure was nothing less than seismic in its
effect on the state. He decreed a general debt moratorium. He
provided free textbooks to all schoolchildren, initiated free
night schools for adults, and hugely expanded appropriations
for public education. He multiplied the programs for free hospital services. He accomplished a panoramic road and bridge
construction enterprise in a state whose interior up to then had
been laced with little more than gullied cowpaths. One observer during those days reported that the common populace of
Louisiana "do not merely vote for him, they worship the
ground he walks on. He is a part of their religion. . . . They
have felt the hand of Huey." More important, in all this he

succeeded in delivering Louisiana for a time out of the thrall of corporations, ransacking their tax privileges to boot. Their despair soon reached the point where they conducted a quiet statewide collection of one-thousand-dollar donations to compile a pot for bribing the legislature to impeach him. Scrambling furiously, Huey managed to confound that gambit.

Most notably, Huey also abolished the poll tax—a contrivance long used to depress the black vote—which, in the context of the time, was perhaps his most remarkable feat. He proved somewhat inert to other needs of the Negro, in particular, to welfare legislation. Huey contended these were issues "you cannot change people on. . . . They must change . . . themselves." But Long's instinct was that "any issue of religion or race was an artificial one in politics," and to him, the grimmer old fixations of Southern politics amounted to no more than distractions. He privately proposed to his aides, "You can't help poor white people without helping Negroes. It has to be that way," and he later declared to parties beyond his state, "A lot of guys would have been murdered politically for what I've been able to do quietly for the niggers."

Actually, however oblique Long may have regarded the issue of race to be, he was still not above the customary reflex of racist posturing now and then whenever it seemed politically convenient or unavoidable. On one occasion, he announced that one of his antagonists had "begun his career as an operator of a Negro saloon and dive," and as a Senator, he resisted a federal anti-lynching law with the brutish explanation, "We just lynch an occasional nigger." Whenever the question of race seriously arose, he readily presented himself as a segregationist and white supremacist—which, by sheer political and social instinct, he very likely was. (He once startled Roy Wilkins, who was then a newspaperman, by beginning an interview, "Let me tell you about the Nigras," his pronunciation lapsing before long into "nigger.") Nevertheless, Williams points out, "the privileges that Huey wanted to extend to Negroes . . . for this time . . . were large, almost revolutionary. . . . He would carry the Negroes as far as he safely could at the time. . . . He would not attempt to extend the suffrage to them because if he did, he would fail as a politician, and everything else that the Negroes had won would be lost."

On the whole, though, racism was a matter that constituted

to him only an eccentric and mischievous irrelevancy. As for the Ku Klux Klan, when one of the nabobs of that particular nuisance announced once from Atlanta that he was coming to Louisiana to campaign against Long, Huey quickly rummaged together some reporters to declare, "Quote me as saying that that Imperial bastard will never set foot in Louisiana, and that when I call him a sonofabitch, I am not using profanity but am referring to the circumstances of his birth"—adding then that if the Wizard did perchance venture into the state, he would shortly depart again with "his toes turned up."

Most of all, though, in the end Huey became "the first Southern politician since the great Virginians of the eighteenth century," says Williams, "to have an original idea." Having elevated himself to the U.S. Senate at the conclusion of his term as governor—installing in that office a crony appropriately named O.K.—Long's Populist vision magnified to a continental scale in his "Share the Wealth" plan:

The federal government would apply a capital levy tax to deny any family from owning a fortune of more than five million dollars, and would add a revised income tax insuring no family gained more than one million dollars in a year. Then, from the revenue resulting from these taxes, the government would stake every family in the country with a "homestead" of five thousand dollars, and additionally guarantee every family an annual income either of two to three thousand dollars, or one third of their average income. Beyond that, it would provide pensions to the aged, subsidize the college education of any able youth, and supply generous bonuses to veterans. More sweepingly, it would reduce labor schedules to thirty hours a week and eleven months a year, thus expanding the need for workers. Also, it would buy and store farm surpluses to balance supply with demand.

It was a political epiphany which had purportedly come to Long in an instantaneous thunderclap at three in the morning in a Washington hotel room, he vaulting out of his bed to scrawl it all down on sheets of yellow foolscap. In any event, it was a program that posed the most traumatic implications for the American establishment in those Depression years of the early Thirties. The travail then in the nation seemed composed of the classic conditions of a pre-fascist society—governmental catalepsy in the face of economic derangement, massive popular dislocations, smoke and gunfire in the streets, leaving a vast harrowed middle class as the potential constituency for a fascist order awaiting only that single galvanic wildcat figure of feral genius to bring it all into realization. As it developed, before the end of 1935 there were Share the Wealth societies in every state in the nation, including a number of black chapters —27,431 of them in all, with a membership of over four and a half million citizens.

Long himself rapidly became a national specter. Here was that singular figure, notes Williams, risen up "out of the middle class . . . who claimed to know the will of the people better than they did, who would save the people by whatever means he had to use, and who would admit to no check on himself except their general approval. He would hope to achieve his goal by conventional democratic methods, but would inevitably have to resort to more drastic methods, and so by stages would become the fascist head of a fascist nation." It was a prospect that seemed to unsettle even Huey to a degree. Whenever what was happening in Europe was invoked in appraisals of his possibilities, he was quick to declare, "I don't know much about Hitler—except this last thing, about the Jews. There has never been a country that put its heel down on the Jews that ever lived afterwards. Don't liken me to that sonofabitch. Anybody that lets his public policies be mixed up with his religious prejudices is a plain goddamned fool."

Discounting Huey as ever becoming a true national demagogue, Williams contends that "the original concept of the demagogue has little validity for the American scene . . . in a country as extensive and varied as the United States." That would seem, at best, a dubious proposition. In Huey's case, it was simply that he occurred in the pre-television age, an epoch that seems as remote from our own now as the Paleolithic Age —one in which presences, personalities, the existential reality of events carried for much shorter ranges, were shortly extinguished like match flames reaching the limit of oxygen, and beyond that were detectable only as carbon prints on newspaper pages, a canned sputtering inside small wooden boxes. Even so, Long's own divination was that his Share the Wealth movement, as a third-party front with or without him as its candidate, would quite likely wreck the Democrats in 1936, and after four catastrophic years of Republican doddering he would at last inherit the whole nation. And Roosevelt's own reconnaissance agents brought back the dire tidings that if Huey were a candidate in the 1936 Presidential campaign, he would draw an undertow of from three to six million votes over the entire expanse of the nation, as deeply from the industrial centers of the Northeast as from the countryside and plains.

Initially, Huey had thought he actually might be able to captivate Roosevelt too. But they were as mutually repellent as two like magnet poles. Roosevelt soon became persuaded that Huey was an incipient fascist leader and proceeded to undermine him in Louisiana with patronage appointments, while Huey, in a Senate speech, suggested that the administration was seeking to crucify him for its own ineptitudes and the disorder of its programs—"What is it? Is it government? Maybe so. It looks more like St. Vitus Dance."

Huey offered a prospectus for his own national administration—an enormous public works program sustained by a ten-billion-dollar appropriation, a central bank, railroads under "absolute government control" with the option of nationalization, heavy federal aid to the states at all educational levels, a vast public health undertaking, and finally a Federal Share Our Wealth Corporation to administer his economic program. It has since become the persuasion of a number of historians of the time that Roosevelt's tax message of 1935, generally considered as signaling his momentous shift to the left, was prompted primarily by the menace of Long and his Share the Wealth phenomenon.

In this and numerous other respects, Long seems to have been peculiarly repeated in our day by Alabama's George Wallace. Both derived directly out of the same Populist vitalities, both hauled themselves forth virtually barehanded out of nothingness into an imposing national consequence through merely their own occult fierce sense of the democratic possibilities for themselves. When Wallace began to assert himself nationally in the Sixties as an annunciation of Populism's mutation into a more meager and rancorous urban variety, he produced the same alarms about a nascent American fascism that Long had before him, and to a degree became a kind of hobgoblin ghost-writer for most of the issues and rhetoric of the '68 and '72 Nixon campaigns.

There was even much the same pattern to their careers, including certain central ordeals: for Wallace, his failure in 1965 to get the Alabama legislature to allow him to succeed himself, which left him almost catatonic; for Long, an impeachment crisis that pitched him into "a state of mental paralysis . . . a kind of melancholia," but which, like Wallace, he survived, though these ordeals left a new coldness and implacability in both their natures. They were even strikingly alike in their impatience with the business of having to eat: Huey, as Williams relates, "usually consumed whatever food was put before him, almost literally not seeing or tasting it, merely because it was there," while one of Wallace's old associates reported, "He never knows what he's eating because he's too busy talking—it could be filet mignon he's eating, it could be hamburger, it could be the end of his tie, he don't know."

Despite these commonalities, Long himself was finally of a magnitude larger than Wallace. It would have been quite beyond Wallace, for instance, to repair to the top floor of a hotel and come back down six weeks later with *Every Man a King*, which was Long's great political testament. Wallace seemed totally empty and innocent of abstractions, large formulations of policy, comprehensive visions—his political life instead consisting of little more than a clamorous racial and class fractiousness. As he once jauntily proposed, "Naw, we don't stop and figger and think about history or theories or none of that. We just go ahead."

Asked once about his sentiments on Long, Wallace paused a moment and then professed, "I don't really know all that much about him—just remember how people used to talk about him a lot when I was a boy. He had some good ideas, from what I recall. A few folks have told me his ideas were a lot like mine, 'bout all I know about him—he was trying to do a lot of the things I'm doing before he got shot over there. . . . " Even so, they are like a curious double image, a twin reflection in history, and it was not quite five years after that spring afternoon in Wallace's office when he maintained he was only obscurely aware of Long that he himself was lying, after a sudden quick chatter of shots, like a spilled puppet on the concrete parking lot of a Maryland shopping center.

In the end, Huey came to take on that blind spot of classic tragedy in his otherwise awesome vision: he could not distinguish, eventually, between his purpose and his power. It may simply be that all mortals, being uneven and flawed constructions, will inevitably distend and destruct as they lift themselves beyond the hold of the gravities of ordinary life and ascend toward those weightless and giddy altitudes near the gods—they lack that ultimate symmetry in their nature, some last degree of composure and balance, necessary to accommodate and manage so much power. With Huey, in those high swimmings of hubris, his pride and his mission, the barbarousness of his means and the benevolence of his intentions, merged at last into a blur of indistinction—became the same thing for him. "They say they don't like my methods," Huey himself once allowed. "Well, I don't like them either. . . . I would do it some other way if there was time."

He was frequently given to spurious flushes of generosity (though he once tipped a theater-ticket girl in the Hotel New Yorker three cents for getting him four tickets to a show sold out a month in advance). But Williams reports, "Once he and a friend passed on the street a poor woman and her ragged brood of children. He went on a few steps and then stopped. 'That breaks my heart,' he muttered. He went back and gave all the change in his pocket to the woman." More expansively, he announced to a student convocation at LSU once, as Williams tells it, that he had arranged for a special train to carry them up to a football game with Vanderbilt: " 'If you don't have the money, we can arrange to lend it to you.' Pulling out a wad of bills, he invited those needing help to come up and get their money and sign an I.O.U. A mob of students engulfed him, and he soon ran out of money. . . . He sent a courier to his hotel suite to bring out more money, in a suitcase. He dispensed finally three thousand dollars and then . . . returned to his hotel. But many students followed him there and clamored for their share, and standing in the door of his suite he handed out another thousand dollars."

There is, to be sure, something elusively exhilarating about

his unabashed and romping celebration in his power—
suddenly bellowing to an unruly assembly of other Louisiana
politicians, "Shut up, you sonsabitches, shut up! This is the
Kingfish talking!" As it happened, for the duration of his
ascendancy among his fellow mortals, rage and greed and cunning and fear, all the hues of human experience were height-
ened as if in some collective fever: death and revolution were
in play, murder lurked in the air. The mere will and audacity
of this single presence touched off a season of uproar and
Caesarian political theater: brawls in the state senate chamber,
with legislators galloping across desk tops and getting clipped
by the twirling blades of ceiling fans; secret midnight movements of private police armies; hip-pocket lumps under the buttoned linen suits of politicians that clunked when they sat
down; courthouses and airports occupied by shotgun-hefting
irregular partisans; an actual abduction or two here and there.
But through it all, Huey could not be dislodged, could not be
flushed.

In the last analysis, Huey was a mystery, indefinable even
to himself. Dozing once on a bed in a hotel room while reporters around him were speculating on who or what he was, he
suddenly grunted, "Oh, hell, say I'm *sui generis* and let it go at
that." Another time, he remarked, as if regarding his effect on
the society around him with a light bemusement, "They think
I'm so smart. Maybe I'm not. Maybe it's just that there are a lot
of dumb people in the world." Whatever he was, he seemed
uncontainable, like some chance unprogenitored byblow of the
race with no estate but his own exorbitant energy. He considered himself, in fact, one up on most others he encountered in
that regard: when he began his affrays with Roosevelt, he
offered, "I can take him. . . . He's scared of me. . . . His mother's
watchin' him, and she won't let him go too far. . . . He's livin' on
an inherited income. I got nothin', so I don't have to bother
about that."

It is somehow particularly eloquent of Huey that he liked to
promote the Jew's harp as carrying "naturally . . . the music of
the soul to the world." Of course, that was because it carried
the music of *his* soul—a brisk spry flat twanging homely war-
ble. Actually, as Williams quotes one source, Huey "couldn't
tell one note from another. He did not play the piano or any
instrument. He couldn't. He had no voice for singing." But

like a kind of eager-hearted Caliban, he was swooningly en-
tranced by the sound of far spiritual realms he could never
reach. Says Williams, "When he could get anyone to play for
him, he would sit on the bench or on the floor and listen with
rapt attention. . . . His favorite composers were Victor Herbert
and Sigmund Romberg, and his favorite songs were 'Harvest
Moon,' 'Smoke Gets in Your Eyes,' and 'Look Down That Lonesome Road.' " A bandleader remembered, "When he was dancing in the Blue Room and I'd play 'Harvest Moon,' he was in
heaven. He would look dreamy and blissful and look at me as if
to say thank you and dance with his eyes half closed."

But in barely four years, he converted Louisiana into a personal fiefdom at least as autocratic and claustrophobic as what
had preceded him. It was as if the system had simply not anticipated him, could not accommodate him. Power became as
easy and casual and intimate to him as his own breathing. An
old friend of his who flinched during the impeachment challenge approached him once during that crisis and urged him to
resign; Huey, who was sitting on the edge of a bed paring his
toenails, pointed to a clipped nail on the floor and said, "Boze-
man, I wouldn't give the value of that toenail now for a sonofabitch like you." Soon he had achieved in Louisiana perhaps
the most totalitarian society ever to develop within the American political structure. Cities were summarily clamped under
martial law. Newspapers were forbidden to print anything that
"reflected on the state government or its officers." Gatherings of
two or more people were prohibited. In New Orleans, the carrying of firearms by anyone other than police was banned. He
eventually appropriated every single purview of authority in
the state, including the courts. When he was done, Louisiana
literally belonged to him—it had become his private backyard.
In Baton Rouge he erected, in less than a year, a new thirty-
four-floor capitol building with the bombastic proportions of a
Mussolini opera palace—the personal temple of his reign.

Increasingly, though, Long was being compared in commentaries to those fascist caudillos who had emerged in Germany and Italy. Against these suggestions he hotly protested,
"A man's not a dictator when he is given a commission from the
people and carries it out. . . . A perfect democracy can come
close to looking like a dictatorship, a democracy in which the
people are so satisfied they have no complaint." Indeed, it was

not so much an institutional as a personal, popular totalitarianism, which has always been the dark side of the South's tribal politics—a totalitarianism no less monolithically oppressive for the fact that it was sustained by general folk consent. Huey, as it were, had loosed the beast in democracy. It disconcerted his faithful not at all that he violated the customary Constitutional scruples, busily pillaged the system. If anything, they delighted in his gamesmanship: he was theirs, and they would forgive him anything. This popular indulgence—transferred later to his brother Earl, and in much the same way accorded yet later to Wallace—has consistently confounded and scandalized more fastidious political sensibilities in distant quarters like the seminar halls of Harvard and the editorial boardrooms of *The New York Times*. What the eminently civilized souls there have always failed to understand is that such tribal leaders as Long and Wallace simply operate in a different, more primal political medium. As an Alabama legislator observed once of Wallace, "There's been a stack of stuff six yards high written on the little bastard, every bit of it true, but it just doesn't touch him. Nothing in print on pages of paper can touch him, whatever it is. 'Cause he exists in just a totally different reality of power."

Nevertheless, even as Long completed the frustration of his adversaries, he always seemed to have a vague uneasy prickling in the nape of his neck as to how impossibly he outraged their feelings. All his life, Huey had entertained a highly developed sensitivity to preserving himself physically intact, to avoiding any risk of actual physical sabotage. He had chosen not to serve in World War I, he announced, "because I was not mad at anybody over there." Williams also notes that "a normal masculine emotion never appeared in him—that occasional red rage which makes a man want to fling himself at the throat of another man." At the same time, though, he was always tensed for those eruptions in others he knew he had to provoke. "He thought . . . his enemies were lying in wait to beat him up." When these encounters came, his responses were usually less than Horatioan. In a hotel scuffle once in New Orleans with a plumply upholstered politician, Huey's head, in the words of one female bystander, "was visible occasionally, but most of the time it was lost in J.Y.'s stomach." More often, he was prone to "hit at" his antagonist, and then scuttle off. But he began now to be haunted more and more by the prospect of ambushes—increasingly sensing the terminal furies he had produced everywhere around him—and came to travel always amid a bristling thicket of praetorian guards in peppy straw boaters and pinstripe suits.

He had returned briefly to Louisiana from the Senate in September of 1935 to attend to some small plumbing problems with the legislature, and on a swampishly hot Sunday night was hustling down a marble corridor with a seethe of minions in the deep vaults of that mammoth Tutankhamenian monument to himself, when a frail young man stepped out from behind a pillar, a stranger with shellacked black hair like shoe polish and circular black-rimmed spectacles, wearing a slightly dingy white suit. His name was Carl Weiss, an ascetic young doctor with a facility in music, mathematics, mechanics, and painting, and possessed of a fine wire-taut rectitude—one of those more exquisitely cultivated souls in the Louisiana aristocracy whom Huey had so insupportably outraged as a crass Visigoth running amuck. One of Long's attendants, a gentleman of considerable bulk holding his Panama hat in one hand as he was swabbing at his damp jowls with a voluminous white handkerchief, happened to glimpse, as Weiss brushed past him with an apparitional swiftness, a glint of metal in his hand, and he instinctively swatted at Weiss backhand with his hat, as one trying to shoo a wasp. But in no more than a blink, Weiss had shot Huey under the ribs with a small pistol. Husey immediately loosed a loud squealing bawl and kept on trotting aimlessly, jogging off down some stairs. Behind him, at two quick pistol-claps from Huey's bodyguards, Weiss slumped flimsily to the marble floor, and then was systematically churned to pieces by a continuing bedlam of gunfire.

Weiss's bullet had found Huey's mortality in his lesser viscera, his colon and kidney. Later that night, in an operating room moiling with the retainers who had tumbled on in after him, one witness recalled, "I thought, what a scene—here was a man maybe dying, and that room was full of politicians." If the testimonies Williams cites are to be believed, Huey would rouse from periods of unconsciousness and "talk wildly, as though he saw visions beyond the hospital walls. He saw people out there, the poor people of America, needing him, wanting to give him power so that he could help them." It was a frantic clattering which did not cease until the very last instant, and as he receded into oblivion, it was with a last bleat of his old desperation as the intractable oppressor he had raged against all his life—time—finally closed in on him for good: "God, don't let me die! I have so much to do. . . . "

In front of his capitol building in Baton Rouge, there now looms a gargantuan statue of him—a bronzed colossus in a double-breasted suit, resembling the effigy of some porkish rambunctious raffish traveling salesman of pans, novelties, cough medicine, enlarged to the scale of the heroic. It is deposited, like a grandiose lid ornament, atop the grave in which he lies, at last pent and subdued.

II
The Hoedown Days of Uncle Earl

In the very next election rites, about a year after Huey's "accident," as some of his cronies daintily termed it, Earl Long came into the lieutenant governorship. Actually, Huey and Earl were about the only members of the Long clan between whom there seemed any real measure of affinity, however erratic and staticky. During Huey's impeachment crisis, Earl had gotten into a spirited skirmish in a corridor of the capitol with one legislator whom, as they were grappling on the floor, Earl proceeded to bite on the face—the man afterward having himself promptly inoculated for tetanus. When word of the scuffle was brought to Huey, he cackled, "I bet Earl bit 'em, didn't he?" Earl once overextended himself in his combatative exuberance, though, by zestfully recommending about one troublesome politician, "Let's take the sonuvabitch and kill him!" whereupon Huey kicked him in the seat of the pants, one bystander recalled, "like I never kicked a nigger in the ass."

Not long after Earl's election as lieutenant governor, a jamboree of scandals among the collection of political dukes Huey had left behind—scandals he had prophesied, averring they would all wind up in the penitentiary if he were not around to restrain them—resulted finally in the resignation of the governor, and with that, Earl inherited the tribal chieftainship at last. In 1948, he won it on his own, presided for four years, and then, prohibited by the state constitution form succeeding himself, assumed it again in 1956. Having managed to induct himself into the office one of these times without a run-off election, Earl was fond of hooting, "Huey never done that. . . . Huey tried that highbrow route and he couldn't even carry his home parish. I carry Winn Parish every time." Old political brokers from those days agreed that "Earl was better at conniving than Huey," but it was the perspective of most of them that "It's like comparing a university graduate and a grade-schooler. . . . They loved Earl but they feared Huey." Indeed, over the years there seemed fey vagaries in the voting for him. Once, in the Fifties, when he committed the perilous presumption of crossing the Southern tribal ethic on race, he found himself suddenly consigned among the stragglers in the lieutenant governor's race; then, just as suddenly, he was restored to grace in his campaign for Congress shortly thereafter. But if the popular fidelity to Earl was capricious, it seemed somehow more spontaneous and fond for that—and it endured.

For the most part, Earl gustily continued Huey's Populist tribuneship—introducing free school lunches, distributing new hospitals about, considerably increasing old-age pensions and veterans' bonuses and teachers' salaries, all of which he provided for by more than doubling corporation taxes. It became one of his most cherished campaign cantos to belabor the privileged for some obscure conspiracy to "cut off the spastic schools." Then, toward the end of his second full term as governor in 1960, confronted again by that constitutional proscription against succeeding himself that posed a bedeviling and arbitrary intrusion into his ministry to the people, Earl suddenly hit upon the ploy of campaigning for reelection anyway and then resigning shortly before his term expired, so he could reinstall himself back into office after a few days' existence as a private citizen, thus nimbly observing the constitutional niceties. It happened to fail in the end, but as A. J. Liebling acknowledges admiringly in his exquisite account *The Earl of Louisiana*, "Even Huey had not thought of that one."

The difference between Huey and Earl, if it can be conceived, was like that between *Die Götterdämmerung* played by a Dixieland band, and a lickety-split hot-diggedy-dog country-fiddle hoedown. Earl was a somewhat more antic and skirling spirit, an obstreperous jaybird of a man even well into middle age, one watery eye usually squinting feistily and waggishly, attired in black mohair suits with flowered ties, with the sober swankiness of a funeral-parlor director or prosperous Baptist parson. Sitting, though, he would cross his legs to disclose drooping white cotton socks. He was disposed to a cuisine consisting of Vienna sausages, salted watermelon, and buttermilk. Whenever he was out on his campaign circuits, it was his habit, while perched restlessly up on the platform among the other candidates on a hotly flaring afternoon, to produce from his suit pockets an inexhaustible succession of handkerchiefs, like a magician endlessly flourishing forth scarves, each of which he would sop in generous splashes of Coca-Cola and then swipe bracingly over his flushed face. After that, with an air of abstract earnestness, he would absorb himself in grabbing at the flies mumbling about him.

He was, on the whole, an open-hearted and affable soul, finally innnocent of Huey's capacity for a mongoose-eyed ferocity. He advertised his campaign appearances with leaflets proposing, "Come out and bring all your friends to hear the truth. Nothing will be said to offend or hurt anyone." At the most, he would direct at his adversaries such scriptural reproaches as "By their fruits ye shall know them. . . . Father, forgive them, for they know not what they do." In his constant peregrinations by limousine over the map of Louisiana, he would repeatedly pause along the roads to purchase such random commodities as post-hole diggers, hams, pitchforks, forty-four cases of cantaloupes once and seven hundred dollars' worth of cowboy boots, occasional livestock like goats and chickens, cases of Seven-Up and Dr Pepper, fifteen pounds of okra—he once kept suspended a press conference at the mansion over two hours while he lingered beside some highway haggling over guinea hens. According to Liebling, his mornings as governor usually commenced with an exhaustive meditation on racing sheets arrayed over a conference table, after which he would place his bets by phone (later dispatching a state trooper over to his bookies to collect if he had fared handsomely). That out of the way, he would then studiously consult the supermarket ads in that day's paper.

In fact, one of the most memorable passages in Liebling's altogether entrancing chronicle is the recollection of a Long janissary about the morning Earl saw that Schwegmann's was selling potatoes for forty-nine cents a ten-pound sack. . . . Earl says, "Come on, boys, I can't afford to pass that up," and he goes downstairs and gets into his eleven-thousand-dollar air-conditioned Cadillac . . . and the state troopers get out in front on motorcycles to clear the way, and he sits in front, next to the chauffeur, the way he always does, and packs those politicians in the back, and they take off. They pull up in front of Schwegmann's —all the sirens blowing, frightening hell out of the other shoppers—and Earl gets out and heads straight for the vegetable department. . . . He buys a hundred pounds of the potatoes and tells a state senator to pick them up and carry them to the car, and then he sees some alarm clocks on sale and buys three hundred dollars' worth, and tells some representative from upcountry to carry them. And eighty-seven dozen goldfish in individual plastic bags of water, and two sets of that sweet Mogen David wine, and he tells the new superintendent of state police to load up. . . . The stuff won't all go into the trunk of the Cadillac, so Uncle Earl sends a couple of senators and a judge into the store again to buy some rope, and they can't find any but the gold kind that women use to tie back drapes with, so they buy about a furlong of that. . . . By that time, Uncle Earl is sitting in his air-cooled seat eating watermelon with salt, and he orders the chauffeur to get out and tell the judge to lie down under the car and get the rope around the best he can. The judge gets down on his knees, and as he does he says, "I wonder what the governors of the forty-nine other states are doing right this minute. . . ."

Nevertheless, during those sulfurous years of racial malevolence in the South through the late Fifties and early Sixties, Earl Long refreshingly amounted to something more than a wheezy Dixified Mad King Ludwig of Bavaria. Like Huey, he was always markedly uncomfortable with the lasting distemper of racism in Southern politics. He once startled Liebling during a banquet at the mansion by confiding, in his glubbing mud-smacking Louisiana brogue, "Between us, gentlemen, as we sit here among ourselves, we got to admit dat Lincoln was a fine man and dat he was right—but don't quote me on dat!" To segregationist evangels who persisted in harassing him on the point, he kept declaring, "But you got to recognize that niggers is *human beings*! There's no longer *slavery*!" And in final blusterous exasperation he took to dismissing these various irritants as "little pea-headed nut . . . little piss-ant . . . common damn hoodlum grasseater sapsucker . . . "

It was heady, if not implicitly suicidal, billingsgate for those times, when the conventional political respectability in the South was represented by the White Citizens Council, a kind of dry-cleaned, cuff-linked Klan. Earl's great capsizing came when—around the time he was also contriving his inspired sleight-of-hand to allow himself to serve a third term—he convoked a special session of the legislature to liberalize the state's voter-registration protocols, which up to then had succeeded in rendering blacks voteless neuters as citizens. At that particular moment he also happened to be a man under considerable harried duress from certain other quarters, not the least of them his wife, generally referred to as Miz Blanche. A somewhat brittle and palely powdered matron singularly indisposed to her husband's rowdier range of ebulliences, the two of them had come to be engaged in a running serial of noisy tiffs—performed, as all Long family tiffs were, to the public eye—which were occasioned by, among other things, Earl's frequent glad galumphings among the strip parlors of Bourbon Street.

When he called his special legislative session to enfranchise the mass of the state's black citizens, then, he was already a man rather nibbled at by frets, and it did nothing to mend those ravelings of temper when the legislature quickly and curtly rebuffed his appeal. In the final hopeless hours of that session, Earl became progressively more exercised—at last snatching the podium microphone and producing a stricken hush over the floor by blaring, "You the people that sleep with 'em at night and kick 'em in the street in the daytime." When the ensuing uproar from that subsided, he honked on, "About 1908 I had an uncle who got killed. He'd been a good man, good to his family, good to me. Well, he got drunk one night, went down to the colored quarters"—uneasy aides began plucking furtively as his coattails now, but Earl was beyond noticing them—"kicked a nigger man out of bed, and he got into that bed"—the yells, the whistles, were rising again around him—"that nigger man was so enraged, he shot my poor ole uncle. And he died. Do you know that's what the colored people resent now most? *They want their womenfolk left alone!*" Earl Long had just uttered—in the legislative sanctum of Louisiana in 1959—the great submerged existential truth of the South's racial crisis, a proposition that at that time was still being only tentatively suggested by the most radical ideologues in the North. And having unloaded himself of this ultimate pronouncement, amid a tumult of howls, he was led gently off the floor, muttering to himself, glaring fiercely about him.

Shortly thereafter, on a soft May evening—through elaborate arrangements devised, as Earl later fumed, by "my sweet little wife and my dear little nephew," this being none other than Russell Long, Huey's son, by then a U.S. Senator—Earl was hastily bundled by deputy sheriffs down the steps of the mansion into an ambulance, whisked to the airport, and from there spirited off to a psychiatric clinic in Texas.

He was not there long, though, before he had somehow managed to palaver a judge into releasing him, on his own fervent vow that he would dutifully deposit himself in a New Orleans clinic straightaway on returning to Louisiana and would refrain from prosecuting Miz Blanche and Russell for kidnapping. But no sooner had he signed himself into the New Orleans clinic than he signed himself right back out again, commandeered a passing state trooper as a chauffeur, and grimly headed back north for Baton Rouge to reclaim his scepter, his vestments of power. Miz Blanche, somehow alerted that he was on the loose again, quickly had new commitment papers drawn up, and two detectives then sped to the parish line, where the pulled off the road and waited, poised to intercept him. Presently, an anonymous white Ford zoomed past them, with only a glimpse of Earl sitting up front by the trooper, a rigid and eager and turkeylike figure with his drab hair fluffed wildly askew—and the detectives slewed out onto the highway, shortly overhauling the Ford and waving it to the side of the road, where they informed Earl they had been dispatched to escort him on his triumphal reentry into the capital. He received this news happily, and jauntily resettled himself in the front seat of their car.

It was only when they pulled into the basement ramp of a courthouse instead of conveying him to the capitol that Earl, after an instant of silence, sputtered, "What's going on?" and then, "Goddam. Goddam you all! Yawl doing it to me *again*...." He refused to budge from the front seat, and as miscellaneous officials bustled off to find a doctor somewhere, he howled, "Goddam, all because of a woman. *All because of a woman. . . .*"

About that time, there had appeared in a national magazine a strangely lyric photograph of an extravagantly abundant woman with a loose lush mane of hair who was gamboling barefoot, in nothing but a smoky white gown, through some solitary glade in a soft Louisiana gloaming, her arms lightly raised and her face lifted in a drowsy-lidded transport. This replete nymph, named Blaze Starr, was tripping there under the live oaks to unheard airy pipes and lyres for none other, as it turned out, than Uncle Earl, gloating somewhere off camera.

He had happened upon her several months earlier, back in the winter before all the dishevelments of May, at an establishment entitled the Sho-Bar during one of his buoyant jaunts through the spangled entertainments of Bourbon Street. As Miss Starr later recounted in a beguiling valentine of a memoir with a somewhat passionate orchid jacket, when she had first spied him before one of her performances sitting at a table up front among a glum clump of plainclothesmen—a weathered corncob of a man, by then in his mid-sixties, with a rheumy mulish glare in his eyes and a slight touch of dilapidation about him, his gray furze of hair like dusty lint, garbed in a baggy sack of an ink-blue suit with his tie yanked sideways— she thought, "My God, I had no idea that little guy was a governor." After she had rendered her artistries, though, she was invited to his table—not the first time, actually, she had caught the attention of some notable, having earlier passed through a somewhat boisterous slam-bang consort with police captain Frank Rizzo of Philadelphia, the tankish dime-store Il Duce later to become mayor of that city. Presenting herself at Uncle Earl's table now, she happened to strike up an instant melodiousness with the governor. Herself having been generously ladled into the world out of West Virginia as a mountain girl named Fannie Belle Fleming, she was heartily reassured by Earl, "Deep down, I'm just an ole country boy myself."

There seemed, indeed, an immediate warm zest of delight in their discovery of each other. During one of her subsequent performances that night, she softly puffed him a kiss from the stage, which brought him flapping to his feet, applauding, curtly waving the rest of his entourage to their feet—vaguely lethal sorts with the inevitable discreet lump under their snugly buttoned coats—to clap with him. And the next evening, he had his limousine pick her up and deliver her to him for dinner at his suite in the Roosevelt Hotel. She appeared before him heroically brimming in a tenuously low-slung emerald gown— clothes on her always having rather the quality of an incidental and superfluous afterthought. After dining with a tableful of assorted other guests—who shortly, with a light dab of their napkins to the corners of their mouths, vanished expeditiously —Earl and Blaze sat on a settee, after the old-fashioned manner of front-parlor courtships, and Earl proceeded to make his presentation: "Honey, me and Miz Blanche live in a big mansion, but she lives on one end and I live on the other. She's one of these high-society women—all the time telling me how to dress and what I should do and what I shouldn't do. I just don't guess I ever adjusted to all those highfalutin customs." He then added the announcement, "We ain't slept together in over two years."

To that, Blaze chimed, in this ceremonious and polite little roundelay, "My husband and I are in the process of getting a divorce. . . . But I shouldn't be talking about such private matters. I'm sure you're not interested in things like that."

" 'Oh, but I am,' he was fast to reply," Blaze later recounted. Administering avuncular pats of his blunt freckled white-wisped hand to her sumptuous knee beside him, he croakingly assured her, "I put my pants on just like everybody else. . . ."

They kept company all that winter and on into the spring, Earl having tucked her into the Flamingo Motel on the out-skirts of New Orleans. After a long marriage to Miz Blanche that was barren of offspring, it had begun to bleakly haunt him that he would die with reedy loins spent, dry and blank and childless. He clumsily carted over to Blaze's motel room a large shabby box of foggy snapshots taken during his youth, so she could at least behold some dim image, these many years re-moved, of the rakish and swaggering young country buccaneer who this worn and gristly geezer she had accepted as her swain once actually was. "I told him that it was not necessary," Blaze says, "that I loved him for what he was now, not what he was then." It developed into a peculiarly idyllic concord. He would pick her up at the Flamingo Motel in the early dewy mornings

—waiting by his limousine with his white hat in one hand while with the other clamorously blowing his nose in a vast handkerchief—and they would set out for long pastoral roamings over the Louisiana countryside, Earl orating to her along the way in his foghorn delivery. He would stop at little back-bush pine-plank stores, where he would distribute candy from the counter jar to the gaggles of children who instantly collected around his frayed droopy coattails, and then purchase every ham in the place and distribute them to the children's coveralled elders. Finally loading up for themselves a case of Cokes, onions, a loaf of bread, and a medley of potted meats and crackers, Earl and Blaze would ride on for a distance and then stop again for a picnic under massive moss-muffled oaks, sloshing down these goods they had gathered off the land with warm soda pop. Having dispatched his chauffeur and police bodyguards on up the road for a few hours, Earl would lean back with Blaze under an oak and mutter, "Blaze, what would you think if an old man told you he loved you?"

"If it was the right man, I might tell him that I loved him too."

"Blaze, I love you."

"I love you, too, Earl."

And so they would cuddle, not unlike two babes in the wood nestling in a simple sun-dappled fairy-tale innocence. "I kept thinking about how strange it was," Blaze recalls. "Here I was somewhere in Louisiana with the governor, lying out under a big tree, in love with a man who was old enough to be my grandfather."

At one such gentle moment in a secluded moss-vaulted bower, they were taken with a sudden whimsy to replay again the skinny-dippings of their mutual long-lost childhoods, and partially peeled—maintaining yet a last modest measure of that quaint decorum that had filigreed their courtship, she ponderously plush in bra and panties, Earl a rickety and raddled satyr in only his trousers with the cuffs lapped up above his thin shanks—and proceeded to frolic splashingly in a shallow black pool. Presently Blaze glanced down to discover several leeches clinging to her. She screamed, floundering back out of the water, and Earl quickly crisped them off with a match flame while trying, with low hoarse croonings, to calm her shudderings.

Not long afterward in her room at the Flamingo Motel, as Blaze in her slip was applying herself to a bit of shirt-button mending while Earl lay sprawled in his shorts on the bed, napping with occasional peaceful snorts, the door suddenly shattered apart and four men toppled in, lugging between them a railroad tie. Blaze shrieked, and Earl instantly came roaring up, his arms pinwheeling, which sent the men crowding back out through the door. Earl reeled on out after them into the glare of the courtyard, where there immediately arose the ringing shrill voice of Miz Blanche: "You have disgraced me! You have disgraced yourself!" He simply stood there, a gaunt apparition in his shorts in the bright sunglare, cawing, "You dirty sonsabitches! Oh, you dirty bastards," as the raiding party wheeled on off. Stumbling back into the room, he became composed again only after Blaze had administered a succession of damp towels to his tempest-beaten brow. He then sat up abruptly and announced he was going to transfer her to a second-floor apartment—"You on the second floor, they not gonna be breaking in with a log."

But while Long's kinfolk were predictably appalled by this diversion of his, the commonry of Louisiana were cacklingly enthralled. Long maintained certain perfunctory pretenses of keeping the whole matter clandestine, but in fact, it was followed by the general populace with all the relish and cheerful suspense of villagers watching the fitful course of an elder's beguilement by a local tavern bawd—there was far more enthusiasm among them for this winsome eccentricity of his than for his racial apostasy. He was, in a sense, enacting the secret fancies of many of them. Once he took Blaze to a racetrack where they watched the birth of a colt together, with Earl suddenly blurting, "Blaze, I want you to have my son," to which she murmured, "I will," and he cuffed her to him with a clumsy hug and gave her a great extravagant noisy kiss, heedless of the grins everywhere around them.

He was a man, at sixty-five, dancing in the last best rainbow of his life. After one jealous ruckus, he sat slumped in a mute and abysmal mopiness through a splendiferous banquet celebrating an imperial visitation to New Orleans by General Charles de Gaulle. Finally, in the middle of the toasts, he bolted up and vanished, to go batting back down to the Sho-Bar to get matters sorted out again with Blaze. And the next day, leading a grand parade down Canal Street with de Gaulle, he abruptly instructed his driver to turn down Bourbon Street, the driver venturing with a quick little cough that it was not precisely the scheduled route and Earl shouting, "I'm the governor, goddammit, go that way." Thus the entire procession, New Orleans dignitaries, bands, de Gaulle carried loftily along with it all, turned after him down the street toward the Sho-Bar. As Blaze recited it later, "I had just got to the club when we heard all the commotion. . . . and here comes Earl and de Gaulle down Bourbon, Earl throwing kisses to me all the way to the next side street when the parade got back on the regular route. When it was over, he came back to the club and told me he had just wanted me to see it. . . ."

Sometimes in the evenings, back in the second-floor apartment in which he had now installed her, he would grumble that Miz Blanche, in cahoots with "my dear little nephew," was somehow conspiring to tinker with his food at the mansion so as to give him dire pangs of gastric distress, and was even smuggling some narcotic into his grits and ham gravy calculated to chemistry him into final and total goofiness. But then he would subside into a heavy-lidded and rapturous repose as Blaze spent an hour tenderly ministering to his fingernails and toenails, leaning to him bountifully like the most celestial voluptuous dream of all aging traveling salesmen in barbershops over the land. He had found his Elysium.

In a matter of a few short weeks, though, he had been clapped into the mental ward in Texas, with his nephew, Senator Russell Long, journeying down from Washington to the state capital to explain it all, in mildly funereal tones, to the legislature. Then, on his return to Louisiana, he had been plopped into another mental hospital.

None of these machinations availed, however. Isolated in a room behind ten locked doors, barefooted and sheeted in a white smock, he yet managed somehow to sneak a call to Blaze at the Sho-Bar ("You still gonna marry me?"—"*Yes yes yes yes.*"). So inspirited, he promptly obtained a writ of habeas corpus and came careening back out of the clinic to fire its superintendent and the director of the Louisiana Department of Hospitals. After thus exorcising and dispelling his tormentors—with Miz Blanche at last hastily evacuating the mansion—and having finally restored himself back into his pride and power, he received Blaze in his suite at the Roosevelt Hotel, opening his arms to her with a whoop—"My fair lady!" —and she, spilling to him, cried, "They have treated you horribly"—old briny Solomon reunited with his Sheba.

Even so, through the following weeks, Earl seemed to become increasingly hoodooed by all the continuing fanfare about his exotic mental weathers. Once in a restaurant with Blaze, in a sudden snit of exasperation, he commanded the waiter to bring him a glass of water, into which, to the captivated gapes of the other diners, he dislodged and plopped his false teeth. He then ordered a brown paper bag, mumbling with a manic wink to Blaze, "I'm really gonna give 'em something to talk about now," and with an elaborate deliberation he tore out two holes for eyes (all forks and knives around him now suspended in midair, chewing arrested, all eyes transfixed) and another hole for his nose and another for his mouth. He then pulled the bag down over his head and so sat for two hours serenely finishing his shrimp creole and sipping wine—it was like a desperate and burlesque last recourse against the gawking public expectation of spectacle from which he was now never free.

And in fact, tribulations were continuing to swoop and flap about his head like bats. He was shortly waylaid by a proclamation from the state Democratic committee that he could not be certified to campaign as a candidate again for governor unless he resigned that office first. It was as if, for all his dogged flailing, his magic, his juju, his potencies were fleeing him. The truth was, Uncle Earl happened now to be presiding over an array of simultaneous gymnastics in his life that would have proved grueling for any man, whatever his age and psychological equilibrium. Rudely intercepted in his gambit to assume the governorship again, he concluded that he would run for lieutenant governor. But in the racist foofaraw the campaign had become by then, on election day Earl wound up an amiable oddity lost far back in the dusty brawl. So all that, for the time being, was over with.

At the least, though, with Miz Blanche having been routed from the mansion, he still had the run of the place for a while, until his successor's inauguration. It was an edifice built by his brother Huey to be a replica of the White House "so he would know where all the light switches were in the bathrooms when he got to be President," and it had become by now almost the Long family manse, a cavernous affair with chandeliered rooms outfitted somewhat like resort hotel lobbies or mortuary reception parlors—pastel brocades of pink and green, satiny sashed drapes of a mauve kidney sheen, a plentitude of gilt mirrors, the pale arctic scapes of the walls totally and amnesially blank of any pictures. All alone here now, on his last night in this dynastic palace before leaving to take up common residence again elsewhere—on the last night of the Longs in these corridors and banquet halls of their tribal chieftainship—he mustered one final, private, caterwauling country-festival saturnalia. Hauling over the whole ensemble of Sho-Bar strippers around one a.m. in his limousine, he ushered them on into the mansion, and there—dismissing the butler, shutting the doors to the attritions and depredations at work in the world outside—they proceeded to romp and frisk on through the hours of the night: scampering with whoops and twitters along the corridors, gusting barefoot up and down the grand carpeted stairways. Earl, with this whole Rabelaisian carnival just to himself, lifted high a bottle of Coke mixed half with bourbon to toast Miz Blanche and his nephew Russell, "May their souls rest in hell!" Glasses then looped up after his flung bottle in a wild shattering among the regal chandeliers. He presently went trundling off and fetched a radio from somewhere, and to Elvis Presley whunking "You Ain't Nothin' but a Hound Dog," Blaze began performing atop a long stately table—"Last strip at the governor's mansion!" Earl boomed—she shortly unwrapping herself baskingly awesomely bare down to her wispy chantilly panties. The rest of them then followed her—all teeming atop the table together, with the high spaces of the room suddenly filled with a soft myriad flurry of clothing like a detonation in a Sears ladies-apparel department—while Earl sat magnificently at the head of the table in the midst of it all: a solitary, parched, scraggly old pine-hill centaur with slips and bras and stockings floating and sifting down about him, a prodigal cornucopian extravagance of female luxuriance surging and rippling everywhere around him. Lunging to his feet, he hoisted high another Coke bottle and wailed, *"Here's to the strippers! Here's to the State of Louisiana! Here's to Earl Long! May he live forever!"*

The morning after this last revel, in a panoramic debris of watermelon rinds and stray garters and broken crystal, they aided Earl in feverishly heaping together all the silver and china and drapes and candlesticks they could snatch, heaved it all into four cars, and made off in an urgent wallowing low-slung cavalcade for New Orleans and Blaze's apartment. A few days later, then, Earl took Blaze back up to Baton Rouge for the inauguration of his successor, a moon-faced and tan-haired country minstrel named Jimmy Davis, most distinguished up to that point for having written the ditty "You Are My Sunshine, My Only Sunshine," and whose campaign platform had consisted mostly of the slogan "I never done nobody no harm." Earl rode with Blaze in a convertible in the inaugural parade, pulling from his pockets an endless blossoming of handkerchiefs in red and white and blue and distributing to the multitude pictures of himself inscribed, "I'd like to be a friend of everybody, Yours Forever, Earl K. Long." Throughout the rest of the day's proceedings, he and Blaze occupied themselves in taking pictures of each other with movie cameras. Afterward, riding back toward New Orleans and the Sho-Bar through an orange sundown and lavender evening, Earl suddenly crowed, "I'm gonna run for Congress. Then I'm gonnna run for President." Shortly thereafter, he shipped Blaze on ahead of him to Baltimore, where, toward the close of his race for Congress, he phoned her to vow that, immediately after the election, he would don a black wig and a black mustache and board an airplane and so deliver himself to her forevermore.

It was the last endearment she received from him.

In August of 1960, only fifteen months after having been captured and confined in that mental clinic in Texas, Earl won the Democratic nomination to the U.S. Congress from the Long clan's ancestral turf in central Louisiana. The night before the voting, though, he had been silently walloped by a sudden concussion in his heart. Throughout the next day's balloting, he made no utterance of it, keeping himself carefully stored in a hotel bed in the glum little city of Alexandria, only grunting, to the occasional uneasy inquiries about his peculiar wanness, that he seemed to have partaken somewhere of a bit of dubious pork. Only when the polls had finally closed, and he had won it, did he have himself conveyed to a hospital. Several days later he drank a cup of coffee, replaced the cup on the saucer, and, lightly closing his dusty pale eyelashes, took his farewell.

With state troopers wailing sirens before him as on those legendary mornings when he set out on his grocery-shopping expeditions, he was transported down to Baton Rouge to lie in state. There, wreaths and garlands and bouquets kept drifting in from far dim reaches all over Louisiana, out of the hill country and the bayous, to envelop his bier. Among those in the vast processional crowding past him was, briefly, Blaze—who paused to detach from the deeps of her billowy bosom a single crimson rose, which she placed among the flowers.

As she was still declaring years later, "I loved the man."

III
Last of the Longs

If Earl himself never did quite get there, over the years assorted other Longs, various marginal cousins and incidental nephews, have moseyed out of Winn Parish into the marbled chambers of Congress—one who harmlessly inhabited its halls for a while being named Speedy O, another named Gillis, who seems to still be around. (When one of them offered himself for a lower state office, Miz Blanche, established in Baton Rouge now as a dowager-eminence of the dynasty, announced she knew nothing about him and had no idea where he had come from and wished to have nothing to do with him.)

But of the direct line of succession from Huey, there remains only that frequent source of indigestion to Earl, Huey's son Russell, Senator since 1948. He carries a muzzy mirroring of his father's ribald mumpish face, something of the same tubby hurrying eagerness, but Huey's raging energies are in him dwindled, compressed. In fact, Huey and his son encompass between them everything that has happened in the South since its primordial days, its processing into the savorless urban modulations of the rest of the country, the old turbulent rogue boars of its politics vanished and replaced by so many dapper technicians. Russell presents, on the whole, a muted, sprucely preened variation of his father—a college man, he was, a fraternity princeling who, associates from then remember, always seemed slightly abashed and wincingly embarrassed about his father's clangorous notoriety.

Ascending directly to the Senate when he was only twenty-nine, Russell eventually endured his way on up into the chairmanship of the Senate's Finance Committee, which officiates over, among other things, all initiatives in tax legislation, and soon became a fixture of that chamber's coterie of grandees amorphously defined as the Club. By then, he seemed as remote from the old snorting Populist pentecostalism of Huey as some plump bifocaled Episcopalian stockbroker would be from Neanderthal Man. Most notably, he had made his own peace with all the dragons at which Huey had so long pitched himself—in particular, as high mediator now over the national system of tax privileges, with the oil conglomerates. Russell has conscientiously taken on the corporate tones and decorums. Rising a few years ago to deplore a measure for expanding welfare provisions, he protested, "It's so hard these days to find somebody to wash and iron my shirts." To be sure, he has been given to occasional guttering afterflares of his father's political humors, including a recent zeal for the Kelso Plan, a notion for corporations to encourage their workers to come into the ownership through buying the stock. Such enthusiasms, though, tend to be errant impulses. Not too long ago, when the Senate was considering whether it should censure one of its worthies, Thomas Dodd of Connecticut, for a rather versatile variety of financial indiscretions, Russell was one of the five Senators who strenuously resisted the whole idea, sputtering at one point that the same charges against Dodd could as well be applied to over half the Senate membership. In the furor this occasioned from his fellows, he rapidly rearranged his sentiments on that count, announcing, "If I have any complaint to make of this body, it's that their standards are *too* high."

One of Washington's savviest and most literate commentators, Robert Sherrill, suggested during a recent period in Russell's life, "His face reflects his troubles"—and indeed, it has come to seem a more pillowy, bleary, wattled, and dewlapped version of his father's, a punched-out sofa cushion. For a while he commonly appeared on the floor of the Senate with a liverish blush, the slightest momentary tilt and totter to his movements, and a distinct bouquet of the decanter about him. It was around that time, too, that he abruptly divested himself of his first wife and then married his secretary. Since then, his

particular bemusement by the tumbler's clink has waned somewhat. But as one veteran Washington liberal activist who is
himself still disposed to certain neo-Populist nostalgias puts it,
"I've just stopped following Russell, stopped even being interested in him, he's been so compromised for so long. All he does
now is hang there in the background with the privileged."

To that epigraph has there come, after fifty years, the rise
and roar and decline of the House of Long.

How Lester Maddox at Last Became "Mr. Somebody"

As MUCH A CREATURE of the Southern Populist ethos that engendered the Longs was, in a later day and in his own way, Georgia's cacophonic political fantastick, Lester Maddox. Ranged against such figures as Huey or Tom Watson or even George Wallace, Maddox of course was rather a dime-store trinket of the real thing, more a noisy Jacobin Jester. But there was no question that he inherently issued out of the Populist sensibility, even if what he finally presented was a kind of tawdry cartoon of the Populist temperament's enduring susceptibility to lurid and self-aborting aberration.

In retrospect, the Sixties now seem a decade in the life of this country which passed like a malarial dream, in which the unthinkable became the commonplace, the surreal the familiar. It may seem, then, a reckless proposition, but there was perhaps no more astral occurrence during those bewitched ten years than the ascension of Lester Garfield Maddox—erstwhile fried-chicken peddler and pick-handle Dixie patriot—to the governorship of Georgia. The nation's only notice of him up till to then had been a single brief glimpse, in the summer of 1964, of a flushed, bespectacled figure with an onion-bulb head lunging gawkily about the parking lot of his Atlanta restaurant, a small black pistol clenched at his waist, shrilly shooing back into their car three black students who had presented themselves as customers. The next time everybody saw him, about two and a half years later, he was being inaugurated governor of the state.

That was in 1966. Invested then with a true and imposing political gravity in Georgia, but constitutionally prohibited from succeeding himself, he was elected in 1970 to the lieuten-

The Saturday Evening Post, April 22, 1967
The New York Review of Books, April 6, 1972

ant governorship to preside over the parliamentary machinations of power in the state senate—posing with an almost Presbyterian probity on that chamber's rostrum, behind sprays of tiger lilies and gladioli vaguely suggestive of the floral gorgeousness embellishing the pulpits of Billy Graham crusades—while he bided his time until he could run for governor again in 1974. In spite of all his consequence, though, the passage of six years had done nothing to diminish the initial incredulity of a lot of people in the state.

In 1972 the Georgia Department of Archives and History produced, as an official tax-subsidized courtesy for governors at the conclusions of their terms, a solemn bound volume of Lester's assorted public ruminations while he was occupying that office. It was not exactly one of the more arresting events of that publishing year. The truth is, at no time during his gubernatorial tenure did Lester really amount to much more in the affairs of the state or the country than a bizarre entertainment, and that compendium of his various contemplations, by any ideological schema yet intelligible to man, simply refused to scan. It was a transcript rather of four years of exuberant static, which actually did not fully reflect the complexity of that static, since Lester acknowledged he almost always improvised on his texts. What's more, Lester did not truly translate into print: in type his pronouncements lacked that singular sound of his voice—a high tinny urgent whanging, impatient and helter-skelter and losing whole syllables with no more trace than a lisp, tight little whistles of air—the very sound of zany irascibility.

Still, however distant that collection of texts was from the actual nature of the man, it did provide occasion for second reflections on Lester—not an altogether bootless exercise, as it turned out: one discovered that, while he had endured as one of the more garish curiosities in recent American political lore, his public hour was attended by considerably larger implications and portents (even though he remained cheerfully innocent of them) and his governorship itself may have meant more than many, including Lester, ever suspected.

Up until the very instant of his election, it baffled alien journalists visiting Georgia that Lester could be taken with any seriousness whatsoever by the state at large. Later, after he had delivered himself into the governor's office, Lester himself was fond of recounting, "I never doubted for a second I would win. All I had to do was beat the state Democratic Party, every major labor leader, the state Republican Party, all one hundred fifty-nine courthouses, about four hundred city halls, all the politicians of rank—*every one* of 'em—every major newspaper, the television and radio stations, the railroads, all the major banks, all the major industries, the utility companies. So that's what I did. I beat *everybody!*" Actually, that fairly well describes what he managed to pull off. Aside from his celebrated little pick-handle Thermopylae with the three black customers at his restaurant, about all he had for political currency was his weekly newspaper ads, in which, with a festively baroque conglomeration of typefaces resembling a carnival poster, he alternated menus with some of the more livid segregationist billingsgate of that day—decreeing almost every significant political figure in the state and the nation to be "cowards . . . no-good dirty bums . . . rascals." He himself had been a compulsive campaigner for office and did manage to get into a couple of run-offs—one for mayor and the other for lieutenant governor. But he could also usually be depended on to show up at all the unseemlier racial altercations around town during those days. There was something about him, on the whole, evocative of the distraught gentleman in the Philadelphia *Bulletin* cartoon ads.

But once again, as with the Longs and Wallace, what all the excellently rational observers from afar failed to appreciate was that Lester answered a certain lurking Southern tribal glee in unruliness and mayhem, a secret jubilant readiness for the rowdy and anarchic. It may not be the most responsible of political inclinations, but the delight Lester afforded many Georgians was that of an irrepressible poltergeist.

There had been several affrays at his restaurant, beginning almost immediately after the 1964 civil-rights bill was signed—Lester on one occasion yelping at two black students seeking entrance, "You no-good dirty devils! You dirty Communists!" On another occasion, Lester merely stood in the doorway with a finger thoughtfully rummaging in one nostril as he watched, on a streetcorner twenty yards away, another small delegation of young blacks being persuaded by a gaggle of whites that a notable case of indigestion could ensue from eating his fried chicken; among the crowd surrounding the three youths—

filling-station attendants, Georgia Tech students in tattered sweatshirts and bermudas, businessmen in shirt-sleeves and loosened ties licking ice-cream cones—were Lester's two stout sisters, one of whom demanded of the youths, "Have you boys been born into God's family? Have you been regenerated?" The rest of the crowd was less theological: "C'mon down to Mississippi, niggers! Six feet under, that's all!"

But that afternoon produced one of Lester's more memorable moments. He and his faithful were expecting a climactic confrontation, and Lester stalked up and down the street in front of his restaurant in the warm August sundown, trailed in his every move by a cheering multitude of some five hundred people. They soon created a colossal, horn-blaring traffic jam. When police began diverting cars down side streets at each end of the block, Lester suddenly became convinced it was all a conspiratorial maneuver to flush customers away from his restaurant, and he charged from one corner to the other to protest, the crowd happily tumbling after him. He tried to shove one patrolman out of the street, and then, to the admonitions of a police captain, squalled, "Shut your big mouth!" with the captain answering gently, "Now, Mr. Maddox . . ." But he was a man now mightily besieged, lost in a great, giddy, reckless transport of outrage. He finally screeched his glassy new black Pontiac out of his parking lot and swiftly barricaded one street through which police had been redirecting traffic, locking the car, pocketing the keys, and, with horns now wailing fearfully behind him, marched back down to his place at the bottom of the hill to deploy the rest of his family's fleet of cars to blockade the other side streets.

It was a countermaneuver that was triumphant for another hour or two. Once he hopped on a small bicycle and pedaled up to one corner to check on the situation there, then flagged a passing bus which police had let through and rode back to the other corner, standing tall and imperious right behind the windshield with his arms rigidly spread before him, holding onto the railing, his pose whimsically suggestive of Lord Nelson on the bridge of his warship as it heaved toward Cape Trafalgar. The police at last called wreckers to haul away his cars, and when the first arrived the crowd converged to block it, with Lester himself swinging up on the heavy dangling coupler and clinging there grimly. Finally the driver, caught up in the occasion's spirit of merry uproar, climbed up on the top of his cab and sat there, plump, legs folded under him Buddha-fashion, chugging on his cigar and waving as the throng applauded him.

As it turned out, no Negroes materialized, but that really didn't matter anymore. Walking back to his restaurant, his shirt limp and gray with sweat and the back of his coat smudged with rust and dirt from the coupler, Lester somehow brought to mind the mayor of some small provincial French town who had suddenly taken it on himself to flamboyantly, if futilely, defy in the town square the forces of Paris' federal officialdom. He strode right down the center of the street, his head cocked high, his face flushed and his balding head shining with sweat, his long legs resolutely scissoring and his arms swinging, as the crowd cheered him from the sidewalks, "Attaway, Lester! Oh, man—whatta man!" Reaching his restaurant again, Lester was met by his wife, and he hugged her, shouting, "Don't worry, hon," as the crowd pressed around them, still whooping in the soft summer dusk—"Don't get knocked down, sugar," he advised her. He paused to pose with her under his flickering neon restaurant sign for photographers, and then on an impulse hugged her to him again and gave her a great smack on her cheek. And his eyes suddenly twinkled with tears.

Much the same spry pipes of riotousness were in the air when, on a sunny January morning not quite two and a half years later, the Georgia legislature gathered under the glinting gold dome of the state capitol in Atlanta, convening there, by constitutional dictate, to select a governor after the two party candidates who had run in the general election had failed to accomplish a majority. In the capitol's marbled, mausoleum-like halls, the Grand Memory was still preserved—massive dusky portraits of Georgia's Confederate generals with melancholy gazes on their bewhiskered faces, dim tattered Confederate flags now encased in glass, but with the ancient grime, the yells and smoke and glory still in them. But scuttling past them this particular morning were television crews bristling with electronic gadgetry, heading for the house chamber where members of both legislative bodies were assembled for the proceeding, ruffling through bags of peanuts and swigging from cartons of milk.

There was, to be sure, a certain giddiness hanging over the occasion, as if everyone had suddenly found himself caught in a political lark, a colossal and questionable prank, which was, however, too outrageous and ingenious and enthralling to interrupt. During the preliminary formality of retabulating the popular vote, ballots from far precincts of the state were reported for Donald Duck, the University of Georgia's football coach, and "miscellaneous local individuals." But the rural legislators there were singularly, solemnly attentive to the progress of the matter. At each small falter in the parliamentary formalities, each uncertainty, one of them would instantly bob to his feet and demand to know exactly how the question could affect the outcome. They had about them the kind of fierce earnestness that is born out of long years of political exile: now so close to ascendancy again after eight years of irrelevancy, they were taking no chances. Standing quietly in the hall outside the chamber was Calvin Craig, grand dragon of the Georgia Ku Klux Klan, wearing a natty bow tie with his hair neatly water-combed above his ruddy face, and he allowed to one reporter, "Well, we finally did it. . . ." At one point in the balloting, as a Negro senator rose to explain why he could vote for neither candidate, an impatient hoot came from the back of the chamber, "Aw, siddown!" And then yet another white legislator arose to proclaim, "I cast my vote for that great American patriot, the honorable, the fearless Lester G. Maddox!"

Meanwhile, down on the ground floor of the capitol underneath the house chamber, Lester was barricaded in an office listening to the proceedings upstairs on a transistor radio as he gradually began to pull away in the balloting from the Republican candidate, Howard "Bo" Callaway. State troopers and swarthy aides with sideburns, their eyes narrowed by rumors of assassination plots and last-minute court injunctions, peered darkly at each new face that arrived outside the closed door. One man with a briefcase strolled up to the edge of the crowd and was immediately surrounded: "Hey, fella, what you got in that satchel there?" He sputtered, "Wait a minue, now, I'm *for* him, I'm one of his supporters, he knows me, just ask—" They hustled him on outdoors anyway, with the explanation, "This here's a restricted area, fella."

The instant the vote was concluded upstairs, Maddox and his party suddenly swarmed out into the corridor, yodels breaking out around them, and began making their way toward the gov-

ernor's office to get Lester sworn in before any possible unanticipated intervention. Lester himself was surrounded by a
flying wedge of troopers and plainclothesmen, and they bulled
their way through the floundering mass of reporters and spectators, grunting, "Get outta the goddam way," repeatedly pat-
ting their hips to make sure their pistols were still there. It was
a rather startling processional—suggesting some unlikely
yawping many-limbed beast suddenly loose and charging amok
through the corridors of the capital—and as it brawled on up
the marble staircase to the main floor, one had a sense of being
in the middle of some Latin American midnight coup: there
was about it a definite, if totally gratuitous, air of some attack,
rush, strike, with a furious urgency of its own, completely detached from the absolute absence of suspense in the procedure
in the house chamber which had birthed and released it. It was
as if Lester's own sense of theater and climax simply demanded
that all his solitary years of struggle be finished in this fashion,
this melodramatic style, no matter how absurdly a storm in a
vacuum. The troopers in their broad-brimmed Scoutmaster hats
carried Lester along in the tumult, buoying him up with their
hands under his shoulders so that the tips of his shoes just
occasionally grazed the floor. In the midst of all this, Lester
himself now had a curiously vague and befuddled gaze behind
his spectacles, a tentative faltering half-smile on his face.

There was a last fitful scrimmage at the door to the governor's
office, one newsman being whacked aside with a billy club, and
then, once Lester and his party were inside, the doors were
slammed and locked. A moment later, a cluster of harried men
rapped away at the door, bleating plaintively, "Colonel, this is
part of the escort committee out here, for the luvva . . ." As
they were admitted, there was a glimpse of the troopers inside,
hats tilted back from their damp foreheads, breathing heavily,
lighting up cigarettes—their load delivered. A second later,
another man grappled his way through to the door, began
whamming away, and was admitted with apologies—he had the
oath of office in his coat pocket.

The first indication that it had been done was the abrupt
emergence of the now former governor, Carl Sanders, who,
buttoning up his overcoat, clapping his hat on his head, bolted
on out of the building and into the night. Then Lester himself
appeared, his smile a bit broader now. He was surrounded by a
company of rural and small-town legislators—a dour party of

men with plain faces the color of earth, the hide suddenly white at a line midway up on their hatless foreheads, their eyes glittering and quick—obscure men who for the past eight years, during the urbane administrations of Ernest Vandiver and Sanders, had been on the far margin of things, political outcasts. But now, at their moment of triumph, there was no mirth among them, their mouths clamped shut, their jaws knotted. With their heavy blunt hands grasping his arms, they led Lester on upstairs toward the house chamber, where the legislature was awaiting his acceptance message—it had been done, Lester was their man, and through him they had now reclaimed the state.

Later, Maddox liked to explain what he had brought to pass by informing audiences, "God was my campaign manager." If so, He additionally intervened through some rather crafty sleight-of-hand with the state's political processes. Lester's improbable transfiguration into governor was actually accomplished through a prolonged slapstick sequence of political pratfalls and bumblings. With a diffusion of other candidates in the Democratic primary (including a likable and moderate but late-declared state senator with a vague resemblance to John Kennedy by the name of Jimmy Carter), Lester emerged, through the capricious lottery of plurality selection, in a runoff election with a former governor, Ellis Arnall, an aging but still gusty liberal from the New Deal days. Now having to choose between Maddox and this affable Rooseveltian relic in the racial dementia of those times, voters in the second-round primary opted for Lester—thus nudging him to a headier elevation than he had ever enjoyed in his life, prompting one stunned state politician to remark, "If Georgia were China, this would be known as the Year of the Cuckoo." Lester's accidental coup, though, still didn't seem to really matter, because the Republican nominee was Bo Callaway—a doctrinaire conservative and segregationist of the more businesslike and oblique variety, whose popularity in the state was awesome and virulent.

The millionaire scion of a Georgia textile dynasty that for decades had been unobtrusively presiding over a sizable plot of western Georgia, Callaway was a tall, trim former West Point cadet with a choirboy's face, a tight little mouth, and chastely barbered hair combed straight back in the lacquered style of a Twenties beau. Callaway, for his part, could not seem to believe his good luck when he found he would be facing Lester in the general election. Not the most complicated of men himself, filled rather with breathless and simple enthusiasms, Callaway began campaigning ebulliently on more or less the issue of school spirit—"I *love* my Georgia," he kept assuring everyone. One state legislator remarked at the time, "Hell, neither one of 'em would know how to pour piss out of a boot—Callaway just might, if the directions were printed on the heel." At any rate, for the duration of the campaign, Callaway's manner was like a prolongation of his reaction when he learned Lester was to be his opponent: incredulous, blinking, dazedly smiling wonder. The thought seems never to have occurred to him that the people could really be serious about Lester—and, of course, as it turned out, the majority of them never were. But there began to gather, among those liberals and moderates in the state appalled at the prospect of either Callaway or Maddox as governor, a write-in movement for Ellis Arnall. As Callaway now regarded the appalling possibility this posed—that neither he nor Maddox would wind up with a majority, which meant the decision would be pitched into a Georgia legislature almost exclusively inhabited by glandular Democrats hardly disposed to elevate any Republican to anything, whether he was Callaway or not— there began to grow in his eyes a certain blank stricken suspicion of calamity.

The general election did, in fact, turn out inconclusively, nobody clearing a majority, though Callaway's vote well outdistanced Maddox's. But Lester now seemed, suddenly and incredibly, inevitable. Callaway kept scrambling, in the face of all futility telephoning legislators over the state, stammering tearfully to one, "Well, I'm gonna win this thing one way or the other! I am!" Up to the very eve of the legislature's dispensation, Callaway was still enthusing—this to a gathering of Jaycees in an Atlanta hotel, with Lester himself also on hand to speak—"Gee, it's so good to see all these familiar faces, I want to tell you. Yawl have worked so hard during this campaign— gee, you know, I still remember yawl riding those motorscooters around in the rain down there at Jekyll Island—all of you out there who've worked with us so long and so faithfully, my goodness, just raise your hands a minute so I can see—" He then became, for a moment, squintingly serious: "You know, a lot of people through this campaign have told me, 'Oh, Bo, you can win this election if you'll just *compromise* a little bit.' Well, I told them, maybe so—but I'm not going to change these principles of mine just in order to *solicit votes*. Because. *I love my Georgia. . . .*" There was a plaintive pitch in his voice as he repeated this news one more time, as if he felt he had somehow not managed to convince everyone—if only he could get it across to them, everything would be different, everyone would see and the whole thing would turn out properly after all. What's more, he reminded them, the punishment of an apathetic public "is to live under the government of bad men." At this suggestion, the polite and genial grin Lester had been maintaining as he listened to Callaway instantly vanished, and he cast a long sober look up toward the ceiling, his hands folded meditatively under his chin. When Callaway finished, there was a spirited booming of cheers and applause, but Lester, in the midst of it all, simply grinned at nearby reporters, lifting his eyebrows briefly, slyly, wordlessly, and began tossing peanuts from his cupped hand into his mouth.

That very afternoon, in fact, Lester had directed one of his aides to drive him past the front of the capitol, where the inauguration stand was already being assembled. As they eased by, Lester, peering at it in fascination, mused aloud, "Just think, I was once just a little ole raggedy barefoot boy down there in southwest Atlanta. And now, in just a little while, I'm gonna— go slow a minute—be up there on that platform with all that bunting and flags, and bands playing. . . ."

When he arose on winter mornings as a small boy, before he could eat breakfast, on a cold stomach he had to start a fire in the kitchen, get eggs from the henhouse, heat water, and take his bath in a tin tub. His father was a laborer at the Atlantic Steel Company, and Lester grew up, with three brothers and three sisters, in the same drab smoky neighborhood where one day he was to build his famous restaurant. But then he was just a boy riding his bicycle—the weightless, effortless glide, the exquisite flickering of light through the spokes—on his daily newspaper route, sometimes hovering at the back of a Coca-Cola truck to snitch a bottle, then veering away, madly pedaling off into the calm flare of a Georgia afternoon.

"I tried to play ball," he once recollected, "but the other boys used to make fun of me, you know, 'cause of my being near-sighted. They used to call me 'Cocky' 'cause of my eyes." He sold newspapers for a while on downtown streetcorners, three cents a copy, but "I never could get me a good spot. Somebody else would always take the good spots." Later he worked at a jeweler's supply house, then as an apprentice dental technician, a soda jerk, a bicycle delivery boy—coasting disembodied, the silent wheels strumming the long afternoon light. His career as a restaurateur had its beginnings in a drink stand in an old pigeon coop, which he stocked with a case of Coca-Cola, a case of NuGrape, mint candy, and bread. His love was then borne to him there on a bicycle, eating an Eskimo Pie. She rode past his drink stand several times, and finally he asked her if he could borrow her bike—he fell off. A few years later they were married.

He was nineteen then, and working, as his father had, at Atlantic Steel—a clanging, fierce, cheerless place, with stark heaps of scrap metal rusting in weeds beneath a murderous sun. He earned ten dollars a week. "Men were afraid to get a drink of water, to go to the bathroom, for fear of losing their jobs," he would later remember.

During World War II, he worked in a plant near Atlanta that produced fleets of B-29 bombers, among them, he later reported, the one that dropped the first atomic bomb. He also gave chicken farming a fling for a while. "I had several thousand broilers once. But I lost every one of 'em. They got involved in this cannibalism, you know." On the whole, it was an accurate assessment, as Lester himself later reflected in one speech, that "if anyone ever had a perfect background for failure, I did."

But then he opened his restaurant on an off-street downtown —a fried-chicken emporium he dubbed the Pickrick ("You PICK them out, we'll RICK them up!")—and began, for the first time in his life, to prosper modestly. All the while, he continued his zest for riding bicycles. Shortly before that pandemonious confrontation with the Atlanta police in front of the Pickrick, he won a neighborhood bicycle race, pumping furiously and ecstatically, quickly gathering the wind and leaving all the others, a middle-aged man in his shirt-sleeves skimming off into the blue summer twilight. . . .

Nevertheless, after the melees at his restaurant following the passage of the public-accommodations law, Lester elected to

shut his restaurant rather than serve Negroes. Over the succeeding months, something seemed to fade within him. His
voice became not exactly quieter but tinier, his smiles somewhat pale and fleeting. One summer afternoon in 1964, not
long after closing down the Pickrick, he showed a visitor
around his rambling home of brick and glass, which was situ-
ated among the lilting lawns and shaded quiet of Atlanta's
expensive northwest section. A sign at the doorway warned,
"Beware of Dog" (it turned out to be a collie with a peculiarly
hoarse and unconvincing bark that ended in a squeak), and
another sign over the carport curtly advised, "Stay in Car and
Blow Horn." But inside, among the deep mist-green carpets
and the cold glow of indirect lighting, Lester shuffled about
somewhat droopily. "I really love this place," he said at one
point, "but I'm probably going to lose it all too." He stepped
out once on his wide back porch where, in a corner, a myna
bird was flicking from perch to perch in a small cage, and as
Lester went by, the bird croaked, "Hello, you rascal!" Lester
paused, grinned fondly, and replied, "Yeah, you ole rascal," but
with an odd unaccustomed dullness in his voice.

He eventually reopened his place downtown, but this time
the mild dining music was replaced by doughty fifes and drums
flurrying through "Yankee Doodle Dandy," and he was peddling
crates of ax handles instead of plates of drumsticks, his stock
including a complete family backlash kit of "mama-sized drumsticks and junior-sized drumsticks—those clubs, you know, that
railway switchmen used to carry." He now considered going
into the patriotism business full-time. "I think I'll probably
turn the Pickrick into a national shrine," he speculated, a
glimmer of excitement setting his damp eyes to blinking behind
his glasses. "We'll take people through on tours, and I'll have
an eternal light burning inside. . . ." Instead, he had to sell the
place after a short, indifferent spell of business. He opened a
furniture store which he also called the Pickrick, advertising,
"You will want Pickrick furniture, because our furniture is for
families who live better."

But he was becoming restless again. Whenever the legislature was in session, he could be found in the capitol's corridors
almost every morning—a solitary, forlorn, but deathlessly
eager figure, handing out patriotism tracts with the indefatigable vigor of a streetcorner evangelist, totally impervious to the

snickers and impatient condescensions of the legislators. The doorkeeper to the house was notified he would be fired for only two reasons: "Laying down on your job, or if you ever let Lester Maddox get past you and loose in this chamber." Nevertheless, Lester possessed that peculiar redoubtability, a ferocious fidelity to purpose, that is one of the askance fortitudes of absolute hopelessness. There was, in truth, a kind of valiantness about him; he was like a cracker Don Quixote. And in 1965, he decided he would run for governor.

"I didn't see any way in the world I was gonna lose," he declared later. "I kept telling the politicians, 'I'm gonna beat every one of you. You either gonna come in now or come in later.'" Believing the secret of genius to be directness, he commenced by drawing up a platform and printing fifty thousand copies, which he mailed to people over the state. Then he got into his dusty white Pontiac station wagon and, with a four-foot ladder tied to the top, disappeared into the backlands beyond Atlanta. It wasn't long before one began to notice along thin country highways a spattering of small cardboard signs tacked up high on telephone poles and pine trees, announcing in simple black print, "THIS IS MADDOX COUNTRY." "I used the ladder," Lester related afterward, "to climb up on and fasten the signs way up there so people couldn't come along and tear 'em off. I'd go down the highway and see all these big two-thousand-dollar billboards put up by my opponents, and I'd just pull off the road and get my ladder and hammer up ten little signs of my own and ruin 'em all—and it wouldn't cost me but a quarter."

His campaign staff at this point consisted, in its entirety, of himself, his wife, his daughter, and a sister. In his odyssey around the state, he stopped for occasional speaking engagements, and slept—raggedly, in two-hour snatches—in a succession of bleary little motels, frequently lunging from his bed in the middle of the night, fumbling on his glasses, and scribbling out a suddenly inspired phrase of fulmination in the small harsh glare of a metal desk lamp. The following day, he would stop at telephone booths along the road and call in publicity releases to the AP and UPI—insistent, unreal, dimly crackling little notifications out of the obscure interior of Georgia ("Oh, hell, it's Lester on the phone again") that were largely ignored.

Astoundingly, he bobbed up as one of the run-off contenders

in the Democratic primary. With that, he drove across Atlanta to the oak-bowered knoll where the new governor's mansion was under construction. He got out and chatted convivially with the workmen, shortly inquiring as to about when they figured they'd be finished with it. They told him, and he got back in his station wagon and drove away. A certain change now seemed to settle over him. "You used to see Lester running around with his eyes wide open with outrage, kind of hysterical all the time, you know," said one veteran reporter. "But then there was a picture of him the morning after he had gotten into the run-off. His eyelids had dropped a full inch, he had this hazy little beatific smile on his face, his lips just parted a little bit—he had the drowsy, peaceful look of a lizard that has just swallowed a blue-bottle fly."

Immediately after winning the run-off, he made another trip out to the mansion site to check on the progress. Satisfied, he now struck off after Callaway. By this point he had a lot more company, and other folks' cars, and other folks' planes. He carried with him everywhere a basket of apples, and as his party approached a town, he would toot happily, "Buster, give me an apple from back there!"

He was hardly dispirited by the fact that, in the general election, he actually trailed Callaway by some 3,100 votes. Showing up for that Jaycee banquet in a downtown Atlanta hotel the night before the legislature was to name him governor of Georgia, Lester—although this was not precisely a gathering of his sort of people—was hugely expansive, slapping backs and shouting, "How are you, boy, you doin' all right?" Then he discovered that he was seated right across the table from the Callaways, at point-blank conversational range. But he was in an invincibly amiable mood. Presently, sitting with an almost military erectness, both forearms lying perfectly straight and parallel on the table, one hand holding a cookie and the other hand wrapped around a glass of milk, he addressed himself to the Callaways: "Bo, yawl ski, don't you?"

This sally met with icy politeness from the Callaways—Mrs. Callaway, in fact, simply didn't speak. Undaunted, Lester continued nibbling on his cookie, beaming and nodding at others up and down the table. But once, for a long moment, as Callaway was whispering to his wife, Lester stared silently at the two of them, a light little quizzical smile on his face, as if he were puzzled by their remoteness, by the fact they would not heartily include him in their conversation. Mrs. Callaway, a handsome, tanned, tawny woman wearing a royal-blue sheath dress, turned to a reporter behind her and breathed, "I don't know whether it's the heat or the food or the situation, but it's stifling in here." She managed to maintain a semblance of a smile, though, her jaw set. For a while, Lester and the Callaways studiously avoided each other's eyes. Lester now was spooning down his food with a kind of absent half-mindful haste, not quite getting his mouthfuls of coffee swallowed as he turned to greet well-wishers leaning over him, his chin discreetly dribbling. Then, for another long moment, he gazed at the Callaways again, bemused, and abruptly said, "Well, did yawl have a nice Christmas?" Callaway murmured something, and Lester listened with a very grave and attentive expression on his face. Holding his coffee cup poised midway to his mouth, he then turned to Callaway's wife and inquired, "How about you, Mrs. Callaway?" She gave him a small, sweet smile. "No, we didn't," she snapped, "thanks to you." He stared at her a second longer, blinked twice, and finally raised his cup up to his lips, took a long sip, and set it down, glancing up at the ceiling was an expression of airy, angelic innocence.

There had been a moment back during his campaign: late one dull gray autumn afternoon after a rally in a small north-Georgia village, Lester had instructed his driver to stop the car, and got out and engaged in a brief, low conversation with a small boy who had a bicycle. Lester then shakily mounted the undersized bike and, as his aides sat patiently in the car, he went wobbling down the sidewalk to the corner, then back, his expression absolutely serene and composed, almost blissful, his knees pumping high as a light snow began to fall like a noiseless benediction everywhere around him in the dim, hushed afternoon. . . .

After Maddox's quirk victory in the primary election, that redoubtable Elijah of the Southern conscience, Ralph McGill, invoked passages from the Scriptures in a column about "a dog returning to his vomit," and sometime later he confessed to a friend, "I am an old man, and I'm not sure of anything anymore." But in a lot of other quarters, including liberal, the advent of Lester occasioned a kind of secondary, dark, perverse glee—something had happened outside the computations, the credulity, the comprehension, even the imagination of the press and the political assessors and brokers. A primitive, unaccountable event, something more *alive* than all analyses, had transpired, astonishing the most meticulous anticipations. It seemed for a while a bracing reminder that the common custodians and bookies of reality owned, at best, only an illusory approximation—that life was, after all, larger than all academic arithmetics. But this slightly mad elation was soon followed by more somber reflections. "My God," noted one Atlanta editor, "we still got us a little ole state here that's got to get through the next four years somehow."

Lester's own initial announcements were not enormously heartening on this point. Beyond assuring everyone that he was "tremendously proud and happy to be Georgia's governor," he confided, "Christopher Columbus found a world and had no chart except his faith in the skies. It is with that same . . . faith . . . that I stand before you as your new chief executive." Given his past, Lester's promise to conduct the whole state through the next four years according to his private communions with the sky was a prospect that substantially unnerved, for one, the state's establishment. The night he was sworn in, he had proceeded directly on to the house chamber for his acceptance speech, and he was greeted with oddly listless applause that seemed to testify to a vague uneasiness among the legislators now about what they'd just done. As soon as Lester reached the speaker's podium, the applause quickly evaporated into stillness. With the light reflecting off his glasses, a benign smile on his face, Lester delivered a brief address—"I need and seek your help and your prayers and your counsel and your advice"—and afterward, as he was being bustled through the corridors, he reached through the phalanx of troopers around him to grasp for the hands of everyone in sight, including even newsmen, imploring, "I'm gonna need yawl to hep me now," his dank clasp clinging as he searched for another hand to seize, "I'll be good to you, and you boys be good to me, heah? Hep me be a *good* guvnuh, now." Watching him, even Georgia's new black legislator, Julian Bond, was moved to suggest, "You get the feeling he's suddenly realized he's an overwhelmed man, and he does want help bad, because he's already begun to wonder if all those things he's been thinking all these years are really right." Indeed, with considerable dispatch now, that array of proprietorial interests that Lester had so startlingly outflanked in his campaign—the banks, the state's political consortium, all the patriarchs of the conventional civic respectability—undertook with a certain hasty muted desperation to amicably absorb him and perhaps thereby neutralize him, cheerfully volunteering to him consultants, aides, speechwriters. Poignantly, Lester seemed not only receptive, but euphoric over the offers.

Increasingly, in fact, there was a sense that Lester had somehow, somewhere, quietly undergone a curious metamorphosis. It was as if he were awash suddenly in warm surfs of gratitude and indiscriminate magnanimity. The morning of Lester's inauguration found the platform in front of the capitol now brilliant with bunting, milling with flags in a cold dazzling sunshine, and some considered it not without import that a section of stands had been erected over the statue of Tom Watson, Georgia's turn-of-the-century Populist demagogue— Watson's graven runtish figure, one foot pugnaciously planted forward, one fist raised in the air in a gesture of oblivious timeless unavailing defiance, now quite hidden. The band played a spirited fanfare, and when Lester was introduced, his speech was bogglingly gentle-tempered and conciliatory, brimming with goodwill for everyone. He delivered himself of such improbable phrases as "respecting the authority of the federal government . . . no place in Georgia during the next four years for those who advocate extremism . . . room enough in this great state for every ideal and every shade of opinion . . . for the right of dissent as well as the right to conform . . ." As his voice went on in a thin electronic whinny over the throng of his supporters, their applause became broken, disconcerted, short-winded, and one had an abrupt fleeting suspicion that Lester's mike was actually disconnected; he was moving his mouth, but, through some sly piece of mischievous rewiring, his voice was actually that of an impersonator crouching somewhere below the platform—an infamous trick, an infinitely more fell conspiracy than the extravagant theatrics of assassination alarms in the capitol the night of his swearing-in, a kind of assassination for which Lester's retainers had never been prepared.

Eventually, as he continued with his speech, the feeling of unreality seemed to overcome even Lester. In a dull, tic-toc voice, he plodded on through his unlikely platitudes, concentrating on nothing so much, it seemed, as reaching the finish, repeating again and again, "I seek your help. . . ." Suddenly it was as if he yearned to abstract himself out of his situation somehow, to disperse his formidable responsibility—the inevitable crises and decisions—among as many other people as possible; in fact, to simply reassimilate himself back into the crowd; even perhaps, now that he had done it, had accomplished it, to disappear.

But he was stranded up there on the platform hopelessly by himself, irrevocably the governor. When the benediction ended —"God Bless America," sung by a former director of the Youth for Christ movement, supported by an unseen electronic organ —Lester's eyes were moist. He called out, "Henry, will you sing it one more time? I didn't get enough of it that time." The singer repeated his performance. Lester asked him to do it yet a third time, and turned to the crowd: "All you people out there wanted to sing, I saw your lips moving. Come on, let's sing with Henry." Haltingly, the crowd joined in, an indistinct rumble lagging after Lester and the tenor, and Lester's eyes batted gratefully.

The rest of the day was given over to rather the same mood —as Lester himself had once enthused, "I really like what John Adams said one time: he said, 'There will be tears, there will be singing, and the people will gather together and be happy.' That's all I want—for the people to gather together and be happy." All day long after Lester's inauguration, the state capitol, at least, was full of people gathering together and being happy—among them, great numbers of Maddoxes. One saw them everywhere, standing in corners in quiet little detached clumps, smiling pleasantly as they looked about them, a bit stiff and uncomfortable, but pervasively there. Shortly after noon in the state cafeteria across the street, diners looked up from their tables and stared as a procession of some fifteen men, women, and children, all dressed with a kind of Sabbath-morning formality, wearing corsages and boutonnieres, filed in through a side door. "What is this coming here?" asked one state employee; a newsman turned to look, and then said, "Just some more Maddoxes." They paused and shifted among themselves for a moment in the center of the room, glancing only for an instant at the other people around them, murmuring to each other, steady bright smiles on their faces, keeping their eyes on the impersonal physical features of the place—the floor, the ceiling, the empty chairs and tables, the food on the plates of those sitting near them—and then, at the arrival of one of Lester's brothers, like starlings that have hung milling in the sky for an uncertain moment, they finally collected, found direction, flowed off behind the brother into the cafeteria line.

A certain quiescence settled over the capitol toward the end of the day. In a back office behind Lester's office, an aide whom Lester had fetched out of south-Georgia oblivion—a long and stork-like fellow with a harsh new haircut, wearing a dull black suit buttoned tightly all the way up—sat drinking a Coke and chatting with a newsman. A clipping under the glass top of his desk read, "I am really on the right path if I practice the Golden Rule of Jesus instead of merely admiring it," and a glaring orange sticker on a nearby wall cautioned, "Get up in the world, but never look down on anybody." As the fellow talked on about his new responsibilities, his eye fell on a book of matches left on the desk by some departed member of Sanders' administration. Pausing, he idly picked it up and studied it—a luxurious packet of matches, stiff and glossy and plump, with SOUTHERN GOVERNORS' CONFERENCE, SEA ISLAND, GEORGIA, 1965 regally embossed on the deep-green cover. He held it in his hand a moment longer, peered at the cover silently, turned it over and peered at the back, and then slowly, casually, his solemn expression never changing, lifted it back to his coat pocket and softly let it drop inside. Then, with a deep little breath of gratification, just as slowly and deliberately his hand returned to the Coke on his desk and he resumed his discourse.

All through that day, certain state officials who had served during the Sanders years, lonely remnants now of the old order, sat behind the locked doors of their scattered offices and whispered about what had come to pass, unbelieving, impotent, outraged—"They're the seediest bunch of characters you ever saw. You go in there to the governor's office for just a minute, and when you come back out, you want to just sit down and weep."

*　　*　　*

The following Saturday evening, Lester set out to make his first official appearance as governor at a national Jaycee banquet on Jekyll Island—a moss-drifted resort along Georgia's southern coastline. Strapped in his seat in a state plane, looking a bit uncomfortably pent in a tuxedo and black tie, with his pink face gleaming and his spectacles polished and his thin faint hair combed back behind his balding dome, he could have been George F. Babbitt setting forth for a Zenith dinner party. Immediately after takeoff, a state trooper brought him a Coke, and he cradled it in his lap with both hands as he continued a discursive, running review of his fortunes.

". . . Yessir. Then when it looked like I was gonna win after all, some of these politicians and so forth starting coming out for me—after 'long soul-searching,' they said." There came a scampish twinkle in his eye, and he briefly scratched his ear. "You know how they search their souls, don't you?" Holding his Coke in one hand, he raised up slightly from his seat and wordlessly, with the barest hint of a smile, his eyebrows arching prankishly, reached his other hand around to grab his hip pocket. Then he settled back in the seat and took a quick pull at his Coke, watching the other passengers chuckle around him. "Gonna have to sell my house, though," Lester abruptly announced. "Just can't keep up the payments. I was out there to the new mansion the other day, and the workmen told me they ought to be finished around March. Probably be longer, though. I'll probably have to make two more house payments." He mused a moment. "We aren't gonna be serving any liquor there, you know. I have seen liquor destroy a lot of good people. I've experienced some of it in my own family. . . ."

He looked out of his window for a while. Then he turned back to the passengers in the cabin and, his face touched with a certain grave wonder, launched into a peculiar recital of various manglings and accidents he had witnessed, narrating them in the most elaborate, reverent detail. "I've seen several people killed before. One dropped right in front of me once when I was working at the steel mill, fella was electrocuted. My brother, he was burned horribly, and he's suffered ever since. One hundred and ten operations. Then, my son, when he was just a little thing, I threw him once right through the front windshield of my car when I had to stop real quick. When I went to pick him up, the whole side of his face here"—Lester carefully traced a diagram on his own cheek with his forefinger—"hung down. I carried him to the hospital like that, holding the meat on with my hand. Then, 'nother time"—he took a swallow of his Coke— "he was out playing in the yard and caught on fire somehow. When the maid looked out the window, he was just standing there with his hands up in the air like this"—he threw both arms up as high as he could in his tuxedo—"burning all over. Then, 'nother time, he was playing up in some rafters on the back porch and fell, and caught his chin on a nail up there. It went all the way through here"—Lester lifted his chin and pointed—"and came out"—he bared his lower gum and pointed —"right here. He was just hanging there in the air on that nail through his chin. You look at him now, the next time you see him, you can see the scar there."

Despite this odd little Grand Guignol recountal, Lester was in an irrepressibly buoyant humor. "I guess in the Thirties was when I got interested in government, attending neighborhood political rallies—I wasn't but about eighteen, nineteen at the time. But my first real intense desire was in 1957, when a friend of mine was running for mayor and wasn't making the race I thought he should—he wouldn't work. So I decided I'd get into it. I read one of those ads about Dale Carnegie, and I went over there to check it out. I got halfway through that class, and I announced I was gonna run for mayor of Atlanta." There was an instant of silence as the plane lurched, bumped. Lester quickly glanced around and lifted his eyebrows alertly. Then the plane smoothed back out, and Lester went on, "When I got in that first mayor's campaign, they thought I was funny. Yessir. But the people didn't think so. Nosir. Everybody thought I was funny but the people." He meditated for a moment. " 'Course, it's been hard for my wife to get used to, my running all over the state. But I told her once, 'Honey, every man should accomplish more than his daddy did. If I was just somebody who wanted to work at a job like everybody else, wanted to just run a private business like everybody else, come home every night and eat supper and go to bed like everybody else, then I'm gonna be like everybody else.' Yessir, taking that Dale Carnegie course . . ."

He blinked. The plane was bumping again, and again his eyes widened slightly in suspense. He waited for it to steady. ". . . uh, taking that Dale Carnegie course, that was the greatest thing I ever did. My daddy told me one time, said, 'You better be careful, you gonna bite off more than you can chew one of these days.' I told him, 'Dad, there's not a job in this state I can't handle.' I still think I can do any job in this state, right this minute—'cept maybe doctor. That's something different, you know, being a doctor. But anything else, I can sho do. You can go to the top in anything." He turned to the state trooper who was sitting on the arm of the seat behind him, tilted forward and listening intently. "You remember that, young man. You just set your mind to it, you can do *anything*." The trooper nodded vigorously. "I'm listening, governor, I'm listening."

The plane was riding level and resistless now, and there was a sensation in the cabin of motionless suspension—like the sensation, almost, of floating along on a bicycle. Lester presently reported, "You know, though, I told President Johnson at least forty times that the trouble going on in the country today was gonna happen. After the civil-rights bill was signed, I sent him must've been forty letters and telegrams. One of 'em I sent cost me *thirty* dollars. But you know what? He never answered a single one of my letters or telegrams. Nosir!" He leaned forward then, his elbows on his knees, and inquired in a low, earnest voice, "Johnson and all these others—I wonder sometimes. Do you reckon they thought I was a nut?"

But the impression lingered on through the following weeks that something had tuned Lester gently, muzzily out of focus. He had a series of nice things to say about state political leaders whom he had lustily termed "rascals" and "scalawags" in the past. His appointments to state party executive committees proved agreeably conciliatory and ideologically eclectic, with Lester explaining, "From the very beginning, the Democratic Party's greatest victories have come when its members have exercised tolerance for their differing views on specific questions. . . ." He even repudiated George Wallace's third-party movement of that time, which prompted Wallace to snort, "Hell, he's just comical, that's all. All of a sudden, he wakes up one morning, and he thinks, 'Why, goddam, I could win this thing, I could actually be *guvnuh* of this state!' He gets frantic and starts trying to make everybody he can think of happy, snatching at anybody, making all these accommodations and stuff. What's wrong with Lester is, he ain't got no *character*."

More precisely, what Lester lacked was not so much character, as any terrestrial coherence of ideological vision. He operated from a political sophistication of the subtlety and depth of a framed wall-sampler homily, and as nebulous of real details and applications. (He once proposed, with a wink of arcane canniness, "You know, Goldwater would have won that thing in 1964 if it hadn't been for that *Fact* magazine. They beat him when they came out with that article on him that had that diagram of all that psychiatrist stuff comin' out of his head.") The state's establishment, for that matter, soon determined that there was really no need to neutralize Lester: his own irredeemable ineffable ineptitude precluded his impinging seriously on the state's affairs in any way whatsoever, either benignly or disastrously—he was as hopeless of effecting anybody else's designs as he was his own. While his state-of-the-state messages were given to such pronouncements as "One strong, fearless, dedicated, and God-fearing patriotic legislature can do the job and return America to its rightful place as the greatest, freest, and cleanest nation on earth," when it came to the particulars of executing such propositions, Lester allowed that "there just isn't much major legislation left to pass these days." At times, when the fancy struck, he did dispatch proposals to the legislature, but by the close of his first year in office he had already lost more bills than his predecessor had in four years.

As a result, the magnetic field of authority around the governor's office began to wane rapidly. Its satellite agencies in the state's government started scattering off into their individual orbits—most notably, the legislature. If Georgia survived Maddox largely owing to his own inability to activate any of his notions, the discovery was made in the process that the state could pretty much run itself without any governor's office at all: a realization that immeasurably diminished and enervated that position. To his successor—who turned out to be that temperate young liberal named Jimmy Carter—Maddox left an office about as sacked and empty as Atlanta after Sherman's passage through.

But such a circumstance was never of much moment to Lester himself, anyway. About midway in his term, he declared to a congregation at Adair Park Baptist Church, "For many years, it was my ambition to be a preacher. . . ." And indeed, it seemed that he considered he had been assigned not so much to legislate and administer, as to act as a kind of full-time lay chaplain to the state at large, conducting a running four-year-long revival for "honesty, efficiency, and morality" in the business of the state. Accordingly, Lester propelled himself over the map of Georgia in a performance—1,200 speeches, twice his predecessor's log—that, looking back over it now, rather resembles a marathon pinball-machine exercise: a ceaseless pinging and chatter of piques, exuberances, prophecies, commentaries, as he plunged and caromed about such locales as the Warner Robbins Church of God, the Hormel Company's Tucker plant, the Philippi Baptist Church of Locust Grove, a new softball field in Cedartown, a Congregational Holiness Youth Camp, a Dunlop Tire and Rubber Company plant, a Penny Catalogue distribution center, the Macedonia Baptist Church. His appetite for audiences was inexhaustible and omnivorous: he appeared for such occasions as the Seminole County Fat Cattle Show, the Sweetheart Plastics' plant dedication, the opening of Horne's South Motor Lodge, groundbreaking ceremonies for the Lovable Girdle and Brassiere Company; he spoke to such assemblies as the Graduate Embalmers of Georgia, Inc., the American Turpentine Farmers Association, the Scientific Glassblowers Society, the National Association of Hairdressers and Cosmetology, the Hot-Dipped Galvanizing Association, the American Society for Aesthetic Plastic Surgery.

On the whole, trying to parse any comprehensive political dialectic from all the effusions of this endless circuit became a kind of gentle flirtation with lunacy, a voyage through outer galaxies of daffiness. While insisting that "perhaps the greatest of all freedoms is the freedom to criticize," Lester could also sturdily add that "any rights to be protected are those of peaceful and law-abiding citizens," a guarantee to be distinguished from "letting this great, beautiful, hard-earned country be spoilt, spit upon, desecrated, and dominated by a bunch of snotty-nosed, stringy-haired, red-eyed, LSD-taking younguns who range in age from thirteen to eighty." Reminiscing once about his own personal pistol-brandishing demonstration in the parking lot of his restaurant, he proposed, "I was fighting against legislation which was contrary to the United States Constitution," but he also maintained, with equal ardor, "I do not think anyone has the right to decide which laws he will or will not obey, or to engage in acts of civil disobedience." He was prone as well to such diverting pronouncements as—this to a Calvary Baptist Church—"If Hitler could poison one generation of Germans and nearly become dictator of the world, if Stalin could poison one generation of Russian Communists and enslave over half the world's population . . . think what one generation of Americans, completely committed to Christ and God, could do for our country and our world."

Over all of Lester's utterances there seemed to preside the watchful shade of some sixth-grade history teacher in his childhood, a prim and righteous spinster with her hair in a bun who provided him with lifelong DAR notions about patriotism and the American system—enlightenments lent additional perspectives later by a conglomeration of miscellaneous extracts from Edgar A. Guest, Billy Sunday, William Jennings Bryan, Paul Harvey, Douglas MacArthur, and the *Reader's Digest*. His divinings of not only world affairs but such social distress as crime and poverty were usually of the old-fashioned tent pulpit variety: "I believe a mighty spiritual Holy-Ghost revival in our land" he announced, "would do more in one day to solve our problems and make us secure against our enemies than all the conferences, deliberations, and treaties of politicians could do in a hundred years." At one National Governors' Conference, as Lester later reported to the folks back at the Glenhaven Baptist Church, "I asked the other governors to stand up for God by signing this statement: 'Now, therefore, be it resolved, that we of this National Governors' Conference rise to personally and collectively draw nearer to God, and . . . by regular deed and daily example, provide the spiritual leadership for which our people hunger and which God demands. . . .' Now, I know you'll find it hard to believe, but a few of the governors at the conference didn't want this resolution to even come up for a vote."

There were times, in fact, when Lester gave the impression of having strolled bodily right out of a fantasy of Sinclair Lewis'. "The American free-enterprise system could never have been established if it were not for the birth of Christ," he once declared. "The Christmas trade alone is an example of this truth. . . . In His name, more activity is promoted, more gifts are bought and wrapped, and more business is advanced, than in any other name in the Yellow Pages of the telephone directory. There is power in the name of Jesus!"

Even while he continued to affirm that "I'm a segregationist and proud of it," he appeared to be deeply scandalized by the angry furor raised by black congressmen over his distribution of souvenir pickhandles in a congressional cafeteria one afternoon; to Lester, it was evidence of an appallingly petty malevolence on their part. He simply could not understand why they should have taken umbrage. He was, on the whole, capable of moments of towering tackiness and tastelessness. After the assassination of Martin Luther King, he felt compelled to protest, "My heart went out to Mrs. King and her four children . . . [but] my heart was heavy too when I thought of the wives and children of the firemen, the policemen, and the innocent bystanders who have died, and will die, because lawlessness has been sanctioned and financed. . . . I did not weep at the death of Dr. Martin Luther King. . . . I felt no need to do penance, for I had done Dr. King and his followers no wrong. . . . And I say to these people . . . I will criticize you when you condone lawlessness and attempt to justify riots, looting, burning, and murder." A few weeks later, somewhat more succinctly, he sniffed, "We have seen representatives of the White House, would-be Presidents, and other leaders weeping and flying all over the nation to mourn the death of agitators who publicly threatened to overthrow the government."

Of course, the grim question prompted by all this was how characteristic such simplicity and rancorous bumptiousness might have been of the general perception of the citizenry about the world and times in which they were involved. Lester himself shortly after his inauguration began producing certain larger speculations about amplifying on the trick he had managed to bring off in Georgia. "Maddox Country has already extended halfway through South Carolina and clear to Miami," he averred. He then availed himself of a Fourth of July appearance to submit, for everyone's sober consideration, "a recent article by Jean Dixon." A particularly voluble admirer of Lester's, Mrs. Dixon, Lester now portentously disclosed, had said "that she sees, quote, resentment and anger building up in the American people. They are searching for a new personality who will act, not react . . . show courage, not fear . . . and who above all will hold high the torch of freedom for the world to rally around. . . . This personality," Lester recited on in awe, "is trying to emerge, and he will be forced to the forefront by the American people. Events are building in his favor. . . ."

While flying that night to the Jaycee banquet at Jekyll Island, Lester had been asked if it were conceivable that he might be able to repeat on a national scale the feat he had worked in Georgia. "Naw, naw," he had answered, waving his hand. He leaned back and folded his hands across the stiff white bib of his formal shirt, gazing for a long moment out of the darkened window of the plane. " 'Course, now . . ." Everyone's head snapped back toward him. He was leaning forward again, a mischievous smile peeping from behind his fingertips. " 'Course, somebody said it once, right after I was born. It was our colored woman. She held me up and said, "This man gonna be President of the United States.' " And he winked.

A little more than a month after his citation of Mrs. Dixon's prognostication, then, Lester—in what was unquestionably the consummate whackiness of his four-year governorship— announced himself a candidate for the White House. As it turned out, he presented himself apparently a bit before Mrs. Dixon's forecast "events" had finished arranging themselves for him. Indeed, the annals of American politics probably hold no more curious scenario than Maddox's two-week Presidential adventure. But as one Atlanta newsman who was close to him through it all observed, when asked if it had occurred to Lester at any point that his possibilities might be something less than momentous, "Look, you suddenly find twenty Secret Service men following you around everywhere you go, and you don't have any trouble beginning to believe it's for real." When it all came to an overwhelmingly unnoticeable collapse at the 1968 Democratic convention, and his entourage of bodyguards vanished back into the air as abruptly and magically as they had appeared, one might have supposed it had at least left Lester— who liked to attribute his ascent into the governorship to "Dale Carnegie and prayer"—with the suspicion that, at times, there are even limits to what Positive Thinking can bring to pass for a man. But as one capitol reporter declared, "Lester operates by auguries. Driving down here some morning, he might see a damn mockingbird on a lawn, and when he gets to his office, he'll announce he's gonna run for President again."

For all that, after his accidental topple into the governor's office, Lester uncannily flourished. Beyond all predictions, he increased, if not conspicuously in wisdom, certainly in stature and favor with the citizens of the state. One municipal poll found an 80 percent approval of the manner in which he had comported himself as governor, and at the close of his term, he won the lieutenant governorship by almost as lavish a margin. While lieutenant governor, he even retained former governor Carl Sanders—an urbane archduke of the Atlanta establishment who, during his own term, had once railed in the privacy of his office, "I'm not about to let the fools and nuts like Lester Maddox take over this state capitol for a while yet, I can tell you that"—to represent him in a lawsuit over infringements of his exclusive rights to manufacture and sell his Lester Maddox wristwatches. These were part of a robust commerce he was conducting from a shop among Underground Atlanta's nightclubs and boutiques, something like the fourth resubstantiation now of his old embattled Pickrick—trafficking in such items as Lester Maddox sweatshirts and "Wake Up, America" alarm clocks.

Lester once explained himself, probably more conclusively than anyone else ever did, when he recounted his boyhood to an Atlanta PTA group: "I can remember how faded blue jeans and worn-out shoes didn't seem too important when the school-day was begun with the reading of a verse from the Bible, reciting the Lord's Prayer, and saluting the flag of the United States of America. . . . I sincerely believed if I saluted that beautiful flag, [it] would extend its blessings to me. . . . My inspiration came from every streetcorner where a small grocery store or a shoe shop or a drugstore was located. I saw men standing in the doorways of their businesses in the early morning, and their faces reflected contentment and pride and security. I wanted to be like them. I wanted to be able to stand in my own doorway and greet the schoolboys as they passed by. . . . My dream came true. I was Mr. Maddox. I was Mr. Pickrick. I was Mr. Somebody."

On more than one occasion, Lester was to betray such egalitarian sentiments as "Democracy is founded on the belief that there exists extraordinary possibilities in the common man." If he finally lacked the political savvy and viscera to count for

anything more than a caricature of such Populist legends as
Long or Watson, it was nevertheless clear that, however mixed
his bag of notions, he essentially answered to the same instincts. During an early campaign for mayor of Atlanta, he was
always belaboring the silvered and patrician incumbent, Ivan
Allan, as "the Peachtree Peacock," flourishing a pair of silk
socks in the air as he did so. And not long after his inauguration as governor, Georgia's informal board of managers recognized that not only was there no need to neutralize Lester, they
would have had a stubborn time of it if they had tried. "That
group in Atlanta," Lester began shrilling, "seems to think that
local government should be run from Atlanta's city hall, their
local newspaper office, and the offices of the financial czars
downtown." But as Emory University political scientist James
Clotfelter pointed out at the time, "One problem with Populism has always been that the people who speak for it tend to
be very unsophisticated and naive to begin with. Their perspectives are those of people who have grown up on the
periphery of power, which leaves them especially vulnerable to
corruption."

Lester's own particular vulnerability, it appeared, was that
lonely boyhood desperation of his to be "Mr. Somebody"—a
condition which was defined for him according to the pinched
rectitudes and proprieties of a popular ethic cultivated by the
system. In fact, the American custodial estate's long, resource-
ful, assiduous diversion of every massing surge of Populist politics in the nation's past—not only through the gambit of
myriad intimations of Marxist and racial menace, but also
through the beguilements of the Horace Greeley romance and
the *Saturday Evening Post* respectabilities, and not only in the
South, but in movements over all the country like the I.W.W.
—constitutes one of the more enormous and remarkable bam-
boozlements in all the archives of political cozenage. Lester
himself was an ephemeral, seedy casualty of this historic flim-
flam. While declaring with genuine passion that "one of the
great tragedies of our times is that the people's voice is far too
weak and too often falls upon deaf ears," yet, like so many
before him, he was impossibly enamored of those mean pieties
and orthodoxies by which, historically, the people's voice and
interests had always been eventually undone. "This administration believes in less government in business and more business

in government," he could proclaim, and "our nation became the greatest on earth not because of big men in government, but because of big men in free enterprise." Also, he entertained a somewhat exorbitant deference to the majesty of the military, proposing, "It is time that we called upon our military leaders to tell us what to do to win this Vietnam war," and once enthused to the Gray Bonnet Regiment of the Georgia National Guard, "I wish all Georgians could have seen your mounted review this afternoon, and the powerful pieces of armor and other equipment. It certainly has heartened me to see such tremendous power . . . to know that our state has sufficient force to deal with any enemy."

Nevertheless—setting aside all his incantations and gaudy posturings—Lester did assume aspects, despite himself, markedly more wholesome, for instance, than Wallace. This may have been largely due to his sheer simplicity of heart and wit. But throughout his tenure, despite his ceaseless shrilling of the more squalid homiletics of the right, he seemed repeatedly to lapse into genuinely large-spirited behavior. Most notably, he introduced through appointments a substantial and unprecedented number of blacks into the middle echelons of state government—nowhere near proportionate to their percentage of the state's electorate, but a meaningful increase nonetheless. For all his baleful forensics on crime and punishment and law and order, he seemed actually disposed to an unusual solicitude for the state's prison inmates, declaring once to the legislature, "Georgia, unfortunately, was one of the last . . . to lay down the infamous 'chain-gang' concept of corrections, with its philosophy of vindictive retribution. . . . We're going to begin anew, if that's what it takes, to have a system which helps inmates shape their futures, rather than reminding them of their pasts." His sentiments in this regard were sometimes ascribed to the fact that his own life had been touched with a similar melancholy, one of his sons having been arrested on more than one occasion for burglary. Whatever the compulsion, he initiated a policy of early probationary releases for a sizable portion of the state's inmates—"a second chance," as he put it in a slightly misty voice, "for those . . . who, for one reason or another, have left the path." At the same time, he admonished graduates of one police academy, "Never allow yourself to regard those you are forced to correct as adversaries or enemies." Not surprisingly, in time he became, for most of Georgia's prison population, their patron saint, and one escapee turned himself in, with a list of grievances he had been delegated by his fellows to bring, to Maddox at the governor's mansion.

This occurred on "Little People's Day"—Sunday afternoons, scheduled by Maddox himself, when he simply threw open the front door of the mansion to anyone who wanted to wander in and chat with him. The same neighborliness prevailed to a degree at the governor's office in the capitol. "There have been more visitors to your governor's office and the governor's mansion in the past two years," Maddox claimed, probably accurately, "than in the past quarter of a century." Also, though he was sometimes seized by such fits of pique as ordering all newspaper racks from the capitol grounds, he was generally quite amicable and sporting about the press' frequent raids on him, gamely allowing, "No matter how bitter, no matter how cruel, and no matter how unfair the editorialist's pen is to me, personally I would sacrifice my career, my fortune—yes, even my life—to keep this symbol of freedom alive and unchained. . . . The small pain which I suffer on occasion . . . is a bargain price to pay for that."

And he was given to other refreshing impulses. Any rumors of regular folk anywhere being hoodwinked, exploited, or bullied instantly and spectacularly animated him. He mounted a number of vigilante ambuscades on reported clip joints, and once erected, at both ends of a town legendary as a speed trap, personally autographed billboards notifying tourists of that fact, with highway patrolmen stationed beside them to guard against their removal by town authorities.

But beyond all this, Lester's mere political arrival was of considerable import in itself, as the first vague assertion of a gathering popular mood that was to subsequently dislodge those arrangements of power which had customarily been managing the fortunes not only of Georgia, but of other Southern states—a phenomenon which was to be called the New Populism, and which would ultimately assert itself even beyond the South in the Presidential candidacies of George McGovern and, finally, Jimmy Carter. Lester, of course, remained wholly unwitting of such implications. But often, the imminence of new political seasons are first signaled by the appearance of such unlikely errant birds. Not long after Lester's election, in fact, that genteel collection of enlightened merchants in Atlanta who had been accustomed to comfortably directing the city's affairs through a succession of proxy mayors was suddenly, rudely confounded when their newest offering was defeated by Sam Massel, a Jew backed by a coalition of blacks and blue-collar unions. Though few could have imagined it at the time, what Lester boded, concluded one Southern political analyst, "were the elections a few years later of all those new-direction Southern governors. They worked it from outside the old familiar structures. And what Lester did, he told everybody—anybody—that they could do it."

It was an irony approaching the bizarre, then, that Lester Maddox in the end was to exercise a generally reinvigorating effect on the democratic process, if not directly elsewhere, at least discernibly in Georgia. With some legitimacy, he maintained, "Behind closed doors you throw your politics and your weight around, and people don't get to see what's going on. But at least I've opened those doors. Let them see the bad when it's bad, let them see the bad as well as the good. Maybe it doesn't work every time to my advantage, but how can I get the people involved if I hold things behind closed doors? Talk about the advantage, instead, of what I promised the people—honesty and efficiency in government, and open government. And after I'm governor, what's gonna happen? What's the next governor gonna tell the people when they come knockin' on his door on 'Little People's Day'? What's he gonna tell the news media that have felt free under this administration to look and look hard, hit and hit hard? . . . They won't be able to kill it all. And you can't tell, if this could happen maybe with every third or fourth governor, it could keep living—could keep on living."

In 1973, Lester tried again for the governorship of Georgia—and lost, in the Democratic primary, to one of that breed of blameless and industrious administrative technicians who by now had inherited the politics of the South. With that, Lester seemed to recede into sudden, terminal eclipse. For the next several years, his time was largely passed in scrabbling to salvage himself from a catastrophic campaign debt. His efforts to revive a restaurant business faltered and gasped out—during which he resorted, at one point, to a touring entertainment act with his black dishwasher. Probably his last intrusion into the public notice was a brief, one-man hue and cry against Jimmy Carter, an old infuriation of his, during Carter's Presidential primary campaign in New Hampshire. Then, in 1978, Lester was collapsed by a heart attack, and it was only after a considerable time that he began to stir about again. Since then, he has been operating a small real estate enterprise in Atlanta.

Southerners at Large

The Charleston Cold-Warrior from Hell-Hole Swamp

ON A MILD, ashen, winter early morning in 1969, South Carolina's durable Congressman Lucius Mendel Rivers, zippered up in a scruffy brown suede jacket with limp trousers reminiscent of Depression soup lines, stood on the brick patio of his home in Charleston and pointed out for a pair of visitors, "See that mockingbird over yonder in that camellia bush? That fella picks him out a backyard, and it's his—he's the boss, and he'll take on anything that wanders into his territory. I've even seen 'em fly at great big ole dogs."

Much the same kind of proprietary instinct has always prevailed in Washington, where Rivers had made his own political nest for the past thirty years: it's a town of mockingbirds, all fiercely attentive to their respective backyards of jurisdiction, however pinched or spacious. Washington is a curious aberration in several respects, one of them being that its primary business is power. That's why it exists. As a result, power tends to become a property, a currency, a measure of men in itself, and only incidentally a means to an end.

Long one of the more obscure but formidable potentates of this peculiar community was Rivers, a tall and austere figure who, one dim drizzling December morning, arrived at his office in the mausoleum-like Rayburn Building, as he always did, in the black and vacant hours just before dawn—solitary and unnoticed, wrapped in a black topcoat with a red tartan scarf around his neck, a sober homburg atop a long lavish maestro's mane of frost-white hair combed straight back to his shoulders.

Life, February 27, 1970

Now sixty-five, Lucius Mendel Rivers had gradually and patiently negotiated his personal political duchy in South Carolina's First District into a dizzyingly larger one, the chairmanship of the House Armed Services Committee—a position actually bearing on the world balance of power. He presided over the processing of every military bill from privates' pay raises to missile purchases; as one of his committee's aides declared, "The chairman—this one man—damn near has the capacity to fortify or disarm America."

For all their parochial novelty, the South's political personalities have always figured much in the life of the whole nation —often memorably so. Indeed, it sometimes seemed as if the South, having been confounded once in the field, then proceeded with an infinite resourcefulness to gradually reverse that verdict—its Senators and Congressmen, through the folk loyalties of the tribal politics back home, abiding through the seasons to appropriate Washington in time through the Congressional seniority system. Of this inner Southern coven of power on the Hill, one California Congressman protested in 1970, "They simply run this goddam place. And so run the whole goddam country."

The over-sized gavel, more like a roustabout's mallet, that Rivers kept on a shelf in the den of his Charleston home was no inappropriate token of his own clout in Washington. He himself had once allowed that his legislative feats as committee chairman outstripped anything managed "by Julius Caesar in all his glory." And after he had single-handedly hauled out of a joint conference committee an authorization bill for defense expenditures far beyond the sum approved by the Senate—a bill that bestowed blessings on every project proposed by the military and even on one that hadn't occurred to them—Arkansas Senator William Fulbright was moved to observe, "Of course, no one can turn down Julius Caesar. Even our Secretary of Defense could not resist Julius Caesar." But Rivers remained for the most part a closet Caesar, invisible to the public's eye beyond Washington, the actual dimensions of his importance generally unsuspected.

Now, outside the tall window of his inner office, the Congressional dome loomed immediately across the street, lit and glowing like white phosphorus in the wet celluloid darkness of this December morning, and from a small washroom in the back came an urgent tiny whine as Rivers briefly ran an electric razor over his jutting blunt chin. There was a certain homey coziness to the quarters out of which he operated—a pasteboard box of pecans stored in the corner of one closet, a refrigerator kept full of dove and shrimp near his committee's hearing room. When his staff began filtering in, he emerged from his office, stroking his chin, to greet them, speaking in a voice like a mossy purr—a voice in whose drowsing and misty depths there abided intimations of enormous authority. Indeed, he probably had the most diverting delivery since Dirksen had departed Washington: an ambient and wraith-breathed delivery, as elusive and stealthy as fog rippling slowly over a swamp of hyacinths and water moccasins. To a neatly dressed Negro, a fairly recent addition to his staff from one of the counties in his district, he snapped, "Isaiah, where's my sausage?"—his voice then tapering into a long luxurious moan—"You told me you were gonna bring up some sausage from home. You didn't kill those hogs this weekend?"

He returned to his office then to scan the morning mail: a letter from Chiang Kai-shek, an appreciative note from Vice-President Agnew for recent remarks at a military base ("You better get to know this fella Agnew—he's puttin' a lot of these armchair strategists like Huntley-Brinkley right where they belong. And he's told me, you gettin' it right from the horse's mouth, he's gonna continue to pour it on"), a note from the FBI inquiring about a nominee to a government post ("They want me to tell 'em what I think of him. Far as I know, he's okay, I guess"). His committee's chief counsel, a Marine Reserve general named John R. Blandford, a stout, sober and somewhat gopherlike man, came in for their morning conference. "About these reports from Camp Pendleton with black prisoners enslaving the white inmates," began Blandford, "what we understand is there are these tough black militants, and they've been put in there with these young farm boys, and so . . ." "Well, get 'em out of there," barked Rivers, "or we'll lower the boom. You tell 'em I said—and something else, these My Lai hearings this mornin', make sure everybody understands we not gonna turn those boys loose to all the media. Already been too damn much about this over the media. . . ."

For a number of years, Rivers had staged in Washington an annual luncheon featuring quail furnished by a Charleston trucker named X. O. Bunch and a Charleston delicacy called she-crab soup. This event, honoring the Speaker of the House, employed the resources of three Congressional kitchens and was attended by the Joint Chiefs, the Secretaries of the services, assorted other admirals and generals, Congressional Medal of Honor winners, and dignitaries from such interests as Signal Oil, Avco, Lockheed, Sperry Gyroscope, and the Chrysler Corporation, all of whom dined amid camellias whisked up by the Charleston postmaster in his private plane. One guest came away from the occasion and remarked, "I used to wonder exactly what they meant by the military-industrial complex, exactly what it was. Now I know. I have beheld the military-industrial complex, and it sits on the right hand of L. Mendel Rivers."

From his arrival in Washington in 1941, Rivers had applied himself assiduously to only two passions. One of them was the military establishment with its attendant industrial community. Nowhere in Congress did the Pentagon have a more dogged and unabashed tribune. "And if that's an epitaph," Rivers announced, "I gladly wear it—I gladly share it." Almost as soon as he became chairman of the committee in 1965, he doubled the Johnson administration's request for a servicemen's pay raise, deflected legislation that would have authorized the merging of Army Reserve and National Guard units, and contrived a bill requiring Congressional review of any cutbacks of military facilities (this last vetoed by Johnson). "We have pioneered in all the pay raises," he happily notified military audiences, "and you ain't seen nuthin' yet!" At the same time, he promised, "We don't want to bankrupt any contractors." According to one former administration official, when the Navy balked once on a Rivers proposal for new aircraft to patrol Vietnamese backwaters, he finally explained to the Pentagon he had already engaged in his own discussions with a manufacturer and "I've told those people they're gonna get those plane contracts."

In a sense, the military estate had become his second, informal, awesomely wider constituency. He lived surrounded by affectionate plaques from far-flung installations ("Thank you . . . from the 44th Tactical Fighter Squadron, Kodina Air Base,

Okinawa") and other mementoes like painted portraits and bags of golf clubs. The array of pictures in his office consisted for the most part of autographed photos of generals and admirals; the main thoroughfare of a U.S. base in Pleiku, South Vietnam, was even dedicated "Mendel Rivers Parkway."

He spoke one evening at a dinner on a South Carolina air base—a gathering of men who, most of them, had made passages through distant jaws of danger, who had dwelt close to the teeth of death, and who, assembled now in dress uniforms with their gowned coltish wives amid the trivial civilian pleasantries of a dance band and linen tablecloths, did seem a special species of clean taut quiet brave men belonging to the old simple verities, now embattled and puzzled and outraged by queasy civilian equivocations about those verities and about themselves. Rivers' arrival, among a sudden flourish of braided sleeves and clapping sedan doors on the curb outside, was like the appearance of their Gabriel of deliverance. Inside, he moved along a red carpet through their applause, a tall somber presence in his black topcoat. Later, he was introduced as a man "criticized by those who are determined to disarm this country," and he began, in a languid succession of sighs, "You the only crowd who must die, you know—you haven't done a thing for me but save me in four world wars. . . . Of course, you have enemies—not just in Hanoi, you got enemies in Washington. . . . There's this crew of not-quite-dry-behind-the-ears boys *se*-lectin' targets for mature men only to frustrate 'em. All the military has been allowed to do in Vietnam is carry out the ridiculous decisions of the children in the Pentagon and die. . . . 'Course, when we took on one Robert *Strange* McNamara"— he paused for the laughter—"we exposed his power as just a lot of pure fakery. . . . But this is a time the military needs friends if it ever needed friends. . . . For the *next* one, I say let's give the boys the weapons, let's give them the mission! . . ."

He finally husked, "Now, about this al-*leg*-ed massacre at My Lai" and there was a general brief rustle over the floor, a scattering of coughs. "I'm not gonna let you boys be tried by tee-vee, radio or the newspapers, I'll see to that." The applause was instant, spirited, and a long time dwindling. "I just don't believe any American boy went into any hamlet and murdered any 109 civilians—I just don't believe that. Of course, I've never been in a hamlet with a child throwin' hand grenades at

me, either. I've never had women and grandmothers shootin' at
me. But these men have already been lynched by the news
media, but *we* got jurisdiction over this, and I don't know how
guilty they are, but we gonna find out how *innocent* they are
too, if we can. . . ."

Rivers' private confession on the My Lai matter was, "We
reapin' the whirlwind we sowed at Nuremberg." Indeed, in the
same way that figures from the Thirties and Forties in Germany have come to be forever defined in terms of their reactions to the barbarities of the Third Reich, it's likely that
history will finally measure officials of the Sixties in the United
States according to their indulgence and apologies for Vietnam. Rivers's own apologias for My Lai seemed, if anything, to
exceed in gusto even those of the Pentagon, and before his
committee's hearings, he demanded of his counsel, General
Blandford, "I'll tell you what I want to know—how come, after
we asked the Army about this thing, they proceeded with such
haste to charge this fella with 109 murders?"

Rivers himself had never been in uniform; as he readily
acknowledged, "I came along in an in-between generation that
wasn't called on to do anything. . . . I don't know squads left
from squads right." Nevertheless, he appeared inordinately
enamored of the military tradition; he tended to regard Mc-
Namara's civilian control of the Pentagon as a kind of offense
against nature, a vague perversion. "Those boys over there," he
once fumed to an administration official, "who are they? Just
smart-alecky kids tryin' to run men who've gone through West
Point." To military audiences, he declared, "The only powder
those people have ever smelled is talcum powder. The only war
they have been in is a *boudo*ir." He was ebullient in all things
military, could recite the speed and range of every war plane in
the air, and mounted over the door to his Washington office
was a souvenir Chinese-made Vietcong carbine sent to him
from Vietnam. It was the opinion of a number of uneasy government veterans in Washington then that "what we've got to
worry about, actually, is a military-industrial-*Congressional*
complex. Congressmen become more mesmerized with the romance of the military than does most of the military. It's the
same thing as guys who like to play with cars—they just naturally want them to go faster as a hobby."

Rivers' own public commentary on the nation's military policies constituted, altogether, probably the most arresting incan-

tation ever to come from any figure of significance in Washington. Early in the Korean War, he urged Truman to unload the atomic bomb wherever necessary if the Communists declined to retire back to the North; after the capture of the *Pueblo*, he proposed that the United States give North Korea twenty-four hours to return the vessel or "I'd make positive that at least one of her cities would disappear from the face of the earth." Shortly thereafter, he introduced legislation providing for bounties of up to $100,000 for the heads of North Koreans responsible for tormenting the captured crew members. When in 1967 two U.S. destroyers on maneuvers in the Sea of Japan were bumped by two Russian ships, he responded, "If I were commander in chief, I'd knock 'em out of the ring." In regard to Vietnam, he ventured that tactical nuclear arms might have to be used to tidy up that particular frustration: "We flattened cities in Germany and Japan in World War II. I don't know what's so sacred about Hanoi. . . . Let world opinion go fly a kite." For that matter, he professed, "Words are fruitless, diplomatic notes are useless," and he gleefully bugled, "There can be only one answer for America—retaliation, retaliation, retaliation! They say, 'Quit the bombing.' I say, '*Bomb!*' "

As it happened, this enthusiasm tended to complement the other chief solicitude of Rivers' career, which was his home district of nine counties in the piney, moss-hung low country around Charleston: some even suggested it was his secret ambition to make the two interests totally synonymous. The Charleston area became one of the most elaborately fortified patches of geography in the nation—one survey toting up an Air Force base, a Navy base, a Polaris missile maintenance center, a naval shipyard and ballistic missile submarine training station, an Army depot, a naval hospital, a naval supply center and weapons station, a Marine air station, a Marine recruiting depot and training center, a Coast Guard station, a mine-warfare center, and the Sixth Naval District Headquarters. Rivers himself surmised, "I brought 90 percent of it in," and one of his local supporters admitted, "Mendel's got a real sweet finger." While Carl Vinson was still chairman of the Armed Services Committee, he remarked to Rivers, "You put anything else down there in your district, Mendel, it's gonna sink."

But as one letter which appeared in a Charleston newspaper around that time proposed, "The Confederate South, conquered by an overwhelming force of men, money and guns, unlike the defeated armies of Germany and Japan, was left to struggle without federal aid. . . . Let us not forget Sherman's visit to Columbia, and his march from Atlanta to the sea. . . . So why not go before Congress and interrupt the sessions and demand reparations?" Rivers, for his part, genially averred, "Anybody who thinks I'm not gonna look out after my own people is crazy." There soon accumulated, along with Charleston's military complex, a substantial symbiotic community of industries: just in the first five years of Rivers' chairmanship, five new plants materialized on the landscape—all defense contractors—and another company was hastily assembling a helicopter factory. In regard to a Lockheed installation, Rivers (who also had in his office the Boy Scouts' Silver Beaver award) once explained, "I just asked them to put a little ole plant here." What it all meant as a mother lode to the Charleston area was estimated in 1970 as a $175 million annual payroll, 63 percent of the area's total, and $317 million a year piped into local business. "If we don't have opportunity in Charleston," Rivers pronounced, "there ain't no cows in Texas. We got opportunity for about anybody who's got a pulse."

There were admittedly a few quiet misgivings that the district may have become too dependent on what Rivers had wrought: as one resident put it, "What would happen to this area if peace were ever declared?" Indeed, Rivers was particularly given to warnings about "the siren call of disarmament negotiations—I would rather be a live American with an empty pocketbook than a dead one with a full one. An enormous military-industrial complex is an inevitable outgrowth of the cold war." This raised the suspicion in some quarters that what Rivers had actually been engaged in, through all his years in Washington, was simply looking out for Charleston on an ultimate, global scale.

Originally settled around 1670, Charleston had been a musing little seaport town of washed lemony sunshine and salt breezes, its some seventy thousand souls dwelling in a web of narrow streets with names like Battery, King, Market, Meeting, even a St. Michael's Alley. It had lingered, it seemed, really closer to Europe than to the rest of the ruffian South at its back, and its usual reaction to whatever ephemeral affairs were transpiring in the interior was one of serene and casual indifference. "They've always had a perspective here," said one native, "which enabled them to sit on their front galleries with a bourbon and water in their hand and from their rockers watch two thousand Negroes march by, and then get up and go back inside and watch the rest of the football game on television, both events amounting to about the same thing for them."

Before Rivers, they were principally occupied with tending to the harbor, a commerce in cotton and fertilizer, historical commemorations, and the pursuit of genteelness, in the course of which they gradually fashioned a social complex of clubs and societies as intricate as a lace fan—like the St. Cecilia Society with its annual icily shimmering winter ball, in which membership descended through the male line of the family, posing a grave calculation to any of its debutantes contemplating marriage to a name not on its roll. Somewhat lustier was the St. Andrews Society, founded in 1729 by the Scottish community in town. It held annual banquets (Rivers would be there in blue-green tartan tie and sash) with fifths of Chivas Regal in steady passage up and down the long head table, where the officers, attired in kilts and getting progressively ruddier, would bluster to their feet each time the bagpipe band circled the auditorium with its great abandoned screeching and thumping, one officer finally reading a passage from Burns in the native thistle-tongue, at the finish brandishing a skean dagger high over his head to an eruption of howls and warlike caws.

For that matter, Charleston in general had always been rather disposed to the martial, and its transformation under Rivers into a kind of nuclear-age garrison was not all that incompatible with its temperament. Even before Fort Sumter, there were almost as many private militia companies in town as ball societies. "People of means," reports one citizen, "would get these outfits together against Indians, pirates, slave uprisings, whatever offered itself as an excuse—there were militia companies all over the place." Rivers himself, who packed a pearl-handled derringer in Washington to attend to any riffraff he might encounter, and whose favorite poem was Burns' "Man

Was Made to Mourn," was in a sense simply part of the general mentality of his hometown. In fact, if there was one figure in the past whom Rivers considered his lodestar, it would have been South Carolina's fractious and obstreperous John C. Calhoun, whose statue—flowing shocks of hair brushed back from his fierce eagle's face—Charleston has placed atop a column in a downtown park; while Rivers may have moved on to Washington bodily, one suspected that the spirit of his boyhood was still standing there at the statue's feet, gazing upward.

Rivers soon overhauled Charleston into a microcosm of America's military-industrial civilization. "You used to ride into Charleston on those old thin moss-covered highways," noted one citizen somewhat wistfully, "but now you come in on dual-lanes past radar scanners and factory smokestacks." At the same time, a St. Cecilia Society member mused through his spidery intermingled fingers, "You know, I went to a party just the other day, and doggone if there weren't five—*five*— admirals in the receiving line." The new style of the city was most conspicuous along a boulevard extending north from town—named, appropriately enough, Rivers Avenue. With only a few scattered incidental hints of the imminence of the sea—an occasional isolated palm, random shreds of moss—it was, for the most part, a long, wide, frowzy and glary thoroughfare of package stores and used-car lots, repetitious brick duplexes under pines, trailer courts where youths in T-shirts sat on the fenders of their viciously bright-painted secondhand convertibles drinking beer in the afternoon sunshine, income tax stands and Swiss-chalet pizza parlors and windowless little cement-block taverns painted pink and aqua tucked off under low trees. On beyond Rivers Avenue—beyond a measureless emptiness of grassy marshes, past the hulks of abandoned swamp tabernacles under long ripplings of moss—one came suddenly upon a military installation set out in a fenced isolation behind two neatly paired replica Polaris missiles, and a short distance beyond that, a completely self-contained community called MenRiv Park: commissary, bank, dry cleaner, barber and beauty shops, bowling alley, movie theater, chapel, along with a residential neighborhood stenciled with an exact geometric orderliness like some vision of a totalitarian future. Acres of brick rectangles were set on plots of lawn all evenly mown and spattered with straggly saplings, a landscape bare to

an unwinking sun that seemed to glare with a strange immediacy, as if the earth had all at once drawn millions of miles
closer to it, a huge quietness over the precise streets in which
the voices of far sprinklings of children were quickly blown
away and lost in the bright spaces. It was all Rivers' handiwork; speaking at the dedication of this project, he intoned to
its inhabitants, "I am happy to see these conveniences being
brought to you—baby food, bread, milk. I am going to see that
other conveniences are brought to you. . . ."

Mendel himself came forth out of the obscure margins of
nearby Berkeley County. He was born near Gumville, in a
pocket of palmettoes and burnt stumps and bogs usually referred to thereabouts as Hell-Hole Swamp, where his father
was a dirt farmer and turpentine-still operator. When Missouri
Representative Richard Bolling described Rivers once in a
magazine article as a "Snopes," a Rivers aide phoned Bollings'
office to say Rivers had seen the piece and was curious about
the Snopes reference, since they had not been able to discover
the word in their dictionary. Bollings' aide replied, "Well, it
means white trash," and after a pause, Rivers' aide muttered,
"Oh. Thank you," and hung up. Rivers was later asked about
the incident, and he tossed back his head: "That sonuvabitch
Bolling, he's always sounding off but nobody pays any attention to what he says up there, 'cause he's a nothin'. Why,
members of my father's family sat in Parliament. We not
tramps, we didn't just come here yesterday, that's what I'm
tryin' to tell you—I wanna show you my family tree." (And he
shortly did, unfurling two large scrolls and giving them to the
questioner for his extended perusal.)

Rivers' father eventually managed to acquire an ample gal-
leried house in Gumville—a small rude painting of it later
hung in the den of Rivers' Charleston home—but he died when
Mendel was only eight. "We had worked awfully hard for that
place," said Rivers, "but the bank got all our property for prac-
tically nothin'. All our property. That's when I decided I was
gonna be a lawyer, when Mother lost our place. I didn't like
the legal advice she got." She moved, with Mendel and her five
other children, to North Charleston, then an area where the
streetcar line ended among sandbed roads and stands of pine

and a light scattering of small tidy houses with cows in the backyard. "She made it out here by taking in boarders," said one old resident. Eventually, she remarried—one of her boarders, a slight, quiet man from Pennsylvania who had come down to install a dust-vent system in a nearby rubber plant. But a friend remembered, "With Mendel her only boy, he sort of stayed the kingpin with her." He worked for a while as a grocery boy and delivered papers on a pony, and in the meantime, as he allowed, "I courted about everything there was to court out there." He played baseball for a while with a semi-pro team fielded by the General Asbestos and Rubber Company: "I was in the outfield, and I'd go after tall flies that nobody else would have tried to catch. They couldn't hit 'em over my head. I could run like a stripe-ed ass ape." One friend from those days recalls, "He could throw hard as hell, but he didn't have no control."

The political depot in North Charleston then was a soft-drink and peanut stand known as Coley's Store, and one old acquaintance recounts, "You'd find Mendel out there about every day during political season when all the candidates would be comin' through. Hell, he never missed. It was like he wanted to just see what they looked like, hear what they talked like." After hasty stints at the College of Charleston and the University of South Carolina law school (where he dropped out after two years when he passed a bar exam), he commenced his political apprenticeship in the state house of representatives—a dark, gangling, jaunty youth who by a lucky accident had something of the glamour of an M-G-M matinee idol, posing in one snapshot with a soft askew half-smile, one eyebrow lifted, his cigarette held at a debonair angle. Before long, he had converted his position as a state legislator into a post as an assistant attorney general in Washington, and while there began cultivating in earnest an acquaintance with a Charleston debutante he had met one summer.

Named Margaret but called Mawee, she was a small compact girl with light hair and pale eyes, precise and soft-spoken and unassertive; as she later admitted, "I suppose I had led a fairly sheltered life." She belonged to one of Charleston's impeccably fine-bred families, her father a gentleman cotton broker and, as she described him, "a very gentle and approachable man." She found Rivers slightly bedazing: "He was very

striking, very tall and good-looking and self-assured. He had
the most unorthodox means of courting a girl—I mean, he'd
show up from a trip in the country with great armloads of corn.
He even came around once in his baseball uniform." Rivers, in
the meantime, announced to one friend, "I'm gonna marry that
girl."

It was transacted shortly thereafter. And as Mrs. Rivers
would later report, "I found out he was a politician the moment we were married—we turned from the altar and I looked
over and there he was, just walking up the aisle and reaching
into the pews and shaking hands and saying, 'Howdy. Howdy.
Good to see you.' And then when we reached the vestibule, a
fella was standing there he hardly knew, but he took me by the
arm and went right over there and pumped the man's hand.
'Why, hello, awful glad you could make it out today—meet
Mrs. Rivers.' "

They were living with her family when Rivers approached a
Charleston political impresario and notified him he planned
now to run for Congress: he was told, "Well, you go back to
the state legislature for a while, and then we'll talk to you." So
he opened his campaign out in the bush beyond Charleston, at
the watermelon festival in Varnville, where a general speech-
making bee was under way, with all the other candidates and
their entourages on hand—including the Charleston power ap-
paratus and their anointed, a former major-league baseball
player and member of a venerated Charleston family who was
named Alfred von Kolnitz. "Appreciate yawl comin' out this
afternoon," Rivers began, "and now, if yawl will kindly get the
mayor of Charleston and the chief of police out of here tryin' to
tell yawl how to vote, maybe I'll be able to get something said."
The year was 1940, and as Rivers continued his speech, he kept
referring to his opponent as "*Fritz* von Kolnitz"—an old associate of Rivers' who was there remembers, "You could almost
hear those Nazi troopers goose-stepping."

He lost some thirty-five pounds during that campaign, but,
says a veteran local newsman, "he whipped the Charleston
crowd out there in the sticks." On election night, he appeared
in the city room of the newspaper, where a radio booth had
been set up to broadcast totals, and an editor asked him, "How
about going on the air for a minute with a victory statement,
Mendel?" Rivers demurred, "Well, I don't think I should say

anything until the folks here in Charleston concede," and the editor said, "You don't have to wait for them to concede anything. You just whipped the hell out of those people." Rivers pondered that for a moment, and then snapped, "Where's that microphone?"

As a freshman in Washington, Rivers was installed on the House Naval Affairs Committee—later to be expanded into the Armed Services Committee—which was presided over by Georgia's wizened, bespectacled, wispy-pated "Uncle Carl" Vinson, a wry and wily autocrat. Rivers, for his part, "was constantly attentive to him," as he readily put it. "I did a lot of small favors for him, like totin' him over one hundred pounds of shrimp once. In life, it's the small things that count, not the big ones." In the meantime, he gained some brief peripheral notoriety for his Ciceronian oratory against the tax on colored margarine, a product made from soybeans from down home, and became known for a while as Oleo Rivers.

But more than anything else, he abided. His hair silvered, Charleston prospered. He began wearing vests. Every now and then, he would flare briefly in the news with improbable Armageddonal wheezings—a Southern curio, the classic caricature of the Southern Congressman marvelously incarnated—and then disappear again. And suddenly, in 1965, he was chairman of the House Armed Services Committee: Carl Vinson, after a half century in Washington, returned to the drowsing shade-flecked streets of Milledgeville, Georgia, and Rivers assumed his new magnitude of power with the same swift and easy nimbleness with which he had recognized his new circumstances that election night in 1940. At one of their first encounters, Secretary of Defense McNamara referred to Vinson in a somewhat brittle exchange with Rivers, and Rivers leaned forward and breathed, "But Mr. Secretary, Carl Vinson's gone. He's *gone.* . . ."

While Vinson had been inclined to be deferential to the White House, Rivers promptly had carpentered on the dais of the committee's hearing room—right below his own perch and in direct eyeshot of witnesses—a plaque inscribed with those phrases from the Constitution assigning expressly to Congress the responsibility for maintaining the military. He also began carrying with him a pocket-sized copy of the Constitution with those same phrases underlined; like a preacher with his New Testament, he would bend toward visitors seated in his office, one hand holding the booklet and the other sharply tapping the visitor's knee—"There is vested in Congress—see here?—the exclusive right to deal with the military. I don't mean quasi-right, I mean *exclusive* right. I'll never as long as I'm chairman presuppose the President can speak for the military—it's clear they wanted to avoid a dictator over yonder."

One former Cabinet official who had contended with Rivers declared at the time, "Mendel just feels our system would run better if civilian control came from Congress rather than the President. Specifically, he wants to be Secretary of Defense. As it is now, a Secretary of Defense is Mendel Rivers' natural enemy like cats and dogs are natural enemies." McNamara, with his brisk and frosty self-assurance and his systems-analysis discipline over the Pentagon, constituted a particularly insufferable affront to Rivers.

Rivers insisted, "The Secretary of Defense can do only such things as Congress gives him the power to do. Under the Constitution of the United States, there's imposed on Mendel Rivers—not the Secretary of Defense, but *Mendel Rivers*—the responsibility for providin' for the military." (Chatting on the phone with an Assistant Defense Secretary once, Rivers remarked, with a soft and lazing singsong syncopation in his voice, "You know, Mr. Secretary, the best friends you got are Mendel Rivers and company. Those fellas in the Senate, they wanna put you out of business. But I *sleep* military, and when I'm awake, I *act* military—I even *dream* military.") Indeed, some suggested that Rivers—acting out of that general possessive mockingbird compulsion in Washington—had personalized the committee and the military as his own private stake-claim, and he presided over his property with the closeness and testiness of a plantation lord. Representative Eddie Hebert of New Orleans, who was next in the Democratic line of succession to the chairmanship—a large, florid, congenial man with a voice like the rolling drum of a cement truck, given to chipper orange-and-yellow ties and cigars the size of a corncob—readily allowed, "I kid him a lot—say, Yes, master, and raise my hand, you know. But the fact is, I'm sittin' in that chair next to the King, I'm his man. He knows he can count on me."

What it amounted to, asserted one dissident committee member, "is here we are dealing with the largest agency of

government, it's fantastically complex, and we hear all this testimony for weeks, and then the chairman gets his little group
together and they draw up the bill, and the rest of us find it
before us, already printed up and semi-accomplished. We walk
in and sit down and here it is, around a billion and a half
dollars, and we have fifteen minutes to discuss it. We got
twenty-four hours to get up a minority report, it all becomes
available to members of the House on a Monday, then hits the
floor on Tuesday."

As one Rivers supporter back in Charleston explained, "He
just likes to keep procedures tidy." Such instances of untidiness
as public complaints about his prerogatives he tended to regard as congenital perversity: "Anybody who fouls his own
nest," he says, "is a sonuvabitch." During a critical speech by a
member in the House, Rivers finally surged to his feet and
began reminding the Representative of courtesies he had extended toward the man's district. He tamed restive members on
the committee, said one member, "by bypassing them when he
names subcommittee chairmen until they cave in, and then
granting them a chairmanship. I know one guy he completely
broke that way. Now this fellow votes with Rivers every time,
and Rivers will say, 'It seems the gentleman has seen the light,'
and this guy says, 'Well, I'm on the team now, Mr. Chairman,'
and Rivers will say, 'Well, you used to be out on waivers, but
you're back on the team, I guess.' "

(Testimony during the more leisurely sessions of his committee tended at times to trail into the ineffable. One dialogue
with an admiral proceeded: "How many cows do you have
over there at your dairy?" and the admiral replied, "About
426," and Rivers continued, "We saved that dairy. Now they
are really building it. I will say this, though—it is the most
powerful ice cream I ever tasted. It really has the cream in it.
We will have to come over and eat some sometime.")

One former Johnson administration figure offered, "On the
record, I'd have to say that Mendel Rivers is one of the most
charming and courtly and easygoing individuals I've ever dealt
with, and I have very pleasant memories of our association. Off
the record, however—he was the most extraordinarily difficult
guy to get along with. I've never worked at anything so hard in
my life. I pretty well devoted my time over there to eating
hominy grits—my God, we ate a lot of grits together." His
aggrievement over McNamara's systems analysis Rivers once

took directly to President Johnson, and as Rivers himself re-counted it, "You know, he looked me straight in the eye—straight in the eye—and said, 'Mendel, I'm gonna listen to my Secretary of Defense.' You wanna know what I told him? I said, 'Fine. And maybe you can get the Secretary to get your bills through my committee, then.' "

Rivers' own serene outlook about his committee was, "We get along just fine. There aren't more'n five or six troublesome fellows on there, a committee of forty. I call that a pretty good average. If I can't meet that, God help Mendel Rivers." Actually Rivers found himself on one occasion vexed by a threat posed by Representative Bolling of Missouri to dislodge him as chairman, this part of a general rebellion of young Congressmen then focusing on Arizona Representative Morris Udall's challenge of John McCormack for the Speaker's chair; Rivers, like McCormack, survived when Bolling withdrew before any actual confrontation. Afterward, Rivers effused, "They not anxious to take on ole Mendel." He then ventured, "They worried about the seniority system, why don't they take it up on the floor? They never have, and I'll tell you why—they know what ole Mendel can do to 'em. They know where the power is."

One of his political brokers in Charleston—a somewhat heterogeneous businessman named Joseph Riley, a large loud man with an empurpled face and pale chartreuse tufts of hair like parakeet feathers—liked to hail Rivers about as "the greatest man in America," and Rivers at times seemed susceptible to the same notion. "I've got a sense of greatness," he would confess. "I'm gonna make my name mean something. I'm not gonna let my name go down to the dreamless silence of the tongueless dust." According to one of his committee members, "You absolutely *cannot* overflatter this guy. He soaks it up like a sponge." Rivers himself suggested, "There's no question in my mind I've got a hell of a lot more on the ball than a lotta people I've met in Washington."

But he seemed curiously to alternate between imperiousness and abjectness; he had a disposition somewhat like South Carolina low-country weather in August, uncertain and mercurial, a play of honeyed sunshine and sullen clouds, gusting dust and heat lightning, as muggily sentimental at times as those warm nights flushed with gardenias and coming rain. In his more mellifluous moments, he was prone to poetry—Keats, Shelley, Byron, Rupert Brooke, and slightly sluggish approximations of Shakespeare like "The actor frets his time up there on the stage and afterwards he is heard no more." In an exchange once with Florida's Governor Claude Kirk over the location of a helicopter plant in Charleston instead of Jacksonville, Rivers produced this vaporish metaphor: "Governor Kirk disturbs the even surface of my mood more lightly than the tilted swallow's wing disturbs the limpid glassy solitude of the sound clear pool."

While his poses on such matters as desegregation and foreign aid and the Supreme Court ("Thank God, they can't live forever") were doctrinaire Dixiecrat, he actually had a sputteringly liberal voting record, with about a 40 percent rating by the Americans for Democratic Action. He was sporadically courted by Wallace in 1969, but avoided any official association with him. "Wallace is a little more inelastic than I am on integration," he privately maintained. "I just don't want to get into all that; you start havin' people callin' you a reactionary and all. Integration's an accomplished fact, anyway. We might have fought it, but it's here. My job now, I'm just gonna try to make it work as smoothly as possible."

"The woods are full of people like me," he once reflected, "but I'm going to do the very best I can. Time passes awfully fast. I can see the end of the world—uh, I mean the end of the road. But I have a few more projects ahead that I want to win, like the security of the Charleston harbor and the Santee-Cooper River."

So he endured. He faced opposition only twice in over thirty years, and they were gestures more than anything else. Rivers enjoyed asking his aides, "Now, once again, who was that fella ran against me last time—what *was* his name?" The proliferation of military installations may have tended to cramp certain municipal facilities in Charleston, in particular the airport: the mayor once went on television to complain, "The Air Force has now made it clear to the city that student training flights at the city field is dangerous to the air safety of their base there." All of this profoundly incensed Rivers: "The mayor don't seem to realize he's got a hell of a bonanza out there. Say the Air Force decided to pull out—he'd be flat on his ass." But when there was a flurry of Drew Pearson columns about Rivers' past marathon drinking bouts (he later studiously abjured any spirits and carefully invited visitors, "Yawl go ahead and have a drink if you want, I just don't touch the stuff"), an indulgent edi- torial in the local paper commented, "We are reminded of what President Lincoln said when the dries lit in on General Grant. . . ." On the whole, the mood in Charleston was, as one local newsman put it, "It's Rivers from whom all blessings flow."

He resided in a comfortable but plain brick home in a small inauspicious neighborhood in MacLean, Virginia, to which he would return from his office in the early evenings after the rush hour had ebbed, greeting his German shepherd, "What say, Mr. Mill? You love yo' pappy? Speak to yo' pappy. . . ." He had two daughters, and a son, Lucius, Jr., who attended George Washington Law School for a while—a quiet lean youth with long hair and a Zapata mustache. Rivers, who frequently re- ferred to anti-war protesters as "bearded buzzards," philoso- phized about his son's growth, "He wants to wear his hair like that, it's all right with me. He's a fine boy—he can wear it all the way down to his ankles, it wouldn't bother me any." Lucius had plans to enter the Navy after getting his law degree, and at supper one evening, he asked his father about a certain admiral to whose home he had been invited for a party; Rivers, dab- bing the corners of his mouth with his napkin, replied, "He's just in charge of the placement of all Navy personnel, that's all he is." Aside from his work, Rivers passed a simple and private existence; what occasions he attended were limited for the most part to military functions, while his domestic surround- ings were decorated with tokens of his central preoccupation— what some would have characterized as reflections of the United States' unofficial accumulation and consolidation of a semi-colonial empire in the Far East: furniture and artifacts from Thailand, the Philippines, Vietnam.

He also maintained another home in Charleston, a modest, pretty residence of old brick and iron-grill railings, set along a street like a quiet cathedral aisle of moss and live oaks. He returned there periodically to repair what small ravages may have occurred, both in his house and his district, during his long absences. He spent the length of one drab bone-cold day there in the winter of 1969 hectically orchestrating a con- glomeration of repairmen, raging about rats that had gotten into his attic ("They about taken over up there. You just can't seem to kill the goddam things"), answering calls from Washington about the situation in the stockade at Camp Pendleton ("They got to get those goddam niggers out of there. Tell him to do it, or I will"), and checking on the progress of laborers laying a new drainage pipe across his front yard, with an Air Force lieutenant appearing in midafternoon with some new pipe in a truck. Toward twilight, the job in the yard was finished, and Rivers brought out a half-full bottle of bourbon for the Negro laborers, sidling over to their white foreman and nudging him in the ribs as he watched them take long swigs at the tailgate of their truck.

With his wife having stayed in Washington, he arose early in the mornings to cook his breakfast—grits and bacon and eggs and instant coffee—in a kitchen with a fishing-lodge decor of yellow cypress paneling and red Formica counters, telling some guests who dropped by, "I got the reputation of bein' the best cook in the hollow—see, you gotta heat up that oven hotter'n a June bride on a soft feather bed, and then you put that bacon in." Afterward, he pitched leftover grits out back for the birds, and ambled for a while over his backyard swinging the pot against his leg, among his Debutante camellias and azaleas and birdbaths, stooping once to announce, "Here's a daddy longlegs. Sonuvabitch must be froze to death."

He spent the early part of that morning in a deep and elaborate fretfulness about his Negro handyman. "Where the hell is Thaddeus?" he kept muttering. "I'm just not gonna give him anything. I don't have the time to be worryin' about his breakfast." Finally, in one of his passes by the window, he said, "Lookathere, there he is. There he is. Actin' like he don't know he's late." Thaddeus was floating down the street on a bicycle in the early-morning sunlight—a gnomish mummy swaddled in old bulky clothes, seemingly without age or sex, his skin taut and waxen and glazed over his cheeks and his small black efin eyes twinkling. He was already chattering as he wheeled in the front driveway and dismounted, with Rivers stalking out toward him, "I'se here, yessuh, I made it. . . ."

"Where the hell you been?" Rivers blared, his eyes flaring wide and his chin shoved forward with that abrupt ferocious querulousness of the aging. "You know what time it is? Look here"—he extended his arm and tapped his watch—"see there? What does that say?" Thaddeus, snapping and flourishing before Rivers with the quick fitfulness of a squirrel, kept up a long unintelligible chirruping, and Rivers turned to a visitor and said, "He can't hear worth a damn. The other people around here he works for, we all went in and bought him a hearing aid, but he won't wear the damn thing." He suddenly wheeled on Thaddeus again, braying, "Where's yo' hearin' aid? I say, where"—Thaddeus began scuffling something out of his trouser pocket—"yo' hearin' aid? Well, how come you ain't got it on?"

"It broke, yessuh, see here, can hear nuthin'."

"It's broke? Goddam, you don't ever use it, how you expect it to work?" He took the hearing aid from Thaddeus to fix it, a glimmer of a smile on his face. Then in the kitchen Rivers towered forward and crowed, "You want any breakfast?" and Thaddeus paused and nodded, "Yessuh. Yessuh. Sho' would 'preciate a little breakfast. Yessuh." Thaddeus sat on a high stool at the counter by the stove while Rivers spooned out some warmed-over grits on his plate, then brought him some toast. Rivers leaned close to holler, "What you want to drink? You want something sweet? You want some milk?" Thaddeus looked up at him, humped forward, but his head tilted back and sideways in a suppliant gaze oddly like that of a cherub in a Renaissance painting: "Maybe little juice. Yessuh. Little juice be fine, you got some." Rivers headed for the refrigerator, and as he took out a pitcher, he said with delight, "Lookathere, he wants orange juice. He travels first class."

Later that morning, before he left for an appointment downtown, Rivers stopped in the driveway and yelled back to the steps where Thaddeus was standing, "You know how to run the dryer?" Thaddeus mumbled something, and Rivers advanced toward him again, yelling, "Dryer! Dryer! You know how to run the dryer—*goddam!*" Thaddeus then began frantically turning and pointing over his shoulder and nodding, "Yessuh. The dryer. Yessuh, don't you worry . . ." Rivers turned away and started back for the car. After shutting his door, he said in a lowered voice, with a vague smile, "He's a good ole soul. Good soul. . . ." And a few moments later, on down the street, he continued, "I like Nigras. I really do. Hell, Southerners are more Nigra than they are white. Notice the way they all talk? You tell 'em something, they say, 'Aww, no-o-o-o-,' " his voice

expiring in a long dreaming breath. "Spanish call that simpatico. It's like music."

The next day, he took to the road to check his district, as he
had his house, for evidence of any infiltrations of rats, any
ruptures in the plumbing. His executive assistant—a hefty and
somewhat harried but genial young man from Charleston
named Trezevant Hane did the driving. As they were backing
out into the street, Rivers tapped his window and said, "Trez,
you leavin' those gates wide open—dogs'll come in there and
piss all over everything." One of Rivers' previous executive as-
sistants had finally retreated back to Charleston with a bleeding ulcer; Trez himself always talked in a slightly gasping
mannner, as if trying to catch his breath. On the road Rivers
barked at him, "Goddam, Trez, you a mighty fine fella, but you
can't drive worth a damn," and Trez, nodding sideways as if he
had just received a small chop on the side of the neck, did not
smile. But Rivers seemed in a generally mellow mood this
sharp bright winter morning. He gazed out of the window and
observed, "Look at those pe-can trees, aren't they pretty? Trez,
I always wanted to own that property over yonder. . . ." Before
they reached the first town, while still out in the flat countryside of scrub oaks and low black creeks, Rivers abruptly said,
"Pull off here somewhere, Trez, and let me take a leak." Trez
slowed and eased the car off the highway, but Rivers, poised
with his hand on the doorknob, sat very still for a long moment,
staring down the road where, in the far distance, a car was
slowly approaching, pausing once at a mailbox. "Oh, Lord,"
said Rivers, "ain't that the mailman? He's gonna know me.
We'll just sit here a minute and let him get on past us. . . ." At
last, Rivers opened the door and stepped out into the yellow
weeds of the roadside, standing behind the opened door with
his homburg atop his head, an Old Crow bottle lying in the
shallow ditch beside him.

His first stop that morning was a watermelon-farming community named Hampton, a little part of which had been
present at the most momentous event in the history of the race
since the first amphibian crawled out of the sea—man's arrival
on the moon—part of the lunar module having been constructed of an alloy manufactured right in town. Entering the
courthouse with a brisk combing of his hair, Rivers was
greeted in the quiet dim hall by fluttering lady clerks and frail
officials resembling faded sprigs long pressed between the

pages of deed books and tax records. "You been told that
Clyde's stepfather died yesterday?" he was asked, and he responded, in that slow and lilting simpatico, "Oh, no-o-o-o-o." A
mother came over with her son, and Rivers, hugging both of
them, said, "Stand close to me, boy, her husband's liable to
come in here with a shotgun." He turned toward one old man
and purred, "Tell Sister to let me know when you havin' yo'
operation."

He seemed, indeed, like some tribal chief on his yearly tour
of his villages. In second-story courtrooms rectangled in cold
sunlight, with wooden plank floors and spittoons and wasp
nests from the vanished summer left in the corners of the ceil-
ings, and tall windows like those in country churches with
panes faintly rippled, Rivers sat among the folding seats and
listened to the assorted tribulations of the worn and distressed
of the countryside, their voices a low small murmur, he responding, "Well, you better do somethin' about that boy—they
gonna put him in jail soon if you don't. . . . Well, I'm gonna see
if I can't do somethin' about that, I'm gonna put in a tree-
incentive measure. . . ." At several stops he encountered local
political fledglings—hearty, glitter-eyed, fresh-faced, flipping
key chains—who thanked him for such small attentions as
funds for new sewage systems: "It's really gonna hep us bring
that little industry in down here—all I can say is, thank yuh."
And Rivers, the patriarch, the granddaddy catfish, would hold
up his hand, palm outward as if in benediction, and pronounce,
"Listen, son, when you lead—you gotta lead."

Inevitably, someone—in this case, a farmer in his middle
years, sitting in the front row of courtroom seats with his legs
crossed, one limp-socked ankle swinging—would refer to Fulbright's remark: "See where that fella up there been comparin'
you to Caesar." Rivers replied, "Well, you know what we call
him up there—Brutus Iscariot. Yeah. Brutus Iscariot. Difference between me 'n' him, he's the favorite of Hanoi radio. I'm
not," and he looked around him with his awry grin. Wherever
he went, the Red Peril seemed the deathless obsession. Rivers
was asked in the Allendale courthouse, "What's the problem
over there in Vietnam, it looks like they've fixed it so we can't
win—things happen in government, I know just as well there's
some fella you can't put your finger on who's calling these
shots . . ." River, holding his homburg in one hand with his coat
slung over his forearm, his other hand falling on the man's

shoulder, resonated, "Listen. The only way to win this thing is beat the hell out of 'em in *North* Vietnam. If you don't deal from strength in this world, you don't deal, and whoever comes in second comes in last. That's the way I look at it, brother. Only way we gonna stop North Vietnam is to go in there and just *destroy* 'em."

Hampton was to have its Christmas parade the afternoon Rivers was there, and he was to serve as its grand marshal. Perhaps a dozen high school majorettes gathered around him in a great din of trilling, now and then fingering his sleeves, their eyes bright and quick, all of them breathless and shivering from the cold and also perhaps from his tall august white-maned presence. He looked down upon them with a sly tilted little smile, one eyebrow lifted, and one of the girls reached up and briefly ruffled the tufts of hair at the back of his neck. When at last they all scattered away, he turned to a bystander, his grin lingering, and sighed, "Ain't they cute little devils?" He rode that afternoon in an open limousine, proceeding slowly up the main street beneath strands of tinsel twinkling in a cold wind, with snappy clattering drums advancing behind him: a somewhat dour figure with his black topcoat, his long histrionic mane of white hair, a red scarf swathed around his neck, wearing depthless dark glasses against the dull late-afternoon sunshine, grinning occasionally with one long arm waving. In the crowd of townspeople banked along the curbs, a small boy suddenly piped, "But where's Santa Claus?" And his father leaned down to him and said, "There he is—that's him right there in that front car."

One year later, following extensive heart surgery, Rivers died in a Birmingham hospital. There ensued a thick press of candidates to succeed to his Congressional seat, almost unnoticeable among them a godson of his. Still in his twenties and with virtually no background in government other than having performed assorted errands for Rivers now and then, he nevertheless routed the entire field, which included the mayor of Charleston and the chairman of the county board, simply by posting billboards around the district advertising little more than his name—Mendel Rivers Davis.

A few months after Rivers' death, at a small dinner one eve-

ning in Washington, a secretary who had long served in his office reported, "You know what the doctors said they found when they operated on him? His heart had been battling all those years, until . . . he had a heart literally the size and strength of a Spanish fighting bull's."

Sam Ervin, Saving the Republic, and Show Business

TOWARD THE END of the summer of 1973, he had returned again to Washington, a cool tint now of autumn in the sundowns there, to finish serving as the presiding elder of the Senate Watergate Hearings' last proceedings. In the mild and traffic-mumbling evenings, he would walk from the Wong Cleaners back to his spare two-bedroom apartment, passing the grand glimmering loom of the Supreme Court Building with his laundry under his arm. According to a counsel on his committee, North Carolina's homey and codgerly Senator Sam Ervin was "inclined now to ease away from Nixon a little bit. After all, he was touching the very bowels of the Presidency there for a while." But more than that, it seemed Ervin had sensed and accepted that the higher, larger drama of the summer hearings—when they had turned into a kind of Constitutional revival meeting, a national confessional and redemptive purging—was now spent and over with.

During that time, though, Ervin had come in the popular eye to be pitted, more than anyone else, against the awesome personage of the President of the United States. And that confrontation brought to Ervin—after a political career passed in serene unobtrusiveness—a sudden continental celebrity.

"It was an absolutely new business for him," admitted one of his aides, "and it left him sort of bewildered and dislocated." Another Ervin admirer was later moved to observe, "Our society, this pop civilization, has found that the fastest way in the world to immobilize and blast any honest figure who arises among us is just to surround him with the media's bright mirrors. Sooner or later, it's too much for any man."

*   *   *

New Times, October 19, 1973

No sooner had the Senate hearings paused for a recess that summer than the White House mounted a massive public offensive to diminish and dismiss the whole proceedings—loosing all its formidable political ordnance and engines, with television manifestations by Nixon from the White House's imperial quarters and from San Clemente's sunny castleries, Presidential visitations about the country in a rousing pageantry of booming motorcycles and helicopters and swarming Secret Service praetorians. In the meantime, the committee's chairman, Sam Ervin—principal agent of the White House's commotion—had receded back into the quiet of his origins in North Carolina's highland country, just where the land begins to lift and ripple toward the distant dim immensity of the Blue Ridge Mountains, with patches of sweet corn on steeply tilted slopes behind frail hillside houses and a faint clinking of belled cows in the low laps of daisy-freckled meadows.

Here, Ervin reestablished himself in his small hometown of Morganton as comfortably as one settling into an old porch rocker. In his 1967 dull-black Chrysler with its 97,000 miles, he drove himself every morning, as usual, from his house—a low neat brick residence set close to the street, on the same block where he had been born seventy-seven years before—to his office in the musty hindquarters of an antique building across from the courthouse. He would make his way up a sagging stairway to his few bleak rooms on the second floor, with thin-ribbed radiators under the dusty windows and shelves heaped with speckled nineteenth-century lawbooks, no more notice on the door than a leftover campaign sticker lettered *Sam Ervin Senator* taped to the glass pane.

On an afternoon when Nixon was to deliver another television address to the nation, Ervin drove over to put his own case about this moment of duress in the Republic to the ladies at a DAR luncheon. When he shambled in with a worn lawbook in his hand, he was greeted uncertainly by his wife, a small sturdy lady known around town as Miz Margaret. "Now, why," she asked with a low distressed squeal, "did you have to bring that old book along?"

" 'Cause," he grunted. "Gonna speak from it."

After a subdued, fork-tinkling meal in a long austere room of polished hardwood floors that reflected pale light from the tall windows, the assembly of matrons retired to a large front parlor and arranged themselves in a circle of metal folding chairs, hands primly folded in their laps, their faces all uplifted with pleasant smiles to Senator Sam. A cumbersome and somewhat rumpled figure, with his haze of white hair adrift over his huge ham of a face, he stood before them, one hand thumb-hooked to his pants pocket, and explained, "Not only are the people required to obey the Constitution, but those who exercise its authority—*they're* required too." Then he read to them, his eyebrows furiously whisking, from an 1866 Supreme Court decision on that point, holding the lawbook with both hands out before him at shoulder level, exactly in the manner of a country preacher propounding from the Scriptures; it was a battered, ancient volume on which his own aged, gnarled hands seemed naturally to belong. Finally, his head cocked back and his large eyes flared and rolling, he declared, "That's why we got to keep the power of government divided down into small fractions. Our government wasn't created to be efficient. It was created to preserve the individual. . . ."

One Ervin devotee admitted ruefully around that time, "Nobody can ever really win a head-to-head match with the President of the United States—which is the kind of situation the chairman has come to find himself in. But what's incredible is that while Nixon is out barnstorming this thing now all over the country and on national television, all Ervin does to answer him is just make talks to little local groups down home—which have about the public impact of somebody spitting into a Nebraska mud puddle at midnight."

Ervin was, without doubt, an unlikely anachronism for that time. In a way, he affronted all the new physics of power and consequence. Throughout the Watergate Hearings, he had presided over what promised to be a momentous gear-shifting in the country's political history as if it were a citizens' meeting in the Burke County courthouse. Watergate itself, whatever the magnitude of its cast and circumstances, seemed to remain for him somehow a colloquial affair. He acted out of that tribal Southern sense of community where transactions between men, including politics, were simple, personal, immediate matters, undenatured by technology or computers, close to the earth and the old common sweats of mortality. He speculated once about Nixon to a confidant back in Morganton, with a wink and chortle, "Now this man might be telling the truth when he says he didn't know all that business was going on, but like I heard somebody say once, you're asking a lot when you ask somebody to believe in the untouched virginity of the madam of a bawdy house."

On the whole, Ervin could not have seemed more devoid of the cold urbane sheens and dapper efficiencies of the Nixon executives who appeared before him, Dean and Magruder and Ehrlichman—that impermeable aluminum composure and nicely machined glibness which had carried them all so far, very far indeed, and which they had good reason to suppose was all that was really needed to carry them, in fact, as far and as high as was worth going in this society. On the other hand, Ervin, when met with one of their deft sarcasms, such as Ehrlichman's half-smirking remark "I've read the Bible, I just don't quote it," seemed to flounder, smitten speechless. Confronted by Nixon's sustained rebuffs and truculence through it all, Ervin could only refer to him incredulously as "This one . . . this President . . . this man . . ." Impossible to exaggerate, then, the astonishment of Nixon and his adjuncts when all their excellent facilities—their sleek Southern California nimbleness and Nielsen sophistications—failed in the end against something absurdly archaic, rudimentary, plain and unassuming, sluggish and sometimes bumptious and even largely unregardful of them up to now, embodied in this fusty septuagenarian Senator from the outlands of the nation.

Of course, it was not the first time that the country had, almost haphazardly, pitched forth briefly a figure out of the ordinary anonymous drifts of its folk to attend to an hour of unease and mischief in the Republic—a redoubtable commoner absolutely tailored to the pattern of the crisis. But "one should stop there," one commentator noted about Ervin, "and be content. To ask for more from Senator Ervin is to be painfully disappointed." He was singularly bereft of any noble splendors—as plain as an old stump. Nowhere near so surgically well mannered in interrogation as the diaphanously parliamentary Howard Baker, Ervin was prone at times to bluster querulously over a witness' temporizings: gusts of crankiness and impatience disheveled his composure, even his sequence of thought occasionally. These falterings even prompted mutterings from the White House that senility had begun to frost the edges of his faculties—most notably from Nixon's Agriculture Secretary, a tight dry little clerk named

Butz. For that matter, there was a certain unseemliness about the haste with which the liberal estate had lunged to hail him, given Ervin's less-than-libertarian barricades in the past against most civil-rights legislation. He was disposed, in fact, to a simplicity that approached, at times, a stunning naiveté. Back in Morganton during the committee's recess, he proposed, "People were impressed with the calmness with which Magruder and Dean testified, but I think the source of that calmness must have been that they had endured great agony for many months, anguish of the spirit—the worst thing for a man must be to live in the fear day by day that some secret of his sinning will be disclosed." It apparently had not occurred to Ervin that their calmness more likely was the serenity of amorality, a total absence of any anguish of soul.

Even so, all their facile Madison Avenue cynicisms about the aboriginal fundamentals of Western law propounded to them by Ervin—such as Ehrlichman's rejoinder, to the proposition of the hallowedness of an individual's privacy, "I'm afraid that's become a little eroded over the years"—somehow suddenly rang, against Ervin's hickory-grained simplicity, with their true cheapness: utterances for inscription on tin. What had happened was that the politics of the J. Walter Thompson Agency had, as it were, just encountered the Old Man of the Woods. Through all those weeks of testimony, Ervin became something like the Druid of the proceedings—the Keeper of the Scrolls. Invoking passages from the Constitution and the Scriptures, musing aloud on the incorrigible vagaries and wiles of the human animal, he would gaze about the far corners of the chamber with his tilting, nodding, ponderous head, seemingly addressing the walls and chandeliers, everything around him but the actual witness before him. What he was engaged in, actually, was a three-way conversation in which the witness was only the third party and he merely the second—Ervin, his elongated rootlike hands stiffly flagging up and down and his eyebrows wildly fanning, conducting them in a rapt colloquy with the other, first party, invisible and larger than them both and that particular moment: sheer history itself, right and wrong, the truths of honor. This, for Ervin, was the finest and most engrossing of all talking, all conversations.

As he stood in the foyer of his Morganton home one morning discoursing about the patriarchs, Jefferson and Adams and Washington and what they had all respectively been up to back then, it was with a strangely easy and natural familiarity, as if he were chatting about fascinating local figures of only two generations back whose singular presences were still remembered around town. Indeed, he had the look himself of one of them misplaced in time: the heavy, flushed, pumpkin-size head of some colonial squire in a Gilbert Stuart portrait. And in truth he had wound up ranged not just against the Nixon administration, but, in a sense, against an entire age in America. He was like a last lingering elder from the time of pre-technological man.

Ervin had always been outraged by governmental vandalisms of citizens' privacy, and this was largely because he was so profoundly a private man himself. The only authentic values in life, to Ervin, were found in the personal realities of individual experience. Accordingly, all governmental intercessions into the lives of individuals, however humanitarian, struck Ervin as nothing less than "the processes of death." Asked once to reflect, at a point much removed, on the wisdom of the civil-rights legislation of the Sixties, Ervin merely grumbled, "Well, we've gotten reconciled to it. The bad thing was, so many things were regulated by men who aren't elected to anything—a faceless bureaucracy." This was only one of the incidental myopias of his Constitutional fundamentalism, which also accounted for his seemingly contrary and capricious obsessions over the years—filibustering against civil-rights legislation while, with equal passion, battling federal policies of censorship and citizen surveillance. His ferocious testiness about the sanctity of the individual against the collective expediency even extended, in one case, to matters beyond the grave: when his church congregation in Morganton was pondering whether, in relocating their sanctuary at another site, to also haul along the cemetery of their ancestors, Ervin heaved himself to his feet to cry, "Nobody ran over those folks while they were alive, and nobody's gonna run over 'em while they're dead."

In fact, the public clamor of politics itself seemed to vaguely offend his nature as an unavoidable vulgarity. Most of the offices he had held, his judgeships and even his Senate seat, he came to initially by appointment, and his reelection campaigns tended to be rather desultory and genteelly grudging affairs.

"All the time Everett Jordan was up there as our other Senator," said a Morganton citizen, "he was much more noticeable and outgoing than Ervin. It was always Ervin who came to mind as an afterthought, as being, you know, the other Senator."

Ervin's stardom, then, came to him at almost the last moment of a political career passed in a sedate obscurity, and, finding himself suddenly in the glare and clangor of national celebration, he had a faintly startled and dazed air. Back in Morganton now, he was trailed, in his customary casual ambulations about town, by tumbling dog gangs of newsmen—he glancing sideways at them furtively, with a look of mild alarm. It was a kind of enduring defenseless innocence that caused him, to the considerable wonderment of reporters, to continue to answer the phones himself when they rang; at anyone's knocking, his front door would presently swing open, and he would be standing there in his shirt-sleeves, a blank quizzical look on his face. After yet another exhaustive session with another delegation of journalists in his home, he would always, before they departed, earnestly inquire out of a compulsive neighborly solicitude, "Would yawl like to, uh, wash up back here now?" One journalist spent five minutes blundering into the closets in Ervin's back bedroom before he finally found the bathroom.

Then, on the Tuesday after Labor Day, Ervin received a rather different deputation of visitors in the library of his home —this one a troop of prospectors journeying out of the murky and hectic middle regions of show business. They were led by a plumpish, kewpie-faced little man in a turtleneck sweater and festive plaid suit who was named Al Ham and who had a constant faintly frantic manner about him. He had ventured down to Morganton from Manhattan in a grime-streaked Mercedes with his wife, a bright-haired and ringingly cheerful sometime songstress named Mary Mayo, who once had finished second to a comedian on *The Arthur Godfrey Talent Show*. Through the good offices of two Charlotte mediums—a television news announcer and a composer of musical scores for state beauty pageants—they had somehow managed to prevail on Ervin to spend two days reciting assorted yarns and drolleries and meditations for a record like that cut sometime earlier by Everett Dirksen, which they then planned to hawk to the record companies. "Our hope," allowed Ham, "is to get this thing out right in time for the Christmas trade."

Ervin's staff, when they learned what was happening, was aghast. "The only word I can think of for the whole thing," said one of them, "is gauche." But there had been more than one hint before that Ervin's almost excruciating reticence and diffidence actually muffled, as in many such shy souls, a hulking and florid vanity. His biography in the Congressional Directory was the most exhaustive of anyone's on the Hill until his staff in 1970 finally persuaded him to compress it somewhat. With word now of his transaction with Ham party, one member of Ervin's Washington office reported, "We tried to reason him out of it, but it was just one of those things the Senator had made up his mind he wanted to do. We only have so much power of counsel with him, you know. We could do absolutely nothing with him on this—in fact, he made it quite clear he didn't even want any of us around down there while he was with those people."

Old associates in Morganton were equally dismayed and baffled. "It's the rankest kind of exploitation," said the local newspaper editor, softly shaking his head, "and be damn if I can figure out why he consented to it. At least Dirksen, when he did that record of his, had that theatrical voice and delivery. But Sam's voice really isn't anything all that special. He oughta know that. This thing is totally unlike him."

Indeed, when the recording reels began to turn in Ervin's library at home, Ham's ensemble at first had a slightly stubborn time of it getting Ervin to unfold and begin performing. The television news announcer from Charlotte, a hefty and manicured man possessed of a mineral seriousness, gently coaxed, "Senator, do you have a favorite preacher story, I mean, here from the mountains?"

"No," Ervin mumbled, "I don't believe I do." He did have, though, two former speeches he thought he might read—one of which he had presented to the graduating class of a female finishing academy in South Carolina, the other a disquisition on Freemasonry.

At these suggestions, Ham gave a quick squinty grin that more resembled a twinge of sciatica, followed by a flurry of blinking. But Ervin reverberantly commenced reading from the texts of the two speeches, and when he had finished, Ham and his entourage burst into a light spattering of applause.

This response seemed to have a slightly inspiriting effect on Ervin. Leaning with elbows on his desk, he then rummaged forth a folk waggery about a courting couple on a porch swing discussing an octopus, which ended with the maiden declaring, "G'wan, John, you aren't even using the two arms you got!" Delivering this last line, Ervin immediately flushed and gave a hugely grinning snuffle of suppressed naughty glee, ducking his head and doing a quick little tickled foot-shuffle from his chair.

From this, he went on to produce some miscellaneous contemplations on marriage, a bit heavingly and humidly sentimental, but obviously quite heartfelt. Whenever he paused, the songstress would croon from the couch, "That's just beautiful, Senator. Just beautiful." When he concluded, there was a brief silence, and finally the songstress murmured, "Why, you've made us *cry*, Senator," and the young girl beside her, another member of the party, echoed, "Yes, it's true. You've made us cry."

Ervin glanced at them in slight surprise, his eyebrows shimmying, and muttered, "Uh . . . well, yes, I, uh . . ." Through the next fifteen minutes, while Ervin forged on and the tapes continued to noiselessly spool, the ladies maintained an intermittent undertone of delicate sniffles. Ham turned once to remark *sotto voce* behind a cupped palm to a colleague, "Just terrific. He's really much better when he isn't reading, just remembering and talking."

At last—only a few moments after Ervin had declared, "I believe in the essential goodness of people, I believe the average person wants to live a good life"—Ham leaned forward and, with another small fit of blinking, gently submitted to Ervin some selected scripts of his own that perhaps the Senator, if he wanted, might agree to look over, and possibly read or recite a little later, of course it was up to him. . . . Ervin, absolutely motionless, peered down solemnly at the sheets Ham had placed before him. Among them was a copy of the lines to "Bridge Over Troubled Waters," and Ham inquired if Ervin was familiar with that particular ballad.

Ervin, after perusing it, allowed as how he'd never heard of it, though he offered, "This does remind me of another little doggerel verse I used to know." Ham's squeezed little smile wavered only momentarily. He proposed that Ervin might like to recite that one after, perhaps, memorizing the lines that night. Ervin was pleasantly agreeable to that idea. As the afternoon wore on, he waxed progressively more animated and obliging, at one point vibrantly reading off the lines to "Hang Down Your Head, Tom Dooley."

Some of Ervin's people later speculated darkly that it had all been a last cunning ploy of the Nixon White House, to collapse Ervin's credibility by luring him by his ego into a lugubrious buffoonery. But it was hardly any designs or lusts of politics that, later that evening, sent Al Ham scampering across the dining room of the Holiday Inn when he spied a journalist who had sat in on most of that day's taping session in Ervin's library. "We'd just hope you won't use any of . . . well, we'd really like to know what you might use, because if anything gets out in print before we . . . well, it will only cause us serious problems with the record companies we mean to . . . I mean, surely you can understand, there are *professional ethics* involved in all this . . ." The journalist wound up sitting briefly at the large table where the rest of Ham's company was gathered, and there ensued something like a quick fierce catfight, their clashing voices turning heads at other tables around them. The songstress, quite dry and brilliant of eye now, shrilled, "You have no right. No right to any of it. We didn't even know you existed when we made these arrangements."

The journalist stood to leave, and Ham, waving both hands swiftly downward to hush his companions, then announced in a level, measured voice, "No, really, you've got to understand now. You don't realize. You see, he's been signed to a regular, formal contract as a performing artist. He's under contract to us. We've made Senator Ervin a full recording artist."

Some days later, reported one of his aides in Washington, Ervin was still grumpily insisting, "Well, I don't see anything wrong with it." But beyond that, said the aide, "the Senator just prefers now that nobody bring up anything at all about him cutting that record down in Morganton."

Near the end of that first day of recording, Ham had presented with a special grave delicacy one of his last scripts to

Ervin, and Ervin, with barely a glimpse at it, took it into his hands and grunted amenably—this one, "A Visit from St. Nicholas." And thus the President's single most imposing Constitutional adversary of that time—the intrepid and Jeremiah-like chairman of the Senate Watergate Committee—proceeded to peal forth, "Now, Dasher! Now, Dancer! . . . On, Donder and Blitzen! . . . His eyes, how they twinkled; his dimples, how merry! . . . He was chubby and plump, a right jolly old elf. . . . And laying his finger aside of his nose, and giving a nod, up the chimney he goes! . . ."

Shortly thereafter, Ervin announced he would be retiring from the Senate at the end of his term. His record appeared that Christmas season, but, unhappily, fared indifferently. He has since been occupied, considerably more profitably, as a staple on the lecture circuit, and in providing his person for appearances in television commercials for insurance companies and American Express.

The Roman-Candle Time of Wilbur Mills

FROM THE VERY first word of that two-a.m. imbroglio along the Tidal Basin in Washington, it was a matter that seemed peculiarly shadowed by ghosts of *The Blue Angel:* Wilbur Daigh Mills—the sixty-five-year-old sober high bishop of the House Ways and Means Committee, whose three decades as Representative from a remote and piney district in the Arkansas interior had become a Washington legend of ponderous circumspection—suddenly discovered disheveled, raucous, and thoroughly snozzled with a dubious party of assorted nightfolk including a shrilly hysterical Argentine stripper, his glasses splintered and his plain homespun face scratched and bleeding. There was something in the stunning and garish implausibility of that news that instantly evoked Von Sternberg's forlorn little melo-tragedy of a middle-aged German schoolmaster, grimly respectable and rectitudinous, befuddled and eventually wrecked in his mesmerization by a cabaret strumpet.

In another sense, Mills was only the latest casualty of that strange general distraction that, by 1974, seemed to have settled over the community of power in Washington. It had been, for several years, an uncertain season of left-handed happenings in the fortunes of its politicians—including Kennedy, Agnew, the entire Nixon administration. It was as if strange voodoos were loose in the air, randomly and inexplicably pillaging.

For his colleagues, though, there were special disquieting omens in what befell Mills. No one had answered more utterly to the discretions of that venerable etiquette ordering the House's inner society of power. And in his undoing, his lapse,

Life, July 16, 1971
New Times, December 27, 1974

were harrowing intimations of their own worst nightmares of vulnerability. For one thing, a certain casual, covert, compulsive rutting had long been simply a part of the town's culture of power, the weather of power itself having always acted as one of the headiest of human aphrodisiacs. Accordingly, there was more than simple compassion at play in the notable reluctance of most Congressmen even to discourse on what had happened to Mills: it was like a superstition against tempting the notice of the fates by discussing the matter at all.

Quiet, drab, unobtrusive, Mills was a perfect utterance of the House. In contrast to the proud and glamorous stags who stalk the aisles of the Senate, the population of the House, for the most part, are prosaic and plodding men. Shrewd but consummate commoners, they still belong—if only because they must renew themselves there every two years—to the modest main streets and town squares, the Rotary luncheons and church suppers out in the ordinary everyday life of the land. But even among this unprepossessing company, Mills was rather remarkable in his inconspicuousness. A sedulously staid man of middling height, with gilt-frame bifocals set on a face as lumpily honest as a boiled turnip, his zinc-gray hair combed straight back, sleek and glistening and parted just off-center, he tended to strike even his House colleagues, in the words of one, as "just some real estate broker or Pontiac dealer from Little Rock, up here paying his respects to his Congressman."

But as chairman, since 1958, of the House Ways and Means Committee, Mills happened to preside over the inception and delivery of legislation for taxes, social security, tariffs and foreign trade, Medicare, interest rates, the federal budget—in short, the means of revenue for financing the Republic. In the estimation of many, he was the man, after the President himself, most strategic in the mediation of such elemental national distresses through the Sixties and early Seventies as inflation, unemployment, and the desperation of the cities. But while the heft Mills carried was as staggering as any to be found on the Hill, he endured as a preeminently private creature, with an almost implacably unassuming manner. After a week with one journalist devoted exclusively to his daily procedures in directing his committee, Mills finally seemed to become somewhat more comfortable and even sporadically expansive, until at the end of one afternoon as they were leaving his Capitol office, the newsman happened to mention a few names out of Mills' boyhood. This sudden ambush of a personal curiosity beyond the formal exercises of his chairmanship startled him, pitched him into a momentary dislocation: he paused transfixed with his hand on the doorknob, and merely stared at the newsman for several seconds with a curiously accosted little smile frozen on his face, his eyes softly and furiously batting behind his glasses.

Inevitably over the years, marveling notice was taken of him —occasional newsmagazine covers, extensive newspaper profiles—but they were like matchflares held up to a sheet of sandpaper: no reflection, no shimmer was given off. He seemed to have a presence that defied celebration, that resounded to such media fanfares about as vibrantly as a plank of cork. In fact, he had left behind him, through his three decades in Washington, a wake uncannily bereft of any flair or anecdotes. "I have never been," he himself conceded, "too much on comedy." As a raconteur, his well of wit consisted principally of delighted narrations of the winsome doings of his grandchildren. Only seldom did he essay any humor beyond that, and then somewhat cumbersomely. One afternoon, another Congressman leaned in the door of Mills' committee hearing room and lightly twitted him about his vote for a bill that had been pushed by a female lobbyist; Mills—a surprised smile lifting on his face in an exact semicircular arc like a child's drawing—reddened slightly and blurted, "Well, you know I've never been able to say no to a lady." The Congressman advanced a few steps closer to Mills and said, "What, Mr. Chairman? I didn't quite get that." And Mills, coloring a violent crimson, blurted again, only somewhat more hurriedly, "Said I've never been able to say no to a lady," giving then a quick cough of a chuckle.

Altogether, noted one House member, "Wilbur has never exactly been the kind to make the party scene around here or in New York. In all the years I've been in Washington, I don't suppose I've seen him show up at more than four or five evening gatherings in town." Indeed, whenever a new administration installed itself in the White House, Mills' office would quietly notify it to strike the chairman's name from its social invitation list. As late as 1972, the single junket he had indulged in through all his terms in Congress was a brief expedition to Baltimore, some thirty-seven miles from the capital.

Mills insisted he maintained this assiduous privacy partly out of a calculated wariness, dwelling as he did at the eye of such a turbulence of interests. "Without casting any reflection now," he offered, in a slow resonant voice in which there still lurked the husking, whanging Arkie chords of the countryside of his origin, "but why do you think they have cocktail parties in this town that they invite me to? You know the answer to that." Beyond this fine scruple, he professed, "My only real amusement is work, anyway. My father always impressed on me that you couldn't do a day's work and stay out all night at parties. I just don't have to have it like some people in this town. I just never needed it all that much."

Instead, arising at the staunch hour of five-thirty each morning, in his apartment he would read through testimony transcripts, economic reports, departmental briefs, and then arrive at his office in the Longworth Building, across the street from the Capitol, around nine o'clock. There he would first seclude himself for an hour or so, to intently stitch his way with swift nimble pencil strokes through the *New York Times* crossword puzzle. As he considered then the immeasurably more labyrinthine crossword puzzles presented him through the rest of the day—revenue-sharing and tax-reform proposals, the myriad entreaties of businessmen and lobbyists—he continued to plot with his pencil on a memo pad endless patterns of careful parallel lines which he would then as laboriously cross-hatch, finally shading in the squares. His manner, while receiving the litanies of appeals and arguments, was unflinchingly polite, officious, and while listening to these involuted recitals through the day, he reposed at the end of a long table, sipping from a cigarette holder in which there was inserted a Madison Little Cigar—dandling and twitching the holder in his pudgy fingers, occasionally lifting it to his mouth at a faintly rakish uptilt oddly reminiscent of the Penguin in *Batman*; it was his solitary dapper flourish.

Around dusk, when his day finally concluded, he appeared as brisk and impeccably pressed as when he began the morning. He would then tuck himself into his black topcoat and be driven directly back home by a veteran committee aide who also served as his chauffeur, Mills riding up in the front seat with his gray felt hat settled on his head. He and his wife of thirty-one years, Polly—a thin, pale lady whom Mills had first met in grade school, and who was, if anything, even sparer of word and emotions than he—had resided in the same two-bedroom apartment on Connecticut Avenue ever since they had arrived in Washington, and they passed their evenings there sedately. "What we do is read together a lot," said Mills, "and watch television sometimes. Also, we like to listen to Lawrence Welk." They still dined, for the most part, on the folk fare of their Arkansas past: okra, butterbeans, cornbread. "Only up here," Mills noted, "we'll occasionally have Brussels sprouts." At one time, Mills had regularly taken long evening walks after supper, "but it's just not safe to do that anymore. So instead now, after we eat I walk around the apartment a lot."

To expect from such an eminently unpresumptuous creature that most towering presumption of all—to run for President of the United States—could not have seemed more unlikely. But sometime in 1971, to the incredulous gaping of all Washington, Mills began evincing unmistakable signs that he was entertaining precisely that fancy—and that was when "Wilbur first went off the radar screen," as one House member recalled. This improbable swoon was, to a degree, prompted and abetted by the White House's florid blandishments of Mills at that time for Nixon's master designs of revenue sharing, welfare reform, and health insurance—a cultivation that was not lost on Mills. When Polly once took their three grandchildren on a tour through the White House, word was swiftly dispatched to Nixon, and he had them all conducted on into the Oval Office. "The President called me a day or two later," Mills reported, "to tell me my granddaughter had jumped up in his arms and said, 'I love you,' and he said, 'I told her, "I love you too." ' Can you believe that? That man actually went on about ten minutes there on the phone, telling me what *precious grandchildren* I got." Then, at an evening reception for Arkansas bankers, Treasury Secretary John Connally abruptly strode in with Nixon's economic adviser George Schultz; Mills, standing off by himself, cupping his glass to his chest, watched them with an absent little smile and a rapt bemused squint behind his glinting spectacles. "Look at that, will you," he finally murmured, "just look at that. . . . 'Course, I'm not saying this out of conceit or anything, but the only reason those fellas showed up is obvious. I mean . . ." And unable to actually utter it, he merely tapped his coat lapel.

"Despite all appearances," declared a veteran Congressional journalist, "Mills has always had a deep frustration about recognition all his life up here." That submerged hankering betrayed itself in small ways. As one of his aides allowed, "Most books he reads by checking for his name in the index. If it's not there, it doesn't get read." Resolutely unassertive in public, about the only discharge of passion he would permit himself would be, when he might meet with challenges during committee hearings or debate on the floor, merely to blush brightly, a small flicker rippling in his right cheek. But no more than that.

It developed then, one Congressman recounted, "that some of the guys began to talk up the Presidential thing to him, first just as a joke. You know, 'You got as good a chance as all the others—why not?' Also, it hardly hurts you as a member of the House to be telling the chairman of the Ways and Means Committee he ought to run for President. The trick is, we all sit up here shut off from the rest of the country, only talking to each other, and we start actually believing each other." Mills at first actually entertained the suspicion that much of the speculation about his candidacy had been instigated by the White House to embarrass him. Before long, though, he began acknowledging with a slight smile, not without some fascination, as he was signing letters returning donations that had begun sifting in, "Hell, look at this, the folks down home think I'm already off and running." He was also increasingly given to relating how, leaving the Oval Office late at night, he would glimpse the President moving off to a far window in the awful solitude of his responsibilities, and Mills would then detail his own aversion to the prospect of ever assuming those responsibilities with what struck some as a rather lavish elaboration. He chuckled one afternoon, "Polly, hellfire, last night she was just pleading with me, crying, begging me to promise her that if I should be nominated at the convention, I wouldn't accept it. I just laughed. I said, 'Polly, you know that's not gonna happen. Not a chance in the world.'" He gave a few more chugging chortles, his cigarette holder pinning the perfect crescent of his grin together precisely in the middle. A visitor inquired if he had, then, promised Polly to refuse the nomination. "Aw . . ." he grunted, withdrawing the cigarette holder now and solemnly absorbed for an instant in tapping it over an ashtray. "Aw, uh, well . . . no. I just told her it was so impos-

sible. I mean, there isn't even any point in making such a promise."

But "all of a sudden," recalled one Representative, "we noticed Wilbur's started styling his hair. He starts making trips
all over the country. I've seen it happen a hundred times—a
guy gets this tickling about running for high office, and first
thing you know they're mortgaging their house, everything
they own." Mills himself began to confide glowingly, "Yeah,
members of the House been coming up to me, begging me,
'Now, don't close the door on this thing. There're lots of us
ready to work for you, don't close that door.' The House deeply
resents the assumption, you see, that only Senators can be Presidential candidates. Deeply resents it. And I think they've
seized on me, maybe, as an answer to their pride. But the
whole art in this thing of Presidential politics is a sense of
timing—knowing when to move."

Against all plausibility, against his entire career in Washington of methodical and unremitting fidelity to the sensible and
temperate and realistic, Mills began now enthusiastically savor-
ing that most extravagant of all tantalizations. "Like I remember somebody over in the Nixon White House saying once,"
commented a veteran Congressman, "power is delicious, and
absolute power is absolutely delicious. This town does get to you
that way. And Mills, after all, had abstained from that deli-
ciousness longer than just about anybody else up here."

To be sure, Mills had always been a creature of rather cir-
cumscribed and explicit expectations. By his own admission, he
had nurtured since the age of seven a single aspiration: to be a
member of the House Ways and Means Committee. This re-
markably somber ambition for a small boy he had contracted,
Mills later explained, from the periodic visitations to his small
hometown of the district's Congressman, then a Ways and
Means member—a gentleman who would appear, out of the
steams of a paused train, like some demigod from that distant
constellation of power in Washington.

So inspired, Mills compiled a respectable array of honors at a
small Methodist academy nearby, and from there vaulted on to
the Harvard Law School. He then returned to work as a cashier
in his father's bank and to try mustering a law practice, while
he and Polly—who was the town's postmistress—continued

their subdued and mannerly courtship. "They had already come right close to a final understanding," said an old friend, "before either of them had gone off to college." Still, it was against the admonitions of their parents that they resolved, after what they deemed a seemly interval, that they would get married. This was done on a blithe, gentle May day in 1934, at the home of a friend, and they swooped off for the night to the Albert Pick Hotel in Little Rock—this constituting, to all available evidence, the single most flamboyant gesture, up until 1971, in Mills' existence. They then arose promptly at six-thirty the next morning and returned home to resume their respective duties there.

Actually, this brief extravagance of spirit could have been partly inspired by the general light-headedness of the moment, because at the same time Mills was running for county judge— his first political venture. He won, becoming the youngest county judge in Arkansas' history. And four years later, he made his ascent on to Congress.

There, Mills immediately proceeded to apply himself, steadily and quietly, to the diverse small wisdoms and decorums of the House's inner cosmos of authority. He suffered one early mishap: when he returned to Washington for his second term, he made his move for the Ways and Means Committee, "but I neglected to talk to the leadership about it, as a result of which I got beat. Speaker Rayburn came up to me afterward and said he just didn't have any knowledge I'd wanted to be on the committee, that I should have told him and he could have got me on it. Next time around, I was put on without any trouble at all."

Through the calm passage of the next sixteen years, Mills patiently prospered—there was, on the whole, something about his progress that suggested the obscure diligence of a mole. By the time he assumed the chairmanship of Ways and Means, he had amassed a personal encyclopedic store of economic expertise that ranged beyond the ken of almost everybody else in Washington; his appetite for the bland and inert matter which constituted the fare of his committee's deliberations seemed inexhaustible and voracious. He would sit through the stultifying recitals of statistics and percentages with an unflagging and omnivorous eagerness that left other committee members stunned. "He just keeps going," one of them declared, "and going, and going. Dammit, he just *outlasts* everybody." At the same time, in shaping his final budgetary legislation, Mills would meticulously assemble complexities of consensus among the House membership with a studious solicitude that left him, in time, with a permanent ideological profile of carefully measured inconclusiveness.

However sizable his consequence now in Congress, he remained almost excruciatingly deferential. Much of this reticence owed to the circumstance of his having muffed two of his first committee bills as chairman—debacles that profoundly traumatized an already religiously cautious man. In any event, it was his style on the committee and in the House always to carefully absorb himself into the collective identity, notifying petitioners and lobbyists, "I just don't know what the committee's going to do on that yet, and I am bound by what the committee decides, you understand."

On only one occasion in his thirty-two years on the Hill had Mills allowed himself to be lured by the possibility of a dramatic personal extension beyond the minimally sensible and realistic. After the 1968 elections, he was urged by close associates to permit them, as part of a wider coalition to overhaul the House's leadership, to pose him for Speaker against the waning and rickety John McCormack. Mills at last agreed to explorations of the prospects, but when his supporters, due to the delicacy of the maneuver, were unable to provide him the clinching number of irrevocable commitments, he demurred. "Hell, we had it," complained one of his backers. "All it would have taken would have been for him just to take that little biddy step and say publicly he was running. But we couldn't tug him over that line. It just wasn't a sure enough thing for him."

As the speculation began to gather then in 1971 about his possible Presidential candidacy, Mills suddenly, dazzlingly, found himself a kind of national pop phenomenon. For some time, a small company of Congressional journalists had been occupied in a diversion they called "Wilbur-watching," which one of them explained as "sort of like hanging around waiting to spot the groundhog emerge." That description, actually, was not inapt: Wilbur's work was largely done in burrows, below all visible surfaces. But in his daily crossings between his office and the House—at a bustling and oddly pitching walk, bob-

bing back and forth like a lightly tapped rubber beach toy, his
chunky arms swinging with cupped palms turned backward,
his head thrust forward and his somewhat bulky nose lifted as
if seeking stray scents along the way—he now trailed along
with him a churning train of newsmen and photographers.
Everywhere he moved, he seemed to be at the center of noisy
congestions of courtiers and television cameras, flurries of
White House emissaries and delegations of local politicians.
And in the end, what probably claimed Mills was that most
ravishing siren of our times: the simple celebrity of it all.

"It was undoubtedly the most spectacular thing that had
ever happened to Wilbur Mills," remarked a sympathetic colleague. "There's a whole basic difference in kind between the
sort of attentions he had enjoyed as chairman of the Ways and
Means Committee, and going into a ballroom and hearing
yourself introduced as a Presidential candidate. And for a fleeting instant there, it even looked like it might almost be
conceivable—he did have an impressive potential constituency: Main Street America, the South, and especially the business community. It was a golden moment for Wilbur there for
a little while. I remember once, the president of a corporation
flew us down to Florida where Wilbur was to make a speech,
and there was this big reception waiting with people standing
in line to shake his hand. Wilbur had just never partaken of
these kind of popular excitements before; it was a totally new
element for him. And God, he was enjoying it tremendously—it
was like some kid who had been waiting on to middle age
suddenly experiencing his first Christmas. Then, when we got
back out to the airport, there was a huge shouting argument
over who was going to transport him back to Washington—
another corporate president had flown his jet down with the
understanding he was to pick him up, and there was this great
fracas about it with both these corporate jets parked out there
on the runway, and Wilbur watched the fuss off at a distance
with this absolutely amazed and wondrous gaze on his face.
That sort of attention, that can get to any of us, believe me."

For his part, Mills was soon submitting, "A man my age, I'd
be sixty-three years old when I was sworn in—but all my vital
bodily organs are actually those of a much younger man. I
mean, that's what the doctor told me."

But Mills' fundamental miscalculation was that his immense
power and stature within the insular community of the House

could be translated into a popular political currency; his eminence in Congress' marbled halls gave him an illusion of some
commensurate continental brawn. In fact, as one member
pointed out, "As important as he's been in this special enclosed
world here for so long, I could walk down the streets out in my
district and not one guy in twenty would have the foggiest idea
who Wilbur Mills was. But he just never understood that."
Then, as he doggedly pressed on, the support of the business
establishment, which was the main energy for his expectations,
began to falter and fade, due to the peculiar disgruntlement, as
one Hill commentator reported, that "he wasn't acting like
himself any longer—he was acting too much like a politician."
But perhaps most conclusively, Mills simply, irredeemably
lacked the final essential political property of a dramatic public
presence. He carried, in an age of romantic politics, all the
electricities and mystery of a pension-fund manager.

As the bloom rapidly paled from the brief small bud of his
candidacy, he must have glimpsed now for the first time glim-
mers of the burlesque in that devout aspiration of his—and
that he would never really be more than what he had been for
the past thirty years. Yet he still could not emerge from the
giddiness of the prospect. He was asked one afternoon if, living
as near to the zoo as he did, he could still hear, as he had
mentioned to a newsman once, the lions roaring and coughing
in the night, and Mills chuckled, "Oh, yeah, and it used to
bother me some, those big fellas roaring out there in the dark.
But they don't bother me anymore." Colleagues would later
remember that he continued his bounciness in the cloakroom,
usually a bit sloshed, possessed of an improbably clangorous
and raffish hilarity, dispensing witticisms about tax breaks for
men keeping mistresses, about marijuana cultists. "I was
honest-to-God astounded," admitted a seasoned House member.
"It was like he had just turned inside out. Up until his Presidential gambit, you know, he'd had this reputation for listening
to Guy Lombardo and reading the tax code every night for
pleasure. But it was like something had simply happened to the
man's perception of who he was, his sense of proportion, something deep that never readjusted again."

It became, in fact, a progressive dissolution which took on an
almost classic Sophoclean symmetry. Directly out of his presumption—out of that one brief headlong lurch of ego which
violated for the first and only time his whole life's rigorous

fortitudes of caution and modesty—there shortly issued a whole conglomeration of woes that began beating like harpies about his head. After so many years of a deaconlike propriety in his own financial affairs, it soon emerged that about $106,000 of the $700,000 financing his Presidential whimsy had been smuggled to him out of corporate funds, with an additional $130,000 donated by milk interests. Most ominously, his hold of authority in the House began, at last, to slacken. The Democratic caucus insisted he establish subcommittees to tidy his committee's processes—a stipulation that, only a year or so before, would have been considered an unthinkable affront. He was even visited, during this time, with a sudden siege of physical travails: a ruptured spinal disc, surgery, a fractured rib with respiratory complications.

In the end, what happened to Mills was a small version of the old story of the Faustian temptation: his Presidential transport had amounted, in Mills' own meager terms, most surely to a compact with the Devil—with recklessness, with fancy, with pride and indulgence and risk. And it only followed that, once surrendering himself to that Faustian beguilement, he would have decided, when denied the power-and-glory part of it, to take at least that other part of it: the sensual and lascivious part. Assuming then as his Helen of Troy a stripper from a tawdry local dive, Wilbur Mills entered into a netherworld that, by all the simple asperities of his Arkansas Sunday-school conscience, had always constituted his honky-tonk vision of wantonness and abandon. "When Wilbur decided to enter nightlife," remarked one Capitol veteran, "he went in at such a level, it was totally below everybody's field of vision in this town. Which is unusual, because Washington is actually so small and there're so many eyes that everybody usually knows what everybody else has done by the next morning. But Mills really picked out an underground entrance." Indeed, like the rigidly proper professor of *The Blue Angel*, Mills wound up seduced as much, one suspects, by the sheer smoky iridescent shimmer of licentiousness, of Sin itself, as by the particular sylph he chose as its avatar.

The Silver Slipper could not have seemed more remote from the chandeliered vaults of Mills' long domain in the House. It was a shabby, rank little cranny tucked between a pornographic bookstore and theater, and its license had twice been suspended, once "for invitation, enticement, and persuasion of persons . . . to engage in prostitution and other immoral and lewd behavior." It was there, in the early summer of 1973, that Mills discovered Anna Battistella—a ripe, olive-eyed Argentine peeling then under the alias Fanne Foxe, at thirty-eight just beginning to show a slightly overworn melt and sag, but still gamely saucy.

Shortly after Mills had first materialized in the Silver Slipper, Anna ceased performing and began working instead for Mills as a "personal secretary." But they continued to be a frequent couple there, showing up about once a week to pass a spirited evening, Mills ordering magnum bottles of champagne adorned with spuming sparklers, the tab usually ranging from two hundred to four hundred dollars—and, on one especially ebullient night, seventeen hundred. On occasion, Mills would bring Polly along with him, she sitting still and vague and mostly wordless amid the ribaldry bawling around her, at the most managing an intermittent thin festiveness. Several times when Polly was not there, Mills and Anna fell into uproarious fusses with each other, Anna once scattering the glasses off their table with a swipe of her arm in a shrill snit over Wilbur's dewy eye-battings at another stripper.

In all, there seemed a certain reeling, heedless, precipitous blatancy to Mills' manner in this frolic, as if he had pitched himself into a kind of casual kamikaze berserkness. He would leave his black-and-silver Continental always parked conspicuously right in front of the Silver Slipper, and inside he would loudly, insistently advertise himself to the tables around him as Wilbur Mills, yes, the Arkansas Congressman, yes, the chairman of the Ways and Means Committee, yes, that's right, who had run for President back there a year or so ago. . . .

Anna herself had grown up in the operatic, Caesarian political clime of Juan Perón's Buenos Aires. The daughter of a marginally prosperous foot doctor, from the time she was five years old, she would later recite in her pleasantly tinkling voice, "I had wanted to be a doctor myself. I have always been a serious person, actually." But as an interim expedient, she began performing as a nightclub chorine—a digression from her medical career in which, as it turned out, she was to wind up enthralled ever after. She married a nightclub pianist, a darkly glossy chap named Eduardo, on whom her father looked most sourly —"He never thought," Eduardo himself would confess, "that I would ever be able to make her really secure and happy." The two of them then set out on what proved a long, haphazard odyssey through the nightclubs and stripjoints of Panama, Puerto Rico, Miami, Baltimore, arriving at last at the Silver Slipper in Washington, which indeed was to provide, in time, a Cinderella-style exaltation for Anna.

Some while after that had happened, and several weeks after it had climaxed with the incident at the Tidal Basin, Anna confided to one reporter that a central fascination abiding through her life had been "Theodora, you know, back in ancient times, who as a little girl of only thirteen became a prostitute, and was only about fourteen when the emperor of the Byzantine Empire made her his mistress. Then after the emperor's wife died, he married Theodora and she went on to become a great ruler. Her husband was very old, and she took over and ran the whole state very wisely, very greatly. Yes, like Isabel Perón in Argentina, who was only a dancer, you know, and yet she met Perón—"

"Yes," Eduardo abruptly interposed, "she was introduced to Perón by a pimp, I believe." He had been divorced from Anna now for a month, but was still sitting in a rather clumsy, extraneous, stubborn attendance on her. "Yes," he announced in a loud and slightly flat voice, "the man who got them together, he was a pimp."

"Anyway," Anna continued, "she was a dancer and that was how she met Perón, and she became his wife and soon was ruling over all Argentina. So see, it can still happen like that, like it did with Theodora." She paused, and then gave a light trill of a laugh. "But me, the best I do is Wilbur Mills. Ahhhh. Well, I have always been like, either I have nothing, or I am wanting more, am wanting too much."

It had been only a month after they met that Mills had transferred himself and Polly out of that apartment they had inhabited now for thirty-five years, and established a new residence in the Crystal Arms—three floors above Anna and Eduardo. It was, at the least, an engaging arrangement. Anna decorated the Millses' new rooms—"for a simple man," she recounted, "with Early American furniture and gold carpets." She also presented to both Mills and Eduardo identical orotund baby-grand pianos. Eduardo would later relate, with a kind of harried but doughty amiableness, that whenever he was in Argentina, Anna would play bridge with Wilbur and Polly, "with the dummy hand there where I usually sat"—emitting then a clattering laugh with his eyes blank—"yes, I would be the dummy. Ha-ha-ha."

When Eduardo returned from these periodic sojourns (in which he was employed, he indicated, in some business vaguely involving "exports and imports"), Mills would greet him effusively. "He would kiss Eduardo," said Anna, "and hug him and say to him, 'Oh, Eduardo, I am so happy to see you!' " With an equal heartiness, Mills would proclaim to Polly, "You know, Anna is just two years older than our daughter. I think we ought to adopt her, don't you, Polly?" At the same time, according to Anna, "he didn't want me to associate with anybody in my old business. He kept telling me, 'Oh, Anna, why don't you get away from that work forever? You don't want your daughters to grow up and do the same kind of thing, do you?' He was really very strict, an old-fashioned man." Also, all this while, "he knew of our problems, between me and Eduardo." In fact, whenever Anna had a particularly roisterous tiff with Eduardo, she would scamper tearfully up to Mills' apartment, and Mills would phone Eduardo downstairs and assure him, with a certain ambiguously avuncular solicitude, "Now you know I love you both, and I want you to get along. . . ."

Nevertheless, a year after Mills had installed himself three floors above them, Eduardo at last moved into an efficiency apartment, and divorce proceedings were commenced—a divorce that became final two weeks after the misfortune along the Tidal Basin. Eduardo happened to be in Argentina again when that abruptly dislocating event occurred, and before it flared in the press, Mills and Anna placed a cautionary call to him, Mills advising him, "Now don't you worry about it, Eduardo, it wasn't like they'll try to make it out in the papers and television." Despite that admonition, the next day Anna received a call from her brother-in-law in Argentina: "What's the matter with Eduardo? He came early this morning to my house so drunk he couldn't talk. What has happened?"

Mills' own explanation, when it was finally produced from his office, had more the quality of a poker-faced lampoon, couched in the filigreed Victorian euphemisms of some account of the intrepidly gallant and gentlemanly deeds of Dink

Stover: "Our new neighbors, Mr. and Mrs. Eduardo Battistella, offered us every assistance during the moving ordeal, and since that time, our families have grown to become close friends. . . . Polly's broken foot prevented our entertaining at home, and she insisted I take our friends to a public place we had frequented before. This I did. . . . After a few refreshments, Mrs. Battistella became ill, and I enlisted the help of others in our group to assist me in seeing her safely home. . . ."

More exactly, according to police, when they stopped Mills' car, several passengers spilled out and promptly proceeded to scuffle among themselves. Anna herself had, first, simply stretched herself out flat on the ground; then, a moment later, with a slapping splash, she was bobbing in the Tidal Basin. While she was being pulled out, the struggling of the others continued, one officer being toppled backward into some shrubbery. Taken to a hospital, Anna explained to attendants that she had sustained her two black eyes in a skirmish with her boyfriend over who would drive the car.

Beyond the statement issued by his office, Mills himself remained mute through the next few days. "He never came back to the House," a colleague noted. "We just didn't see him during that last week or so that was left until the House mercifully adjourned." But like the taunts and smirkings of the professor's once-reverential students in *The Blue Angel* when they discovered his infatuation with Lola, Mills became the subject of sniggers now from his previously venerative House colleagues; one jingle tripped through the corridors of Congress: "She was only a stripper from the Silver Slipper, but she had her ways and means."

With his reelection to the House also suddenly imperiled for the first time in three decades, Mills hastily returned to Arkansas. He encountered there some scattered instances of unpleasantness, was greeted with howls and whistles at one high school in his district, but on balance, he was spared such moments of discomfiture. If anything, the episode actually seemed to have had a certain endearing effect on his constituents: as one of them put it, "Hell, I never dreamed ole Wilbur had it in him."

He survived. And with that, there was a general assumption in Washington that he would return now, chastened and sobered, to his customary sedate and prudent instincts—that, surely, it was all over. When it was announced that Anna was opening as the featured attraction at a Boston strip palace, it seemed only that Mills might now have to endure her forever touring about the country as a gaudy antic haunting image of his past folly, a Mardi Gras bagatelle left from the hallucinations of his vanity in that Presidential adventure of his once.

She was appearing at Boston's Pilgrim Theater—an aged, spacious, dank hippodrome with frumpish rococo balconies painted a dingy candy pink, its deep murks tinged with a sour staleness—which in itself offered certain symbologies for any Calvinist's apocalyptic vision of what had happened to America since the simple righteous austerities of Plymouth. Between its successive stage acts—solitary females expeditiously undressing and executing various copulatory heavings and leg-gapings—there were nameless movies whose single common plot consisted of a clinical series of fornications and fellatios in livid butcher-counter hues, interspersed between repeated breathless phone calls. While one of these films was dimly undulating and smacking on the screen, down a sagging stairwell past leprous plaster walls, Anna was sitting on the edge of a cot in her basement dressing room, where a star had been hastily crisscrossed on her plywood door with a felt-tip marker. She was wearing a drab pink terry-cloth bathrobe and crimson slippers, her bare shins glistening pale as paraffin. With her was Eduardo, her recently scuttled husband, trimly outfitted in a snug sweater and slacks, but with a slightly frenetic cheerfulness about him, a glazed glare in his eyes. In fact, both of them—as much as Mills himself through those earlier months—had now the distracted and faintly manic air of still being caught in the relentlessly continuing performance of some large mistake not yet quite comprehended.

"Please, I'm sorry, I am a little mixed-up," she murmured as she fumbled for an eye-liner pencil she had dropped on the floor. "He called me several times this afternoon from Washington. He does not want me to go on with this, he said. He was worried about all the interviews with television and the newspapers. He would actually prefer, I think, that I go back to Argentina. But this is the biggest chance I have ever had. I don't believe this will last too long. But I must work as long as this lasts, that's what I told him."

To all appearances, Eduardo had returned from Buenos

Aires to try perhaps reclaiming her one last time. Indeed, in her dressing room now, there were intimations between them of some possible nostalgic scrimmagings just a little earlier— "Yes, you serving champagne this afternoon," she sniffed at him once, "it always gets me tipsy, I know now why you did it," and Eduardo assumed the slightly sheepish, abashed look of someone who has managed to pull off an irresistible bit of mischief. . . .

Nevertheless, the next morning after her show, a caller paused in the corridor just outside their motel room, overhearing some immense fracas proceeding muffled behind their closed door, which, after a few tentative raps, Eduardo yanked open, standing there in nothing but pale-peach bikinis in a fog of steam and reek of cologne. "We are busy," he snapped, adding the faintest flicker of a pained polite smile before briskly shutting the door again. After several minutes had passed, the door reopened and the visitor was admitted. They were dressed and finishing breakfast at the small table beside the chiffon curtains of the window. Anna was without her wig now, and her face, under her harshly close-snipped hair, had a bleak frail purged look, taut and glazed like the skin of a healed burn. She arose to take a call from a newspaper in Los Angeles: "Well, I'd rather not right now. . . . Well, okay, if I must. . . . It went just fine last night. . . . Yes, he called several times. . . . No, we are still very good friends, yes, of course. . . ."

Several minutes after hanging up, she became sick, and quickly padded in bare feet into the bathroom. With dim sounds of her coughing and hacking coming from behind its closed door, Eduardo declared that he would be leaving for Argentina the next day. He allowed with an unhoping smile, "The reason her father did not want me to marry her was because he said I was not strong enough, and her father was right. I have not been able to give her the strength and confidence she should have had, I have not been able to take care of her like her father knew she needed to be taken care of. He was right to tell her not to marry me. I have failed. But yet—yet, I hate to go tomorrow. I hate to leave her alone like this. However, it seems I must. She does not want me here."

That night, then, she was called onstage at the Pilgrim Theater around eleven-thirty for her second performance—*You've read about her in the newspapers, and now, here she is!*—and she bloomed forth into a swooping spotlight, glittering in a voluminous billowing swim of white feathers, gladly grinning. Soon down to a G-string with a white plume on her rump, she pranced and pumped and shimmied through a strenuous routine that was vintage 1948 Havana Tropicana. Her bare, oddly bulbed breasts tautly buoyant, she proceeded to twitteringly distribute, from a frilled Little Bo-Peep basket, lollipops to the men along the ramp, all of whom seemed middle-aged—in fact, a rank of elders who, as she leaned down to ruffle their thinning fluffs of hair, all seemed in that smoky half-light to bear a startling resemblance to Wilbur Mills: a whole gallery of Wilbur Millses. And then, abruptly, she was wearing nothing— afterward, she would fret in a small whimper back in her dressing room, "This manager, he made me show too much, I don't like to go that far, but he said I had to"—and so with no scarf, no G-string on her ample tufted lap, absolutely spankingly bare, she began coiling and twining. . . .

And the next night, suddenly, incredibly, Mills materialized on the stage with her. His bifocals glinting in the stagelights, he brayed to the audience, "She's my little Argentine hillbilly, and I've come to see her dance!" It was stupefying, it was as if he were, after all, enacting to the very end those last sad scenes of *The Blue Angel*: the professor, his position and reputation and all respectability now vanished like a half-forgotten dream, enlisted in Lola's troupe, playing a dumpy clown, reduced to amusing his new fellow mummers by imitating a rooster, cawing and flapping his elbows.

With that, on his return to Washington his colleagues in the House swiftly, and with persuasions as delicate and discreet as the movements of gamekeepers enclosing a lame boar, managed to softly settle a net over him, delivering him at last into a barricaded and etherized sanctuary in Bethesda Naval Hospital, in this operation acting with a gentleness for a casualty— the least likely among them—of those private furies of hubris and avidity forever tempting, luring them all.

Mills shortly resigned from the House and retreated back to Arkansas, where he submitted himself to a protracted treatment for alcoholism. Similarities between what happened to him and to Earl Long seem to suggest themselves, of course, but in the end, they were wildly divergent political personalities. Mills devoted himself for some time then to touring about, discoursing on his struggles with drink, while in the meantime being quietly retained as a tax consultant by a Wall Street firm. In October 1979, it was announced that his former colleagues in the House had decided to restore him to a marginal measure of duty on the Hill—on a committee deliberating the assignments of Secret Service protection for Presidential aspirants.

THE RACIAL PASSAGE

FROM THE OBSCURITY of the South's very beginning, for almost three hundred years until the end of World War II, whites and blacks in the South were left more or less alone together, dual protagonists interlocked in a mutual though unarticulated private experience isolated from, and in a sense more real than, all the larger machinations of history proceeding around them. This old and secret intimacy—a continuing underground interplay of existential frequencies of style and wit and spirit—amounted to the vast unlit other side of the moon of the South's past and character.

Their common sensibilities derived, to a degree, simply from their common long labor with the earth itself, an ancient relationship like that which still lasts over the Mississippi Delta—that colossal flatness stretching off infinitely into hazed summer mornings under toweringly heaped molten white clouds, and nights with lightning hinting stealthily far on the horizon; the primordial and fathomless wilderness of cypress and cane and sweet gum here once long since erased, conquered by wide combed fields of soft cotton sprawling off like the floor of an unremembered sea, a grandiloquent landscape where the days languish in the heavy air of a slow, timeless, sensual, consummate marriage of man and earth.

But over the course of time, the white Southerner also became increasingly occupied in the accumulation of liens and buildings and machinery and cash, investing so much of himself, so much fierce calculation and energy, into that accumulation and then into the protection and increase of it that he took on, in a sense, the quality of those things, as Marley's ghost came to be slyly possessed by his possessions, so that something about his being seemed to smell faintly of metal, of rust and machine oil and pocket-change. No doubt all people become Snopesian at a certain point in their transition from the land to the city; the white Southerner was simply arrested at that point—between the mild earth and the vicious electricities of the city—much longer than most. But all that while, the black Southerner had little to distract him from the ripening of his own simple humanness. For centuries, in fact, he had nothing else to live with and know other than himself and his kind, and earth and air and the seasons—and thus had always known more immediately what being mortal means, had become more accomplished in laughter, gladness, lonesomeness, grief, endurance, love. So in the long spiritual commerce between the two peoples of the South, much of what remained quick and spontaneous and lusty in the white Southern nature was the secret continuous gift of the black man. "Like every other white Southerner," an elderly and patrician Atlanta attorney pronounced in the early Sixties, "I got a Nigra personality. Ain't any getting around it. We got the same way of living close and easy to our skin, same kind of humor, same relishments in food. It's been the Nigra that's really made the white Southerner so different from whites in the rest of the country— we much closer to them, by damn, than we are to the white folks up yonder in New York and Minneapolis. Hell, we even get the way we *talk* from them. We just a little *paler* in all these things, that's all."

Whether consciously or not, then, whites and blacks in the South became, over three centuries, a single people—or rather, two halves of a single people artificially divided by the arbitrary laws and institutions of fear and guilt and greed. Indeed, precisely from their unspoken kinship issued all the viciousness that characterized the white Southerner's open and public transactions with his shadow-brother, the black man. Simply to abide the otherwise insupportable indecency of the black man's debasement in his midst, the white Southerner had to make his life in a twilight margin of reality between the actual and the illusory, had to contrive a baroque facade of legalisms and technicalities and then believe in that facade against all evident human truth. One toll of this effort was to render the white Southerner a perversely mixed creature, with deep and myriad dualities in his nature. It may be that all human personality is haphazardly mixed, at bottom in unceasing chaos, but few people are ever called upon to actually enact that ambiguity so fully with their own lives as was the white Southerner. Necessarily, he kept himself hung in a kind of fierce and harried irresolution—between the exuberant and the dogmatic, the large-spirited and the mean, the Dionysian and the Calvinistic, the lyric and the base: between life and anti-life. And much of the violence in the white Southerner's nature came from the tensions of these dualities of spirit that he had for so long, almost unthinkingly, to sustain.

As much for the white Southerner as the black, then, slavery became a many-dimensioned curse quite demonstrably, in the most literal Old Testament sense, passed from father to son on down through the generations. For the white Southerner, that curse consisted of all the deliberate little deadenings of his heart and mind—the numberless small violences, like self-mutilations, against his own soul—that were necessary to bear the natural outrage of slavery and then its camouflaged sequel, segregation. Possibly the only true capital crime is the assumption of an aptitude for converting the personal into the impersonal, the human into the abstract; from that subtle decadence, all other sins derive. And it was a facility in which the white Southerner became well practiced—a nimble and instinctive knack, retained from the slave-system mentality, for rupturing that natural connection between oneself and other men—the original Cain Act, in that it allows then any manner of violence against them.

A Death in
Lowndes County

OF ALL THE tribal ceremonies by which the white Southerner comported himself through the Black Awakening, few had the spectacular plainness and primitive purity of the trial, in 1965, of a middle-aged white townsman in Hayneville, Alabama, who had shotgunned two young white Northern clerics involved in the local civil-rights movement. Tom Coleman, a fifty-two-year-old state highway engineer and part-time deputy sheriff, had confronted the pair from the doorway of a general store one hot August afternoon right after their release from jail; after a short and uncertain exchange of words, Coleman suddenly simply lowered his shotgun and began booming away. One of them—Father Richard Morrisroe—was blasted virtually in two, but somehow lived, paralyzed. The other—an Episcopal seminarian named Jonathan Daniels—died instantly in the dust in the store's front yard. It seemed a curiously abrupt, gratuitous, arbitrary violence on Coleman's part: only a short while earlier, he had been quietly playing dominoes at the courthouse.

The trial was held in the fall—pale mornings and dreary afternoons flicked by drizzles, with a small dim sun suspended over drab fields of dried corn stalks: a cool and quiescent weather strangely abstracted from that glowering summer afternoon, the instant astonishing flash and roar and blurting blood of the deed itself. Hayneville's courthouse—a spartan, chalk-white, two-story edifice erected by slaves in 1833— hulked over a trivial clutter of repair garages and dry-goods stores and filling stations, and the courtroom inside on the second floor was bare and old and high-ceilinged, full of light and airiness, with iron-jointed ranks of wooden folding seats and

Newsweek, October 11, 1965

tall narrow windows like those in the school auditoriums of one's past. The brigade of national newsmen who converged here for the trial never quite realized, once it commenced, that the reality of what they were witnessing actually lay apart from and beyond the systematic and familiar legal protocols proceeding before them. Instead, what was really under way was the performance of a kind of unspoken folk rite—a commemoration and sanctification and reaffirmation, not only of Coleman's act, but of the whole communal mythology to which it had answered.

The first morning, before the trial began, Coleman stalked restlessly about the front of the courtroom, pausing once for a long moment to gaze, alone, out of a window at the nearby football field named for his father, once the county superintendent of education—a post that was now held by his sister. He had a weathered leathery face, with pouchy eyes and a small mouth drawn thin as wire and crisp beige hair that had recently been barbered. There was about him the burnt, spent, almost drowsy detachment of a man who had finally committed himself to a single act of ultimate irrevocable violence —an unreachable solitude. Whenever someone came up and spoke to him, it seemed to startle him slightly, and he would stare at the person for an instant as if not recognizing him. One friend, after shaking his hand and whispering something in his ear, turned to leave, but Coleman clung to him for an extra moment, wordlessly and not even looking at the man's face, before finally and reluctantly releasing his hand. During this wait, he smoked Raleigh cigarettes ceaselessly and hungrily, all the way down to the filter, stabbing one out in an ashtray with one hand while with his other rummaging for another in his pack. As the judge and other court officials began to take their places, a relative of Coleman's stepped close to him and slipped a tranquilizer into his palm.

The judge was a slight frail man with a soft blur of white hair and a small sparrowlike face, his head barely reaching above the top of the bench, and he announced before commencing the trial, "Members of the court and the jurors will have priority in using the upstairs bathrooms, just so's there's no misunderstandings." With that, a deputy sheriff hoisted up a window beside the judge's bench and shouted down to the yard below, "All you witnesses in the Thomas J. Coleman case, come on upstairs. We fixin' to start." This particular deputy had with him a small, stubby, muddy bobtail bitch of indeterminate breed, which, during the course of the trial, stiffly trotted about the courtroom, wandering over to the state troopers to be patted, circling for a while through the legs of the jurors, sitting below the lawyers' tables and scratching its ears. The deputy checked once more out the window—"Any more witnesses down there?"—and it began.

As the jurors were being selected, one elderly spectator leaned forward to reassure a friend sitting in front of him, "One thing for sure, gonna be a little bit of twine running from everybody in that box to that there chair where Tom's sitting. 'Course, might be one of 'em prejudiced—could be his kid was kicked out of school by Tom's daddy once a long time ago. You can't never be sure." The circuit solicitor who was to prosecute Coleman was himself part of the community—a large, convivial, sunny-faced man named Arthur Gamble, Jr., who was commonly addressed by witnesses as Bubba. One of Coleman's three lawyers, a young man from Montgomery with a peculiarly undersized head and tight pinched-together features, introduced himself to the assembled jury by pointing at the defendant and declaring, "This is my uncle, Tom Coleman," and then adding, "I'm just a beginning lawyer, just out of law school, and I've never argued a criminal case before. Bubba over there, now, he's a real fine lawyer, and there's lots a young lawyer like me can learn from him."

After these neighborly pleasantries, Coleman's nephew summoned the first witness, a deputy sheriff named Joe Jackson—a squat porkish man with bristling gray crew-cut hair and a slightly liverish complexion, who meditatively chewed on his thumb between his answers to questions. "Joe, did you notice anything unusual that especially attracted your attention when those people were released from jail, anything particularly about Jonathan Daniels?" Jackson, taking his thumb from his mouth, chuckled. "Well, one thing. He kissed that nigguh gal." A twitter spread over the courtroom, then through the jury box. "On the cheek or on the mouth?" Jackson answered, "On the mouth." "They'd been separated about a week, is that true?" Jackson confirmed this, and the jurors exchanged grins with spectators in the courtroom.

A doctor from the state crime lab followed Jackson on the

stand, and after describing the fatal wound—"a ragged hole, one and one-eighth inch in diameter"—he began lifting out from a large cardboard box at his feet the clothes that had been taken off Daniels' body. A total hush fell over the courtroom while the pieces of limp, empty, shapeless clothing were extracted out of the box one by one: old khaki trousers, tightly rolled belt, red-and-black plaid boxer shorts, a black clerical shirt with a gaping hole in the chest. In implausibly theatrical accompaniment, a sudden darkness of wind and drizzle soundlessly lashed the leaves outside the tall shut windows. When Daniels' blood-sprinkled clerical collar was lifted from the box, Coleman's daughter—a pretty schoolteacher married to a Selma boy—blushed, her eyes glimmered with tears, and she fumbled a handkerchief out of her purse. At that, Coleman's wife, a spare, narrow, somewhat astringent-looking lady dressed in severe black, with narrow-lidded eyes behind silver-rimmed spectacles, reached around and stroked the back of her daughter's hair. The blood-flecked collar was placed on the rail of the jury box along with the rest of Daniels' clothes, and one of the jurors carefully moved his knee a few inches away from it. Coleman himself, sitting hunched forward with his elbows propped on the arms of the chair, kept his eyes averted in an absent gaze across the courtroom, smoking a cigarette and chewing a tiny wad of gum with a barely perceptible movement of his small closed mouth.

When this awkward business was concluded, there was a short recess. In the crowded hearty clamor of release and relaxation in the upstairs bathroom, filled with the hiss of cigarettes dropped in urinals and a continuous tumultuous flushing, one townsman whooped to his fellows, "Any of yawl see that black bastard with the beard try to sit down beside my wife out there? I told a deputy to get him out of the courtroom or we were gonna have another trial around here." Back in the courtroom, there was a brief bit of commotion before testimony resumed, when an old man with a battered felt hat in his hand suddenly snapped his head toward a black man sitting a seat away from him, and demanded in the unsteady blare of the aged, "Move yo' foot, nigguh." The black man simply stared at him, whereupon the old man kicked his leg. A deputy sheriff hurried over, snatched the black man up by the back of his shirt, and hauled him on out of the courtroom, telling him at the door, "Now git yo' black tail on outta here." Then the old man was escorted out, the deputy giving him three comforting pats on his back at the door. Altogether, it was as if Coleman's deed, and now this deliberate ceremony of vindication, had unleashed a contagion of milder imitations through the community, everyone feeling some prompting to validate himself with his own token simulation of Coleman's act.

When the proceedings commenced again, Mrs. Virginia Varner—a beautician and owner of the Cash Store, where the killing had occurred—took the stand to testify. She was a trim, handsome brunette wearing a modestly chic blue dress, black gloves, and a fixed pleasant smile. She spoke in a very small voice. "Well . . . uh . . . yeah, I heard a shot. I was actually making change when the shot was fired, and I continued making change, and then I went all to pieces." Gamble, the prosecutor, asked her if she had called and requested that Coleman come over, and she said crisply, "No, I did not." She was then questioned by Coleman's chief attorney, a state senator from Montgomery named Vaughn Hill Robison—a man with a long homely houndlike face, lank scraggly sandy hair combed straight back to the turtle-hide nape of his long neck, and a shrewd little furtive twitch of a smile, who resembled nothing so much as an old-fashioned fire-and-brimstone Saturday-night backwoods preacher. A diligent country-style charmer as well, he beamed at Mrs. Varner: "Now, you got a daughter at Auburn, yawl educatin' that child, unh hunh? Yes. And yawl just got that one little store, idn't that right? Yes. Believe you got a beauty parlor there in the back of that little store, haven't you? And the operators there are wimminfolk, aren't they? And you had called yo' daughter and told her to lock the doors of yo' house because you knew these people had just been released from jail, hadn't you? And there were no men there in the store, were they?" Whether or not she was beginning to get Robison's drift, Mrs. Varner self-consciously pushed her skirt an inch or two further down over her knees, and her answers became progressively more bitten and frosty. When Robison was done with her, he swooped forward in a nimble little clog-shoe jig of gallantry and escorted her down from the witness stand with a light touch on her elbow.

But Abell Williams, an elderly black grandmother, got no escort whatsoever from anyone. She approached the witness stand with a home-whittled walking stick, slowly and painfully mounted, and then massively settled herself, feet planted flat and wide apart with the walking stick leaning against the sling of her skirt between her knees. Asked by Gamble if she knew Coleman, she replied, "Well, I stays home most all the time, and I don't know many of the white folks." Asked if she had seen the shooting, she said, "No suh, I knew there was gonna be trouble when I got there, but when the shooting was going on, I was laying with my face over the counter," and she leaned far over to demonstrate, folding her heavy arms about her head, which elicited a number of grins from the spectators, including Coleman's daughter, whose spirits had now revived somewhat. The third defense lawyer, a chunky man named Phelps with a toothpick in his mouth, arose to inquire, "And there weren't any menfolk in that store, were they, A-bell? . . . All right, I believe that's all, A-bell. Thank you." She looked uncertainly at the judge, who told her, "You may go back home now, A-bell."

At the end of that day's session, a few reporters took a stroll around town. The afternoon was gray and misting, and they walked, not talking much among themselves, past the seed mill where Morrisroe had been dragged that savagely hot August afternoon to let him lie in the shade, and then on down along the road's weedy oil-mottled ditch to the Cash Store. It was a small shacky structure of old lumber painted a rust red, with a scrappy tin roof curling at the edges. While the reporters were standing there, Mrs. Varner emerged from the front door in fur-covered slippers, carrying a box of trash. They watched her take it over to a rusted and flame-scorched oil drum, dump the trash in, start it burning, and then walk briskly back to the store, disappearing inside with the empty box in her hand. Something in her manner, during that brief simple performance, imparted a sense of a larger distaste and repudiation— a feeling that she had been vaguely uncomfortable in her role of furnishing Coleman's lawyers with someone they could contend Coleman was protecting, and she was now greatly relieved that it was over with for her. What ensued now in the courtroom did not concern her—she had discharged her small duty and had detached herself from the whole disagreeable business, had dumped it as deliberately and simply out of her life as that load of trash, left to vanish unregarded in smoke behind her.

On the second morning of the trial, Coleman's family arrayed themselves in direct eyeshot of the jury, and Coleman's son, a state trooper called Little Tom in the community, watched from the back of the courtroom, surrounded by friends and other troopers. As the jurors filed in, one of them leaned over to the bailiff—a wiry old man with tobacco stains around his mouth—and muttered behind a cupped hand, "You better have sumpum left in that bottle from last night, you ole fart," and the bailiff cackled, "Aw right, now git on up there in that box." The day's first witness was summoned by the deputy sheriff shouting to the courtroom at large, "Where's Leon?" Someone in the back yelled, "Here he is. Here he comes." Leon Crocker, short and squarish, retired after twenty-five years with the U.S. Department of Agriculture, lowered himself into the witness chair and snugly folded his hands over his stomach. Gamble asked him how long he had known Coleman. "Since 1918, 1920," said Crocker, and then he looked at Coleman and smiled. "It was back in the old days. . . . Yes, we've played a few games of dominoes." After this reminiscent preamble, Crocker proceeded to narrate what he had seen of the shooting, his voice quick and flat. He was wearing glasses, and whenever he turned to answer a question, the light stamped a momentary blankness over his expression. "The one they call Daniels, he took the lead. I heard Tom tell him, 'This store is closed.' He stood there for a second, and then took another step, up on the first step. I heard him ask Tom, 'Are you threatening me?' And Tom told him, 'No, I'm just trying to get you to leave.' Then Daniels opened the screen door and tried to go in—and then I heard a shot."

With only an instant's pause, Crocker continued, his face empty of expression, "The other one, he made a break like he was going to Daniels' assistance. Then he made a kind of twist, you know, like he was careening over to his left. That's when I heard the other shot." Morrisroe, as it happened, was hit from behind—and the only way to explain that rather unhappy circumstance was to have him executing such a sudden and eccentric gyration right before the shot. When Morrisroe dropped, said Crocker, Coleman stepped from the door and told him, "Here, you take the shotgun. You might need it. I'm going over to the sheriff's office." Gamble then hefted the weapon into the air for Crocker's identification—a curiously inert and cumbersome object now that seemed to have no real active connection to the rage and blood of that summer afternoon, to the killing it had done. In fact, the killing itself had somehow slyly begun to seem a merely academic matter. The judge managed to produce a scatter of laughter in the courtroom when he piped from behind his desk, "Gentlemen, I hope somebody's seen to it that the gun's not loaded."

The defense then took its turn with Crocker. "Yes," he offered, "there was a kind of bright shiny object in Daniels' right hand that resembled a knife blade, about three or four inches long." To illustrate, he closed one fist and measured under it with his other hand, invoking thereby the unlikely picture of Daniels holding the knife clenched for downward stabs in the manner of turn-of-the-century melodrama villains. "I heard Daniels say, 'Are you threatening me?' and then I heard a shot, just before he made his move to go in." Crocker neither blinked nor swallowed, merely sat motionless with his hands clasped across his stomach, talking on in a steady level toneless voice. "The other one ran forward, and just as he made his move to go into the store, he just kind of twisted around, like he was trying to dodge or something. He had something in his right hand. I took it to be a pistol. It was a round object like a gun barrel. A few minutes later, some Nigras came up and went over the bodies, like they was hunting for something. . . ."

Sometime later in the trial, a statement was hastily and perfunctorily presented from Father Morrisroe, who had dictated it from his hospital bed in Chicago. He recalled that he and Daniels had gone to the Cash Store to buy a soft drink and something to eat; that when they arrived there they were stopped by Coleman, who told them the store was closed; that Daniels had asked him, "Are you threatening me?" and Coleman replied, "You damn right, I am," and with that, began blasting away; that Daniels had neither knife, gun, nor stick in his hand, and as for himself, "the only thing I had in my hand was a dime."

But at this point, not only the killing but the victims themselves were losing all their reality. It was like a second, formal, larger crime of extinction and effacement—in a sense, in that courtroom, Daniels died a second and more final time, became no more than the empty and meaningless clothing lifted out of the coroner's cardboard box, and a garishly sinister caricature in the recollections of his executioner's friends. One other thing of himself, however, Daniels had left behind: a handful of books, which Robison introduced as evidence. As he held up each volume, Robison would intone in his deep hound's bay of a voice, "And what's this one? *The Fanatic*, I believe." He knelled each title slowly and significantly—Richard Wright's *Native Son, The Life and Times of Frederick Douglass, The Church in the New Latin America*—not once during the trial referring to their contents, just pronouncing those heavy ominous mysterious titles which loosed their own shuddering connotations about the Hayneville courtroom. When he asked one black witness what Daniels had been holding in his hand when he approached the store, he was told, "He had a Bible, I think." Instantly wheeling around, Robison began scrabbling up Daniels' books from the clerk's table, crying, "This the Bible he had?" and holding up each book for a moment before letting it drop in disgust. "This? *The Fanatic*? Or this? *Native Son*?" It was still true in many small Southern communities like Hayneville that people presumed books—all books—were supposed to more or less instruct people on how to behave, since that was the preeminent function and use of the only book most of them had ever read with any seriousness.

The time came to call the first of the black witnesses that day, and the deputy bellowed out of the open window to the yard below, "Tell Joyce Bailey to come on up here." A moment later, she entered the courtroom, hugging a blue raincoat around her—a long slat-thin girl with large luminous eyes which were filled now with a quiet terror. When she mounted the witness stand, the judge snapped, "Throw your chewing gum out." She bent her head and simply let the clot of gum fall into her palm, holding it awkwardly as if she expected she would have to sit there with it resting in her hand until they had finished questioning her. The judge finally said, "Throw it out the window there." She looked around, then leaned and flipped it outside.

After a while, it began to seem that the black witnesses were to be trotted up before the court more for everyone's general amusement than anything else. Asked what she had heard that afternoon in front of the store, Joyce Bailey said that Coleman had told Daniels to "get off this property, or I'll blow your goddamn heads off, you sons of bitches," and there was a rippling of laughter over the courtroom. Again, asked what she was doing when the second shot was fired, she answered, "I was running," which the courtroom found equally diverting. She, surprised by the second eruption of laughter, could not suppress a brief smile herself—a lapse, an entrapment, a betrayal that struck her an instant after it happened and left a new hopelessness in her eyes. For the remainder of her interrogation, she confined herself for the most part to a single soft "Yes" or "No," simply staring at her interrogator with a wide-eyed despair. Once, when Robison badgered her about a small circumstantial detail, her helpless and bewildered floundering finally brought a loud solitary snort of laughter from the foreman of the jury. Realizing he had guffawed all by himself, he quickly recovered his sober composure, shifted in his seat, tugged down his coat, and gravely bowed his head for a moment, as if with his laugh he had all alone delivered the summary announcement that her testimony was just too much.

All of the subsequent black witnesses, when asked what they did when the shots were fired, answered, "I run . . . I turned and ran," and the spectators, with their infinitely alert and inexhaustible sense of humor about the nature and aspects of black people's fear, would snicker deliciously. Each gust of mirth from the courtroom invariably startled the black witness on the stand; it was one reaction to their testimony that not even they had expected—entertainment. Coleman's family allowed themselves flickering smiles now and then—except for his wife—and even the judge's face occasionally reflected the merriment around him: he could not resist a few faint smiles.

It was not totally a light-humored interlude, though. To establish the position of Daniels' companions shortly before the shooting, Robison presented a photograph to an eighteen-year-old black named James Lee Baity and asked him to point out where they had been standing that afternoon. But Baity could not keep from glancing over the courtroom, at the expectant amused faces of the spectators, until finally Robison brayed, "Now, look hyer! Look hyer, now—this way." Baity slowly turned his head toward Robison, as Robison continued, "There was a big gang of yuh under that mimosa tree, weren't there?

About twenty, twenty-five of yuh?" Baity made a reply, his voice sunk to almost a whisper, and Robison didn't catch all of his answer. He caught the yes, but he didn't catch the rest of it. Robison's head whipped up a few inches higher, and glaring down at Baity, he demanded, "You said, 'Yes *sir*,' didn't you?" And Baity sputtered, "Yes sir. I said 'Yes sir.' "

That afternoon, the calm choreography of perjury began in earnest, with the most meticulous and exhaustive testimony of the entire trial now focusing not on the shotgun blasts but on those elusive glints on fleeting objects that could have been a knife or pistol—and on the vision of a Catholic priest and Epis-copal seminarian balefully advancing on a small store filled with defenseless women. Beyond any question, the iciest wit-ness during the whole proceeding was one Billy Cooper, twenty-five, a stockyard worker dandily dressed this afternoon in a glossy gray suit and tab-collar shirt, who commenced al-most idly, "As I pulled out into the street, I saw several Nigras running up toward Hayneville. It looked kinda strange to me, all these Nigras running up the street, you know. . . ." But there was something so cold and metallic and machined about Coop-er's composure, it seemed to discourage any laughter over this observation, any jollity whatever during his testimony. His hard clean polished face was absolutely passionless, as heatless as chrome, and he regarded the courtroom with a pale gray-eyed gaze. "Then I saw this kind of trim, dark-looking Nigra kind of leaning over Daniels' body. I could see the blade of a knife protruding out of his hand." When he looked over at Morrisroe's body, said Cooper, "I saw another nigguh down on his hands and knees trying to pick up something. When he straightened up, it looked like he had a pistol, but he turned his back real quick." When he strolled over to where Morrisroe was sprawled, said Cooper, "I could see that he was bleeding a little bit. He said, 'Where is the gun?' " Then, with only a bare glimmer of a smile, Cooper added, "He seemed to be in a dazed condition." While he was standing over him, reported Cooper, Morrisroe began pleading for a drink of water, "but I didn't think you were 'spose to give people water when they have some kinds of injuries"—Cooper briefly raised his hand to scratch his eyebrow lightly with his little finger—"so I didn't."

But if anyone became a symbol of the entire trial, it was Joe Bell Coker, a first cousin of Coleman's. Coker suffered from a nervous tic in the left side of his face which was particularly activated by moments of stress during his testimony. Like an unusual number of other Haynesville denizens who had preceded him on the stand, Coker too was short, squat, lumpish of features, with bristling gray hair—as if there had developed in that community some vagrant subgenus of the race. He was wearing for his courtroom appearance this afternoon a cheap bright-blue suit and red tie. To begin with, he was asked what he did for a living, and he answered, with a flurry of tics, "Right now, I'm unemployed." It turned out he had been sitting on a bench in front of the Cash Store when his cousin shotgunned Daniels and Morrisroe, and he recounted, in a dull tick-tocking monotone, how that had come about: "Daniels attempted to open the door. He had something looked like a pocketknife. Had it in his right hand. Tom told him to leave. . . . Then, after the first shot, Morrisroe kept coming forward. There was a shiny object in his hand looked like a pistol. Tom shot him just as he swerved away to the left. . . ." At the end of each sentence, like an automatic punctuation mark, Coker's tic flickered. When Gamble began questioning him, he answered while looking fully and steadily at Coleman's nephew behind the defense table. Nevertheless, his tic, which he had almost managed to master when he was being questioned by Coleman's attorneys, now became progressively more pronounced under Gamble's interrogation, innocuous as it was, until finally, with every twitch, his lips were pulled back in a savage grimace over his teeth. Released at last, he ducked his head and, his eyes dodging only once over the crowded courtroom, retreated hurriedly toward the back door, taking surprisingly long strides for so stubby a man.

The testimony was concluded just before nightfall. With a low general shuffling over the courtroom, people turned to chat with their neighbors and light up their Camels and Old Golds. It was growing dark outside, the dusk dissolving in the tall windows in a long continuous weeping of rain. As the day had begun to die from the windows, the last black spectators in the rear of the courtroom had, one by one, filtered away, and now at the edge of night, in the sallow tired antique shine of the courtroom lights, there was not one to be seen. There was no one there now but the white folk of Hayneville, and a few reporters. In the window directly behind the judge's bench, the steeple of the Hayneville Baptist Church loomed against the dim evening sky without color or depth, a shape black, flat, geometric, as though sawed from asbestos.

There was nothing left now but the final arguments. Coleman's third lawyer, Joe Phelps, approached the jury box. He was a plumpish, balding, supremely self-contented young man, with a round-cheeked baby face and a tiny precisely pursed mouth. He orated with abrupt short quick gestures, like a chubby marionette, and the stance he assumed during his interrogations—his back rigid and chest at full pouter-pigeon expansion, his coat unbuttoned and his cupidlike hands grasping the lapels—was a dumpling caricature of that stalwart statesman's pose struck by the graven green-dappled effigies of such patriarchs as John C. Calhoun and Jefferson Davis atop granite columns on state-capital lawns all over the South. "It's an honor for me, gentlemen, to be associated with a man like Tom Coleman," he began. "You knew his mother, you knew his father. Some of you knew Tom Coleman when he was growing up, some of you knew Tom Coleman when he married his sweet and fine wife. Some of you knew Tom Coleman when his children were born, and when he began raising them. . . . And you know he had to go down there on that Friday afternoon, had to do what he did down there. . . . These people come into our community and agitate and terrorize. Where do we draw the line? Do we stand by and let them cut us, cut our friends? The law doesn't say we have to. We can say to them, 'Thus far shalt thou come and no further—here all evil must cease!' Tom Coleman made a decision to protect Jenny Ed Varner, to protect the other ladies in that store. . . . We all ought to thank Almighty *God*! that we've got a man like Tom Coleman in this state today. . . ."

When Phelps had finished, Robison arose. "You are men," he whispered to the jury, "you are not IBM machines, you're not computers, but you're men, and as men, you have a mind, you have a heart. You . . . have . . . a . . . *soul*!" This last word was breathed with an almost ecstatic urgency. As he proceeded, Robison gained the amplitude and steam of a one-man camp meeting: he gasped, quavered, snorted, whinnied, bellowed, twisting and kneading his interclenched fists behind his back while stretching to his tiptoes like a crowing rooster, then suddenly crouching low to slap the rail of the jury box. All that was missing was the wail of a pump organ. "Gentlemen of the jury, this is an unusual case, the most unusual I have ever tried. There is no conflict of testimony! . . . Now, you can believe that knife was there or not. . . . But when those folks came down there and started in on Mrs. Varner, Tom Coleman did no more under this threat to him and to her and to the community than we would. God give us such men! Men with great hearts, strong minds, pure souls—and ready hands! *Tall men . . .*" (The latter part of this incantation, it turned out, was lifted intact from the invocation for Klan rallies.)

When Gamble ambled forward to give his closing argument, several people walked out of the courtroom, like spectators beginning to file out of the stands in the closing minutes of a 56-0 football game. After first proclaiming, "I feel like I have to apologize to you for the way this case was presented by the state," he went on with all the animation of a cigar-store Indian, in a leisurely and even undertone, "There is no evidence here at all that Jonathan Daniels was making any attempt to actually *cut* him with that knife"—Gamble thereby accepting, assuming, a vitally incriminating detail which not even Robison, after the performance of his defense witnesses on the stand, could quite bring himself to pretend he totally believed.

After the jury had shuffled out to begin their deliberations, Coleman stood up and paced about the courtroom a bit, his trousers slung low and baggy under his paunch, his face weary and pouchy. At last he wandered over to sit for a while among his family, his wife on one side of him and his daughter on the other. They immediately leaned in close to him, as if to enfold him in their midst, rapt and anxious and attentive to his every breath, but he refrained from looking at either of them, keeping his eyes instead on a point of empty space directly in front of him. Now and then, without moving his stare, he would interrupt their solicitous murmuring with some short, gruff, grunting remark. And suddenly, watching him, one felt that the reason he had done it—what had finally impelled him to that sudden inexplicable act of profligate pointless violence —was that it had been the only way he knew, not calculated but somehow sensed, for a fifty-four-year-old man, his youth and energies and significance dully expended and almost lost now over the long tedious attrition of the years, to reclaim once more the avid undivided notice of his family and his women-

folk. Even if it were to last for just a short while—only a tem-
porary reprieve from middle age's dreadful intimations of
nothingness—he was back in the warm and critical center of
their lives again. So he lounged there, luxuriously affecting indifference, as they clustered around him, as if out of that
August afternoon there had been born to him a last Indian
summer of his youth. And then—final glory and sweetness—he
suddenly lurched up and left them without a word, their arms
shelteringly entwined now around a vacant chair, to go over
and huddle with his attorneys and his son. For a moment, he
clasped Robison to him almost amorously as he whispered
some commentary into his ear. Not until twenty minutes had
elapsed did he deign to return again, briefly, to his women.

The jury stayed out one hour, and then returned to tell the
judge they needed to talk about it all a little more. When they
were dismissed for the evening, they shambled past Coleman,
so close a few of them brushed his tie, and nodded to him,
smiling a bit sheepishly like schoolchildren going through their
appointed motions in a Christmas pageant who are unable to
resist smiling at each other's costumes and lines. The last jury-
man glanced at Coleman as he went by, and winked.

The next morning—the last morning of the trial—was chill
and dank, and the rain had become peppery now, prickling the
puddles in the yard outside the courthouse. In the courtroom
itself, there was a listless air of anticlimax. Only a smattering of
citizens had returned for this last closing gesture of the ceremony, and their voices rang in high stray echoes in the bleak
washed light. There were no blacks whatever in the room, save
for a jail trustee who was sent to fetch Cokes for the judge and
the deputies while they waited for the jury to report. Twenty-
nine minutes after resuming their deliberations, they emerged.
A slip of paper was given to the clerk of court—a thin cranelike
lady with shell-rim glasses hanging from a beaded chain
around her neck, herself a relative of Coleman's through
marriage—and, dead-pan, she read out: "Not guilty."

Coleman's wife, lowering her head, clasped her hands together and stretched her arms straight out in front of her, then
raised her head and produced the only approximation of a
smile to be seen on her face for the entire three days of the
trial. She got up with her daughter and began pushing toward

her husband. But when the two of them reached him, they had to wait until he finished shaking the hand of each juror. When he had completed this, Mrs. Coleman seized him, a bit clumsily, her head pressed against his arm, and she muttered, "Oh, God, I knew it all the time." He patted her vaguely on the back, a cigarette smoldering between the fingers of his hand, while looking over her shoulder at one juror who had lingered to tell him cheerfully, "We gonna be able to make that dove shoot now, ain't we?" A townswoman reached Coleman and took his face between her hands as she congratulated him, "Good ole boy. See? Didn't I tell you not to worry?" He looked down at her dully, holding his cigarette carefully and delicately away from her, mumbling, "Yes, ma'am. Yes ma'am. Thank you." When she released him, a newsman asked him if he had anything to say about the verdict. He turned to the reporter with a cold squint from his baggy eyes and rasped, "Naw," thought' a moment, and then added, " 'Cep' I'm happy."

Downstairs in the clerk's office, Leon Crocker, witness for the defense, was dispensing money to the jurors—from twenty-four to twenty-five dollars each, according to mileage. They were generally raising a festive and good-natured hubbub until the press walked in, whereupon they instantly fell silent, their faces glazed, and they assumed assorted church-usher poses. The jury foreman, a short blunt man like so many of his fellow townsmen, was ashen-white with either rage or embarrassment, or both. He kept his narrowed eyes averted from the reporters around him with a scrupulousness which suggested he felt the very sight of them might soil him: "There'll be no comment," he clipped, "ever." But a slight man with a blithely happy face and a thin thread of a mustache, when asked how much he was getting paid, chirped pleasantly, "Not enough!" Asked what had been discussed in the jury room, he replied with a silly little innocent smile, "I'll tell you the dog story that fellow over there told us, if you want." He nodded at one of the jurors, who was, at that moment, scowling at him very pointedly. Presently, another juror engaged him in a brief but spirited conversation in a remote corner of the room, and the man disappeared shortly afterward.

*   *   *

So, over the short passage of five or six weeks, Jonathan Daniels' total effacement from the life of Hayneville was finally accomplished—his murder amounting to no more, in effect, than the quick and meaningless and unremembered death of some small animal idly shot by adolescent boys one evening in a field before supper. But no matter how correct and systematic the legal process of their civic sacrament exonerating Coleman, it is impossible for a community to engage, as did Hayneville, in such a sedulous, elaborate, tacit collaboration in falseness, unreality, absurdity, without its collective life being savaged in some way. A certain price was necessarily exacted— a strange distance and awkwardness between old friends, encountering each other on the street now as accomplices in a counterfeit trial; an uneasiness between husband and wife over the breakfast table in the morning; a flatness in the greetings and an avoiding of eyes at Sunday-morning church services. Over all meetings, all communal gatherings, all conversations, there would hang that secret unspoken mutual knowledge of what they had all, together, done: the lying. They would still refuse to admit even the possibility of any guilt over something that was to them both necessary and honorable; rather it was a disquiet simply over what was required of them to do it. Therefore, in arranging together to vindicate one of their own for the slaughter of a menacing and detested alien, and to reaffirm again the cabals of the old tribal ethic, the entire community necessarily suffered a death of a kind itself: a little more was stolen from their collective spirit and lives, and they carried around with them a new exhaustion, in a community that could not stand that much more exhaustion. That was how the curse had worked down through the generations.

Not very long after the trial, it turned out that Joe Bell Coker, after his tic-stuttering testimony, had left the witness stand not only to stride hurriedly out of the Hayneville courtroom, but out of Hayneville, out of society, out of life altogether. On a winter midafternoon, he went into his bedroom, sat on the edge of his bed, put the barrel of a .22-caliber pistol in his mouth, and committed suicide.

A group of reporters, flying back to Atlanta the morning after the trial's conclusion, sat in the back of the plane talking to a man who, after a few minutes, announced that he was a native of Hayneville. He was now working for a dairy firm in Montgomery, but his father had been a country doctor residing in Hayneville, and that was where he had grown up. Dressed with the starched neatness of a middle-class businessman, he quietly explained, "You know, I'm just tired of seeing Negro faces. I truly don't have anything against them. I believe —in fact, I know—they were put on this earth with the same rights we have. When I was growing up, I guess I did everything with them that any other young boy growing up in a small Southern town did back then. We were real close, and nobody really thought anything about it. But over these last several years, I've just gotten tired of seeing their faces. I can't really explain it. But I just want to get away from them, be somewhere where there isn't a one of them for five hundred miles around, where I won't have to see a single black face for the rest of my life."

He gave a small smile. "I'm sorry if that sounds ugly or prejudiced. I don't feel any hate toward them, or anything like that. But I was up in Vancouver not long ago, and every single face I saw up there was white, and I felt absolutely wonderful —it was like, for the first time in years, I was able to draw a full deep breath again. When I retire, that's where I'm heading. It was like paradise."

Largely as a result of the voter-registration campaign that had brought Jonathan Daniels into Hayneville, blacks in 1970 came into most of the offices of authority in Lowndes County, and continue in those offices—including that of sheriff, tax assessor, county school superintendent, and two of the five posts on the county commission.

Coleman, now retired from the state highway department, has dwelt on quietly in his home on the fringes of Hayneville, a plain brick residence under two pecan trees. He continues to be intermittently importuned by journalists for some reminiscences of what happened back then in 1965, but he crustily refuses any commentary on that. He keeps a police radio scanner which he listens to late into the nights, and occasionally he will phone the black sheriff to alert him to some disturbance he has picked up. He will allow now that the concord between the older whites and blacks in the community seems somewhat improved, but he is irritated by the manner of the younger blacks: they will, he complains, deliberately slow their walk while crossing an intersection in front of his car.

Nightwatch in
Greene County

THE LONG INTERCOURSE between whites and blacks in the South may have largely been compounded of violence and exploitation, as brutalizing in a way to the white Southerner as the black. Nevertheless, unlike the more studied and detached civilities of the North, it was at least a warm-blooded play, made up not only of violence and outrage, but also common savors and syncopations of spirit, and a love for their common earth. Accordingly, there was some speculation that, with the civil-rights movement, the white Southerner might at last begin to be delivered from the old oppressive curse by finally realizing and officially affirming in open daylight—even if it was under federal constraint and impressment—what had been a kind of covert and trouble three-hundred-year-old common-law marriage.

In 1966, the white citizens of Greene County, Alabama, were confronted for the first time, in that spring's Democratic primary, with a black majority of registered voters—and a slate of five black candidates for local office, including a lean and gangly twenty-six-year-old Baptist preacher named Thomas Gilmore, who was running for sheriff. It would be hard to exaggerate the harrowing implications in those days for the rural white Southerner of a black running for sheriff of his county: the sheriff was a kind of absolute totem image of all authority and order out in the Southern countryside, the towering Big Daddy figure. One white citizen of Greene County blustered a few days before the voting, "Goddam, nothing could be worse than this, this is *Armageddon*." But Gilmore, for his part, quietly insisted, "This election is actually gonna help the white man as much as us. You know why? Because he's gonna find out that Negroes don't have that automatic fear of white folks like he's been thinking for so long, they ain't gonna take any longer what they been taking all these years, they through with getting beat and clubbed on bridges, and they ain't putting up any longer with all that 'nigger-nigger' talk. And this discovery is gonna be good for the white man's soul, because he's gonna realize a man is a man, black or white, and this is gonna change the white man in ways he ain't even thought about. It's gonna re-create and make stronger than ever before his *own* self-respect. When you can start believing in man, that's when you can really start believing in yourself. We gonna help the white folks around her believe in the *whole* race of man."

As it turned out, though, not only in Greene County but all over the South, the white Southerner negotiated his way through such challenges of the Movement, hardly as a moral adventure, but as a simple, elemental tribal matter of embattlement and survival.

Greene County is a pastoral expanse of lush and lilting pastureland in northwest Alabama, over which, in the spring, there pass hushed and softly brooding rains, and which in May is briefly hazed over with a mist of pale-lavender field blossoms. The county seat, Eutaw, is a leafy little village of some 2,800 more or less neighborly souls, with a whitewashed stucco courthouse reposing in the center of its lavishly shaded square. The original courthouse, erected in 1839, had quickly vanished one night in 1867 in a sudden instantaneous boom and glare of flames, along with a number of federal indictments against local Klan leaders that had been thoughtlessly stored inside. After a seemly interval, a new courthouse was built exactly duplicating the old one, and that is the edifice which stands now on Eutaw's square.

Gilmore had pitted himself, in his campaign for sheriff, against what had become a forty-four-year-old family dynasty, embodied at that moment by a huge, wispy-pated, bright-cheeked and affable figure with cauliflower ears named Bill Lee. "My daddy started this business around 1922," Lee explained one afternoon, "and then my brother swapped the job with him every four-year election. From about 1935 to 1947, I was doing some rasslin' off-season from playing with the Green Bay Packers, but three years before my daddy died, I came back. My father and brother and me have worked this thing all this time, and not once in forty-four years have the cullid folks 'round here seen a gun. I mean, I don't think no more of walking into one of these nigger joints without a gun, and a hundred likkered-up niggers in there, than I would think of walking into a church—because they know ole Bill's gonna be fair with them."

But Lee campaigned little among blacks. Instead, he employed the services of a wealthy black cattleman, whom he had appointed a deputy shortly after news of Gilmore's candidacy got around, and a buff-colored mulatto named L. C. Ball who, shortly before the campaigning began, had returned to Greene County from Los Angeles, where he had been a Bunny scout for the Playboy Club. For the most part, L. C. Ball simply strolled about the streets of Eutaw in a snappy straw hat and a checkered sport coat, always alone, only pausing occasionally to casually expound to small groups of blacks in a deep leisurely pontifical voice, rolling an unlit cigar between his fingers and tapping his hat back with a curled forefinger, while they regarded him with a mixture of abashment and awe. "You know, I learned a whole lot of things out there in Los Angeles. And when I got back here, I spotted right away that there's some undesirable elements at work amongst us. . . ." The week before the voting, Martin Luther King swung through the county one afternoon, addressing a congregation in a swampishly hot little church on the outskirts of Eutaw, "We are not Bill Lee's children. We are no white man's children. We are *God's* children. And for all these years, the white man has been bloc-voting to keep us down, has been trampling us under with the iron feet of oppression. . . ." (The genius of King's ponderous rhetoric was that it was consummately the rhetoric of the human spirit faced by enormous challenge, by slow massive terrific struggle—that was the brilliance and perfection of his otherwise cumbersome metaphors.) "Now we gonna engage in a bloc vote to get back up on our feet. Because we have suffered too long, we've had too many mountains to climb and too many oceans to cross, to let this opportunity pass from us now." While King was speaking, L. C. Ball watched from across the street, alone, leaning over the back of a pickup truck and meditatively sipping on a straw in a milkshake cup. But by the time King finished and people began coming out of the church, he had disappeared.

The Saturday before Tuesday's voting, Gilmore was already aglow with the impatient exhilaration of a small boy on Christmas Eve. "This election is going to work so much good, for everybody. I even had a city policeman come up and start talking to me the other day. He's been on the force for sixteen years, and I think he was worried about what might happen to him after Tuesday. His whole mind, while we were talking, was pointing toward him being my deputy, but he just couldn't get himself to the point of saying it, you know. He said he'd devoted his life to law enforcement, and then he said he'd even work for nothing if he had to, and then he said, 'I reckon they'd run you and me both outta this county if you made me deputy, wouldn't they?' I told him I didn't think so, but all he could do was give a little laugh. He'll get around to saying it sooner or later, though. Man, we gonna be clearing away a lot of junk and rubbish in folks' heads come Tuesday."

In the evenings after his rounds about the county, Gilmore returned to his little white frame house, set well back from a country road, where a woodstove in the bare plank-floored kitchen filled the dim rooms with a constant fragrance of burning pine kindling, and he would greet one of his small sons paddling about in drooping cotton underpants and wetly running nose, "Yes sir, there he is—this is the boy who's gonna be the first Negro President of the United States." The boy would simply blink up at his father with an expression of blank uncomprehending delight. For his part, Gilmore declared, "I hope to be in the legislature in Montgomery before too long. If I get in there and do a good, strong job, I might be the first Negro governor of Alabama. Anyway, I think I'm gonna enjoy politics. I don't see how we can miss on Tuesday. Unless . . ." He paused.

"But I can't believe they would do that. I just can't believe they'd actually take this thing away from me now. Not that kind of way. Not even them now."

It had long been an election-night tradition in Eutaw for whites to gather at the square and watch as returns were posted on a blackboard set in the main corridor of the courthouse. But on this particular evening, the cars and pickups were a little slower in arriving, and the small clumps of people scattered over the lawn were a little quieter than usual. Clus-

tered in the shadows under heavy spreading leaves that stirred
easily in an evening breeze under the calcium-white glare of
streetlights, they talked and waited, taking a little longer to go
in and check the blackboard—their voices a low and scattered
rustling over the lawn, their white shirts luminous in the dark
and their cigars and cigarettes describing abrupt tense arcs like
stray brief sparks. "You know Sam Amerson—that nigguh out
at Mt. Hebron who was always asking Miz Sally's daddy if he
could call the dogs whenever Miz Sally's daddy went hunting?
Well, damn if he didn't show up this morning at the polling
place out there where Miz Sally was tending the boxes. Said he
wanted to vote—yeah, ole Sam Amerson—only he didn't exactly know how, asked Miz Sally to mark his ballot for him.
When she asked him who he wanted for sheriff, he said Gilmore. She just looked at him a minute, and then went ahead
and marked it down. According to Miz Sally, Sam Amerson
ain't gonna be calling nobody's dogs again for a long time. . . ."
Finally they would stroll on into the courthouse's blank bone-
bare shotgun corridor, where a dog was snuffling about the floor
and a sweet breeze from the rich May evening combed cleanly
in one open door and out the other, and they found the blackboard gone. They would stand for a moment with a vaguely
lost expression, and then amble over to a policeman to remark,
after a few genial observations about the nice night outside,
that the board didn't seem to be there. "Yeah, that's right," said
the policeman. "We just thought we'd skip the blackboard this
time with all the nigguhs voting and all." Muttering "Well,
hell," and "Shucks," they would then mope on back outside with
a slouch of disappointment and deprivation.

But inside the probate office off on a corner of the square,
with its tall green shutters hooked shut this evening, a more
private watch and count was being kept. Probate Judge Dennis
Herndon sat at his desk—a placid youngish man with a fresh
bland soap-scrubbed face and furry gray hair with a bald spot
in the back, coatless and tieless but with the crisp cuffs of his
shirt still buttoned, steadily chewing gum as he took the telephone calls coming in from far-flung polling booths over the
county. A few local officials and sheriff's deputies were gathered tensely over him. But word of this special tabulation soon
filtered over town, and as the evening wore on, other citizens
wandered in—lawyers and doctors in soft pastel sweaters and
canvas sneakers who had arisen from their supper tables, from

color television sets in pine-paneled dens, and driven over. And then, a bit later in the evening, the humbler folk in the community arrived, mechanics and gas-station attendants, somewhat more subdued and studiously cordial and deferential. They formed after a while a kind of haphazardly democratic Judgment Day assembly of Eutaw's white townsmen, all crowded together in a rare general fellowship in Herndon's office.

The first two boxes to report showed Gilmore leading by a total of twenty-four votes, and as other citizens began phoning Herndon to find out what was happening, he told them, "Well, it's looking real sad, the colored are leading right now, but we got a little ways to go yet." Gilmore's lead continued to hold, and around nine o'clock, a local attorney declared, "Dawgonnit, we all used to be drunk by this time. But this one's too serious—this one ain't any fun at all."

Spirits lifted notably in the room when the absentee vote was delivered: there was only one black vote among the more than two hundred cast, and, not surprisingly, only one vote for Gilmore. The Dairy Queen sent over commodious cups of Pepsi-Cola for everyone, and the shuttered room—high and narrow, painted a drab institutional mint-green—became even more crowded, smoke gauzing slowly up to the long harsh fluorescent lights, the talk rising to a loud dense buzz. Then the phone rang again, instantly arresting all voices, and Herndon began scrawling down figures, with faces suspended over him in a breathless motionless attentiveness. Herndon's rapid arithmetic showed that Lee's lead from the absentee ballots had faltered, and the room asssumed the gravity and stillness of a mortuary parlor. Then, with a quick series of calls, Lee began to pick up steam again, and the room became uproarious. Now, when citizens phoned in, Herndon told them, "Yes, ma'am, it's looking a whole lot better now, I'm still scared to death, we still got some real woolly-boolly boxes to come in yet, but it looks like Bill could pull it out. . . . Yes, ma'am, you welcome, and give us a call later, we'll be right here."

Among those calling was, every now and then, Gilmore himself. After picking up the phone, Herndon would notify the rest of the room by declaring in a suddenly louder and more formal voice, "Oh, yes, Gilmore. Well, Gilmore, let's see what I got here. . . ." And everyone instantly went silent, listening with small smiles as Herndon recounted the latest news, which became progressively more cheerless for Gilmore. After imparting to him one particularly bleak set of figures, Herndon hung up and announced, "Well, he sounded downright encouraged." The room erupted in guffaws—"Sho. He's been scared to death he might actually win this thing and have to be the sheriff. He's gonna be the happiest man in the county when he loses."

By midnight, Lee was some four hundred votes ahead. Polling officials from some of the more remote precincts in the county, who had called in far handsomer counts for Lee than anyone had expected, now began arriving in Herndon's office with their ballot boxes, flushed and wind-blown and blinking and a little whiskey-eyed from their long pell-mell drive through the night. Herndon congratulated them, "Yawl did real good out there, I'm telling you we really need those votes," and quickly directed someone to pour them some bourbon, which they mutely and gratefully accepted, straw hats held in callused hands, swiftly bending their long ropy necks to sip from the small paper cups, then wiping their mouths on their flannel sleeves and stepping back along the wall to hang around until it was all over. Serenely and tidily chewing gum, refraining from the paper cups being passed around, Judge Herndon continued to sit behind his desk taking calls. But everywhere else in the room the whiskey now was beginning to splash. A few people would quietly excuse themselves and, after a short absence, reappear, abruptly and totally drunk. One citizen took a call from his wife in a back office, and returned to report, "It was like trying to talk to a parrot. She went home tonight just knowing we was gonna wake up in the morning with a nigguh sheriff, and proceeded to get tighter'n hell. She called me just now to tell me she's decided she can't face it, we're gonna have to move to Rhodesia. I kept hollerin' to her that Lee was gonna win, not Gilmore, but she was too tight to hear a word I was saying. I finally just had to hang up on her."

Suddenly, L. C. Ball was discovered in the room, talking quite soberly and intently to a white man in a far corner. One of the few there who was wearing a coat and tie, he rolled his unlit cigar between his fingers as he cast an occasional uncomfortable glance around him out of the corner of his eye. But he was abided. One townsman, nodding toward him, confided to another, "Hell, that L. C. Ball, he used to sell dope, but he was the best worker Bill had." Only a moment later, the black cattleman appeared just as abruptly and inexplicably—as if he had been hanging somewhere in the air outside waiting to see how L. C. Ball would be received, and then, at an instant when no one was looking, had spirited himself on into the room after Ball. Someone chided him for not being sterner with the blacks he had arrested after Lee had appointed him a deputy, and he grinned, casually hunched forward in a soft Orlon golfing sweater with both hands shoved deep in his expensive shimmery gray slacks. "Well," he drawled, "I had to stay in good with them, but I'll be getting tough enough with them from now on, don't worry. We can't let this riffraff get on top of us, you know." He refrained from even observing the general jovial circulation of bottles around him in the room, but at last a cup was presented him, and he quickly, calmly accepted it. A moment later, L. C. Ball, still in the corner across the room, was also holding a cup.

Eventually, it was clear that not only Gilmore but all the other black candidates had been defeated. "I'd kinda hoped they might get at least one little ole bitty office," announced someone in the room. "It'd been good for their morale." Another voice yelled, "Aw hell no. We don't want to help their morale. Not one bit." What had begun as a grim political nightwatch had, by now, long since eased and expanded into a common celebration, and they remained there in the probate judge's office—bleary, hoarse, rumpled, red-eyed, bewhiskered, jubilant, bottles lifting and paper cups passed sloshing from hand to fumbling hand—until shortly before dawn. Then they began shuffling out of the office, on out into the cool and limpid darkness with the sky just beginning to pale, scattering off with a few final happy calls, to their homes, to their beds, to sleep at last. They had survived.

The next afternoon, blacks in the community offered a range of explanations to the troop of astonished newsmen who had come down to cover the election: "Well, see, I been knowing Mr. Lee for almost forty years, and I used to foxhunt with his daddy, Mr. Frank. . . . Mr. Lee, he been a pretty fair man. He don't believe in overriding somebody like some of them other lawmens in Alabama, he a different kind of man." In the cool of the evening, Lee himself reposed massively in a white metal lawn chair in front of his rambling white house to receive the congratulations of neighbors happening by: "Yes, ma'am, we were right fortunate. I 'preciate you dropping by, now." His own benign appraisal of the outcome was that "we never really had a problem here with our colored people. We in this county feed 'em and take care of 'em, they get their groceries for nothing and the government gives 'em their luxuries with their welfare checks. They know the law's not gonna bother 'em here, and they got the best climate in the world. It's just the best place in the world for a colored person to live, and we've got a different set of very intelligent social colored folks in this county who know that. Naw, it was these teenage woolly-boogies running amuck all over the place. Why, I must of had at least a hundred darkies come and tell me that Hosea Williams, that fella Martin Luther King sent in here, had threatened to burn their cotton and corn in the fields."

He tugged thoughtfully at one of his wadded ears. "But back when Johnson struck the civil-rights bill with his pen, that very day I carried a bunch of colored folks into the only two eating places here in town and sat down and ate with them. Yessir. And I carried colored children at a rate of four a day, twenty-seven of 'em all count, in there to the picture show and sat down and watched picture shows with them. I been a moderate in all this business. Why, when we were having our own little demonstrations here, I even joined in and sang with them —did that for a solid year. Once, I even knelt with them, got down on one knee and prayed with them. For a whole year, I'd lie awake at night and fight that thing knowing I was gonna have to face them again the next day. They just couldn't get ole Bill mad, 'cause ole Bill'd join in and do everything they was doing. But I asked them one day, 'Why? Why? Just tell me *why* you marching, and I'll give up everything and march full-time with you.' They just looked at me. I never could find out why, 'cause they couldn't tell me. . . ."

He shifted in his chair, a vast amiable ruddy-cheeked country man. "But you know—I don't understand a bit of it. This thing's so *massive.* I mean, you just can't expect fifteen hundred people to be able to keep beating off twenty-seven hundred. It just stands to reason they bound to win something eventually."

Four years later, they did. Gilmore not only dislodged Lee in that 1970 round of voting, but Judge Herndon and most other white officials in Greene County were replaced by blacks. Gilmore has remained sheriff since then, while Lee now works his cattle in the mornings and plays golf in the afternoons. "He says," remarks one townsman who was in the room that election night of 1966, "that he's never been happier in his life."

Martyrdom by Accident:
The Advent of Julian Bond

HIS BREAKFAST, that bright bare January morning in 1967, was a cup of coffee, sparingly sipped from between long tapering fingers in which a Salem cigarette smoldered, as he sat strangely quiet and withdrawn amid the cheerful clatter of Paschal's Restaurant, deep in one of Atlanta's Negro neighborhoods. In an hour, Julian Bond was to become a member of the Georgia house of representatives. But the night before, while other Georgia legislators who had come rollicking into town from the far corners of the state were smacking down an epic supper of barbecued wild hog up on the fourteenth floor of the aging and raffish Henry Grady Hotel, Julian had stayed alone at home, finishing off a bottle of bourbon left from the Christmas holidays. As he had confessed with a light laugh to a friend who had phoned him, "I'm feeling a little rocky about tomorrow. . . ." Now this morning, he was wearing a sober blue suit with a vest that was looped at the bottom with the chain of a pocket watch, a guise that only increased his look of boyish vulnerability—the vest drooped a bit loosely, and his slender neck lacked perhaps an inch of filling his collar. He had rather the appearance of a fledgling banker. And in the din of voices around him, with the cash register pinging furiously nearby, he muttered, his words barely audible, "It's here at last—and now, none of it seems real."

As a matter of fact, for the past six years the Georgia house had been engaged, one way or another, in shooing Julian Bond from its midst. In 1961, he and a small delegation of other Negro students were making their way to seats in the "whites only" section of the house gallery when a representative on the floor below noticed them and bayed over the buzz of business,

The Saturday Evening Post, May 6, 1967

"Mr. Speak-ah! Git those niggahs out of the white section of the gallery!" Julian and his companions were promptly flushed out of the balcony by capitol guards—indeed, they were pursued, at a brisk but decorous walk, all the way out of the capitol building.

Four years later, shortly after a court-ordered reapportionment of the house, Julian was elected by his home district in Atlanta to sit at a desk on the floor of the chamber itself. But the house membership, on a day reeling with hot emotions, voted to eject him as unfit to be among them when he refused to disavow a statement—issued by the Student Nonviolent Coordinating Committee, the company of angry young civil-rights activists, called "Snick," to which Julian still officially belonged—that denounced America's involvement in Vietnam as criminal and urged all of America's alienated not to participate in it. Though the statement had been drafted by Snick in Julian's absence, when he was confronted with it by a radio newsman, he had given it his qualified assent. As it happened, though, among the troops in Vietnam the percentage of boys from small communities over the South was about as over-proportionate to the general population as the percentage of Negroes. One legislator on the day of Julian's eviction from the house said simply, "I'll tell you what I think about this fella Bond—I've got two sons in Vietnam, my uncle was killed in war, my brother was a prisoner of war and I had to take the telegram to my mother, and I joined the Army myself at seventeen. That's what I think about Julian Bond."

There was a small number of legislators—mostly those who happened to know Julian personally—who quietly labored to salvage him from what they regarded as a melancholy disaster, both for Julian and for the Georgia legislature. One of these was the house speaker, George T. Smith, a south Georgia fellow himself with a face as plain and frank as a wooden bucket. "I got to know Julian as a young man who was articulate and extremely intelligent—though a young man who had also certainly felt the personal sting of segregation. I went back and forth on the phone all that weekend before the house was to convene, and I realized finally that I was beat. He was gone, even if he had come out with a retraction."

For a while following that initial repudiation, then, there threatened to be the spectacle of the house grimly, interminably tossing Julian back to an electorate that would just as interminably be tossing him right back to the house—he was elected a second time, there was another rebuff by the house, he was elected a third time. One thorny-knuckled rural legislator snorted, "They can keep on electing him till Gabriel blows his trumpet, they ain't *ever* gonna get him in here."

But what finally ended Julian's successive incarnations and evaporations as a Georgia legislator was a Supreme Court decision that the house had acted unconstitutionally the first time they refused to accept him on the floor. Even then, though, one back-county representative vowed, "It don't make no difference. He's done ruined hisself in here. All he'll be doing is sitting in that chair for however many years playing with his pencil."

An oddly mute and nebulous figure throughout the course of this whole affair had been Julian himself. "The entire matter could have been greatly ameliorated by Julian's personality," said the then chairman of the Atlanta delegation, Jack Ethridge, a genial and urbane young attorney with horn-rim glasses and a Kennedy-like mop of chestnut hair. "I found him, when I finally got to know him, very easygoing and open, and a young man of great sensitivity. But before it was over with, somehow we had reached a point where, if you had anything good to say about Julian Bond, you were un-American." To many in the Georgia house—especially those men from the state's outer reaches who were described by one state official as "hard-drinking, hard-praying folks who are patriotic in the old-fashioned way"—Julian represented a special, exotic evil. Declared Representative Jones Lane, a burly Primitive Baptist from sandy, gnat-humming little Statesboro in east Georgia, "I'm scared of him. I'm scared of all those people." But there was something finally uncanny about the hostility—its general contagiousness, its startling vehemence, its curious impersonality. Seeming to lurk at Julian's elbow, of course, was the specter of Snick, whose master design for America, such men as Lane were convinced, was godlessness, disruption, and "interrace sex." Even one moderately liberal representative from Augusta asserted, "Julian's their Manchurian candidate. All they got to do is flip that queen of spades, and he stiffens."

But despite all the fulminations he had touched off, Julian himself presented a rather whimsically improbable revolutionary. Tall, willowy, almost wraithlike, with a quiet and finely modulated voice textured, it seemed, of flannel, he was the son of one of the nation's most distinguished Negro educators, Horace Mann Bond of Atlanta University, and the Bond family itself, according to a white Southern dowager versed in such matters, was "among the few genuine old aristocratic Negro families in the South." The members of the Georgia house heard him amiably admit on a taped radio interview replayed for them, "I like fairly well the life I lead now, you know. I don't want to see too many abrupt changes in a direction I don't like take place." In contrast to most other members of Snick, he usually seemed, even now at twenty-seven, to have a difficult time taking himself or his situation seriously. He more suggested one of those languid, leisurely, bright, introspective, and exquisitely detached young men in Henry James novels, always preferring to dwell on the periphery of passionate events and conflicts. He was the kind of young man who in another society, in another time, would perhaps have been delicately described as "still finding himself." He once remarked, "The ideal life would be to have the freedom to be a dilettante —the freedom to go wherever I want to go, whenever I want to, and do whatever I want to do."

The most discernible interest in his life up to then had been a certain sporadic literary hankering. Listing himself in the house directory as a "writer," he was an occasional correspondent for *Ramparts*, and thought he might like eventually "to own a Southwide weekly newspaper with editions in every Southern state." After dropping out of Morehouse College just one semester away from graduation, he worked for a while at a Negro weekly in Atlanta, writing sports and a column of advice to the lovelorn. Sometime earlier, he had begun an autobiography, but shortly found it kept going out of focus on him. There was also a period when he considered he might be a poet. He had spun a few slight verses of a somewhat diaphanous excellence that were published in several anthologies: "When rain comes creeping in . . . mewling and wetting my body, I have sneezed in Cambridge. / Damn . . . / A Bard girl who thought I was sweet comforted me / I asked her with my eyes to ask again / Yes, yes, yes, yes—I was hungering like mad. . . ." And then there was "Look at that gal shake that thing / We cannot all be Martin Luther King."

At the least, as his father exclaimed to a friend on the day of

Julian's first confrontation with the house, "My God, I didn't raise my boy to be a Georgia legislator. I'd hoped he would go into a more academic occupation." Julian's childhood was a relatively snug and insulated one. When he was five, his father moved from Georgia to Chester County, Pennsylvania, to take the presidency of Lincoln University. "We had a great big old white house like a Southern plantation house," Julian remembered, "and there was this long porch where we'd sit in the evenings in the summer." And growing up in Chester County, "I never really knew what a segregated school was until I entered high school."

It was at George School, a Quaker institution where Julian was the only Negro student, that his comfortably buffered childhood came to an abrupt end. "I started dating this white girl from Virginia who was also a student there. We'd go into Philadelphia on Saturdays or Sundays, just mess around all day and then get back to school around six or seven in the evening. Then one afternoon the dean of men called me into his office. He was sitting behind his desk—he looked like a tennis player or a country-club golf pro who had just begun to age. He told me, in a very calm and polite voice, that he'd appreciate it if I didn't wear my school jacket on those trips to Philadelphia. It was just as though he had slapped me across the face. All of a sudden, you realize all the talk there's been, all the whispering, without your knowing it. And also, that you're a Negro. That moment, that was the first time I really realized it—that distance I hadn't ever suspected. I simply couldn't speak anything to him. I just stood up and walked out of his office."

The shock of that moment lingered through the following years. When his father moved back South to Atlanta to accept a post at Atlanta University, "I was scared to death," said Julian. "Mother'd ask me to go down to Rich's to get some clothes, and I'd say, 'No, no, I got enough clothes now, don't need any more.' I thought that down here people stopped you on the street and lynched you just for the fun of it." But Julian's experience at George School—which amounts to the great common trauma, in one form or another, that comes in the lives of all American blacks—befell him more or less belatedly, and so did not seem to blast him so profoundly.

He enrolled in Morehouse College in Atlanta, majored in English, and took a philosophy course under Dr. Martin Luther King, Jr. About that same period, he later confessed, "I began spending a whole lot of my time in drugstores." What kept him lingering in one drugstore in particular was a bright-spirited co-ed named Alice with a freshly pretty face. After the passage of a few months, they drove up to a little north-Georgia town to be secretly married—not living together for another four months. (By the time of Julian's tribulations with the Georgia house, they had three children and were settled in a small, plain frame home in Julian's district, with a curtainless front room cluttered with new Mediterranean furniture and brick-and-plank bookshelves brimming with paperbacks.)

What nudged him to drop out of college was, Julian would explain simply, that it was "boring." More exactly, though, he had become caught up—as any other sensitive and politically aware young Negro in the South then had to be—in the sudden windy drama, the lyric days of courage and danger, the grand righteousness and breathless inevitability of the Movement. It was, he told a friend, a splendid moment to be alive. Before long, he discovered Snick, and thereby seemed to have discovered himself at last.

"They were in this grubby little office, this tiny room with no windows, and they were doing things out of that room that had never been done before. People would call up about somebody missing in some south-Georgia county, and they'd swing into action—it was something to see. I just liked their style of life. And that was a great neighborhood—there was a numbers racketeer who would cash our checks, up to five hundred dollars, no questions, and a restaurant owner there would sometimes let us eat for free, we even got free laundry service. There was the Royal Peacock nightclub across the street, and we'd have these big parties there when Snick people came in from the field. . . ."

But from the first, Julian was regarded with a faint measure of suspicion by the fire-breathing young circuit riders of Snick. Installed in Atlanta as communications director, drawing the highest salary in the organization—seventy-five dollars a week —he tended to betray certain bourgeois instincts, most particularly an undisguised affinity for the lilting good life that was more appropriate to the Pepsi Generation than to a civil-rights guerrilla. (Indeed, while in Snick he posed in a sunny poster ad for RC Cola.) He also had frank expectations for his own eventual prosperity—"I'd like," he would readily profess, "to be a millionaire"—and answered to a kind of adolescent, indiscriminate awe of celebrities, proclaiming, "I like being around famous people." On the whole, he seemed notably to lack the order of angry soulful commitment that had always character- ized Snick; he never seemed exactly prepared to make a career out of alienation. He entertained no great urgency about getting personally involved in the street confrontations then in Ala- bama and Mississippi, and he cheerfully acknowledged it, once observing about the 1961 Freedom Rides, "You'd have to be a fool to want to go on a bus trip through those states."

In fact, according to the late Ralph McGill of the Atlanta *Constitution*, Julian was "privately hoping to get out of Snick. He'd privately been talking to a rather successful advertising agency about taking over a department dealing with a very substantial Negro market." Julian himself later allowed, "I had gotten to the point where I wanted to be independent. I don't know, I just thought by now I might be more my own man." At one point, he even insisted to a white friend, "I don't think of myself as a Negro. I'm a Southerner. I just like the Southern way of life."

When he decided after reapportionment to become a candi- date for the Georgia house, it was at least partly out of a wist- fulness to arrive at a more serious and substantial self- realization. At the beginning, there was a degree of grousing from Snick about his venture. "They objected to my running as a Democrat," Julian reported, "and they even objected to my campaigning in a coat and tie." But the enterprise was not without its beguilements for Snick, and when they realized that Julian had made up his mind, they finally pitched in, ex- pansively, to help him.

His district was a dense, glum neighborhood in southwest Atlanta, at least 80 percent Negro and with a level of unem- ployment four times that of the city at large. His principal opponent was the dean of men at Atlanta University, and against him Julian conducted a freewheeling campaign in Snick's classic skin-to-skin style—strolling sidewalks morning and night, lingering with people on front porches, holding after- supper block meetings. He won the Democratic primary hand- ily, and in the general election, hauled away to a thumping 2,192-to-967 victory, with his district producing the highest popular turnout of any in Georgia in the house races that year.

Now a representative-elect, Julian found the immemorial small rites of legislative politics exhilarating. At preliminary

meetings of his county delegation in the house before the session was to open, "fellows would come up to me," Julian gleefully related, "and they'd say, 'Step on outside here in the hall
with me a minute, son, let's talk a little bit.' They love to be all
the time forming these little instant coalitions, you know." He
was openly expecting the best. Despite the fact that he was
still a member of Snick, he amicably assured his colleagues,
"I'm not going to be leading any marches and sit-ins." One
afternoon shortly before the session opened, Julian later recalled, "I was having drinks with the rest of the delegation
from my county up there at the Top of the Mart. We had just
finished a meeting, and everybody around me was talking and
laughing, and it suddenly occurred to me, 'What a great bunch
of guys these are!' "

It's doubtful that Snick expected its statement on Vietnam to
detonate such a violent reaction in the house against Julian.
But it was also apparent that, on second thought, they found
the turn of events not altogether disagreeable. They lived in a
reality of spontaneous, existentialist conflict, and what they
seemed to expect of Julian now was consent to a kind of magnificent crucifixion. Over the weekend prior to the opening of
the house session, there was a series of fractious, ragged-
tempered meetings between Snick and those members of the
legislature's black delegation who, with the encouragement of
House Speaker Smith and other white officials, were trying to
persuade Julian to rescue himself by issuing a moderate and
patriotic statement of his own. Early Monday morning, before
the house convened, James Forman, who was then executive
secretary of Snick, appeared in the halls of the capitol—
looking, in these surroundings, eminently subversive in a rumpled denim jacket and frayed serge trousers, suggesting some
hulkish, baleful angel of retribution with his hair flaring with
an angry electricity about his head—and throughout that day
continued to prowl the corridors in a lingering uneasiness about
Julian's susceptibility to compromise. He got word early that
afternoon of a private conclave in Speaker Smith's inner office
between Julian and his principal accusers. Suddenly Forman
was looming in the speaker's reception office, and with secre-
taries recoiling behind their rosebud vases and Smith's aides
gawking with wetly chawed cigars held at paunch level, he

demanded to see Julian. Smith's secretary replied in a very high, very thin voice, "Well, I'm terribly sorry, but the speaker said they were not to be disturbed in there." Forman then manded that she take a note in to Julian. It was not Julian who emerged, but his attorney, and he and Forman went out into the hall, where Forman, slumped sulkily in one of the benches against the stairway railing, instructed him, "We've made a commitment. Julian's made a commitment. Now you go back in there and tell him, tell them that."

As it developed, then, Julian's final confrontation with the house that afternoon was the climax of a career that had always been largely a pattern of caprice and accident. And he moved through it with the faintly bewildered and pained air of a young man who suddenly finds himself in the middle of complex furies he has unwittingly invoked, who has discovered the harrowing unsuspected perils of casual commitments. He had acquired a genuine excitement about being a legislator— but the Snick statement, and then his almost offhand defense of it, and then the house's quick blustering reaction, had all converged to impress him into a role he would have more happily abjured. He had become a martyr by happenstance.

"But I still never really thought they'd do it," he later said. "It was like being in a play, a movie. Everything was so formal, you know, with that 'Mr. Speak-ah!' and 'We will ask Mr. Bond to please step aside for a moment while the oath of office is administered. . . .' And all along, I wasn't going to bother anybody or cause any trouble. I still couldn't believe it. But they went ahead and did it."

That had happened on a cold, glistening afternoon, with the house chamber—a vast, airy affair of an indistinct architecture best defined as pastel Dixie-Grecian—a trifle overheated. Though the house membership had never been noted for its composure, there was now a peculiar peace over the floor as representatives gathered for the event; they had the patient serenity of a stand of hunters waiting for the appearance of some still-hidden but cornered game. Occasional discharges of cigar smoke drifted up over their calm faces.

Earlier that day, Julian had presented himself for a press conference in a committee room down the hall, discussing his situation with just the slightest tremor in his thin fingers, a faint shine of sweat glimmering on his temples in the glare of the television lights. In fact, he had not slept since the previous morning, and he was now sustaining himself on Coca-Cola, cigarettes, and "nerve pills." Once or twice, he stepped back from the mike and briefly closed his eyes, lightly rubbing his eyelids with the tips of his thumb and forefinger, blinking as he looked back up again. Inevitably, a newsman asked him a question that seemed to be nosing around the larger question of whether he was a Communist, and Julian's gaze glinted with anger for a moment. "I want every one of you in this room to hear this. I'll answer this question now, but this is the last time. I'll tell you that I was never a Communist and am not now a Communist. Now I'll never answer that question again. I resent it. It implies that I don't have the intelligence to arrive at the position that I have taken without having been manipulated into it by someone else."

But that afternoon, as he stood at the lectern before the assembled members of the house, in a somber brown herring-bone suit and vest, he had the look of a defenseless, doomed yearling deer. There was a matchstick frailness about his neck and wrists, and his forehead seemed as fragile as a thin bulb of glass which could be splintered with the flick of a finger. "Do you admire the courage of persons who burn their draft cards?" someone demanded from the floor.

"I admire people who take an action," he answered quietly and carefully, his accents crisply precise, "and I admire people who feel strongly enough about their convictions to take an action like that knowing they face pretty stiff consequences. But I have never suggested or counseled or advocated that anyone burn their draft cards. In fact, I have mine in my pocket and will produce it if you wish. . . ."

The house then listened to the tape of the radio interview Julian had given shortly after Snick had issued its statement. Julian, seated at the front of the chamber, leaned forward with his elbows on his knees, lighted a cigarette, and steadily tapped it over a Lily cup between his feet as he reheard his voice, now disembodied and amplified over the house's loudspeaker system. This should have been the moment of truth in the matter, after all the sound and fury. And his pronouncements, as they unfolded on the tape, seemed singularly mild and civilized, almost excruciatingly reasoned:

I like to think of myself as a pacifist who opposes that war and any other war. . . . But one of the many reasons that I oppose the war in Vietnam is that it seems to me that we *are* at a war declared not by Congress, as wars are supposed to be declared, but war declared by President Johnson. It seems to me that there's something wrong with that sort of situation. . . . Now, I'm not taking a stand against stopping world Communism, and I'm not taking a stand in favor of the Viet Cong. . . . I oppose the Viet Cong fighting in Vietnam as much as I oppose the United States fighting in Vietnam. If I lived in North Vietnam, I might not have the same sort of freedom of expression, but it happens I live here, not there.

What was immediately striking about the tape was that it disclosed in Julian a nature and disposition wholly out of character with the lurid notions that had accumulated pell-mell in the house over the past few days—and for that matter, a perspective quaintly out of character with Snick's own bristling statement. But when the tape ended, there was the sound over the house floor of a unanimous letting out of breath, a low general shuffle, with a number of exchanged glances—it was suddenly apparent that they had heard merely a voice, a tone, that was simply a physical piece of supplemental evidence whose real larger sense they had already, long before, determined. Several legislators left the chamber for a moment and returned with bottles of Nehi strawberry pop which they passed out to loudly appreciative colleagues at neighboring desks.

Then Representative Bobby Pafford—a bulging man with large white soft hands who was an oil distributor from south Georgia—stepped up to the lectern, his eyes batting as if he were on the verge of tears. A little tremulously, he began, "There is blood that runs down the trenches in a far-off land that causes tears to run down mothers' cheeks. . . . And yet, there are those in this land that love not country more than self, and advocate *doctrines*. . . . Usually these creatures are far, far away from this land of beautiful rivers, great cities, pine forests, fresh air and pleasant living known as Georgia." This was getting a bit thick even for the Georgia house, and there was a certain amount of uncomfortable squirming and coughing over the floor. "But now we find not only our state, our counties, but the legislature itself has been invaded by one whose Snicking pursues not freedom for us but victory for our enemies. I regret to say that reapportionment ousted noble and distinguished statesmen from our midst, and has shoved in their stead, that this state might see darkness rather than light, the *infamous Mr. Bond! . . .*" Pafford fairly plunged back to his seat, blinking furiously in a warm flush of indignation, embarrassment, patriotism.

The vote was 184 to 13. The infamous Mr. Bond, sinister fruit of reapportionment, arose and left the chamber. A rural legislator then snatched from Julian's desk the metal name tag that Julian would have worn as a representative, and presented it to Jones Lane. After a second of tantalization, Lane declined it, and his colleague declared, "Well, least I can take this tag home and hang it on my outhouse door."

Eating lunch the next day at Paschal's Restaurant, Julian dropped his wadded napkin on his unfinished tomato sandwich, lighted another Salem, and began torturing a paper clip between his fingers. "You know, when they asked me after my testimony to stand up there for questions from the floor and nobody had anything to ask of me, I thought, 'Well, this is a pretty good sign. They all understand it now, maybe.' The funny thing about it, I wasn't even going to run again next time. I just had a few little bills I wanted to introduce to see what would happen—something on better housing, more moderate rents, equal jobs and pay, the abolishment of capital punishment maybe. How innocent can something be?"

In the months that followed, Julian pursued his new role of martyr, however accidentally occasioned, with an apparent vigor and earnestness, making speeches across the country. In private, however, he fretted, "I feel trapped by this thing. People are always paying so much attention to me now. If I used to do something wrong, I was just a young man getting in a little trouble, you know. But now—why, it's Julian Bond, the ousted legislator! In airports and places like that, people are always looking at you and whispering. The ordeal didn't end that afternoon in the house. It just keeps going on and on." There were times, in fact, when he longed to drop the whole matter. "I didn't really want to run again after I was kicked out. What was the use? But my father wouldn't let me. He held my feet to the fire."

Whatever else, the experience had left Julian with only a deeper sense of personal isolation, apartness. "I guess, from the beginning, I never thought I could function with those people up there," he conceded. "Anyway, I'm not as naive now as I used to be. I'm more suspicious of people. And I don't believe in the soul force anymore. You'd like to think people would do things for the right reasons, but they won't." Before long, he also resigned from Snick, without ever explaining why.

One Saturday, while the final judgment on his exclusion from the house was still pending before the Supreme Court, Julian sat in the gloom of a nearly empty bar in his district, twirling a bourbon and Coke between his fingers as across the room a pianist and a pallid, limp-haired white female vocalist discordantly tinkered with arrangements for that evening. It was a dully drizzling winter afternoon outside, but Julian had arrived at the bar wearing no topcoat—only a tweedy sport jacket with a crew-neck sweater pulled over a white dress shirt. "You know, for several weeks after they kicked me out, I kept having this recurring dream that while I'm in my house sleeping, a lot of white men come up on my front porch and begin banging on the front door. I get up and crack the blinds and say, 'What do you want?' and they say, 'We want you, buddy.' So I get my shotgun and go back out there and open the front door and tell them, 'If you aren't gone off this porch by the time I count ten, I'm gonna blow you to kingdom come.' I count to ten, and they don't move—I count to ten *three times*, and they still won't move. So I let them have both barrels and blow them right back into the street. Then I put up my gun and go back to bed and fall sound asleep."

Julian ordered another bourbon and Coke. "See? This whole business has almost made a paranoid, a psychopath, out of me. I was just so damn much happier before all this happened."

It was only a few days later that the Supreme Court directed that Julian be installed in the seat to which he had been, now three times in successive special votes, elected. But curiously, the morning of his investiture at last as a member of the Georgia house had the quick, quiet, incidental quality of an afterthought, and Julian himself, at this moment of arrival, seemed oddly extraneous to the event. After serving for over a year now as so vivid a symbol to those forces he had inadvertently aroused—a shadowy provocateur to the Georgia house, an embattled young St. Sebastian to the civil-rights community, a Constitutional principle to the Supreme Court, a mere prop in the political gamesmanship of other state figures—through all this, it was as if Julian's own identity had disappeared. "The experience devoured him," one observer put it. Now, Julian seemed peculiarly removed from what was finally to transpire that day. Legislators, instead of taking the oath of office as a single body, were called up to the front of the chamber in clumps—a concession to the abiding distaste of some of them to being sworn in with Julian. When his turn came, he arose, looking at no one, his face vacant in the sudden dazzling of flashbulbs around him, and made his way to the front. After taking the oath, he started back toward his desk, his eyes on the floor. There was scattered applause from the gallery. He didn't look up. It was all over.

That afternoon, he appeared at Paschal's Restaurant where Snick was about to issue another statement, this one denouncing Congress' investigation of Adam Clayton Powell. Julian was greeted with a hug and great claps of laughter by Snick's new executive secretary, Stokely Carmichael, and they crossed the street together to the parking lot of a filling station where the press conference had been set up, Carmichael's arm slung around Julian's shoulders. But as Carmichael began reading the statement with much vigor and animation before the thicket of microphones, Julian detached himself to one side and stood there silent, a small musing smile on his face, looking away into the middle air above the roofs around him.

At the capitol the next day, as other representatives thronged noisily in the corridors during a house recess, Julian remained alone at his desk in the nearly deserted chamber, concentrating on a long letter to an acquaintance in San Francisco, which he was composing on his new official house stationery. A little later, when a friend stopped by his desk, Julian reported with a kind of low tentative excitement, "Hey, I put in my minimum-wage bill today to be drawn up." But weeks later into the session, it still had not gotten out of committee. Julian even confessed at one point to a certain sporting readiness to temper his attitude on the Vietnam war: "I'm a weakening pacifist now—I've been rethinking a lot of that lately." But though he was assigned to three major committees, "the chill," he said, "is sure still here."

Julian had ended that day of his final admission into the legislature at the Bird Cage, the bar of a motel that had just been constructed in Julian's neighborhood. It had materialized there, among the dirt yards and tin roofs, like a mirage of Las Vegas or Miami, with a long, sprawling lounge in peacock hues of green and aqua and purple, suspended in a kind of murmurous, tinkling, submarine twilight, given over to a gorgeous lavishness only likely to be found, in a town like Atlanta then, in the black community, where in their delights and dreams they could begin from nothing, with none of the white man's restraints of cultural nostalgias for Europe or the old South, and leap instantly to such a frank, free, extravagant opulence. At the bar, young Negroes in liquid cashmere sweaters and calfskin shoes, silver chain bracelets on their wrists, their faces masklike behind dark glasses, were listening to Billy Ekstine songs as the winter day dimmed toward night in the curving glass wall behind them. "What I wish is that I had a place like this," Julian observed.

Suddenly Carmichael appeared, looking somewhat ambassadorial now in a trimly tailored sheeny gray suit and vest, but carrying with him still that sense of great velocity, a headlong vitality, a huge restlessness. He announced that Powell had lost his committee chairmanship. Loosening his tie with a yank, he stood for a moment over the table where Julian was lounging with a couple of friends: "But did you see the man on TV? I mean, he comes up to those mikes after they've busted him, and he gives it this, you know . . ." Here, Carmichael mimicked Powell shooting his cuffs, daintily adjusting his tie knot with an air of fine disdain, elegantly flicking his cigar. "Man, he don't blow his cool for *nothing!*"

At that point, a middle-aged Negro businessman came over —not quite drunk, but almost—and cackled to Carmichael, who had seated himself beside Julian, "Yeah, what they can't stand up there, the man done gone off to Europe and Bimini with their Miss Ohio, that's what it is. He's a cat. Am I right? How many of them got beauty queens for secretaries? He's out of sight. Am I right?" He and Carmichael then went into a rapid, spinning, dizzying exchange, Carmichael lashing back and forth in glee over the table with his wide white grin like a cobra striking, extending his palm for the businessman to slap at each flourish of delicious irony: *"Lemme tell you, brother. . . . The man, he just got too much of it for them crackers. . . ."*

But Julian remained leaning back quietly, an absent little smile on his face, one arm hung over the back of his seat. Somehow, subtly, he had again withdrawn himself to the periphery of the passions before him, now this uproarious laughing flat-eyed rage of Carmichael and the businessman. A few moments later, squinting through the slow curl of smoke from his cigarette, he offered, "Actually, Adam Clayton Powell's got it made. He's not worried about any of them—they can't touch him. He's got himself that island down there. He's out of it all now. That's what I really wish I had—an island like that."

Taking a sip of his drink, he then reflected, "You know, back when I was writing that sports column for that weekly paper here, I invented a fellow named Sam Bernard. He was the first Negro to enter this college in Texas, and he was the only Negro there. And boy, he did everything—I mean, he broke a record every weekend, swimming, tennis, high jump, running. The only thing was, he wasn't too good at team sports. What he liked, where he excelled, where he was *great*, was just him out there—all by himself."

In a similarly inadvertent and sideways fashion, Julian was to experience a brief second apotheosis at the Democratic convention in 1968, when a delegate from Wisconsin, simply as a ploy to get anti-war exhorter Allard Lowenstein to the convention microphone ostensibly for a seconding speech, nominated Julian for Vice-President. Julian was then obliged to point out that, Constitutionally, he was not yet of age. Nevertheless, he had become the first black in the Republic's history to be so distinguished, and found himself something of a political sensation for a period afterward.

Despite that, while wending about the country on personal-appearance tours between house sessions, his actual circumstances continued somewhat alist and indefinite. He dallied variously with finding some regular position as a journalist, as a network television personality, even essayed a fried-chicken-

franchise operation for a while. In the meantime, he was elected head of the Atlanta chapter of the NAACP, and moved into the Georgia state senate—an even more becalmed cloister than the house. Even these years distant from that winter morning in 1967, he will still confess, "I'm just sort of in limbo."

The Judgment of
Jesse Hill Ford

Outside the windows of the courtroom, out in the white flare of the June morning, the town's modest skyline of gabled tin roofs and steeples wavers in the rippling windowpanes like a mirage, a separate world of calm and innocence. In the courtroom, with its sweltering impactment of spectators convoked out of this small west-Tennessee community of Humboldt, there sits waiting at one of the tables before the judge's bench a man with the thick heftiness of a honey bear, his charcoal-gray suit a bit snug around his shoulders, with a clipped thatch of sandy hair lightly dusted with a pale ash of age. Yet he has, at forty-two, still some air of lingering boyishness about him. A native Southerner who has been for over a decade now a fellow townsman to the folk filling the courtroom behind him, he is a writer whose stories have been made out of the humor and tribulations of Southern villages much like Humboldt. Then he leans forward with his hands tightly clenched together atop the table as the district attorney arises and begins, "In the case of the State of Tennessee versus Jesse Hill Ford, whereas Mr. Ford has been indicted for murder in the first degree . . ."

THE EVENING BEFORE his trial was to begin, Ford had presided over a large conclave of newsmen and friends at his commodious home on the outskirts of Humboldt. Seven months had passed since he had shot to death a black man parked in his driveway late one night—a bizarre and imponderable act by a writer who for years had been regarded as one of the most thoughtful and compassionate chroniclers of his region's racial duress and tragic violence. But now Ford moved through the

Life, October 29, 1971

swarming of his guests with an improbable, oblivious festiveness, even playing the piano for a while as his elder daughter, Sarah, sat beside him singing. At one point, as he finished "On a Clear Day You Can See Forever," his eyes blurred with tears, but he quickly wiped them away with his knuckles.

The party's hectic, noisy incandescence lasted on until the first thin chirpings of birds before dawn. Finally, with the start of the trial less than five hours away, a newsman suggested to Ford that his guests might be overtrampling his hospitality if they stayed any longer. Ford murmured, "No, no, God, no—it's like when someone close to you has died: you need to have people around you. . . ."

When word that Jesse Hill Ford had killed a young black man first appeared in the newspapers in New York one Wednesday morning in November of 1970, the conversations in the sanctums of Manhattan's cultural curia were, for a time, unusually preoccupied with the incident. Ford's most memorable novel was *The Liberation of Lord Byron Jones,* published in 1965 during the high pitch of the Movement in the South—a folk tragedy exploring the mindless violence that plays through a small Southern town after a black undertaker named Lord Byron Jones commits the unthinkable presumption of naming a local white policeman as co-respondent in his divorce suit; Jones' execution then becomes inevitable, and in a way the policeman merely acts as the assassin for the affronted social canons of the whole white community, which subsequently conspires to absolve him from any punishment.

It was a tale, in fact, which Ford had conjured from an actual episode in Humboldt, and the book produced no small discomfort and indignation in the town's white community. Thus, with the news that Ford himself had killed a black man, the initial reaction in Humboldt was, as one white matron pronounced, "Maybe he can write about hisself now." And soon the local district attorney—with a spirited enterprise unique to that region in any instances of white mayhem against blacks—charged Ford with homicide, which embraced all the counts from involuntary manslaughter to first-degree murder. From afar, it appeared that Humboldt's white citizenry had availed themselves of a grotesque accident to attend to Ford, at long last, with an especially lively vengeance.

The mishap itself seemed no more than a sourceless flash

happening. Ford's initial explanation was that, following the publication of *Lord Byron Jones*, sporadic anonymous harassments began to be directed at his household—refuse scattered at night over his lawn, taunting telephone calls, "unknown people in cars who'd drive up here and try to frighten us." These casual mischiefs—which increased when the movie adaptation of his novel was shown in town—were all clearly the doings of whites. But when the city's schools opened for their first year of real integration in the fall of 1970, suddenly it became blacks who, quite openly, began harrying his family. It had proved a troubled transition for Humboldt's students: the blacks had not only lost their own high school but, eventually, all the black players on the football team were dismissed when they failed to appear for a practice. Their resentment came to be focused on the captain of the team, Ford's seventeen-year-old son Charles, an All-State halfback. As Ford recounted it, Charles began receiving threatening phone calls, and during a Homecoming parade downtown on a November afternoon the car in which Charles was riding was stoned by blacks along the sidewalks.

It was four nights later, around ten o'clock, that George H. Doaks, a twenty-one-year-old Army private, turned into the long driveway of Ford's home a mile outside Humboldt. With Doaks was his sixteen-year-old second cousin, Allie V. Andrews, and a four-year-old girl with whom she had been babysitting when Doaks picked her up. Miss Andrews later in her testimony insisted that they had gotten lost returning from a dairy bar. In any event, when the car reached Ford's house, it turned around, drove a short distance back down to the second sharp bend in the driveway, and then parked off in the grass.

Charles wasn't home yet, Ford later declared to the press, and the Doaks car "was in a perfect position for an ambush." Ford, striding across his front yard with a .30-06 Enfield deer rifle toward the rear of the car, fired a warning shot. Then, reaching the car, he banged the rifle butt on the trunk—and the car suddenly surged forward. With that, Ford fired the second shot, which shattered the back windshield and exploded the left side of Doaks' skull. Afterward, laboring to explain the blind impulse of that second shot that night, Ford betrayed hints of a larger tension in which he had been living: "I just pulled off a quick shot, just trying to stop that car. I was just damned sick and tired of all that had been happening to us. I wanted to know who was doing this to us, and I thought whoever was in that car was a part of it."

As it turned out, the event considerably intrigued the distant covens of the Manhattan culturati for a season, a fascination largely owing to the titillation of a writer's having been overtaken by the engines of his own fiction, ambushed by the very fevers he had loosed into play in his work. One evening a few weeks before Christmas, there was a party at an East Side mansion several blocks off Central Park, which was attended by composers, publishers, television commentators, magazine editors, and others just anonymously rich—an informal convocation of that infrastructure of Manhattan Island that functions as the invisible Vatican of the American sophistication. It was raining heavily outside, a black blowing banshee night, but the roar of the rain in the streets was heard, inside, as no more than a dim monotone under the intricate sibilances of their voices. And as they moved about—excellently preened esthetes, gauntish and vivid women with enameled faces, drifting through high, tapestried, candle-lit rooms—through their conversations there filtered a kind of rapt delicate twittering: *"Have you heard about Jesse Hill Ford, that Southern novelist who . . . Isn't it the strangest, most monstrous thing . . . My God, how in the world do you suppose that thing came about? . . ."*

As it happened, all this was noted by another writer from Ford's part of the country, a journalist not yet turned thirty who had wandered by circuitous chance among this company, something of a provincial stray. But when, only a few weeks after that East Side party that raining December night, he found himself flying to Humboldt to write about Ford's situation, it was as an emissary—whatever his own inherent nature as a Southerner—of that other community's curiosity and sensibility. As the plane began tilting down toward the level drab snow-spattered map of west Tennessee, his assumption about what he would find was that Ford, since the wanton flare of the disaster that autumn night, had been passing through a personal ordeal of the most rare convolutions.

Along the expressway out of Memphis, dull-brown fields spanned past emptily, rutted like washboards and rippled with scanty snow, with intermittent quick spangles of swamp water winking through marooned cypress trees in the cold and brilliant February morning. An hour and a half east of Memphis, fifteen minutes off the expressway, Humboldt was announced by a water tower perched over a spidery webbing of winter trees. It was, for the most part, indistinguishable from all the other meager little towns littered in endless reduplication over the South—a few leisurely monumental homes on the outskirts, the main street a brief unprepossessing gallery of cafes, bargain clothing stores, drugstores, a single movie theater with a rusty marquee, a few new banks of glad pastels and glass.

When the journalist entered his motel room, he found resting on the window table a festively beribboned basket containing fruit, Portuguese sardines, champagne, and a small note signed, "Jesse and Sally Ford." Half an hour later, rapping lightly and almost shyly at the door, Ford himself appeared and invited the journalist out to his home for drinks. He had the full round innocent face, with the faintest sly crinkles of mischief around his eyes, of an affable unfrocked friar—a look of altarboy freshness mixed with a twinkle of the roguish. But he was dressed with an odd formality in suit and tie, as if for an appointment with his banker. There was about him a certain uneasy air of precise and studied politeness. He said, with a small cough into his fist, "I'm certainly glad to be meeting you finally, even though I wouldn't—I mean, I'm certainly sorry it had to be on such an unfortunate occasion."

After driving along meandering back roads, Ford turned through an unfinished gate of two brick pillars onto the driveway of his place—a rather baronial twenty-seven-acre spread which he had established for himself five years earlier out of the movie sale of *Lord Byron Jones,* and had christened with the name of Canterfield. It was testimonial, once again, to that old inveterate covert hankering of all writers, for all their chronic social brigandage, to invest themselves ultimately with the equipages of local nobles—like Shakespeare in the end eagerly setting after a coat of arms and the best house in Stratford. Ford's home loomed beyond the two sharp elbow turns in the drive, a square two-story edifice of dark brick with a gabled slate roof, still looking a bit raw and new this winter afternoon, sitting strangely bare and isolate on grounds stripped of all trees. Two tawny mastiffs came loping clumsily across an adjacent field strewn with dried cornstalks as Ford pulled up to the house.

The journalist followed Ford through the moiling of the

mastiffs, past a quiet clang of the iron-grill barricades at the front door, on into the foyer, where Sally Ford appeared—a short, dumpling woman, who greeted the journalist with a vociferous cordiality like a bedlam of small bells, the lens of her glasses fogged with a faint dampness. They then settled themselves in the living room, with a certain chill elegance to its pale tints and French engravings, a papery floral spray set in a vase by the gleaming cold fireplace. A black maid presently emerged, a large impassive figure in white uniform, bearing drinks on a silver tray. As they began to talk, two blond gaunt whippets floated and alighted about the room with a noiseless tensile grace. Ford's older son, Jay, was off for his first year at Vanderbilt, but Charles and the two daughters were at home—Sarah, sixteen, a tall Junoesque honey-hued girl with already a deep smoke of womanhood in her gaze, and Elizabeth, ten, slim and grave and pixieish with yellow shingled hair. Enclosed now by his household, Ford seemed to subside into a complacent stillness, merely sipping from his scotch and soda as he listened to Sally exchange enthusiastic pleasantries with the journalist. But he had not removed his coat, and was still perched somewhat tensely on the edge of his chair. Now and then he laughed—an abrupt, total, whooping laugh, erupting forth it seemed from some constant, poised, ready glee. But even then, in his frost-gray eyes there remained a certain secret remoteness. And as the conversation went on, the circumstance that had actually placed the journalist here in their living room—the fact that Ford had killed a man—somehow became gradually more impossible to refer to.

At one point, Charles entered the room—a pale, taciturn youth built with the compact brawn of a bobcat. Ford told him, "I was talking to the coach over at Trenton today, and he said you were the finest football player he'd ever seen." Charles merely stared at his father wordlessly. After a moment, someone else spoke, and Charles strode back out of the room.

Ford at last invited the journalist to ride with them over to a nearby town for a late dinner at the Ramada Inn. Before they set out, as a kind of departing flourish, Ford sat down at the living-room piano and pranced forth a homemade little tune with curlicued mincing chords, while Sarah and Elizabeth stood beside him tamping tambourines and chiming in small voices like meows, "I feel *ver-ry* better nowwww . . ." Back outside then, night had closed coldly over the countryside, and the journalist got into the back seat of Ford's station wagon in the darkness with an obscure uneasiness of something around him totally outside the spectrum of those expectations he had brought with him to Humboldt. When they passed back out through the unfinished gate, Ford explained that it would eventually be equipped with iron-lattice doors and electronic controls and a two-way intercom to the house. "Well, Jesse," Sally chirped, "that's what I call locking the barn door after the horse has got out." Ford replied, "Well, maybe after all this is over with, I can go into the electric-gate business. Fact, maybe I'll go into the deer-stand business. . . ."

Then, during dinner, Ford finally began to discourse on the aftermath of the shooting, noting once with an incensed air, "Do you know that not a single one of the blacks around here for whom we found work during the filming of *Lord Byron Jones*, not a *single one* of them has called me since this trouble began?" More than anything else, he and Sally seemed to regard the incident as some capricious vandalism of fate against the orderly pattern of their lives. "My God," said Ford, "I make half my living on lectures, but all of a sudden I'm an untouchable. This business is just about to ruin us."

Sally reported, "A lot of people have called us saying, 'Oh, what a terrible thing, I'm so sorry, it's such an awful thing.' But this one friend of Jesse's over in Trenton, he called right after it happened and said, 'Goddam, Jesse, you should have done this *last* year, before they integrated the schools!' Oh, Lord!—" She laughed, a high splintering laugh. "And the other evening, we were playing Botticelli with some friends, and this one fella had us stumped for almost two hours—we just couldn't guess who in the world he was. He kept telling us, 'I'm somebody who's become very close to you, Jesse, very important in your life. I'm somebody who's lost their head over you, really.' But we just couldn't guess, so he had to tell us, and you know who it was? My God, it was that nigguh Jesse accidentally killed!"

Once Sally paused to lean close to Ford, hugging his shoulders quickly and muttering, "I *love* you," and he twisted in his chair to put his arm around her waist and lightly kissed her cheek, murmuring, "And I love you, *too*." They maintained a resolute gaiety throughout the dinner. Then as they were leaving, Ford struck a jailhouse pose behind the wrought-iron partition of the dining room, his hands gripping the grillwork as he grinned through at them with suppressed little grunts of laughter. Sarah, noticing him, squealed, "Oh, Daddy—*quit*! Momma, look at what Daddy's doing!" and Ford gave an impish snigger of delighted gratification.

Sarah drove them back to Humboldt. Ford was slumped low in the darkness of the back seat, with Elizabeth's head lying on his shoulder. So nestled now in the mellowness of his family, he remarked drowsily to the journalist, "You know, they're all that's real. Nothing else is real, finally. Nothing else is worth anything." And a moment later, Ford himself was asleep, his head resting atop Elizabeth's.

The journalist awoke into a dank and bleary morning, a slow drizzle puddling the empty weekend parking lot outside his motel room. After breakfast, he sat staring out of the picture window in a mood of deep dreariness. Ford had seemed, in his jauntiness of last night, brazenly implausible as the same man who had written *Lord Byron Jones*. There was no way to rhyme him with his work. . . . Perhaps all writers, if they happen to stumble personally into the kind of crises through which they put their characters, would always turn out to be weaker and more trivial than those characters. Indeed, that could be why they wrote in the first place: they perceive honor and bravery and endurance all the more urgently—so urgently they spend their lives endlessly inventing instances of them— precisely because they happen to be more defective in them than most of their fellow men. Perhaps they were more inadequate in those values because they were more aware of them— in the way a coward might be one who simply has a much wider appreciation of all the things that could possibly befall him. But maybe all writers were merely undertaking to exorcise the specter of their own baseness with the proxy fortitudes of their characters' performances in travail. Indeed, some peculiar wistfulness seemed now to hang over the quote which Ford had chosen to commence *Lord Byron Jones*: "Blessed are those who died in great battles,/Stretched out on the ground in the face of God. . . ."

Nevertheless, what the journalist felt, on this dim dissolving morning, was a terminal despair about the whole story. Ford's sentiments, at the least, seemed hopelessly oblique to what had actually happened. The journalist called New York and notified his editor he was returning home.

But only a few moments after he hung up, Ford phoned him and, with some odd thin tone of entreaty in his voice, ventured an invitation to accompany him to a nearby town to pick up a butchered hog. And the journalist—feeling, now that he had dropped the project, a delicious lightness of release, noticing then that the wearily drizzling morning outside had been translated abruptly into a thickly milling snowfall—told Ford he would ride along with him, and decided that he would linger on in Humboldt this one day more.

The processing plant, a small cement-block shed, was lit against the muffling snowfall outside. In the bleak shine of its bare bulbs, several black women in shapeless baggy smocks were hacking, with a silent deliberation, washed slabs of crimson-marbled meat, while the proprietor—a man of ample bulk in a white coat—packed Ford's sections of hog. Ford then followed the proprietor to another ramshackle paintless wooden shed with a floor of oil-stained dirt, shy whisks of snow whispering dryly through the paneless windowframes, and picked up two tins of lard. As he went about these simple attentions, Ford—with a freshly scrubbed look this morning, his hair neatly brushed—had an air of chipper coziness, as if comforted by retracing once more the small rites of normalcy that had structured his daily life in Humboldt before the accident in November. That single instant of marauding craziness, and the prospects of ruin it had evoked, all seemed dispelled into a distant unreality this morning by the vast hushed falling of snow, downmurmuring in a calm continuous obliteration, leaving a world around him from which all sound and motion and time had vanished.

But returning to Ford's house, they approached again the turn in the drive where the shooting had taken place—a site now permanently interposed between Ford's home and the community like an unavoidable toll gate of recollection. And as they moved past the turn, Ford for the first time began describing the event itself in detail, but in a toneless and bemused voice as if he were recalling, in the quiet shadowless anesthesia of this snowing afternoon, an episode that had happened to someone else. . . .

*　　*　　*

He had worked on past sunset, into the night, and then had come downstairs to watch television, while in the living room a pianist practiced in long ringing trills for an upcoming "musical evening" the Fords were planning. Around nine-thirty, the pianist finished and left. About an hour later, Ford clicked off the television set, and he and Sally went upstairs to bed. He had already fallen asleep when Sally gently shook his arm, whispered, "Jesse, I don't think that's Charles," and he heard, at the same moment, the slow rumble of a car passing in front of the house. He scrambled into a jump suit and a plaid jacket, grabbed the deer rifle, and went out into the night. It was a black autumn evening, moonless and blind, with a breath of frost in the air.

"What frightened me was that after I had fired that first shot, then after banging on the trunk and shouting, still there was no response whatsoever. Then it just all of a sudden started forward. And when the second shot was fired, the car stopped just as quickly—just stopped. Its lights were still on, and the motor was still running, but there wasn't a sound from inside. Nothing. I thought, 'Oh, my God—there's something wrong. Something's happened. . . .' Suddenly, the side door flies open—bam!—and this girl with a little child is running like hell down the road. I thought, 'My God, is this a family? What've I done?' I went on back up to the house and told Sally, 'Sally, I think I just shot somebody.' She went all to pieces. After a while, the ambulance got here, and the police came up to the house and asked me, 'Did you shoot at 'em?' I said, 'Yes. Didn't anybody get hurt down there, did they?' and they said, 'Looks like this fella is in pretty bad shape,' and I said, 'Oh, my God. Oh, my God.' I never went back down there to the car. I just waited for Charles out in the front yard, and when he finally drove up and asked me what all those cars and people were doing down there, I told him, 'Charles, I think I just shot somebody, I think I just killed a man.'. . ."

But now, this afternoon three months later—during a long lunch of grits and eggs and sausage and coffee and honey, with a quiet clinking of forks and cups in the pale light of a large window looking out on the snow—it did seem somehow only the brief phantasm of a night long lost in the departed autumn. Ford took on, through the lunch, further aspect as a man of civilized enthusiasms, given to generous flushes of feeling, who derived a special hearty delight from his family. It was well into midafternoon when they all arose at last from the table, and Ford then wandered down to his barn and began pitching fistfuls of unshucked corn to his livestock while his two daughters swirled off on their horses with a quick smothered battering of hooves in the blowing snow. Returning to the house on numb sodden feet, with the mastiffs blundering through deep drifts around them, the journalist told Ford, "This is not a bad life. You have a good life, you know—it's really what we all want, this."

"It was a great life," Ford replied, "and when we get through this thing, it'll be great again. "Look"—he stopped for a moment—"I didn't want that fella dead. I wish to God he were alive now. But we've gotten tough about the whole thing because we've had to." Ford resumed his booted trudge through the drifts toward the house, breathing a little unevenly with the effort. "Yes, sir. We're tough as hell on it now. I happen to be in a situation, and I've got to get through it. And until I do, by God, I can't afford to have any human feelings."

The journalist's plane did not leave until the next morning, so he stayed on into dusk, he and Ford sipping a thin sweet amber wine as they talked—even though he still felt removed into that melancholy of a final alienation that had brought him to the decision he could not write the story. Then after supper, Ford determined that one of the mastiffs, Rosie—who was now two days late delivering puppies—would have to be taken into town to the vet's office for a cesarean. Wrapping her in a blanket, he hoisted her, staggering under her wallowing struggling weight, into the back of the station wagon. The night was a deep soundless gong of cold, and with Sally sitting up front with a kerchief swaddled around her head and the journalist driving, they eased carefully along roads that lay under the endless dim sheen of snow like vague traces of almost-forgotten secrets.

When they pulled up at the small white-frame clinic, the vet came tromping down from his house—a long, languid figure with a mustache like those in daguerreotypes of frontier sheriffs, wearing a red jump suit and galoshes, his only heed to the night's cold a shabby fedora plopped hastily atop his head. He kept the hat on, only nudging it back a bit from his forehead, as he proceeded with the operation in a brightly lit room. Ford and Sally and the journalist watched it, taking raw swigs from a bottle of Canadian Club fetched from the vet's pine-planked kitchen. Rosie lay sedated, a heavy inert load, on a high table as the vet slowly enlarged the incision into a wide spillage of blood, a glistening muck of exposed rent viscera that had the appearance of an abrupt profound violation, a violence, which it seemed impossible the dog could even survive, much less that any new life could emerge from it. But then the vet was withdrawing from this mangled gore of disruption two gray-gauzed plump sacks like sausage skins, and an instant later he had snipped from them what seemed two uncannily precise artificial replicas of the puppies Rosie should have produced— two cunning but meaningless counterfeits. And now a sudden muted frenzy like a desperate skirmishing filled the small room, a wordless commotion of lifting and slapping and kneading that absorbed them all for a long suspended moment. The journalist found himself holding cupped in his own hands the damp light form of one of those perfect imitations, blowing his own breath in urgent pants into its miniature muzzle, and then felt his wrist surprised by the small faint stirring of something not himself, saw the timorous brief movement of a forepaw, and then heard a tiny sound like a kitten's sneeze—once again, that most primitive but most stunning of miracles: out of noth-ingness, abruptly, existence.

The night around them now seemed astonished, stricken with wonder. They again passed around the bottle, flushed and slightly disheveled and filmed in a light chill of sweat. To the journalist, his pulse still dimly hammering like that of a runner who has just completed a long sprint, it was as if he had awak-ened to discover himself transported light-years away from the fretful moral ponderings in his motel room that morning. They drove back to Ford's house in a fine exhilaration startlingly alive to everything around them—to the cold pang of the night, the solitary glows of the streetlights, the mild whimper of the puppies in the back seat with Rosie, the small noises of their existence already becoming absorbed into the familiar and commonplace,—and Ford himself boomed with a tremor in his voice, "Godamightydamn, those precious sophisticates up there in the salons of Manhattan, you think a one of them has ever gone through a night like this? Holy *Jesus*—delivering two mastiff puppies by cesarean operation in the middle of a frozen winter night! But things like this are happening to us all the time down here, it's just been a normal day for us. But it's more real than anything they'll ever know up there on Park Avenue. . . ."

About an hour later, as the journalist sat alone in a darkened downstairs room finishing his drink before returning to the motel—noticing in the faint glow of a hall light that his clothes were now flecked with small red stains—he knew that he would be staying in Humboldt for yet a while longer. It was not so much that in the feverish elation of that night's business he had sensed himself suddenly and unexpectedly born into the full quick of the Fords' life here. Rather, there had been a moment back at the clinic after the vet had injected Rosie with the sedative: she had begun sagging slowly to the linoleum floor, her haunches sinking and her head drooping, yet still struggling vaguely against her inexorable descent into sleep, her sides heaving and nails fitfully scrabbling for steadiness on the linoleum, giving now and then a long fading whine; and then Ford was kneeling beside her, speaking in a low moan, "Rosie . . . Rosie! Don't. Don't be afraid. Look at her—she doesn't know that she's ever going to wake up, that she'll ever be back home again. It's awful, the most terrifying thing in the world for man or animal, going under into unconsciousness. It's like the dawn of death. . . ." Suddenly he was weeping, kneeling beside her sprawled form, looking somehow like a small boy with his head hung low and his hands lying flat and still on his knees as tears glanced down the front of his jacket.

It had been in this abrupt quiet shattering that the journalist at last sensed—as he had expected from the moral vision in *Lord Byron Jones*—deeper, darker desolations and travailings within Ford.

But even yet, while it seemed clear there was much more at play in Ford than had been indicated that first night, the journalist for several more days hung in an uncertainty about undertaking the story. "I am convinced," said one Humboldt civic figure, "that the instant Jesse Hill Ford pulled that trigger, the novelist began taking over." Indeed, it appeared that

Ford was increasingly inclined now toward rather extravagant flourishes of self-melodrama. Shortly after the shooting, he had accepted an invitation to ride in a steeplechase outside Memphis, a highly cavalier whim since it was his first gallop ever through that forbidding exercise, during the course of which he was clouted off his horse by a low-leaning limb; his arm was in a sling for several weeks following. "But what you find," he proposed afterward, "is that life is never so luminous as in the presence of danger. I'm not going to be alive four years from now, anyway," to which Sally cried, "Oh, Jesse, for God's sake!" and he snapped, "Look, I live every day like it was my last day to be alive. That's all. I'm a guy who's up for murder one, why the hell should I be worrying about getting hurt in a steeplechase?" It was as if he had begun enacting himself as the protagonist in the story of what had happened to him, developing it and himself into yet another literary work—out of a writer's inevitable instinct for self-dramatization, a kind of furtive but incorrigible and absolute narcissism that prompted Ford at one point to notify the journalist, "You know, there's another fella who's been around here who's gonna write about this thing. Very likable guy, and a liberal, from what I gather. But I just don't want him to do it, and the sole reason is, he simply can't write worth a damn. It's not that he's a liberal—I wouldn't care if he were a Trotskyite, a Rosicrucian, or a Knight of Columbus. It wouldn't make any difference. I just want somebody who'll write about this thing *well.*" It was as if, to almost monstrous lengths, the story was the thing.

But Ford, after all, was not the actual victim in this affair, and it seemed to the journalist that exploring Ford's own ordeal would somehow have the effect of rendering the true victim invisible, irrelevant, and thus doubly dead, the fact of his death ceasing to really matter in itself. Thus, the investment of so much concentration on Ford's experience would be a collaboration, even if of a devious sort, in that essential perversity in the mentality of all white society that was the central outrage in Ford's own work: the final inconsequence, to the critical truth in any matter, of the black man.

Then, late one night, they sat talking of what it meant simply to be a Southerner writing out of that condition, of having been formed by a land that had passed through an immense tragic experience that had left it the one region in the nation with its own ancient native mythology of pride and fire and doom. "Hell," Ford cried, "we grew up in another culture, where those *old* reflexes of the human heart still govern. We act from blood and the earth, and we don't forget. That's the thing—*we don't forget.*" Soon, some primal yawping joy seemed loosed about them in the night, a skirling of bagpipes in the heart, celebrating the South's mad and haggard honor, its unflagging passionate follies. Ford suddenly said, "And by God, when we're faced with a threat to our *home*, to our own *family*, we answer with the same reflexes—look, now, if you thought somebody was out there to waylay *your* son, you know you would have done exactly the same thing. . . ." The journalist, momentarily tasting some old half-forgotten brine of unreckoning fierceness, quickly replied, "Yes. You're damned right. Of course I would have."

And in that instant, he knew at last that he would write it. Because the act was in him too. He was not, after all, that finally removed across a divide from Ford. Now, in remaining to explore what had happened to Ford, he would, in a sense, actually be exploring, and then writing about, what lay implicitly as much within himself.

Ford was born in Alabama, but grew up in Nashville, about 150 miles to the east of Humboldt. As a small boy, he had been a compulsive contriver of stories, artifices, episodes. "When he was about four," his mother later recounted, "he invented this camp, with its own camp people and camp animals. He'd go off for a whole afternoon visiting this camp, and come back and tell us all about what was going on there."

He had casually expected to become a lawyer until, after graduating from Vanderbilt, he learned—"with," he said, "this sense of great relief"—that he had failed by a few points the entrance exam to law school. There then followed a wandering and indefinite season: service in the Navy, newspaper work, studies at the University of Florida under the aristocratic tutelage of Southern literary priest Andrew Lytle. Eventually, after foundering as a public-relations executive for the American Medical Association, he leaped into the open uncertain seas of writing fiction.

In 1957, he and Sally, whom he had met in a sophomore literature class at Vanderbilt, moved in with her father in

Humboldt. Sally was the only child of Dr. Charles W. Davis, a widely venerated physician who had ministered for nearly thirty years to the pains and maladies of the countryside's population, many of whom he had also delivered; when he was killed in a car crash in 1968, the Humboldt High School gym was named for him. After their arrival in Humboldt Sally began teaching school, and when it was discovered that Ford, who was working in a back room in Dr. Davis's clinic, was a writer, "people here tolerated him," says one resident, "largely out of consideration for Sally's father."

But Ford's move to Humboldt was made out of a special calculation. Such small communities are particularly felicitous locations in which to set up in the business of writing novels. They really contain, in microcosm, the whole of mankind's career; all the history of the human heart is replayed within the passage of one small-town generation. One can perceive the full course of lives, the rise and fall of ambitions, the strugglings and spoilings of lusts—one sees and knows the beginnings and the ends. Curiously, it is in a small community that a writer's sense of the mortal experience on this planet can most nearly assume universal perspectives.

But it is a mixed blessing. Small communities like Humboldt also become, for any writer who chooses to stake himself out there, just as immediately a microcosm of society's immemorially troubled and testy truce with the artists and seers in its midst. Ford would insist to friends, "What I've liked about living in Humboldt, there just isn't all this inbred, tortured literary discussion going on around you all the time. Somebody will find out I've had a novel or short story published, and they'll say, 'I heard you sold an article. That's good. I sold a tractor today myself.' " But even if he actually entertained this fancy, the difficulty was that he finally wasn't trafficking in such plain commodities as tractors or shingles or hardware. His was a more inscrutable enterprise, whose solitary regimens gave him a character of occult reclusiveness. One morning, the owner of a narrow little cafe on a backstreet of Humboldt paused behind the counter to remove his toothpick and observe, amid a savory sizzling of grills and a quiet clacking of billiard balls from the tables in the back, "Damn, I don't know, the man's just different. Keepin' to hisself all the time, stuff like that. He acts real funny sometimes. Only time he ever came in here, I never could figger what it was for, but I sat talking with him right over there for must of been like two hours, and he used words, you know, I didn't understand half of 'em. And I know I ain't all that ignorant. He walked out of here, and I still ain't got the goddamnedest idea what the hell he actually said."

Also, though Ford and Sally were members of the country club, they seldom appeared there, and on the few occasions they did, reported one acquaintance, "he'd just sort of barge around real noisy and clumsy for a little while, or sit off at a table kind of stiff." All this while, said a Humboldt attorney, "people around here would see him walking to the post office every morning in a sweatshirt and tennis shoes to pick up his mail, and they'd say, 'Look, there goes that deadbeat again.' When he started getting successful and built that big house out there, the only difference that made was, he was a rich deadbeat now."

There was also the matter of what Ford happened to be writing while living there in their midst. A local business elder —a stumpy, puckish, spiffily garbed troll of a man with a certain worn raffish look in his crinkled face—proposed one morning in the office of his bank, "Thing about Jesse, just like all these writers, he's a sensationalist. I've read some of his works, but all that kind of language he uses in there, and all this stuff about Nigra women sleeping with white men—I mean, most people around here had just rather not read such trash as that. We don't think we're like that, we got a wonderful little community here. Truth is, he's been bad for us. He doesn't really care about helping or fitting into this community. Why, not long ago, we rented this fine old hotel down in Jackson and gave a black-tie ball, we went to a great deal of trouble—and Ford shows up, dressed in a tux and tie all right, but wearing these goddam bright-yellow hunting boots! What I'm telling you, the man *tries* to be peculiar, like all those writers. . . ."

He added after a moment of reflection, "My wife, now, she comes from this little town down in Mississippi where they had this fella who was a writer, and she tells me he acted exactly the same way as Ford—half the time wouldn't speak to you on the street; Sunday mornings folks would come out of church and pass the drugstore and he'd be sitting in there all by himself with a three-day growth of beard reading magazines. Just like Ford."

The journalist, after a pause, ventured, "What little town would that be in Mississippi your wife is from?"

"Aw, little place you probably never heard of," the businessman said, "name of Oxford."

"And that fella—the one who was a writer—his name wasn't Faulkner by any chance, was it?"

"Lemme think—yes, by golly, I believe it was. That was it, sure was—James, Robert, something, Faulkner."

Too, Ford had inevitably enlisted Humboldt's private history —its events and personalities—for the stuff of his tales, in the way that all writers instinctively appropriate their surroundings for the performances of their own imagination. But Ford's work was particularly specific to Humboldt: not only incidents, but locales in his invented community of Soperton duplicated with an unusual precision locales in Humboldt. Not surprisingly the assumption soon developed among Ford's fellow townsmen that what Ford was actually up to was more or less a direct secretarial transcription of local figures and affairs, only thinly veiled in fictitious names. Perhaps as a result, as if to subtly disconcert and dislodge his supposed claim on them, the appearances of his books and short stories would be quickly followed by small alterations of physical features he had described in the town, quiet little revisions and rearrangements of the props and furniture in his stories—paving a parking lot he had described as dusty, suddenly repainting a civic building a different color, even once dismantling an entire filling station. Ford himself complained, "They keep tearing up my goddam set on me—every time I bring out a book, they decide to make another little municipal improvement downtown."

In the end, Ford seemed to have most deeply affronted the citizens of Humboldt not by writing out of compassion for the black man's ordeal and an anger against white viciousness, but simply by writing about them and their town at all. His offense was that of making stories out of their lives from a distance of amusement and pity and irony, even while still living there among them. His place became that of an alien informer in their midst. "Everybody thought he'd sorta been making fun of the town, holding us up for ridicule in the eyes of everybody else," one citizen said not long before Ford's trial was to commence. "There's no doubt about it, that's why there's a great deal of gratification around here about the position he's in now."

Ford lived then in a kind of compound, twice-forlorn isolation in Humboldt: his estrangement did not even derive finally from the passion and indictment of his work, but, hopelessly, from a simple trespass against good manners. At the same time, even before the shooting and the trial, Ford was also regarded with some suspicion by Humboldt's black community. One young black educator asserted, "In *Lord Byron Jones*, what he did was low-rate blacks in that book. Like the way he portrayed that undertaker's wife, that was low-down and just crude and insulting to black women. And black men too, the idea any black man would let a white man carry on like that in his own house. That just shows there's no white man who can understand the black man."

Yet it seemed likely there might at least be found a few covertly cosmopolitan souls in the white community who, sharing similar sophistications with Ford, presumably could have provided him some refuge and company—those thoughtful and urbane spirits one happened upon even in the smallest Southern towns then, quiet subscribers to *The Atlantic* and *The Saturday Review* and *The New Yorker*, who lived the gingerly existence of inner exiles in their own communities. But Humboldt's sole specimen, apparently, was an attorney with a certain hygienic neatness and pleasantness, ashen-haired but youthful, who had long been attempting to construct some semblance of a biracial committee in town. Sitting one summer Saturday afternoon in the Freon-chilled calm of an Early American den, the man's entire family, in fact, appeared the sort of gentle, temperate, eminently sensible folk on whom perhaps the humanitarian health of any community finally depends: impeccably rational, of unfaltering goodwill, an almost cellophaned quality of decency about them. But the attorney submitted with a polite smile of mild wonder, "You know, that Jesse, sometimes he would call me up at all hours of the night, from all sorts of places like Chicago or Los Angeles, just wanting to talk. Good gracious, how he'd be wound up, talk on and on. You'd never know when one of those calls would come in from someplace at three o'clock in the morning. He's always been like that—a *volatile* kind of person, you know. . . ."

And suddenly there was the realization, as the attorney went on with the same air of cheerful incredulous amazement to narrate other such novel impulses of Ford's, that this surpassingly civilized soul was actually as remote from Ford, as uncomprehending of him, as the local business elder who had sat in his bank's office deploring Ford's yellow boots. Like most who are authentically taken up into the obsession of writing, Ford belonged, more or less, to the Dionysian disposition, a nature tending toward the unruly and ecstatic. Most of all, what separated him from this good attorney, with his fastidious humanitarian liberalism, was that Ford worked out of an older understanding of man—that primitive, profoundly reactionary, pagan vision in which virtually all true story-tellers have probably been working since Homer, which has evolved not an inch since Ecclesiastes: that the race is basically unimprovable, and its condition an inalterable mixture of meanness and nobility, violence and compassion. Ford himself once remarked, "I've been invited to sessions before to discuss biracial committees and all those other causes, yeah. But I've never gone. I'd just rather not hear them mewl and whine."

The final fact that confronted Ford in all this was that the natural locus of any serious writer in his society is always outside of it. But Ford seemed strangely reluctant to accept his inherent estrangement from his fellow townsmen. Curiously, he was still contending up to the very eve of his trial, "One thing I've never done is violate any of the proprieties around here. I know the difference between mores and morals. That's why I've been able to get along with these folks." With all the rancors so evidently arrayed against him in the community, it seemed a boggling blind spot in Ford's perceptions. But even as he waited for the grand jury to meet and return an indictment, Ford remained doggedly impervious to the probability that there was a general animosity at work against him in the matter. "Hell, they *know* me here. And I've brought too much damn money into this town. People just got the wrong idea about my standing around here. All these people calling me and saying I ought to get tried somewhere else, damn, it's ridiculous. I know these people, by God, and they don't." While this determination still seemed from afar to suggest suicidal longings, one sensed in it a simple fierce refusal by Ford to accede that he might be so much an outcast in his own community that it would now scourge him in such a total way. In a critical respect, he could not afford to flee to another venue: that, in itself, would be an affirmation of the direst estrangement that would, in effect, formally and forever dispossess him of Humboldt and the life he imagined he led there—he would never be able to return afterward and dwell among them again with any real pretense of belonging there.

So, with the barging awkwardness of one who has largely passed his years living in his own inner fathoms of imagination, Ford now began groping out for the community. "After he shot that nigger out on his place," a local filling-station manager recalled, "I happened to pass him on the sidewalk downtown, and I nodded and spoke to him. I don't suppose I'd spoken to him more than once before in my life, but he stopped and grabbed my hand and shook it and started talking to me about the whole thing. Hell, I didn't want to know his life history, I'd just meant to say howdy—but he stood there telling me about it, explaining all kind of stuff about how it happened and everything, like he wanted to talk until sun-up again, all the while hanging onto my hand like he was afraid to let me loose. It was weird, I can tell you that."

Even so, while Ford had sought to make his life as a writer settled peaceably in Humboldt, some dull undertone of sourceless dread had begun to pulse through his days there. When they were beginning the designs for their new house outside town, Ford reported, he and Sally read Truman Capote's just-published journalistic novel, *In Cold Blood,* about the late-night massacre of the Clutter family in the Midwest. Ford subsequently had his architect revise the arrangement of the upstairs bedrooms to provide for what he termed "clear fields of fire around the house. Jay could cover almost the whole backyard out his window, Sarah could cover her side of the house from her window. . . ." When they moved into the house, parents and children both slept with rifles and ammunition under their beds. "We discussed what we would do if somebody got in anyway," said Ford. "We weren't going to be slaughtered in our beds like the Clutters, whatever happened. If somebody did manage to get in the house, they sure as hell wouldn't get out again—we'd either hold 'em or kill 'em. We all decided this, Elizabeth and Sarah and everybody, in an unanimous family decision."

Ford allowed one day, "Maybe it just goes with being a writer, but I think I've been paranoid all my life, probably—a paranoid manic-depressive schizophrenic." While Ford seemed to relish all his children with an almost poignant avidity—their humors, their small inventions of wit, their peculiar piques, their simple presence around him—he had always suffered a special anxiety, he maintained, for Charles. "It so happened that we came close to losing him right at the beginning, and ever since, I had this terror, I've never been able to get over it."

Charles confided, "Aw, sure, I know I'm his favorite. I always have been," and gave then an odd little flat smile like a fleeting wince of discomfort. He remained, throughout the months before his father's trial, a silent and shadowy presence, a peculiar morose air about him of displacement. Sally declared once, "Lord, how glad I'll be when Charles can leave for college in August. He just needs to get away from here, get out of all this. As soon as he's away from here, he'll be all right again." One afternoon, Charles confessed, "I wish it could be me. It'd be so much easier to stand, instead of him having done it for me. I tried to get him to let me say I'd done it. I pleaded with him. . . ."

There are times, though, when certain anxieties and tensions gather into self-combusting disaster. "For several months before the thing happened," Ford related one night, "I was having these dreams. At first, I would suddenly awake in the middle of the night—just like you'd snap your fingers—at a sound like some godawful clap of thunder. It happened two or three times—about three o'clock in the morning, *blam!* and I'd jerk straight up in the bed. Then, after several weeks, it happened again, and this time the whole dream came with it. Somebody was chasing me through the kitchen, through that back hallway that leads to the door out to the garage. I didn't know who it was, but they were trying to kill me, I knew that. Then, just as my hand grabbed the doorknob to snatch the door open, there was this incredible explosion in my head. I had been shot in the head, I knew this in the split second before I died, before I passed into nothingness. And then all of a sudden I was awake."

Ford paused. "You know what was actually happening in those dreams? By God, I believe I was actually dreaming what was going to happen out there that night in November. I *dreamed* it. Only, instead of it happening to me, it was me who did it—I shot Doaks through the head."

Now, after that night in November, it remained for the grand jury to decide whether Ford would be brought to trial on charges that could range up to first-degree murder. "They've got to return some sort of indictment, hell, I know that," Ford professed. "I want 'em to, actually. If they returned a no-bill, Christamighty, in the East they'd say, 'Look, a white man can kill niggers down there and get off scot-free.' I'd never be forgiven for that." By the day the grand jury convened, he and Sally had reached generally buoyant expectations of indictment on one of the lesser charges, perhaps involuntary manslaughter.

But late on a February afternoon when the grand jury emerged from their deliberations, the district attorney, W. R. Kinton—a large man with black frame glasses set on a face resembling, with its backward-combed tufts of frosty hair, an irritable osprey—casually pronounced, "Oh, we got a number one. That's right—first-degree." Out at Canterfield, Ford was upstairs taking a shower when Sally was brought the news. She merely sat very still for a moment in her chair in the den, her knitting lying in her lap between her spread knees, her hands resting flat on the chair arms as she stared at the television screen where *Truth or Consequences* was still clamoring with an oblivious canned hilarity. Then her eyes watered. "Oh, God. Oh, God. I just can't believe it. I can't believe they would do that to us. These people were supposed to be our *friends*." Ford's mother, visiting from Nashville, was sitting with her—a fragile lady with white hair like spun glass—and she merely gazed out of the window beside her into the late afternoon, and then softly, briefly, wordlessly shook her head in that manner of elderly Southern dowagers that is perhaps the most eloquent affirmation of disaster and finality yet devised in human expression. Sally continued, "I've never in my life been mean to anybody, not in my whole life—but, boy, am I going to learn how to be mean now. I am going to be the meanest . . ." And Ford's mother interjected quietly, "Now, Sally. We must not forget, we have always been genteel people. Don't let them drag you down to their level, Sally. You lie down with dogs, you get up with fleas."

Ford came downstairs, his brushed hair still damp from his shower, and he simply stood silently in the middle of the room for a minute after Sally told him. "Well," he said at last, "now we know where we are, what we have to do." There was a light airiness in his voice. "We know how the land lies now, there doesn't need to be any more guessing about that." He went to the other end of the room and sat by himself for a long moment on the ledge of the fireplace hearth. Then he suddenly, loudly announced, "Goddammit, I think I'll just plead guilty to the charge and get the goddam thing over with. I'll just take their goddam fun away from them and go ahead and plead guilty to murder one and go to jail. . . ." He quickly rose to his feet again. "Let's get away from this place for the rest of the day. I don't want to be here, anywhere in this goddam county. We'll drive to Memphis, that's what we'll do. Because you know how I feel right now? Like the Count of Monte Cristo. After this thing's over with, I'm gonna pick 'em off, one by one." As he started back upstairs to change, his mother called, "Jesse, now, don't say such things," and he shouted from the stairway, "Well, goddammit, Mother, I'm sorry, but I *mean* it. . . ."

With Sally driving, Ford sat alone in the back seat with a scotch and water in a milkshake cup, staring out the window as they rode through the calm wide fading of the day, the late afternoon lengthening across the winter countryside in a cold red sunset. Presently he said, his voice softer, "Well, we sure as hell took a hit today, no doubt about that. . . . Sally, you remember several years ago when we went up for that governors' conference in Hot Springs, Arkansas, when I was doing that piece for *The Atlantic*? God, we had such a wonderful time. We didn't have a worry in the world then, did we? That was when we were happy. But those times are over with forever now, I guess. Those sonsabitches mean to see to that, obviously." He spoke now as if from a distance of impersonal bemusement. "Of course, I know what they're doing to me, I'll tell you exactly what it is: I've made 'em mad all these years writing about their double standards of justice, throwing all these poor blacks in jail and beatin' 'em for traffic offenses while they let any white man who kills a black go free. So now that I've killed my nigger, they've decided, by God, they'll just show me what that single standard of justice is like. All I've been writing about, they're gonna put it on me now and show me how it feels. Yessir, that's exactly what they think they're doing—they're stickin' it to me."

Later that evening, as they were sitting around a fireplace in the back of a Memphis supper club waiting for a table, Ford— by this point, after uncounted additional scotches, somewhat ruddy with prickles of sweat on his forehead—watched a man seated across from him talking to Sally, someone with large eyes blurrily bottled in thick glasses, whose two companions were listening with smirks and bobbing heads, and finally Ford hissed to the journalist, "I want to know who that sonuvabitch over there is." Clapping his glass down on the table, he made his way with a lunging clumsiness past the knees and feet of the others seated there, leaned over the man, blaring, "I'm Jesse Hill Ford," and shoved out his hand. The man, a witless little grin clinging to his face, gazed up at Ford muzzily, and then piped, "Ford? Ford? Yeah? Well, let's see your driver's license. . . ."

The waiters tried to wedge their way through the small mob of onlookers who, with the sudden scuffling thumps and clattering of furniture and shouts from the back of the restaurant, had crowded to the end of the bar, some standing atop chairs. The man's two companions were trying now to grapple their friend away from Ford's grasp, Ford reaching across the tangle of arms and hands for the collar of one of them too while howling something unintelligible. This abrupt little melee was gradually tugged apart by the waiters, and the three strangers, still sputtering in disbelief, took their leave. A moment later, Ford was sitting again on the sofa by the fireplace, perfectly composed and chatting pleasantly with the others around him, taking easy sips from his drink. It was as if he had merely engaged in some gesture now accomplished and complete, and had returned satisfied to what he had been doing before the humor had taken him. He was presently joined by a couple who had been drawn over by the fray, and he fell into an extended exuberant literary discussion that seemed to have a particularly restorative and refreshing effect on him.

Perhaps more desolate than the alienation from his community that Ford at last had to face, though, was the isolation in which he also dwelt as a writer from those of his own blood

—an isolation he could never acknowledge even to himself. His mother—once a teacher of "expression" in public high schools —had always managed to remain cheerfully vague and uncertain about what he was actually writing. "Some of us in the family were talking down home the other day about his *Lord Byron Jones* book," she offered, "and I told them all, 'You know, when I read it, I got the impression it was *pro*-Nigra.' But somebody said, 'No, no, it's not that at all. You just read it again, and you'll see it's actually not pro-Nigra at all.' So I did, and I see what they mean now." And his son Charles admitted, "I've heard people say a lot of stuff Daddy's written is supposed to be for the niggers, but I don't know. I started *Lord Byron Jones* once, but never was able to really get into it."

It may be the lot of almost every serious writer that he leads a separate clandestine existence even within his own household —his very business, after all, is that of voyaging alone out to those far edges of the mystery of the human heart where few have gone. But there still seemed an astonishing fundamental gap between the feeling in Ford's work and the recognition of it by his family. It was as if, in this most important sense for any writer, they had never really known who he was.

Yet more sobering, though, was the fact that Ford was not only a stranger to his community and to his family, but was also finally a stranger even to himself. The afternoon of the grand-jury indictment, Sally declared, "If you ever write another thing that's sympathetic to the nigguhs, Jesse Hill Ford, I'll have you committed to the insane asylum—I swear I will." He replied, "But dammit, Sally, it *hasn't* been sympathetic to the Nigras. I don't write as a liberal or conservative or integrationist or any single person. A writer's not just one person— hell, he's three, four, any number of people if he's any good. He doesn't know himself who the hell he is."

But if all writers tend to live diffused into a whole spectrum of characters, possible identities, Ford had long been working in a tension of potential identities involved with the violent seethings of the South and its past, all the sirens of guilt and racism and fear and fury at play over his land. "And it takes a very stable person," as Ford once proposed, "to flirt with that kind of instability. A great degree of self-knowledge is required of any writer to keep him this side of insanity." To negotiate it all, a writer must always keep himself—as Ford described the young white lawyer caught in a moral maze in *Lord Byron Jones*—"like the original mold of a creature as yet untainted, as yet uncommitted, having in him the penultimate possibilities for either good or evil. . . ."

It is a writer's peculiar unease, then, that while potentially any number of people he is finally none of them, belongs in the end to none of their worlds, but hangs in an endless abeyance among them all. He lives in a kind of anarchy. Beyond whatever order and intelligence takes form in his work, he is without any real sense of himself. And in this would lie the last and most fearsome loneliness—a suspicion sometimes that, passing before a mirror, he will see nothing but an empty room.

Ford, then, already led a tenuous enough existence before that shattering night in November. And it's very rarely that any individual, much less a writer, is pitched into the kind of crisis, as Ford was now, that calls for such an ultimate personal validation of his professed faith and decencies.

Toward the close of *Lord Byron Jones*, Ford's liberal young white lawyer, Steve Mundine, observes, "From the first, I've been afraid something would happen to make us—all of us—have to choose sides," and as he declares at one point, the trick, for any man of civilized conscience who has chosen to make his life in the lap of a different and more brutal society, is "not to be beguiled." But as Mundine is warned by his wife, "Fear, Steve, they make nets of it and once you become entangled then it's too late to struggle."

In Ford's case, those invisible webbings lay slung about him with a particular subtlety and complication. "They just aren't gonna get me in a jail," he asserted once before the trial. "The same thing would happen to me that happens to a fox you capture and put in a cage—something would die in me. I couldn't stand it." But the treacherous risk for anyone, like Ford, choosing to live out in a community like Humboldt was that, once caught in the sort of peril in which Ford found himself, all the hope that is offered by that community is deliverance on its own terms.

Lord Byron Jones was, if nothing else, a passionate testament against the pervasively corrupting effect of the duplicity of the law in the South. Steve Mundine anguishes with his own uncle about the town's collaboration in sanctifying Jones' murder: "This business of protecting one man because he's white and putting off another because he's black, how many generations of intellectual cripples is the South going to produce? . . ." But now, improbably, awaiting his own trial, Ford began to lament the fact that immediately after the shooting he had not possessed the presence of mind "to go right back down there and get this thing straightened out when the police arrived. If I just hadn't stayed up there at the house—that was my big mistake. All I'd have had to do was just walk back down there and tell 'em, 'Look, now, I can't have this car and all this mess on my property—that dead one there, let's get him on out of here, and that girl there, I want her arrested for trespassing.' They'd have said, 'Right, Mr. Ford, you bet, we'll take care of this for you, just don't you worry about a thing.' I could have stopped the whole damn business right there and wouldn't be in this fix now. Instead, I let 'em stay down there three hours taking pictures of the car and measuring the goddam road and all that stuff, and after that, it was too late."

An apostate in any society faces extra liabilities should he blunder, even through accident, into the hands of that society's judgment. And now it was as if Ford had made the determination that, if he undertook to negotiate his way out of his jeopardy in fidelity to the feelings in his work, he would become even more hopelessly isolated not only from the community but from the comfort of his own family, who belonged inextricably, and in this emergency even more vehemently, to the common ethos of Humboldt. Thus, in the last weeks before the trial, Ford listened without demurral, indeed with an appreciative heartiness, to the commentary of his family around him: "That little nigguh floozie that was in the car with Doaks," Sally told him, "when this whole thing is over with, her little ass is gonna land in jail, we gonna *see* to that. . . . Nigguhs—*nobody* hates 'em as bad as I do." In *Lord Byron Jones,* returning home after listening to some especially rabid railings at a party, Steve Mundine's wife, Nella, whom he brought into the South from San Francisco, implores him, "I can't breathe in this climate. I can't talk, I can't think. . . . and tonight, when you just sat there through it all, when you never raised your voice. Can you spend your whole life like this, Steve?" But Ford's own house now was increasingly occupied by the same variety of local citizens—"handsome and princely

sometimes, and attractively bigoted"—who populated the an-
grier passages of *Lord Byron Jones*; Ford kept himself surrounded by their company, the same "loud arrogant voices"
of his novel now ringing through the rooms under his own
roof—the local high school football coach, a huge figure with a
closely mown transparent stubble of bruise-gray hair, booming
one afternoon, "I don't care what anybody says, they ain't ever
gonna be able to make us live with 'em, we just not gonna
accept 'em. Funny thing, though, they beginning to find out up
North what we been saying about niggers all these years down
here."

Moreover, it was as if Ford himself had set about assuming
the mien, the mask he sensed necessary for escape and survival,
which was the countenance of the community around him. He
decided to become them, as a chameleon in danger takes on the
coloring of its surroundings. And in this surrender, Ford acted
with the precipitous exorbitant enthusiasm of an excommuni-
cant's recant. In the whiskied miasmas of one late evening, he
called a friend and blustered, in a lurchingly loud voice in
which, though, there was a thin uncertain rattle, "Well, I'll tell
you what, how I feel now is I just wish I'd shot a hundred of
'em, that's all I regret. The black bastards, what we gotta do
down here is just wipe out about a dozen more of 'em and get
things back to normal. . . ."

So it was that the old curse that had abided over the South
from its aboriginal crime of slavery—that debasing legacy
about which Ford himself had written so knowingly—
cunningly began to claim Ford too, from a grim accident which
itself was triggered in a way by the continuing ramifications of
that ancient crime—perhaps all the more savagely because he
had sought for so long to exist outside of it, as a writer instead
telling about it. Now, he seemed to have calculated, out of his
instinct as a writer for the fullest authenticity, that for true
reprieve he must transliterate himself totally and without reserve into this society—truly covenant now with all the old
demons and dark glees of violence at work in the South, with
which in the past he had been only tentatively in communion,
but which now could absolve him of his act and deliver him
from punishment.

In Memphis one morning, Ford drove out to meet a casual
acquaintance of his, a man called Sonny Waldrop, who owned

an automobile scrapyard on the fringes of the city. "Now this sonofabitch you about to see, all he's *about* is violence," Ford enthused, "just simple and natural *violence.*" While Waldrop's daylight occupation was technically that of presiding over his junkyard, Ford explained, his true moonlit passion was arranging pit-bulldog fights, most of them held in Sunday pre-dawns on deserted plantations in northern Mississippi owned by absentee Northern landlords. A legendary brawler in Memphis' neon stretches of honky-tonks and roadhouses, Waldrop had lost one eye in a long-ago altercation. Ford had first encountered Waldrop during research on a novel, and he greeted Ford in the gray-cindered yard in front of his place with a delighted bray. "Guhdamn, Jesse, what you doin' here?"

He was himself strikingly evocative of some overgrown bulldog, with the same brutal impacted massiveness, the clamp of his lower jaw like the prow of a tugboat. His hair was oil-combed back to fat black locks on the nape of his neck, and he was wearing corduroy trousers that drooped below his billowing belly, his thumbs hooked in the pockets. "Hell, yeah, I got a dog out back there now," he offered in his amiable wheeze. "Ain't even full-grown yet, but the goddam meanest dog I ever had—I mean, two German shepherds jumped on him both at once while he was tied up to the doghouse, and he killed both their asses, by God. Wanna see 'im? C'mon back, I'll show 'im to you."

They followed him on into his place, making their way through the cavelike twilight of a narrow aisle past dim begrimed shelves laden with an infinite collection of amputated machine parts, and emerged out back into a small enclosed wasteland—a landscape of furious static disruption, dismembered cars, innards of engines, rusting skeletons of body frames, the haphazard and quiet flotsam of numberless unremembered collisions and explosions accumulated here in weeds and oil-bruised dirt in the pale sunshine of this February morning. Pointing to a small hummock ahead of them, Waldrop declared, "Over yonder he is, the sonbitch, right there. . . ."

Beyond a battered sheet of corrugated tin roofing, they saw, still chained to his hovel of a doghouse, the form of a half-grown bulldog with a hide the dull-gray color of old dishwater, lying on the top of the small rise in the cold sunlight—a third of his neck gnawed away. Still, an instant or two passed before the realization registered, as Waldrop idly nudged the dog's stiff flanks with his boot, that it was a carcass—had been lying out here a carcass, chained to the doghouse, for at least a whole day. "Greatest goddam little ole dog I ever came by," Waldrop whooped, and for some reason, no one seemed able to bring himself to note out loud that it was actually dead, to call this disappointing fact to Waldrop's attention. "Mean, *mean* little sonbitch, I wanna tell you," Waldrop went on. "Right after I got him, fella had this Doberman pinscher said he wanted to fight, and he fuckin' tore that Doberman all to pieces," and as Waldrop continued narrating the dog's performances, he gave delighted little dips and pumps of his hips and his shoulders, simulating his dog's fighting lunges, while in a pinched sour kennel near the rise where the dog lay, two German shepherds were whirling, lashing, ravening against the fence with urgent abject moans.

Presently another man appeared—built, oddly, exactly like Waldrop—only his head was cauled in a waxen glaze, his face blurred and disfigured like a tallow effigy that had begun to melt, with merely an indefinite nub for one ear. When Waldrop introduced him, there was a sudden awareness, in the man's handclasp, of a disconcerting absence of several fingers. "This fella here now, he got burnt up in a car wreck, that's what happened to him," Waldrop eagerly announced. "Hell, the bastard ain't even spose to be alive now. His head swole up big as this"—Waldrop measured the approximate volume of a jack-o'-lantern pumpkin—"they was waiting for him to die for thirty hours. But sonbitch, here he still is!" While Waldrop was so celebrating him to the two strangers, the man nodded and mumbled obligingly, " 'At's right. He's telling you the truth," but in a soft, subdued, almost abashed voice, with an air of vague embarrassment and dislocation, as if he felt he were lingering there before them improperly, like someone who suspects that in the interest of everyone else's comfort he should have left a party long ago. Then the man peered around Waldrop, at the doghouse atop the knoll, and after a moment said quietly, "Sonny, what happened to your dog?" Waldrop grunted, "He died," and went on talking.

They wandered back through the building out to the front lot again, where Waldrop called over an elderly man, somewhat flimsy and sunken, like a balloon that has begun to leak air, a mouse-brown hat on his head: "Coly, c'mere, want you to meet a fella, this here's Jesse Hill Ford. You know, that writer over in Humboldt shot that trespassin' nigger, killed his ass." Shaking the man's hand, Ford told Waldrop, "Damn, though, looks like they've indicted me for first-degree murder, Sonny." Waldrop clapped one heavy clublike hand on Ford's shoulder like a benediction and wheezed, "Listen, Jesse, been me, I would of shot the bastard *eight* times. They'd never of even knowed who the hell that nigger was, they'd never been able to find enough parts of him to put back together to tell. Don't you worry about that grand jury over there, they just tryin' to look good. It's gonna come out all right. And anybody gives you any trouble, all you gottta do is call ole Sonny—you know that." Ford murmured, "Well, thank you, Sonny. Goddam, I appreciate that. I really do. . . ." And as he smiled in the winter sunlight, his eyes dampened with tears.

Ford, perhaps because he spent the most intense part of his life alone and within himself, had always seemed to relish intervals of companionship with a swooping and slightly inflationary elation—and now, during this time of danger, his urge for company seemed ravenous, obsessive. "My God," he confided at one point, "it's like I can't stand for anybody to be out of my sight for over eight hours. . . ."

In the home of acquaintances one evening, Ford and the hostess—a small tidy blond lady who had the brittly gay air of having passed through valleys of her own—sang together in a small palmy alcove, the woman playing the vintage upright piano with crisp chords and Ford leaning over her, belling, "Diamonds Are a Girl's Best Friend" . . . "Yes, Sir, That's My Baby." Watching them, one had the recognition that Ford's disaster had, in fact, brought him an unexpected gift: the chance, in his strategy to survive in Humboldt by merging himself into it, also to indulge in a luxurious surcease from aloneness. It had offered him an opportunity to truly come in out of the cold. He began congregating with his friends as never before, suddenly became visible everywhere, seen at parties, in homes around town, on the downtown sidewalks.

Before long, though, it began to seem that Ford, in contriving to recede indistinguishably into the common face of the community, was seeking deliverance from more than just his legal crisis. More than once there were signs that, after having regarded that community for so long with the secret intelligence of a third eye, this solitary knowing part of him still pursued him like an unquiet shade. So that in his retreat now into the order of life around him he was undertaking not only to rescue himself from disaster, but at the same time—with the same stroke—to rescue himself from the deeper enduring consciousness of that third eye from which he had always written: a torment not only about what he had done, but about the means to which he was resorting to extricate himself.

In the end, guilt may be the most insupportable of all mortal griefs. On the night after Ford's indictment for first-degree murder, after that small skirmish in the Memphis supper club, they had all stayed over at the apartment of a friend of the family. Sometime before dawn, the journalist, sleeping on the couch in the living room, suddenly became aware that someone was standing over him, and opened his eyes to see Ford peering at him anxiously: "Goddam, you awake? Look, I got to talk to you a minute. . . ." The windows of the room were just beginning to pale, the room dimly gathering depth and detail like a photograph beginning to emerge out of solution. But Ford was already fully dressed in tie and tweedy coat and crinkled yellow shirt, though he was still unshaven, a tan smudge of beard on his jaws. Holding a glass of grapefruit juice and gin, he dropped into a chair across the room and abruptly announced, "You know what I just heard on the radio back there? About my indictment yesterday? They're saying I killed a *young soldier*, for Christ's sake. Just think how that sounds—my God, a *young soldier!*"

Ford lunged back up out of the chair. "Why aren't they saying an AWOL private? That's what he was. . . ." He began striding back and forth flourishing the hand holding the grapefruit juice and gin. "You wanna know what he was? Christ almighty, he was a drug-addict deserter out with his second cousin two weeks after marrying the mother of his bastard child, that's what he was. We got to get that across to the press somehow, goddammit. We got to do something about this—we just can't be having this *young soldier* stuff."

Ford's desperation had apparently become reduced to a compulsion to defame, vilify his victim. But as he continued talking and pacing about the room in the gray light of dawn, the journalist suddenly sensed that this reelingly extravagant alarm over so innocuous a designation as "young soldier" actually spoke of some other horror that had reached Ford in that early morning—a more profound dread that had waylaid him in that first unwary defenseless instant just after awakening when he had turned on the radio. He had, this time, indeed taken a true hit—immeasurably more damaging than the indictment the day before: a blow of some unbearable guilt and sorrow.

For the next two hours, he sat rigidly on the edge of a dinette chair—drinking his grapefruit juice and gin, getting up once to shut the venetian blinds against the growing brightness of the morning—while he watched the succession of local and national newscasts on a portable television set resting in the center of the room on a metal trolley. "All right, now, that's good—a marijuana story, that's gonna help us. That's great. . . . Ah, good, great, they didn't mention a thing about the indictment, they kept it off. That's perfect. I have a friend in the news department up there with that network, he's looking out for me, by God. I can count on him. . . ." He continued this running monotone commentary, lost in a ferocious concentration, a private spinning play of surmises and arcane computations, sitting in the dimmed room and staring at the ceaseless flickering mercurial glow of the television screen, while the journalist, watching him, felt a chill wash of suspicion that Ford was actually going mad before his eyes. . . .

What seemed obvious now was that, however that trial turned out, the real ordeal would only then begin for Ford. In any journey back into that detachment in which he had dwelt and worked before the shooting, he would have much to pass through.

Four months later, then, in June—and the low hushed woolen skies and silent snows had passed into a heat and glower like the instant before some terrific immolation. On the afternoon before the trial, Ford was visited at Canterfield by a local Baptist minister, a thin dark young preacher who had once admonished his congregation from the pulpit to stay away from Ford's works. He sat now on the end of the couch in

Ford's den, his long black hair combed back from his scythe-like face, attired in a somber suit with the dead luster of black swampwater faintly bronzed by amber late-afternoon sunlight. "I must say, I have never read any of your books, Jesse," he pronounced, "but I understand yawl are without a pastor right now, and I just wanted to come out, and bring you a few thoughts from God's Holy Word. . . ." He spoke with a tense unremitting urgency, a kind of ethereal ferocity that seemed to have already wasted him of all softness in its unabating burn. Now, one hand clenching a black Bible, it was as if he were conducting an impromptu invocation here in Ford's den: "Before you came in, Jesse, I was just sharin' with Sally here that God's at work in this thing. Yes. You know, the Lord says in His Holy Word that we may not always understand the workings of God, but all things are in His design. Yes. And so I just wanted to come out, Jesse, and share with you and Sally here, that you're in our thoughts, yes, and in our prayers. . . ." He finally leaned forward and intoned, "Could we just stand now for a word of prayer?" And when he was finished, in the absolute stillness that lingered for a moment, he husked to Ford in a sunken moan of jubilation, "God bless yuh, Jesse."

Early the next morning, they began gathering out of the surrounding countryside into the columned whitewashed mortar hulk of Humboldt's city hall, proceeding through the lobby with its old railroad-terminal benches and pale-green Coca-Cola clock, up the narrow creaking flight of worn stairs to the courtroom on the second floor, steadily and murmurously filling the rows of varnished wooden folding seats in the cool of the new air conditioning, the ceiling fans overhead motionless. Finally a deputy lifted his walkie-talkie and thumbed its button and shouted into it, "All right! Send all the jurors up!"

The 134 prospective jurors—only six or seven of them black —began to be called in one by one, summoned from name slips drawn out of a pencil box, and each was questioned, in what was like a long processional out of the anonymous unchronicled life of this land—farmers with weather-seamed faces, young filling-station workers in crisp white shirts and lavishly combed hair, an insurance drummer and a cigar dealer, a barber, an affable banker of imposing girth with his cream-white Panama hat placed politely on his knee. During this slow assembly of the jury, Ford—wearing his gray business suit, sitting in the small area at the front enclosed by a lacquered oak railing, the meager mundane arena now where the course of the rest of his life would be deliberated—heard the prosecution for the first time officially pronounce the word "death." During a short exchange between the attorneys and the judge over whether the state should disclose at that point if it intended to seek the death penalty, Ford listened with merely an empty, impassive gaze while the prospect that he might actually be made to die sounded repeatedly in the air around him.

Beforehand, one black citizen had proposed, "What this trial's gonna prove is who's less unpopular in this town—us, or Jesse Hill Ford." But through the questioning of the prospective jurors, it soon became apparent that Ford, despite all his years as an outsider in Humboldt, had at last come into the pale of the tribe.

"Have you been prejudiced, or personally offended, by any of Mr. Ford's novels or writings?" one venireman was asked, and the answer came ready and level, "Nosir. Sure hadn't." Gradually, the pattern of an elaborate entwinement of secret kinship in the community began to appear: "Well, his boy and my boy are real close friends. . . . Well, yes, Mrs. Ford taught me while I was in school, and now she's teaching my boy." Many of them turned out, in fact, to have been patients of Sally's father. "Well, sir, do you feel this relationship to the Ford family through Dr. Davis would in any way affect your judgment in this case?" "Yessir, I'll be honest with you. It sure would."

Finally, though, it seemed to be Ford's deed itself that, even beyond its racial inflections, had redeemed him, commended him to the acceptance of the community. Prospective jurors declared, in almost uninterrupted succession, that they had already formed an irrevocable judgment on the matter: "Nosir, I'm sorry, there's just some things I been brought up to believe, and one of 'em is the right of any man to defend his property." The district attorney, W. R. Kinton, would then ask, "You mean, this opinion you already have as to Mr. Ford's guilt or innocence is so strong that, even if proof was presented in this courtroom directly and positively *refuting* that opinion, you still could not set it aside?" "Yessir. That's exactly what I mean."

Only one black was on the jury that was finally selected. Not very long into that first day, the victim's father, George Doaks, Sr.—a motel chef and country preacher, a man with a round smallish head set on boxy shoulders, wearing his Sunday suit and sitting with his wife and his son's widow immediately behind the prosecution attorneys—dropped his gaze and did not lift it again above the level of the tabletop before him for the length of the trial, withdrawn, unhoping, even though still necessarily pent in the procedural formalities that remained until it was all over. Doaks made one brief appearance on the stand, and was asked by the prosecution, "George, when was the last time you saw your son alive?" Doaks recounted the evening at their house, stretching out his arms as he said, ". . . and he held his little baby out to me . . ." and then he began crying. The prosecution waited a moment, and then asked him the rest of their questions, which he answered in a cracked and empty voice, his hands slowly twisting together in his lap. After Doaks' testimony, Kodachrome snapshots of his son's body were passed among the jury—the event thus diminished to depthless prints on tidy squares of glossy paper.

With that out of the way, the trial became more like the occasion of Ford's formal presentation at last, after twelve years, to the general community. Taking the stand, he cited his service with the Navy during the Korean War, and presently explained why he had moved there to Humboldt among them: "I wanted to write fiction . . . and I had no reputation. So, Sally could teach school, while I wrote. . . ." Then, with his attorney, a graying former judge named John Kizer, acting as interlocutor, he chatted pleasantly to the jury about what he did out on his place, the livestock he had and the crops he grew. And finally, he invoked the supposed arcane wizardries of his art— to authenticate his testimony that many of the anonymous calls to his home had actually come from Allie Andrews, the girl who had been in the car with Doaks: "Yessir, that's my work, a fiction writer. I recognized her voice not as an average person might, but as one who makes their living by listening to other people talk. . . . Many American critics have noted that I have the finest ear for dialogue of any American writer." He dilated on that to them: "It takes years of study. . . . You'll see in your mind the pattern of that voice. . . . You have to communicate the exact texture of that voice."

The closing day of the trial arrived with the surprise of a cool glistening morning, touched it seemed with a premonitory tinge of November, the time almost eight months ago now when it had all begun. Ford had shed his staid charcoal-gray suit, and was wearing another the dusty light-green color of newly mown hay. It was obvious at this point that the prosecution had come to suspect they had made a fundamental miscalculation somewhere along the line. Their final exhortation to the jury had a certain winded and, by now, obsolete quality about it: "Some people seem to gloat over the fame they have, the property they have, the trouble they can cause. ... Mr. Ford may be a hot-tempered man who wants no invasion of privacy and went way out in the country—that's all well and good. ... We know he's headstrong. ... But gentlemen of the jury, people must be held responsible for their actions, whether his imagination runs away with him or not. ..." And then, for a moment, it was as if Ford were being posed for judgment by the very angers and appeals of his own work: "Ladies and gentlemen, we've got to make the laws apply equally, to *all* sides. ... Do we believe in justice, disregarding all prejudices, all races and colors?"

But the defense closed with, "Gentlemen . . . God placed this strongest instinct of them all in the human heart: the instinct for self-preservation. . . . How far can a man be driven until he loses his mind? . . . The human heart, gentlemen, is not exposed to the law. . . ." And then there came the final apology, the explanation that climaxed this public induction of Ford into the society of Humboldt: "Gentlemen, he's just a person trying to make a living like everybody else. Just because he's going about it a little differently shouldn't be held against him."

And with that simple proclamation, it was accomplished: Ford's self-willed assimilation, against all the persuasions and sensitivities of his work, into the conventions of the community around him. But there are instances when dread assumes a chaotic ferocity that begins to consume all about it, including that which it meant to protect. Ford, in his duress, had resorted as a defense to those same habits of the white Southern ethic that he had always deplored with apparently genuine passion. And in this, there were truly tragic intimations: that through the means with which he sought to save himself, he would find that he had lost that portion of himself most worth saving.

The jury was still secluded as the afternoon sank into a hot languishing dusk. Below the courthouse, a crowd was gathered in the twilight, standing along the sidewalk across the street in front of the loan offices and used-clothing stores, sitting on the fenders of cars in the filling-station lot. Inside the courtroom, the windows had blackened now, and the courtroom reflected itself in them, while the night seemed to hang in the chamber in the weary shine of the ceiling lights in some stale and muggy vacuum in time. Waiting, Ford muttered, "I'm terrified. I sit here, and terror comes in little spurts. . . ." There was an odd dullness in his eyes. "I'll tell you exactly what it's like—it's like sitting around in a front parlor waiting for somebody to die."

He was silent for several minutes. Then he suddenly leaned forward and whispered, "That fella over there—that young deputy who's been keeping his eyes right on me. He's the one who's supposed to do it." With his eyes now flicking over the courtroom, Ford went on through drawn taut lips, "We got another anonymous call this afternoon—telling us that as soon as the jury reported in, an attempt would be made on my life before I left the courtroom. The police will be involved in it. That little fella over there, he's the one who'll actually do it. . . ." He nodded, just perceptibly, toward a chubby and boyish deputy chatting amiably with some newsmen. "It's always the one you least suspect," Ford went on in a stealthy undertone. "Every time, it's the one who looks the most unlikely. . . . What I did, I called the governor, and he's sent some state troopers in. I think we might make it, but . . ." He was crouched sideways now in his chair, almost huddling, his head lowered but his eyes still tossing about in a furious scrutiny all about the courtroom. And there was a sudden chilling sense that there had stolen out of this wanly lit night, once again, that same delirium which had taken Ford in those dim pre-dawn hours four months ago in Memphis, the same berserkness, in fact, that had seized Ford that autumn evening over seven months ago. He pulled his eldest son, Jay, close to him, and whispered in his ear, "We got to watch that far corner over there now. What they'll do is distract everybody's attention with a disturbance over there—that's when they'll make their move. So we'll have to move fast, out the back way. Make sure there's a car parked right outside the door back there. And make sure somebody's keeping their eyes on that little sonofabitch over there every minute of the time. . . ."

At nine-fifty, the jury shuffled back into their box, a switch was flicked, the air conditioning ceased its hum, and, in an absolute hush, the foreman stood and announced *Not guilty*.

But Ford did not seem to hear him—those short syllables of his survival, his freedom, the termination of his anguish, no more now than the idle and meaningless puttering of a stranger's breath. He continued glancing with a ragged covertness around the courtroom, and then rose with the others and started out, surrounded by a seething of friends and newsmen that spilled with a clattering stampede of footsteps after him on down the wooden stairway, then down the back stairs, surging out now into the warm flush of the night in the rear lot of the courthouse, where two state troopers were waiting with a car, its engine softly muttering. Ford pitched into the back seat with Jay and the journalist, and with a rapid battering of car doors, the car lunged forward out of the lot and up a back street, speeding away under a calm repetition of streetlights.

Jay began yelping gleefully, but Ford remained leaning back in his seat, silently watching the road ahead of them and the side streets that blinked past. He turned once to look out of the back windshield, and said, "There's somebody behind us." One of the troopers, without looking around, said quietly, "That's our car, Mr. Ford." Nevertheless, as they hurtled now with a vicious haste down narrow streets, they seemed, despite the verdict in the courtroom, in some wild flight through the gentle summer evening of Humboldt; it was as if the lit front porches and shadow lawns blurring past Ford—the small white houses, all the simple familiar facades of his town—were rushing away from him past the windows irrecoverably into the measureless maw of the night.

There were already the clustered gleams of many cars in front of Ford's house when they arrived, flashlights flinging and yawning over the grass, and Ford climbed out of the patrol car into embraces in the darkness, tears, a nuzzling of his mastiffs, and then a small startling rustle of clapping from a throng of unrecognizable figures, a company of dark faceless shapes collected from somewhere out of the night and milling now on the lawn in front of the lighted windows of his home.

Two days later, the journalist drove through a late declining afternoon out to Ford's place for a last visit. "Jesse's down at the pond swimming," Sally said. "Go on upstairs and wait while I send somebody for him." A back stairway led to Ford's study, a cramped chamber of harsh unfinished cypress-plank walls, tucked under a corner of the roof like the captain's cabin of a privateer galleon, with a simple severe cot and papers thumbtacked to the walls and strewn across a table beside his typewriter. In a tall glass cabinet by the door, there was encased an old Confederate saber—a plain talisman of this land's ancient holocaust of glory and doom, propped upright at a rakish tilt with its sharp point resting beside a skull.

Returning from his swim at the pond, Ford showered and then sat on the edge of the cot, barefooted, wearing white duck trousers and a sky-blue turtleneck sweater, twirling between his hands a bell snifter of ruby brandy. "Of course, I always figured these people were like they proved to be," he said. "These people are Scotch-Irish, English—these are *my* people." Outside, the sky had suddenly darkened, with the bright-green tops of trees lashing under a lowering sullen immense haste of clouds, and shortly the storm clapped down on the house, a battering everywhere at once of rain with cuffs of wind and drizzle coming through the curtains of the small window over Ford's typewriter. Ford got up to close the window, and continued, "I feel closer to the people around here now than I did before this thing happened. Suddenly, when they were selecting that jury, I knew that I knew them. I didn't know them by name, but I *knew* them. They had started to hate me, and I knew they had started to hate me, but in all this, we discovered something that we really didn't know. That we are kin."

But later that evening, in a back-street tavern, there was a folk chorus of commentary that intimated Ford's acquittal owed actually to a white communal instinct far older and larger than Ford's particular ordeal—and that all his own feverish attempts to come into the common tribe of his fellow townsmen had been finally gratuitous. A wizened and dusty-booted native snorted, "Tell the truth, I still don't like Jesse Hill Ford much worth a damn. But I sure as hell liked that verdict."

On another afternoon after the trial, the journalist drove out of Humboldt, out into a wide countryside heavy and sluggish now with the molten shimmering green of summer. Turning down a thin graveled road, he found the Doakses' home—a small scanty structure of white clapboard with a porch of

cement blocks, set in a grassless broom-whisked yard. Beside
the house, a ramshackle wooden fence enclosed a mud lot of
grumbling hogs, and a rickety green pickup truck rested under
a nearby shed. Reverend Doaks, wearing a plaid flannel shirt
and black wing-tip shoes powdered with dust, arose from a
cane-bottom chair on the front porch to greet him, and Mrs.
Doaks, in a maid's white uniform, invited him inside.

They sat in a long front room whose dim walls were patched
with white plaster, the light sockets in the ceiling vacant of
bulbs. But a profusion of artifacts adorned the room: a miniature ceramic bust of a thorn-garlanded Jesus, a brilliantly hued
print of the burning Sacred Heart, a waxen floral arrangement
set on the coffee table, and a tangerine-tinted porcelain Si-
amese cat deposited atop the television cabinet. Across the
room rested the cap-and-gown graduation picture of their
son.

"He was our oldest boy," said Mrs. Doaks. "He was our
first boy. He loved to roam these fields around here. When
he was little, he'd get off in these fields and bottoms with little
white boys and play all day long. . . . But it was real strange
when he came back from the Army this last time. The Thursday night before that Monday, he went to church with us, and
after the singing, he stood up and said there was a song sung
that night that specially impressed him—'Swing Low, Sweet
Chariot.' " Mrs. Doaks was sitting on a nickel-plated kitchen-
ette chair, and she started rocking slowly back and forth,
folding her arms about her, the chair creaking faintly under
her as she spoke with tears welling in her eyes. "I just couldn't
understand it, you know. I remember looking back at him and
wondering, Now, why did he say that song? 'Swing Low, Sweet
Chariot.'. . ."

Before he left, the journalist told Doaks he was sorry for
what had happened, and Doaks replied, "You sorry? Then
maybe you can guess how I feel. He was my own flesh, my own
bone and blood—and Jesse Hill Ford spilled it. But what can
you do?" A rooster was crowing intermittently somewhere in
the yard outside, a dry insistent monotonous sound in the
drowse of the afternoon. "My boy was shot down in cold blood,
but we don't have no justice. Nowadays, they just carry it a
little further, you know what I mean. But that's the only difference. Now, we be Christian people, we believe vengeance be-

longs to the Lord. But Mr. Ford's conscience won't let him forget this. . . ."

"It is Monday, some nine months since it happened," Ford wrote to the journalist several weeks after the trial, "and here I am about in the same situation I was in after Doaks was shot. Then I could not be decently sorry about it for having to defend myself. But all that I got out of killing a man and the months that followed is diabetes mellitus. It didn't teach me a damn thing. It was just an interruption that permanently destroyed a vital balance of body chemistry: this used to be called 'a broken heart' until science 'discovered' that it was something else just as dimly understood. . . .

"Something is wrong in my world and I don't know how to fix it. I just keep hoping the two parts of it that have seemed always of late to be so out of step will soon, somehow, come back even again, so that I can cope with it even if I cannot understand it. . . .

"My feelings have been dammed up so long that I feel almost helpless. I feel such an overwhelming and ineffable sadness when confronted deep in myself with the fact of this loss and the fact of this damage to a creature self—in short, the hurt that was done to the me that writes—that I cannot bring myself to admit it publicly nor speak about it. . . . As for the man who fought in court and the man who raged and lost sleep and health, as to that Viking self, it did him no hurt. Turned loose, he would go along and spend the rest of his days wreaking some sort of vengeance of one kind or another on those who oppressed him. . . . But there is a part of me, a self, a deeper being, that does not yet understand what it was that came between it and the reason for its existence. That self is wounded and will not soon heal. That self is puzzled, and will not soon see the straight of things again. That self only knows that it was hurt and damn near killed. . . . Just now I feel it quietly weeping like a woman on a dark plain, widowed in war and her dead lying all unburied. I must go to her and somehow, if possible, assure her that I am still alive. . . ."

Some two years later, Ford and Sally were divorced. Ford left Humboldt for good, passed nine months teaching creative writing on a Birmingham campus, and, having made another marriage to a young lady from Nashville, he has spent each year since drifting between there, Los Angeles, and the Virgin Islands.

Canterfield was lost to foreclosure by a Humboldt bank. Sally now resides in town.

Charles, now married, has moved to Wyoming, where he is studying for a doctorate in chemistry.

Aside from the publication of the novel he had been working on before his trial, no writing by Ford has appeared since. Returning briefly to Humboldt in 1979 to answer a legal action brought by Sally, he explained to the court that he had been suffering from a psychological block. The last word was that he had been privately commissioned to write the biography of a founder of a Nashville bank.

What Happened That
Summer to Warren Fortson

No LESS THAN IRELAND, the South has been a sow with a propensity for eating its children—especially the brighter and more restive among them. One of the most familiar stories of the Sixties was that of the solitary and earnest white Southerner who wound up involved, from whatever prompting, in the Movement in his hometown, and quickly found himself ruined and outcast. Many of these gentle, blasted souls eventually took asylum in the calm insulated preserve of liberal agencies, like the Southern Regional Council or the Civil Rights Commission, which had offices then in Atlanta—Atlanta itself coming to serve as the common refuge for such casualties from all over the South.

One of this number—a droll, waggish, Falstaffian figure, commodious of girth and gusto—took charge of the Atlanta bureau of a national legal-rights organization, where he soon gained a measure of celebrity for his zestful libertarian skirmishes in a series of Constitutional cases. In his office late one night, after a small birthday party there for Georgia's dapper young black legislator Julian Bond, which was observed with pimiento-cheese sandwich wedges and scotch in waxy Dixie cups, he decided to place a long-distance call to a black friend —an old associate back in that state and city where, eight years ago, he had committed his own fateful apostasy. It was almost midnight, and, save for two lingering friends, he was alone now in his office, blearily drunk and slumped behind his desk, a huge blowsy heap, his glasses askew and slipped down to the tip of his nose. He blared into the phone with a blurry grin, "Dalzell? Hey, you no-count nigger—goddam, you drunk again? Nigger, you never gonna amount to anything, are you?

Newsweek, September 20, 1965
Atlanta Magazine, July, 1969

You just a no-count black-ass nigger. . . . Hunh? Well, I know it, I ain't wurf a shit, thass right. But goddammit, that don't matter, 'cause I'm *white* folks. But you just a sorry ass-scratchin' country nigger. . . ." After he hung up, he sat for several minutes with his hand still over the phone, staring at it silently, with a suddenly dreary, sagging face. Then he looked up and murmured, "You know, that don't get it, does it? That ain't exactly bringing in the kingdom either, is it? . . ."

Among that company of white excommunicants left scattered over the South by the Movement, there was one man—Warren Fortson, of Americus, Georgia—whose ordeal became a singular parable of what can happen when someone a bit more restless of conscience than his neighbors nevertheless undertakes to make his life comfortably that of Everyman's. Fortson was not, in fact, an especially imposing personality—just fairly thoughtful, fairly decent. For the most part, he was indistinguishable from his fellow townsmen. Any lust for crucifixion, for striking lonesome bravado poses, could not have seemed more alien to his eminently conventional and placid disposition. All through his difficulties, and even after his capsizing and exile, he still gave one the impresssion that it had all been a bizarre accident. But what happened to Fortson holds a pertinence that, actually, goes beyond those times in the South: it really tells of common men of goodwill and some perceptiveness in any community, in any age, who wander unwittingly, out of simple alarm and anger, into a moral involvement that gradually captures them completely, leaving them in the end devastated and separated forevermore from the familiar settings and cherished people which once sheltered them.

Like so many other of those sparse towns strewn numberlessly over the South's backland, Americus had the appearance of having been abruptly plopped down intact, out of nowhere, into the negligibly inhabited spaces of south Georgia, and left there static and changeless under a vast oblivious silver-shimmering sky, in an emptiness of piney flatlands and fields of cotton and peanuts. The center of town had remained a paltry collection of brick and stone buildings inscribed with dedication dates from the turn of the century, all of them long since weathered to the drab uncolor of snuff or dead leaves or the earth itself, and along its idle streets, there weighed some abiding lassitude of brute tedium. As in the blank lost wastes of Scandinavia, the number of suicides in Americus had always been extravagantly disproportionate to the population.

For many decades, the old gentry had grimly kept at bay any intrusions of industry from afar, out of a wariness about the "undesirable elements" it might infiltrate into the community. The last aging survivors of that finely mannered order still produced for a guest monumental eight-o'clock suppers of home-baked bread, plump chicken crackling-fried in buttermilk batter, young sweet corn picked early that morning from the garden, sweet-potato casseroles dusted with pecan flakes, and home-steeped dusky scuppernong wine in ancestral cut-glass decanters. But their sons and grandsons had enterprisingly pursued more sensible arrangements with the times: while Americus still remained principally a farming town, it had managed to acquire a shirt plant, several mobile-home enterprises, and a coffin factory. One local young attorney, suddenly come into a flush of money, contrived to have transported from a neighboring county the entire main floor of an antebellum manor house, mounting it a few miles out of town on a mortared elevation in a newly razed plot of raw red earth stippled with spindly saplings and still rubbled with plank ends, where it loomed like a hastily clapped-together movie set. There the young attorney and his wife would entertain friends after supper in its splendid high-ceilinged rooms, rustling winter-evening fires winking over polished hardwood floors, the young attorney recounting in bemused detail over a bell snifter of cognac such drolleries as how their dog kept breaking wind under their bed at night, the menfolk periodically retreating out to the back veranda to relieve themselves over the banister railing.

Even before the summer of 1965, Americus had long been noted for the special malevolence and durability of its racial strife. As early as 1958, an interracial communal farm a few miles out of town began to be besieged by firebombings and shotgunnings that lasted, off and on, for several years. During civil rights demonstrations in 1963, five local Movement leaders were arrested and charged under a century-old Georgia law with "insurrection," a rather total measure since conviction could have carried a maximum penalty of death. A former state legislator from the area was personally given to slugging marchers in picket lines, and the sheriff who attended to the community's racial dislocations, a studiously surly man with a pinkish bulb-eyed Boston terrier's face, his trousers tightly lashed high up on his waist, several inches of nylon sock showing, referred to journalists and all others curious about Americus' style in racial difficulties as "buzzards." In the lulls between street confrontations, Americus conducted its business with blacks in the same quaintly blunt manner. For instance, landlords in the black neighborhood, who had converted chicken sheds into five-unit apartments with no toilet facilities other than the yard out back, discovered that the surest way to collect their money was simply to remove the front door from a delinquent's quarters; one winter a child was found in these dwellings frozen to death.

Then, during a local election in the late spring of 1965, a black woman who was a candidate for justice of the peace was promptly arrested when she stood in the "white women only" voting line, and kept pent in jail for nine days. There instantly followed the familiar reeling fever of mass meetings, twilight marches surging down the main street past a gallery of young whites lounging on parking meters outside the pool hall and chili cafe and movie show; the first scrabblings of violence quickly brought wholesale tumultuous arrests, while other white citizens, bankers and merchants, looked down from behind dusty second-floor windows with pale jaw-clamped faces and small hard eyes. There was the usual desultory mock attempt to form a biracial committee, but it shortly sputtered out, as all the others had before it—the last such effort had rapidly died on the vine when the whites couldn't agree whether to call their black counterparts by their first names or to address them as "Mr." and "Mrs." Finally, on a savagely hot July night, a white youth standing in a street-corner filling-station lot with a group of his fellows was shot to death from a passing car of blacks.

With that, all the massive klieg lights of the national press swung on Americus, and presently came to fix their fierce arrested lightning on the personal beleaguerment of one of its white citizens—a local attorney named Warren Fortson.

"Maybe it was because I was one of those few people in the South who had lived on both sides of the equation," he reflected later. "I had been part of the mentality of the establish-ment, and then, somehow, I came to know the other side."

The youngest son in a family deeply seasoned in Georgia politics, Fortson had a wheelchair-confined brother, Ben, who had been Georgia's secretary of state almost as long as there had been Talmadges in the capital. Fortson himself, after a tour in the Marines, arrived in Americus in 1959 to begin a law practice and raise his family—deliberately selecting it for its calm leafy snugness, reminiscent of the small town of Washing-ton in Georgia where he had grown up. "I wanted to get back to that way of life—the closeness and healthy informality you find in small towns. That was the way it had seemed to me as a boy. Of course, I was acting out of one of the great illusions of nostalgia. I wanted to go back and live in a calendar picture." In Americus, he and his wife, Betty—a tall, sleek, tanned, effu-sive brunette—soon became almost a cliché of Southern small-town respectability: country club, Rotary Club, Junior League and Garden Club, school board. Fortson began teaching the men's Bible class at the Americus First Methodist Church. In time, he was also presiding over a robust household of five children. By 1962, he had been appointed county attorney.

He was a heavy, bearish man usually a bit tousled and crinkled in the heat, with a bland full-moon face, a perfectly circular retreating hairline, and eyes narrowed to a thin squint behind black-framed glasses. He had a small, light voice that seemed somehow misplaced among his bulk and energies. Whenever he happened to remove his glasses, it gave him a momentarily exposed and defenseless look, and presently, as if he too suddenly sensed some subtle vulnerability, he would snap his glassses back on with a blur of his hamlike wrist. He moved with a certain blundering lunging impetuousness, stuffing himself into his too-tight coats with almost a slapstick urgency, the lapels pushing up his collar tips, a stray strand of hair dangling over his forehead.

But more than anything else, there was about him an essen-tial quality of mildness. As much for that reason as any other, probably, Fortson began to indulge in a gingerly dissent from the general disposition of the community. While on the county board of education, he had gently harried his colleagues into desegregating the local high school. At twilight patio parties, he would fret the tinkling gossip with notions about urban-renewal programs. But he was more than a cocktail-party provocateur—he initiated a tour by a busload of the town's civic leaders through the black neighborhood, during which, at one point, a burly businessman suddenly bolted out of one hovel, snatched his collar open, and vomited in the front yard.

What disconcerted Americus more than all this, though, was Fortson's increasing willingness not only to accept black clients, but to involve himself in their cases with unmistakable seriousness. This eventually led him to defend two local black youths, a boy and girl long vigorous and conspicuous in the Movement, whom authorities supposed they had finally cornered by whimsically charging them with fornication. The charge was eventually dropped. But however Fortson unsettled the white community by such extensions beyond the pale, his behavior was still regarded as one of only intermittent eccentricity. There may have been something a little erratic and awry in him, but he remained, in the Americus tribal context, essentially wholesome.

As it turned out, what was awry in Fortson was that he had a simple incapacity for detaching himself from what was happening to other people, and in a place like Americus, a susceptibility like that is likely, sooner or later, to consume one. During 1963's summer of demonstrations, Fortson walked to and from his office every day past an abandoned two-story building that city authorities had improvised into a general storage bin for masses of arrested student marchers. "I'd look up there," Fortson later recalled, "and see those windows boarded up with plywood in that August heat—and behind them, all those high school kids, hundreds of 'em, up there in the dark and the heat and the flies, getting only two hamburgers a day. But all you could see from the sidewalk was the plyboard over the windows. The idea that something like this could go on, not way out in the woods somewhere, but actually right here in the stark middle of town . . . That's when I decided that nothing like that was ever going to happen again in Americus, ever, if I could help it."

After that, there was no way for him to extricate himself from what was to come two summers later.

That glistening green June of 1965, even as demonstrations were again spilling through the downtown streets of Americus, Fortson's own circumstances had reached their highest tide; he moved his family into a handsome sixty-year-old brick home with nineteen airy rooms, set on a softly sloping, shaded side street just around the corner from their church. It was as if, whether illusion or not, he had finally managed to recreate, reconstruct into reality, the nostalgias of his own small-town boyhood.

Then, barely a month later, the white youth was shot to death at the street-corner filling station. Fortson instantly made a public appeal for the formation of an authentic biracial committee. It was the only way, as he saw it, to forestall the customary blundering of blind reflexes on the part of a white leadership insularly absorbed in grappling with the apparitions of their collective paranoias. But as innocuous and almost touchingly naive as his proposal seems now, at that time for most of Americus it was attended by assumptions and implications that approached the apocalyptic: that there could be some legitimacy to black discontent, that blacks should be dealt with on an equal level of manners and respect, as if they were actually white citizens—in short, that the old accustomed order and vision of things might be fundamentally suspect. The white community in Americus simply could not believe that this crisis, like all the others before it, had not been externally and artificially induced, and to consent to a valid biracial committee would indicate they were actually taking it seriously. Even more ominously, as Fortson persevered, inevitably there took shape behind him that great dark ultimate menace to remote embattled white communities like that in Americus: being overwhelmed by the blacks around them. And their patience with him snapped at last.

Fortson's appeals for a biracial committee were soon answered by a petition, signed by two thousand members of the community, demanding that he be fired as county attorney. This prompted a small, motley company of temperate souls to collect around him—as one of them put it, "When we heard about that petition, that was it. If that could happen in Americus, right here on Taylor Street, it was time to do something." They gamely undertook to counter the first petition with another, asking that Fortson be retained as county attorney, but could muster no more than a hundred names. Nevertheless, a delegation of them appeared with their meager roster to answer the first petition when it was presented one afternoon at a meeting of the county commissioners.

Spectators were crammed steamily in the room—a small chamber in the modern new courthouse, with a clinical and anonymously antiseptic look about it. Fortson himself sat off at a far corner of the conference table. The five commissioners, all of them in their shirt-sleeves, shifted a little uneasily in their chairs, chomping on unlit cigars. And when the two petitions were presented, the commission chairman quickly and tidily tucked both of them away with vague thanks, indicating the commission would consider them at a later and somewhat less public juncture.

The chairman had started to move on to other business when one of Fortson's supporters, a housewife, suddenly leaned forward and called, "Wait a minute. Is that all? What about a biracial committee?" This slapped a deep silence over the room. The woman glanced at her husband, who had cautioned her before the meeting just to sit there and be quiet. They were young landed gentry in the area, Russell and Mary Anne Thomas. He was a tall, genial, drowsily drawling conservative Democrat who had voted for Nixon against Kennedy, but, as he explained, "My daddy told me once, 'Son, for God's sake and the sake of your own children, don't make the mistake that I and my generation have made down here.' And when this business against Warren started, I figured this was exactly one of the things he was talking about." His wife, Mary Anne, after bearing five children, still had the fresh impervious imperishable vivacity of a debutante, and it was in precisely that eager bright-eyed manner that she now accosted the commissioners. The chairman, a plump little chipmunk of a man, allowed as how there would have to be a "cooling-off" period before any consideration of a biracial committee, and added that they didn't have the authority to set up such a body anyway. "Why can't you?" blurted Mrs. Thomas. She was poised on the very edge of her chair, her large brown eyes hotly flaring. "I mean, here. Right this very minute. If you don't have the authority, who does?" From several seats away, Russell mumbled, "Uh, Mary Anne . . ." The chairman, a faint look of despair in his eyes, essayed a small witticism, "I always heard women started the French revolution," and then laughed a bit too heartily. "That's right," snapped Mrs. Thomas, "and we had to demonstrate to get the right to vote too, and we weren't always nonviolent." His laughter rapidly evaporated, and Mrs. Thomas, crackling with impatience, persisted, "Can't you see? Now is the time to just do what's right—just to act like *men.*" This produced a general shuffling around the table, one elderly commissioner removing his glasses to vigorously polish the lenses with his handkerchief, pursing his lips and giving tight little sniffs. The chairman cleared his throat and said, "But Mary Anne. Who really knows what's right and what's wrong?" (Later, that night, she would declare, "Now I know why that remark sounded so familiar—that was Pilate's question too, wasn't it?")

Finally, from the far corner of the table, Fortson spoke for the first time that afternoon. "Gentlemen, anything I would say at this moment would be manifestly ill-advised, but I'm going to say it anyway." He leaned massively forward, his heavy head lowered and shoulders humped, and made one last entreaty for a biracial council in his thin wispy voice, thumping his clasped hands on the table only a few inches away from the petition with the two thousand names demanding he be fired as county attorney. "You all know that sooner or later we're going to have to sit down together and talk this thing out. The only question is, how long will the violence last before it happens? The city is disclaiming authority. The county is disclaiming authority. So who are you waiting for? If you're waiting around for Jesus Christ, I'm afraid He's not likely to show up, gentlemen. . . ." The five commissioners merely snuffled and glared and shifted in their chairs, crossing their legs and intently flicking invisible specks from their knees. At this point, the chairman noticed the president of the local John Birch Society slipping into the room, and he quickly announced with considerable firmness and finality that they would have to move on now to other business.

That night, Warren and Betty Fortson were visited, in the scantily furnished front room of their just-occupied home, by yet another deputation of out-of-town journalists—like a sudden rackety arrival of migratory birds, they had been flurrying for several weeks in and out of the local motel, effectively appropriating it for their stay with the sheer swarm and sleepless noise of starlings. Fortson leaned back with loosened tie and damp wilted shirt, and confessed, "What's beginning to worry me is, I haven't seen a client for three weeks. Part of it has been the fact I've been wrapped up in this biracial committee, but also there haven't been that many people calling the office here lately. That's the way it really starts—not petitions. These things don't happen suddenly, they happen gradually. I'll know in about three months whether they really meant that petition or not." Betty, wearing a crisp orange pantsuit, had slipped off her sandals and was sipping a bourbon and water on the sofa beside Warren. She began talking about the anonymous phone calls they had been receiving for several weeks, assuming an air of light blitheness that, nevertheless, seemed somewhat thin and feverish. Fortson reported then that he kept a .45 now in his desk drawer in the living room, and they had sent the children off to stay with relatives until the temper of things ebbed a bit.

Around eleven, Russell and Mary Anne Thomas dropped by with a box of T-bone steaks to cook for supper. Russell Thomas propped his heavy buckskin boots on the coffee table, took a long swallow of Johnny Walker and water, and then drawled, "Dawgonnit, the thing about all this mess, Warren—all the time, way deep down you feel like you're doing something wrong, even though you know it isn't. You gonna feel guilty any way you go. Damned if you do, damned if you don't." He grinned. "Why'd you have to pick Americus to move to anyway, damn your hide. . . ." It was almost midnight when they finally settled down to supper in the front room, eating the steaks from plates set on newspapers spread over their laps. Suddenly, the phone shrilled in the back.

Betty swiftly slipped on her sandals and disappeared to answer it. The talk ceased while they listened to the dim intermittent undertones of her voice. Then she returned, smiling, her eyes dewy, and announced, "Well, that was our old neighbor, Dr. Collins, the John Birch leader. I can take everything but people being nice. I only start to come apart when they're nice to me." Collins, who was still Fortson's doctor and whose backyard had adjoined his before the Fortsons moved, had seen Fortson on a television news show early that evening, had then proceeded to toss down a number of drinks, and had finally called to tearfully burble, "They had folks on that program calling Warren a Communist, Betty—but it's an absolute lie, I know that. He's no more a Communist than I am, and you tell Warren I said so. They trying to pit brother against brother. It's all these press people, Betty—they Communist-inspired. It's ructions they want. But aw, Betty . . . Me and you and Warren, we might disagree, but we've known each other six years. Why, yawl's dogs used to bite my children, for goodness sake!"

"I think that's perfectly charming," said Mary Anne Thomas

after she heard this. "The pity of it is, Bob Collins will be sober again in the morning."

"Oh, I don't know, Mary Anne," said Fortson. "I think most people would rather be kind than unkind, if they had a choice." He had finished his steak, and sprawling back on the sofa now, he mumbled wearily, "That's the tragedy of this thing. It goes for Collins just as much as for the little fellow who owns a corner grocery—if he happens to have his own personal feelings about what's going on, he can't speak out even if he wants to, because he knows he'll be wiped out. It's a strange kind of tyranny, faceless. But it's so strong that to get around it, Collins first has to get himself plastered and then make his call over here at midnight. But he did it, however bombed he had to get himself to do it, however late the hour. What we're trying to do is just make it a little easier for people to be decent, that's all. It's when a system, for whatever self-interest or cooked-up dogma or ideology, makes that choice so difficult for the common individual as to be no choice at all—in other words, a choice between kindness or survival—that's when you get what happened in Germany. It effectively paralyzes a population for whatever godawful mischief the state then chooses to prosecute. How tiresome the German analogy is becoming— but it could happen here. Hell, some of it has already happened in Americus. But what will undo it, and what can always undo it, is, I repeat, this one little simple thing: the average person, goddammit, does want to be kind, rather than unkind, and he *will* be kind, if he is given just half a chance to be. And that's all I'm after—to open up that possibility a little bit."

At the least, Fortson had managed to effect some discomfiture in the consciences of a few white citizens in Americus. While Fortson was eating a late lunch one afternoon at a diner on the outskirts of Americus, he looked up to see looming over him one of the town's more forbidding conservatives, a segregationist of the Paleolithic variety—a millionaire whose fortune had been made in the shadows between politics and business, a huge ungainly man with a look of Lazarus about him, glazed sunless skin and thin lank sorrel-dyed hair, with a blind man's dark glasses and a jackal's sepulchral grin. "I been trying to chase you down all over town," he said, sitting down across the table from Fortson. Without further ceremony—in a low hurried voice, with frequent quick little grimacing grins—he proceeded to confess that, hell, maybe Warren was right about the whole damn business, a lot of times he'd gotten the feeling himself deep down that Nigras weren't really being treated fair at all, that they were actually just like everybody else but things were just fixed around here so they didn't stand a chance from the minute they were born, and sometimes he didn't really know why there was all this ugliness about the Nigras, where it came from, even the ugliness he sometimes . . . And then he suddenly stopped; his mouth clacked shut. It may have been that he finally noticed the astonished gape on Fortson's face. Whatever it was, without another word, as abruptly as he had deposited himself across from Fortson, he heaved himself back up and strode off. He took a table at the other end of the diner, where he ate a rapid solitary lunch without so much as another glance in Fortson's direction.

But almost in inverse ratio to its growing hopelessness, Fortson's idea for a biracial council increasingly obsessed him. Ironically, with the passage of the Voting Rights Act late that summer, blacks suspended their demonstrations, and community officials, who had hitherto professed they would consider forming a committee only when the marches ceased, now declared there was no need for one—ever. With that, Fortson and three of his friends hastily rummaged together their own makeshift bootleg committee—an ephemeral, poignantly meaningless affair, since it was recognized by no one but themselves. And by now, the smaller, personal excisions had begun. Fortson was relieved of his Sunday-school class at the Methodist Church. Betty found herself studiously ignored at meetings of the Junior League, "as if I had suddenly become invisible." Their expansive social life in Americus had quickly been reduced to a single meager civility: as Betty defined it, "being careful that you don't put people you see on the street, in the stores, in the embarrassing position of having to speak to you."

The summer burned on into September. Someone in town photocopied a *Chicago Daily News* article about Fortson and distributed it in all the cars parked outside the stadium during a high school football game. When Betty took home movies of their next-to-youngest child entering the first grade, the word around Americus the next day was that she was there filming the desegregation procedures at the school. And finally, the county commissioners—while not firing Fortson formally—hired a second law firm to discharge the county's business. "We felt we needed an additional attorney," explained the commission chairman, "because Warren's . . . uh, had a lot of things he's had to do lately. But I'm certainly still a friend of his. Why, he's even brought his kids out to ski on my lake." In the meantime, his law practice dwindled away to virtually nothing —his office empty, day after day, even of black clients. Now Fortson took to sitting up by himself through the long hours of the night beside a downstairs front window of the new house they had moved into only three months ago, all the lights out, the .45 in the desk drawer near him, long gauzy white curtains softly and soundlessly furling in the large, half-furnished rooms around him.

Finally, to one last flare of national publicity, he and his family fled to Atlanta. And with that, the klieg lights on Fortson flickered out for good. Perhaps there lingered for a little while in the general mind an incidental memory, a waning afterimage of a large mild man beleaguered and dogged and unbelieving even up to the instant of his absolute ruin. But soon there was not even that recollection of him. Several months later, a New York magazine editor pondered, "Fortson, Fortson—now, who the hell was he? Wasn't he that newspaper publisher down in Mississippi they ran out of business? No, of course not—that liberal lawyer down there in Georgia somewhere. Sure. Whatever happened to him, anyway?"

Abruptly landed back into quiet everyday anonymity, Fortson in Atlanta began trying to repair as much of his life as he could. It seemed a natural and felicitous transition to join that community of similar refugees working in the various civil-rights agencies of the day, and before long he enlisted with the Lawyers' Committee for Civil Rights as a kind of circuit rider in Mississippi, offering his services as a counselor and mediator to white leaders in communities caught in racial whiplash.

As it turned out, this time in Mississippi proved crucial to him. Already he was beginning to suspect of his ordeal in Americus that never was so much lost for so little. "But I never fully comprehended what was happening to me there, and why. Just all of a sudden, boom—it was over, I was in Atlanta." So Mississippi began to afford him, in town after town he visited, a kind of second sight of what had happened to him, and served in a way to affirm the necessity of what he had done, despite its costs.

"I'd go to those mass meetings religiously over there. I don't think I'd ever understood what the movement really was until then—sitting in those little crackerbox churches crammed with maids and yardmen and old janitors all clapping and singing those songs, and some tall black starved-looking woman standing up front by the pulpit like a rigid hat rack and leading off each verse with this unearthly soul-shivering voice, 'Go down, Doctor King . . . say, let my people go.' Never in my life had I been that hotly close to love and courage and goodness, looked it that full in the face. I thought I had understood why the Negroes in Americus had taken to the streets, I thought I knew how they felt, but I never really found out until those mass meetings over there in Natchez and Fayette and Laurel. It's funny how, a lot of times, it's only when you're through an experience, and exhausted—only when something's over with and behind you—that it really starts opening itself up to you, too late."

The spiritual weather in the towns he called on seemed to him interchangeable with south Georgia's: "that same edge of meanness," as he put it, "that utter lack of any genteelness under racial duress." It was probably inevitable that sooner or later Fortson, from his position now as interlocutor, would find himself trying to restage Americus in Mississippi—"only this time, make it work out somehow." Instead, he came in time to a profound pessimism about the ultimate effectuality of the Movement. For one thing, "I found out there was nothing really exceptional about Americus," he recounted months later. "The whole white South—maybe all of white America—was Americus. Because in all those troubled little towns, I wasn't sitting there talking to men, I was talking to a system which was acting through these fossils of what had once been men. They had ossified into a part of that system long ago. I remember sitting down with the town elders in Fayette and trying to tell them, 'Look, I'm a Southerner, and not very long ago my town went through exactly what you're going through now, so I can tell you a little bit about why this is probably happening, and what's probably going to happen if you don't at least *talk* to them seriously.' But all they wanted to talk to me about was Communists. The Movement to them was anything in the world but a genuine popular arising against conditions there. In fact, it was only intelligible to them as a manipulated conspiracy because that was how they, as systematic souls, operated. Everything was machinery. And after a while, this got to be consoling, in a sort of backhanded way, about my own failure in Americus, because I came to realize the hopelessness of anyone—not just me, but anybody—trying to say to the city and county officials there, 'Look, boys, this just isn't fair, let's do the right and sensible thing now.' That's Greek to the system, and all its officers, high and low. Those words are understood only by the private individual, alone."

At the same time, confessed Fortson, "I came to suspect that the Negro really wasn't going to win—at least, not in this generation. The United States itself is supremely a white society, in the sense that it is a systematic society. But I began to feel in the black movement this careless looseness, a total lack of program and predictability, this reliance simply on sheer energy and emotion, that became part of my despair with the whole thing. Of course, that may have also been precisely its genius— the spontaneous over the structural. It may have been beautiful, it may have worked miracles over the middle distance, but I couldn't see it defeating the system over the long run. The truth is, I have myself that Western Anglo-Saxon personality that demands orderliness and sequence, patterns. Maybe it's just become a part of the white man's nature. But what turned out to be the hardest and most conclusive disappointment of all was the fact that those mayors and county commissioners weren't entirely wrong about one thing—the movement just *didn't* suffuse the whole black population. That would enrage me. It was like they were watching the whole question of their salvation as a people being contested and decided right there before their eyes, and many were totally indifferent to it, except in the most nebulous way."

During his tours in Mississippi, Fortson lodged at an aging, gabled boardinghouse near downtown Jackson, leaving Betty and the children in their apartment back in Atlanta. After he had been working there abour four months, a newsman from the Americus days happened to come across him one evening in a restaurant in Jackson, sitting alone at a small table along a wall, and they had dinner together—Fortson awkwardly pitched sideways in his chair, eating hastily and spottily, vaguely restless, as if he sensed he was actually supposed to be somewhere else and was trying to recall exactly where it was. Later, over a beer, he said, "I realize it may seem I have a vested emotional interest in what I'm about to say—you know, everything important ended with me in Americus. But dammit, here in 1967 the Movement as we used to know it just doesn't exist anymore. I've been all over Mississippi, and all that's left of it here is a few scattered seedy students who never went back up North, cranking out leaflets on mimeograph machines in a few grubby back rooms. As for the Negroes, they're moving into themselves now, you see it everywhere, they're introverting. They've quit the field. Birmingham, Albany, St. Augustine, Americus, Selma, the March on Washington—all that is gone now, it's passed away."

Each time Fortson returned to Atlanta, he found that he and Betty had become even more strangers to each other in that city. Their marriage began gradually unraveling, as if its texture had been too much a part of the texture of their life in Americus to be extracted from it. After some six months in Mississippi, Fortson signed on with an Atlanta law firm whose interests, mostly corporate matters, were distinctly removed from any welterings of racial conflicts. It all seemed now truly over for him at last. He and Betty were divorced.

But after a time, his work and Atlanta itself began to grow stale and oppressive to him, and finally, even at this remove, he passed once more into the eclipse of his defeat in Americus, more darkly than ever before—he seemed filled now with a nausea of soul over it. "I did what I did, but what difference has it finally made to anybody?" he explained. "Absolutely nothing's come of it, and nobody remembers me but my enemies. Not even all those liberals I'd get phone calls from while I was down there. When I finally had to leave, and I began approaching them, I got this odd little feeling of distance, a slight coldness. I began to wonder if it'd been all the press coverage, if that once you're spotlighted, they have no more use for you." He was hulking over a cup of coffee in the clash and steam of a cheap corner diner in downtown Atlanta. It was midafternoon. "I ought to be back at the office. But I'm sitting here whining over something that ended over two years ago. I

admit it, this is whining. But god*dammit!* Maybe my disappointment is just that of being left behind after the band moves
on. I understand that's the way it has to be—events have got to
move along and the real parties concerned can't be taking the
time to dwell on what you tried to do for them. White people
like me who make these decisions have to live with them, and
know there isn't going to be any special solicitude for them
later. But what I'm speaking of is the fact that not one of the
Negroes I tried to work with down there hardly even remembers who I was. One Negro attorney—I probably spent more
time with him that summer than I did with my family—he
wouldn't even return a call last week. That's one irony that's
hard to take. I just never was built to be a martyr, that's the
whole trouble. It was just that Negroes became like a burden
on my back down there—what we were doing to them, what
we'd been doing to them for three hundred years, it got to be a
burden after a while I couldn't get off my back. Now, I'll tell
you how I feel sometimes. Sometimes, I find myself hating
everything Negro—everything that tastes, smells, sounds, looks
Negro: hate their suffering, hate their patience, all their ag-
grievements, all they've had to endure, all their righteous demands for redress now. I feel sick unto death of them
sometimes."

One weekend, he visited a friend in Boston—that old brown
city of chestnut trees and postage-stamp parks and foggy windows along narrow wet brick streets, with its pale English
weather and breath of wharves and sea. Fortson sensed, in his
rounds there, a tone of life like the weather: quiescent and
almost autumnal, tamed and composed, nourished by fine measured subtle flushes of energy. After dinner one evening at the
Kennedy Institute, he sat talking with a small group in an
apartment long into the night, and he remembered later, "God,
it was great. There wasn't that enormous labor, like there
always was down in the barrens of south Georgia, to make the
conversation as excruciatingly intellectual as it could be. What
we used to put ourselves through down there in Sumter County,
trying to keep ourselves alive and the emptiness out. But with
those people in that apartment that evening, there was just this
confident anticipation of change, a careful excitement about
the truth—they really believed in what they were saying, it
wasn't just witmanship and gymnastics. I felt good there—felt

really good for the first time in God knows how long. I thought, boy, this is the place for me, I could love it up here." But after he returned to Atlanta, a suspicion gradually chilled this exhilaration: that very likely in Boston there merely lurked a stasis of another order from that of the South's. If what was lacking in the South was a calm precision winter-twinkling excellence of wit and mind, Boston was as lacking of another intelligence: that sensual intimacy with human experience made up of the strivings and appetites of a heart kept simple and so more alive.

In 1967, after a year and a half in Atlanta, he moved to New Orleans, where he joined another law firm—and then, barely nine months later, abruptly resigned. After a while, he drifted back to Atlanta. "I think I want to orient myself toward something not really involved with the practice of law now," he suggested. But he had foreclosed for himself any further work in a civil-rights agency, finding himself vastly uncomfortable, for one thing, in the relentlessly didactic and conscientious company of those other liberal derelicts like himself who had managed to reach a peace of sorts by becoming institutionalized apostates. For Fortson, it was as if the matter could never actually be real except as he had lived it—merely as a citizen in one's community. He admitted, "To be able to make your life as a professional liberal, you have to have a certain amount of permanent personal anger in you, you have to be able to be intense and mad underneath all the time to sustain you in that line of business. I don't have that. Also, when I come up on an issue or confrontation, after a while I begin seeing nuances, complexities, implications, which stall me and just sort of take the steam out. That can be considered a form of corruption, I know—a corruption of will. Anyway, you sure as hell can't live in that kind of work being susceptible all the time to moral equivocations."

What this long and inconclusive aftermath of revelations, loss, fitful plans, despair, and rancor all portended, finally, was that Fortson would probably pass the rest of his life as a kind of Flying Dutchman. The unrest would probably never really end. This was a possibility that had occurred to him by now. But he had also reached the recognition that "I actually had no choice down there. It would have been far worse for me, for everybody, if I hadn't done what I did. It got to be a simple basic matter of treachery to myself. The sad thing is, there are thousands of people in communities everywhere, quiet and responsible people, who fail to answer that call to the truest part of themselves when some really difficult problem seizes their community—and this means nothing less, the tragedy to the community aside, than their own quiet sure death. It comes down to a matter of acting to save your life. Because saving your life, in the last analysis, is saving what counts in yourself, even if you lose everything else."

But in the end, Fortson still had not been able to really leave, take himself out of that Southern small-town ethos—that myth and idyl of his boyhood he had almost managed to realize in Americus, but from which now he had irrevocably exiled himself. Whatever his heresies, he had become simply too much a part of Americus to ever feel at ease, at rest, anyplace significantly different. (For that matter, all the ambitious and fugitive sons of the South's small towns, even long after they have repudiated those forlorn and insular places in their con- science and tastes, secretly continue to carry them in their hearts.) What seemed most likely was that Fortson would always be suspended between Americus and the sensibilities that made it impossible for him to remain there.

"It's true, I don't know anymore if I'll ever again have that feeling of truly being home. I wonder sometimes if Americus didn't leave me like some person who writes his big novel, a novel of such magnitude in his life and the lives of those around him, that everything after that is anticlimactic. In a sense, emotionally, I reached a climactic point in Americus which I know I can never again duplicate. If I went through exactly the same experience again, step by step, it wouldn't really be the same experience, I could never again feel that alive. Something like that happens to you only once, and the question is: what can ever happen to you again to match it? I was innocent then, and full of expectations and a belief in possibilities, in a way I can never be again. Sometimes you feel a nostalgia for that—you wish sometimes you could be inno- cent that way again."

Fortson subsequently joined one of Atlanta's largest and most elite law firms, and has resided in that city since. About his only extension beyond the almost totally private life he now leads has been service on the Atlanta board of education.

He still makes occasional calls to old friends back in Americus, but has returned there only a few times over all these years—his last visit being in December of 1979, when Russell Thomas, one of his thin company of supporters during that summer of 1965, was elected mayor of the town.

A Meeting of Strangers
in Americus

ON A CHILL Friday evening in November of 1970, the football
team of Americus High took on the squad of a neighboring
south-Georgia town, the Cairo High Syrupmakers, in what has
long been in such small settlements over the South a kind of
seasonal demireligious folk festival—an occasion amounting to
about what bull-tumbling rites meant in ancient Minoa. With
the flare of the stadium lights now washing high into the night
sky, latecomers, hearing ahead of them the rowdy thumping of
the band, hurried across parking fields of grass already faded to
a pale beige but still plush underfoot, with a musty tang of
autumn. The two shallow banks of bleachers were filled mostly
with small family galleries: wives whose faces were wan of
makeup, their neutral-colored hair fiercely scalloped and rippled from their afternoon beauty-parlor appointments; the men
beside them, with cleanly clipped haircuts under little flannel
fedoras and quilted rayon jackets zippered snugly up under
their chins, tending to look like merely enlarged versions of the
small boys sitting at their elbows. Along the waist-high wire
fence immediately below the bleachers, there passed a ceaseless trudging processional of men holding white Styrofoam
cups who by halftime had become a bit ruddy and blusteringly
convivial—while others periodically retreated behind the
stands to the rear of a Sunbeam Bread truck, where they
passed around a half-pint of Early Times for quick high tilts
under a bright cold moon.

But there was, this Friday night in Americus, a certain surreal alteration in this immemorial weekend pageant of small
Southern towns in the fall. In the midst of the whites in the
stands, there was also a large population of blacks. They sat
somewhat more sober and subdued, but produced now and

Life, February 12, 1971

then patterings of circumspect applause. What's more, about half the players on the field below them were blacks—among them a sixteen-year-old halfback named Calvin Prince who had already that season averaged 127 yards a game rushing. Now, as he was running back a punt for the first of his three touchdowns that evening, the cluster of primly groomed white matrons who had been dispensing hot chocolate and slabs of homemade cake in the concession booth began bobbing up and down with ecstatic little fluttering handclaps under their chins, squealing, "Calvin Prince! There goes Calvin! Who else!"

Somehow the storms and implacabilities of only five years ago, when Warren Fortson had been harried out of Americus, seemed on this Friday night like a fantasy: between that summer and now, there was some impossible gulf of incoherence. Of course, it had long been speculated that football, being the folk mystique it is in the South, might one day provide the wand-waving grace for dispelling the old intractable racial impasse there. "All it would have taken to undo George Wallace in Alabama," asserted one Southern journalist, "would have been Bob Hayes running halfback for the Crimson Tide." Also unlike the mammoth isolations of large city stadiums, between the stands and the field here this evening there was an immediate intimacy—to the two black girls among the Cairo cheerleaders who came skipping across the field at halftime, to the strutting and swirling of the integrated bands. As Calvin jogged off the field after his third touchdown that night, one white father announced loudly to his wife in admiring celebration, "Lookathere—he *still* ain't smiling."

Larger than these moments, however, were the implications of this Friday night in Americus. At the previous summer's end, that ultimate Doomsday which had been impending for white Southerners ever since 1954—the massive integration of their public schools—arrived at last in communities all over the Old Confederacy. Thus once more, after a quiet suspension of several years, the South found itself again at the center of that national moral struggle which had spasmodically proceeded ever since the founding of the Republic. But after the passage of several startlingly serene months, a suspicion began to gather that something at once ironic and momentous might be taking place in the deeps of Dixie. For all the violence and evasions of those years after the Montgomery bus boycott, for all the scattered rearguard skirmishes, what seemed to be hap-

pening in such Southern communities as Americus posed, even
if flickeringly, the first authentic suggestion that it might be
the South, after all, where the nation's general malaise of racial
estrangement would first find resolution—in the formal emergence there at last of the single people, unique and richly
dimensioned, they had really always been.

Now, five years after that long glowering summer of marches
and gunfire that had ended with Warren Fortson's exile from
this town, Americus had accomplished a total integration of its
schools with an uncannily quiet dispatch. With about 1,850
black students in a general enrollment of 3,105 in the city's
school system, the ratio ranged from one white to four blacks
in the classrooms of the lower grades, to about one to one at
Americus High. More, in the system's administrative offices, on
the second floor of a turreted downtown edifice of mustard-
colored brick with corridors of bare wooden floors that creaked
underfoot like a frigate's deck, there were displays of black-
studies programs, including pamphlets on Martin Luther King
and Dred Scott and Frederick Douglass, brochures entitled
Racism in America, and children's novels about black cowboys.
In one English classroom at Americus High, there was a poster
of James Baldwin, with a quote from his work: "It is a terrible
and inexorable law that one cannot deny the humanity of another without diminishing one's own; in the face of one's victim, one sees oneself." It was, altogether, nothing less than
giddying in a community that only five years before could be
thrown into paroxysms by a mere proposal for a biracial council. Mary Myers, the daughter of Americus' mayor—a tall,
coltish girl with long butterscotch-brown hair who was now a
junior at Americus High—declared, "Back during that summer
five years ago, I remember everybody seemed so scared all the
time—if you needed anything downtown and they said on the
radio there was going to be a demonstration that day, you'd
dash up there before two o'clock and get back home as fast as
you could. It's never going to be the way it was then. Never
again."
Actually, when it had become obvious that the hour of total
integration was at last inescapably at hand for Americus, there
was a minor evacuation of some administrators and teachers
out of the public school system, and they were accompanied by

about 375 white students. Private schools multiplied over the area like an overnight backyard rash of mushrooms, most of them glum and makeshift affairs. "They the sorriest damn schools you ever saw," declared one civic leader, "but as downright pathetic as they are, they maybe been a blessing. They've drawn off the reactionaries for a while and allowed us to go on about our business, so that when they fold up, we'll have the whole thing more or less stablized, and those folks will be coming back into the system on *our* terms."

Fortson, at least, had the rueful gratification of one particular five-year-delayed vindication. "All that disruption five years ago," as one town leader put it, "showed us the consequences of letting a situation develop without any positive and responsible leadership." Americus's new mayor that fall of 1970 was attorney Frank Myers—an amiable, portly, deliberate man with a flourish of sideburns on his round face—who had essayed his election through a scrupulously maintained posture of moderate discretion. "We decided we were going to have open house in all the schools right before the term began," Meyers reported, "just to let folks rub shoulders a little bit, let 'em go smell each other and look each other over, you know. At the elementary school my boy goes to, we had a meeting of the nominating committee for the PTA in the home of a black family—four blacks and two of us whites there. And after the tea and cookies, we went on about our nominating business just like nothing had ever happened in this town." During the open house at the formerly all-Negro A.S. Staley High School, which was converted into the city's integrated junior high, "some of the white parents would come into the office to meet me," said the black principal, Kelsie Daniels, "and though I'm sure they'd heard I was black, somehow it still wasn't real to them until they actually saw me standing there. I just let 'em sit down and compose themselves after the shock, and one lady finally said, by way of starting a pleasant little chat, 'Well, Mr. Daniels, how did you get to be an administrator, anyway?' "

Even so, that first week after the opening of school, said one student at Americus High, "there were folks all over town who were all the time calling up the white parents asking if the colored kids had started bothering us yet." At the same time, a white principal reported, "we had maybe half a dozen parents just standing outside every morning after they let their children out—not white parents I'm talking about, but colored ones. So finally one morning I went outside and asked them what I could do for them. They said, 'We just want to make sure our children are all right if there's going to be any trouble. We still just a little uneasy about leaving our children here.' I told them, 'There isn't going to be any trouble here, I'll see to that. You can go on home now.' "

But the president of the Americus High student body, a heavy and clean-combed white youth named Johnny Sheffield who also played fullback on the football team, would insist that the school negotiated the merger as gracefully as it did owing not so much to the precautionary policies of officials but to "the little personal moments among the students when they first got together. For instance, about a month before school started we had a football meeting with the black players in the gym. We started talking about how, if we could really put their team and ours together, we might go all the way to the championship. Then when we started our preseason practice, one of the drills was getting down on your hands and knees and locking heads with another player. I think I was the first one to come up on a colored boy, and I did feel a little funny there for a second—I mean, just to *touch* them was such a totally different situation. But I got down on all fours and locked heads with him, and after that everything went along natural." Before long, some of the white players had even begun arriving home after practice with black teammates. "My folks got kind of disturbed the first time," one white lineman later recalled. "Said I didn't have to actually bring them in the house. I said, 'Well, what reason would *you* give them for not inviting them in?' "

Certain awkward hesitations still lingered in the transition, though—the retention of all-white cheerleaders and majorettes elected the year before, a moratorium on all social functions, the withdrawal off-campus of school clubs sponsored by local civic organizations like the Kiwanis and Civitans. But these expediencies, almost exclusively, were taken out of a solicitude for the paranoias of parents. Johnny Sheffield related, "Before school started, the Key Club had a dance inviting both black and white football players and their girls, and a lot of the older people got upset about that too. They had a discussion afterward about how right now that sort of thing might be too *dangerous*."

Lurking at the center of this abiding uneasiness on the part of white elders was the old bane of interracial liaisons. Mary Myers allowed that "before school started, a lot of girls I talked to were scared to death because of all these horrible tales they'd heard from their parents." Not long after school had begun, though, a group of white girls selling cakes for their club on a downtown sidewalk one Saturday afternoon, happened to spy Calvin Prince a short distance away, affording Americus the unnerving apparition of their flurrying after him with delighted shrills—"Calvin! Calvin!" Still, some teachers and parents continued to cultivate a ferocious vigilance, and this fretfulness on the part of white adults produced the one serious episode of dissonance during the early fall. Johnny Sheffield later explained, "The white kids decided we'd have a big dance for homecoming. I don't know what was wrong with us—we didn't really mean for it to be a restrictive kind of thing, but we just weren't thinking." When the letters of invitation were prepared, some white parents intervened to add to them, "This dance will be private—no blacks admitted." A few of the letters even bore the further notation, "Make sure no blacks see this." Inevitably, though, some did. It precipitated several days of disarray, chants by black students in the halls between classes, a threat of black defections from the football team. The signature of a white student leader—a sandy-haired youth named Charles Warren, who like most other youths in Americus was staunchly deferential to the inclinations of his elders—had been printed on the letters. "Somebody's parents told Charles this was the right thing to do," asserted one of his friends, "and he just took their word for it." Finally, at a tempestuous student assembly, Charles arose and labored to explain and to apologize, finishing with tears in his eyes. "Afterward," Charles recounted, "a lot of the black girls came up to me crying too, and said they were sorry for me and would help me the best way they could."

Nevertheless, a mood of precariousness remained through the fall of that first year of full integration, and there were increasing indications of a smoldering cynicism among some black students—a resentment arising from a final gap between their own expectations and the blithely optimistic assumptions of white students. A black girl declared, "Whenever I'm with nothing but girls, all the white girls seem to be as friendly and out-going as they can be. But just as soon as we get mixed and there're white boys around, they seem to turn and get nasty. It makes you wonder sometimes, if *this* is all it's come to, whether it's all been worth it—all those years of demonstrations and getting hit on the head and thrown into jail."

Calvin Prince himself was an irrepressibly jaunty young spirit—during one practice session, a white coach yelled to him, "You all the time hollering about throwing the ball to you, Calvin, so why don't you get in there and see how you do trying to throw it yourself," and Calvin, not given to abashment, crowed jubilantly, "I can throw it if the receiver can get out there. If he can't, I can throw it and get out there and catch it myself." Later, loping down the field for practice kickoff returns, briefly all by himself in the waning gray frosty afternoon, he executed happy little heel-snapping leaps sideways in the air. . . . Still, standing in the grassless front yard of his family's asbestos-shingle house one cold Sunday sundown, Calvin confided as he rolled a Pepsi bottle back and forth in the dust with the toe of his tennis shoe, "The fact is, the whites seem to love you long as you playing football. But beyond that, I don't trust 'em. I really don't. That homecoming-dance thing— we been putting up with mess like that for three hundred years."

But whatever their disenchantments, the experience brought to black students, as much as it did to whites, the one incalculable gift of a liberation at least from the old illusions entertained by the generations before them. "After all these years now," said one black girl, "we realize the whites are just human beings, not supermen without any faults or weaknesses. I can sit there and look at them now and think, 'You're not like we been told—you're no different from me.' Maybe this is what the whites have been scared of all these years, us catching on to that fact—and that some of 'em are just as dumb as anything ever walked on two feet. Why, a boy in one of my classes, he just sits there all the time eating on pencils—*yeah!*"

At the same time, the presence now of blacks in their schools promised to tug white students out of those anesthesias that had for so long insulated small Southern communities like Americus from the critical throes at work in the affairs of the nation—a parochial simplicity of perspective reflected by one junior high student's poster with a scissored newspaper photograph showing helmeted police flailing away with high-swinging clubs at a scattering covey of young demonstrators, with lettering beneath it explaining, "The police caught the people." It was a kind of innocence perhaps most eloquently hinted by the fact that, at that time of Huey Newton and Eldridge Cleaver, the ironic connotations of Americus High's nickname —the Panthers—seemed not only not to disconcert anyone, but not even to have occurred to them. At the least, white students in Americus seemed rather more likely now to feel themselves closer to the actual urgencies in which the destiny of the country was involved, if only because one of the principals in those conflicts, the black person, had to become a more personal and immediate reference for them. Further, this release into a larger awareness, while occasioned by the circumstance of blacks among them, was not likely to be confined to the realities of racial dispossession. One such illumination tends to beget other curiosities, which beget a legion of further curiosities—a process not easily restrained. There was really no measuring the emerging small sophistications that might now begin to add dimension, however tentative and rudimentary, to the lives of Americus' youth.

Also, Mayor Meyers observed, "Competition now between blacks and whites on the faculties is going to weed out the incompetents sooner or later. In the past, no one really cared enough to check whether a teacher was really incompetent— just so they satisfied that social requirement of being white or black. It was strictly a social arrangement. You see? There just ain't any way to count all the varieties of ways in which this business of keeping up two separate societies has stolen from all of us."

Intriguingly, one even began to hear some conjecture, from both blacks and whites, that one of the serendipitous effects of the merger might be the imparting of a measure of Black Soul to the white youth of Americus. Before that autumn of consolidation, the band of all-black Staley High enjoyed a legendary notability over the whole area. "At the Christmas parades downtown," recalled one white citizen, "there wouldn't be a band that could touch that outfit from Staley. Now they'd be just a little stiff and proper passing through the white part of town, you know. But just as soon as they crossed over to head down into the black section of town, it was like Resurrection Day—they'd cut loose with sounds and moves you couldn't believe. So whenever they'd come along uptown, all the white folks on the sidewalks would just sort of start casually drifting on along with them toward the colored section, until finally there was this great mob of white people clumped up there on the edge of colored town kind of wistfully watching the Staley band busting loose on down the street into the Nigra section.

"Unfortunately," the white townsman added, "when they combined the schools this year, the white band director said you couldn't play in the high school band unless you could read music. Hell, most of those kids from the Staley band, as soon as they found out what the song was supposed to be, they'd just pick up their horns and blow—they'd never looked at a piece of written-down music in their life, all they knew to do was just play it. But as a result of this music-reading business from the white director now, we only got a few black kids in the band this year, and it's got just about the pizzazz of a month-old opened half bottle of Nehi orange pop."

For that matter, perhaps the deepest misgiving among Americus blacks was that integration might actually effect a progressive dissolution of black identity. "When we got over there," declared one black student at Americus High, "it wasn't really our school. Like we had lost our own school, you know, and all we had now was the whites' school. Because somehow it just seemed like *everything* was white there. It was like a jigsaw puzzle to me." But one black matron in town—the wife of a prosperous funeral-parlor owner and a redoubtable partisan herself from the old civil-rights battles there—pronounced one afternoon, her eyes glittering like bright agate, to a living room full of disgruntled black girls, "Oh, no, no, we're not gonna be losing our identity. Instead, we gonna give all those whites a little soul. We gonna give 'em some *tone*."

Indeed, one Friday-afternoon pep rally in the Americus High gymnasium began with a series of skits by white women teachers, costumed as beribboned dolls, which possessed about the hilarity and lustiness of a Methodist Sunday school's social hour. But then, when three other women teachers—two whites and a black—tripped out on the polished expanse of the basketball court to perform a similarly airy dance to "Glow-Worm," suddenly a black drummer in the bleachers broke into the startlingly glad battering beat of a honky-tonk stripper number, bringing an explosion of cheers and howls and clapping. The three teachers, captured in the center of the basketball court by that sleazy gleeful beat, began to twine and prance with fingers snapping high over their heads, and the entire band now was squalling and thumping after the drummer, while a billowing exhilaration was set loose, surprised and free and wheeling in the gym's high ringing tumultuous spaces. "When that Nigra boy up there suddenly started hitting that drum," Mary Myers declared afterward, "it was like every one of us in that auditorium came to life."

So there began occurring in Americus such casual and accidental moments intimating mutual frequencies, a potential for community beyond the bulk of the actual available evidence, beyond the agreeable concessions of whites, beyond even the disappointed pessimisms and exasperations of the blacks. The custom had evolved at a local radio station to have in the Americus High team members, on the mornings after their games, to act as auxiliary disc jockeys on a program playing phoned-in requests. On the Saturday morning after the Panthers had won the regional AA championship—with wintry old men in army surplus jackets and bibbed coveralls leaning in the thin sun against the brick store-walls downtown while from a distance came the faint clash and boom of shuttling freight cars—the boys arrived one by one at the station, a squat building set at the weedy edge of a Negro neighborhood. They waited in the small reception area to go on the air, all wearing their bulky blue-and-white letter jackets, and presently one of the white players, who had about him a hominy-fed heftiness, his sockless feet shoved into loafers, turned to a black player sitting beside him and drawled, "Amerson, I noticed last night you had them four wimmin waiting for you after the game again. Four wimmin, and dawg, if you didn't go and pick out the ugliest one *again.*" Amerson chortled, rubbing his knees, "C'mon, man, you can't tell *me* about that woman. That woman, she so ugly she smoke a pipe. She a *tree.* . . ." A black teammate returned from the record room with an album that he waggled in one hand at Calvin, announcing he was going to dedicate it to Calvin and a certain girl. "Better not, man," said Calvin, "you'll mess me up good tonight." One of the white boys whooped, "Gonna mess up

your night plans, Calvin? Haw!" And he leaned all the way
over to slap the floor with both hands as he unloaded a long
guffaw.

After another moment, a white youth asked, in regard to the
game to be played the next week for the south Georgia AA
championship against the town of Statesboro, "Yawl played
their colored team last year, didn't you? What they like? They
any good?" And a black answered, "We gonna take 'em. They
tough, but we'll take 'em." When they finally wandered on into
the broadcast booth, a black player called Lightning hooted,
"Man, I'm gonna put on some *soul*. I'm gonna put on 'Heaven
Help Me.'" One of his white teammates said, "I ain't ever
heard of that one," and Lightning squawked, "Man, you mean
you ain't ever heard that done by Little Stevie Wonder? Where
you been, on the South Pole?" The white youth gave a faint
smile, "Well, yeah, I guess I have heard it before, but I just
couldn't understand the words too good. It's sure got a good
feeling to it, though."

"It's unbelievable," Mary Myers once reflected, "that in a
small town like this, whites and colored were living right together all these years without ever actually knowing each
other, doing anything together. But our own experience now in
school, it's bound to change the community when we get up
there—bound to open it up. Because we're going to know better." As it happened, the homecoming-dance crisis proved a
particularly protean event at Americus High. Charles Warren,
for one, later admitted, "People just weren't used to thinking
very carefully about how something we might do or say would
hurt a black man. We just hadn't ever put ourselves in their
place. If we had, we would have realized it was going to make
them mad, was going to hurt them, because it would have
made me mad."

What it all intimated, in the end, was that, through the simple happenstance of this fresh generation of Southern whites
finally and fully encountering the black Southerner, there
might at last be worked a release from that old curse enduring
from the South's aboriginal system of slavery: those myriad
and devious reflexes of mind, dullings of spirit, by which white
Southerners managed the necessary trick of transforming other
human beings into objects having no real connections to them-

selves. But of course, even while unrealized and unacknowl-
edged, the white and black Southerner had long ago become
one people. It seemed possible, then, in that fall of 1970, that
what was beginning to be transacted in the south was the
affirmation at last of their common identity.

It had always been the lot of the South to serve as the crucible
for the nation's ordeals of conscience over race. And if it remained true that a racial dichotomy was the single most profound crisis the country faced, then it could have been that in
goading and impelling the South toward an integration of its
people, the rest of the nation had actually been prompting the
South to deliver the entire country itself finally out of the danger of total racial schism. As with the schools of Americus, the
peril was that the impatience of blacks might constantly out-
strip the pace of what whites regarded as painful and substantial accommodations and accessions on their part. But through
the next two or three years, Americus and numberless other
communities like it over the South would be embarked on a
desperately critical and suspenseful voyage—and the real toll
and duress of that adventure was to fall on the students, both
black and white, whose lot it had become to purchase, with
their own patience and compassion and endurance and belief,
the future of the South itself.

In his law office that autumn of 1970, with the venetian
blinds of a window behind him opened to the yellow leaves of
a November afternoon, Americus Mayor Frank Myers conceded, "I can't deny to you that I'm still probably about 40
percent bigoted. There just ain't no way to grow up like I did
without having prejudices. All I can do is just fight 'em the best
I can. But I'll tell you one thing—my daughter, now, and my
two other kids, they absolutely rid of *all* of them." And just as
it took the passing of a generation during forty years in the
wilderness to purge the Israelites into a people prepared for
the Promised Land, Myers proposed, "It's gonna be our children finally who're going to deliver us out of this thing that's
been going on down here ever since slavery. They the ones
who'll do it. . . ."

That situation of 1970 has continued to hold, if not actually
improve, in Americus' schools, with blacks wholly involved
now in student government and extracurricular life, and no

260 □ THE RACIAL PASSAGE

defection of white students from the public system. In 1979, Americus High students elected a black homecoming queen, in 1978 a white; "They just sort of swap it back and forth each year," said one parent. In all, it has passed since 1970 from a matter of wonder to a matter of course.

An Alabama Marriage

> *Maybe in a thousand or two thousand*
> *years in America. . . . But not now! Not*
> *now!*
> —WILLIAM FAULKNER, *Go Down, Moses*

IT WAS ONLY one of many similar occurrences, back in that shadowy age in the South before the Civil War, that were never inked in spidery script into the front-leaf dynastic chronicles of the parlor Bibles. In this instance, it was the young heir of a thorny and grizzled old patriarch who presided over a plantation with a multitude of slaves down in a south-Alabama Black Belt community called Union Springs, and who, having already exhausted and buried several wives, was preparing to take yet another. A few days before the wedding, his son notified him that he was himself in love with one of their slave women, and meant to make his life with her. The father, in a reeling fury, dispossessed him, and promptly dispatched the female slave to another owner. The youth lingered until the day of the wedding. Then, during the marriage feast, he poisoned his father— and fled, vanished, never to be seen again.

Generations later—wars, occupations, movements, marchings, assassinations, countless tides of legislation later—on a bright and winey Saturday morning in the autumn of 1972, a trim pale young woman, herself a direct descendant of that dour and implacable slaveholder, was playing tennis with her husband in a city park in Tuskegee, Alabama. Raised on the same plantation site at Union Springs some twenty-five miles away, Frances Baldwin Rainer had been styled and toned according to the timeless protocols of Alabama ladyhood—the tidy decorums of her local Methodist church, the cavalier rituals of football weekends and Alpha Gamma Delta sorority dances at the University of Alabama, where she came to be called Tas. Married now three years, she had that medium unfocused prettiness generic to the Southern belle. Her two-year-old son—an elfin child with large luminous eyes, named John-John—was happily paddling about the swings and sand and slides of a nearby playground, while on the shaded court under tall hushed pines the spaced taut pongs of rackets echoed with faint rings, the ball drifting in long white soft blurs back and forth across the net in a measured and almost formal exchange, as calm and exquisite as a minuet, between Tas and her husband, Johnny Ford, who was the mayor of Tuskegee, and who was black.

It was quite probable that Johnny Ford's own forebears, as he pointed out, were among those slaves on the plantation of his wife's ancestors. A tall man in his early thirties, built with the sleek brawn of a welterweight, deeply and glisteningly black with a suggestion of a film-actor's handsomeness, he was quiet and self-contained in manner, spare of word and gesture —although given to a certain rainbowed Carnaby Street nattiness in attire. The son of a menial assistant at the local veterans' hospital, he grew up on the fringes of Tuskegee in a glum ramshackle neighborhood of water wells and scrap-plank outhouses, dishwater-puddled dirt yards, with a constant vague whiff even in summer twilights of smoke from unseen pine-kindling fires in dim back bedrooms. The city's park was segregated then behind a high, bleak stone wall that had the gothic look of a medieval rampart, with a dedication plaque mortared into a buttress by one of its iron-spiked gates, and Ford recalled, "I'd stare up at that plaque, with the mayor's name right up at the top there, and think to myself, *If that man can keep all of us out of this park, he must be one powerful dude. Yeah, that's what I'm gonna be, mayor of this town. . . .*" But that prospect could not have seemed then a more remote and implausible whimsy. Ford and his friends would sometimes climb a chinaberry tree by the park's wall to watch the scions of the town's white gentry playing baseball inside, "and I can remember," Ford says with a small smile, "how the white folks would point at us and holler, 'Hey, look a-yonder at those blackbirds up there.' "

*   *   *

Now in 1972, when one paused to take account of what had actually happened in the South in only the past fifteen years, history seemed to have somewhere, unnoticed, calmly somersaulted into realms of the psychedelic. It was as if, since those summers of danger and outrage in the Sixties, a whole century had quietly passed in the deeps of Dixie. The stumpy figure of George Wallace striking his sullen pose at a doorway of the University of Alabama in 1963 to deny entrance to two black students, all the convulsions and travails of those feverish days, seemed to belong to some lost simpler age. If nothing else, it left one at least with a hopeful suspicion of how ephemeral, after all, were the old human furies of intransigence and irreconcilability.

At the same time, many of the apocalyptic pronouncements of the brimstone-eyed segregationists of those days were, in a sense, actually turning out to be fulfilled—though not precisely in the way they had in mind. It appeared now that the South had all along held within itself, unuttered, the answer and resolution for its own ancient racial duress, not through sustaining and fortifying its old order of division, but in delivering itself at last into full daylight as the single society and single people, black and white, it had really always been, privately and tacitly and furtively, from its very beginning.

For the white citizens of Tuskegee, at least, being presided over by a black mayor married to a white woman would have seemed a realization of their most garish nightmares of the Sixties. But there had hardly ensued a stampeding white evacuation of the town. Over a cup of coffee one afternoon in a Tuskegee restaurant that had once been the local Klan lair, Ford himself was moved to speculate—after a nearby tableful of ruffled and talcumed white matrons had greeted him with a flurry of cordial chitterings—"I've long felt that the South is the real new frontier in this nation. I don't know if it's so true in the rest of this country, but there's been a personal relationship between whites and blacks down here for so long—lot of meanness in it, sure, but a lot of compassion too. Main thing is, it's been *warm*, you know, whether hate or love—it's been close and *personal*—and whenever you have that, man, that's when you got the only true and vital basis for achieving a real community, a real *human* society."

And even if there should materialize now in the South that last and most ominous hobgoblin in the conjurations of the segregationist exegetes during the Sixties—intermarriage—the particular marriage of Tas and Johnny Ford suggested that it would come with a surpassing normalcy, a casual ordinariness that, given the South's ferocious past, was yet spectacular. "I don't know, maybe some people are marrying now interracially because it's the politically stylish thing to do," said Tas, "and that's okay, I suppose, if it helps in creating a wider acceptance. But with me, it was just that Johnny happened to be the man I loved."

Like most small Southern towns, Tuskegee's square had at its center that runic totem of a Confederate soldier wearing a graven blind scowl, leaning on his rifle with a kind of Greek, slant-hipped languor. Immediately off the square, with its vast yellow-brick citadel of a courthouse horned with gables, the original residential streets led off under arches of water oaks like long still caverns, filled on summer afternoons with a green aquatic gloom, on each side the ranked galleries of discreetly moldering manorial homes from that lost age before the doomed gray Crusade, where on summer evenings old women would appear in the sideyards after supper, wearing shabby woolen shawls, their hair like dim white smoke in the twilight as they slowly floated among their gardenias and muscadine arbors.

For all that, Tuskegee had also long been something of an anomaly among the South's small communities. Reposing in its midst was the oak-shaded campus of Tuskegee Institute, founded in 1881 by former slave Booker T. Washington and his onetime slavemaster as a vocational school for blacks. Considerably amplified since then, with some 3,350 students, the college had provided Tuskegee with a black population notably more sophisticated and assertive than that in most other small Southern settlements. In 1966, on a gray wet morning after the fatal shooting the night before of a Tuskegee student, there was the then-extraordinary spectacle of Tuskegee's white mayor standing on the front steps of city hall with his three white councilmen in a prickling rain, before the bobbing umbrellas of some 1,700 students massed below, gamely mumbling his way through "We Shall Overcome" along with everyone else. "I'd never sung that particular song before," he confessed later as he sat in his dim clothing store just off the square, "so all I could do was just try to read their lips. I did the best I could, though, and I know the other fellas behind me fell in too, 'cause I could hear them—singing it real low." Some observers back then were already suggesting that the statue on Tuskegee's campus of Booker T. Washington lifting a cloak from the upraised face of a crouching freed slave could as well have had the figure of a white man kneeling beside that of the black. But as the mayor opined, "Trouble is, there's just a lot of folks here who, I gotta admit, still hadn't realized yet they were freed the same time the Negroes were."

Indeed, outnumbered by blacks about four to one, the mentality of most whites in Tuskegee during those days approximated that of the whites in Southern Rhodesia. As black voter registration gradually began to pull abreast of white registration, the reaction of local authorities was simply to arrange with the Alabama legislature for a redrawing of the town's boundaries—the result of which was a municipal map vaguely resembling a Picasso abstract of a chicken, but which nevertheless managed to place outside the city limits almost the total black population of Tuskegee. The town's lone swimming pool, after a court had ordered its desegregation, was found drained the next morning with its bottom strewn with garbage, cow manure, and puddles of sulfuric acid. And in a state which had compiled one of the heaviest records of lynchings to be found in the nation, a quiet and sedulous accounting kept since 1882 by Tuskegee Institute showed that most of those lynchings, both in Alabama and in Tuskegee's own Macon County, were precipitated by purported ravishments of white women by blacks and instances of interracial romance.

Tas' father, the principal public accountant in Union Springs, had himself been a robust member of the White Citizens Council, which constituted during that time a kind of white-collar, Rotary-version Klan. Tas sat with Johnny one evening in the primly neat living room of their small brick home, her pale face bare of cosmetics under her long sandy hair, and recounted how, as a little girl and her parents' only child, she had listened to her father's racial discourses with fellow townsmen over midmorning coffee in a Union Springs cafe, and had accompanied him on drives to Montgomery for conferences with the state senator from Tuskegee who was executive director of the Alabama Citizens Councils. "I worshiped my father then. I would never question what he said on such matters." One of his close acquaintances in those days was a clamorous segregationist judge in neighboring Barbour County named George Corley Wallace, who was producing an inordinate amount of smoke and noise for so modest an office— issuing injunctions against the removal of segregation signs in railroad terminals and threatening to order "the arrest of every member of the FBI or other federal police" who might turn their attention his way. "Of course, I strongly verbalized my own support for Wallace," Tas would later admit. "There's no question about it, I grew up thoroughly seasoned in all the prejudices."

After her father's death when she was twelve, Tas and her mother moved to Miami, but Tas eventually returned to graduate from Union Springs' segregated high school. When she entered the University of Alabama, as her father and grandfather had before her, it was during the high surgings of the civil-rights campaigns in the South. But Tas existed with her sorority sisters at the university in serene detachment. When the Selma-to-Montgomery march was proceeding like a huge motley pageantry of the American conscience just a two-hour drive from the campus, it simply never occurred to Tas that she had any reason to be there. She was, then, hardly one of the young partisans of those impassioned days—indeed, there was generally a peculiar absence of Southern youths among those great legions of intense young evangels who appeared over the land for a season. Tas' only real nudge out of the honeysuckle-perfumed coma at Alabama came from the rather soft-focused and airbrushed movie fable, *Guess Who's Coming to Dinner*. Even so, she would recall, "Discussing that movie with my sorority sisters, not even the most liberal and progressive of them could project themselves into that sort of situation except from the parents' point of view—you know, like, gosh, can you imagine what you would do if it were your child?"

With a degree in political science and history, though, she was not wholly without gutterings of altruistic sentiment. But unable to find any openings in Montgomery in the sort of mannerly social work she had in mind, it wasn't until she wound up by casual happenstance as a welfare case worker among the destitute in Tuskegee that she at last came by her own full illumination of conscience. "It suddenly became quite clear to me, because it was right there in front of my eyes, bodily and physically, day after day, what the civil-rights movement had actually been about all that time." She was commuting from Union Springs, where she was boarding with some old friends, and at a routine planning session between welfare agents and officials of Tuskegee's Model Cities program, she first met the program's twenty-eight-year-old director, Johnny Ford.

Ford had only recently arrived back home in Tuskegee after a long and circuitous pilgrimage of his own. He had grown up in an insularity as intact, in a way, as Tas': passage through the hermetic isolation of Tuskegee's segregated school system, then an academic scholarship at a small black college in Tennessee, where he played quarterback on the football team. But after graduation, "I headed straight for New York"—fleeing, like numberless other black youths in the South, from what seemed to him then the brutal and unalleviated exhaustions of his region. In New York, after a few uncertain weeks, he managed to acquire an assignment from the Greater New York Council of Boy Scouts as a street counselor in the grim precincts of Bedford-Stuyvesant. "There were a few knives pulled and stuff like that, yeah. But I could handle 'em, and they realized after a while, I think, that I was for real, that I actually cared." In fact, his conspicuous success invited the notice of aides to Senator Robert Kennedy, and before long, Ford found himself an advance strategist for black communities in the high political lyricism of Kennedy's brief barnstorming Presidential offensive. "I believed in that man," Ford later reflected, "and I can't stop mourning him. It still hurts. He was the best, like nothing we'd ever seen before or we've seen since. It's almost like he was too good and too fine to be allowed to last." Ford was in the throng tumultuously impacted in the hotel ballroom in Los Angeles when there came those light dull cracks from somewhere nearby. "What it sounded like, I remember, was just balloons popping in a corner. . . ."

When he finally returned to his hotel room several hours later, "all of a sudden I got down on my knees by the bed, like I hadn't done since I was a little boy, and I started praying. And I was still praying, still wondering all through that long flight back across the continent, *Oh, Lord, what's going to happen to this country now, who's left, Lord?*" Back in New York, he desultorily occupied himself for a while with work for the Humphrey-Muskie ticket. But "it was empty, man. There wasn't any meaning in anything up there anymore." And that Christmas, when word reached him that there was an opening in the Model Cities project in Tuskegee, he headed back home.

"In the beginning," said Tas, "if I had taken a step back and realized what our friendship might be leading to, I probably would have shied away in total shock. I don't think either one of us really recognized what was happening." They began seeing each other, casually and unobtrusively, at the home of mutual friends in Montgomery. Both of them were of rather subdued and reserved temperaments, and after a time, when in a kind of second take they began to sense the actual dimensions of their feeling for each other, they both recoiled. "I didn't have any doubt at that point about how I felt about Johnny," said Tas, "but it finally hit me what effect it would all have on the people I love, how many of them would be hurt." Indeed, by now certain appalled mutterings about Tas' attachment were rippling through Union Springs. "I started getting terrific pressures from down there, from my family and friends. It started just tearing me apart—after all, these were my people. I began to feel almost a panic to get out of it somehow."

Ford had already begun to entertain speculations about actually realizing now that improbable hankering of his boyhood—running for mayor of Tuskegee—and "I knew the fantastic hassle I'd probably have to go through with the black community over something like this." But beyond that, when he confronted the more personal implications of the prospect, he was left, if anything, even more unnerved than Tas. "I thought, wait a minute—what am I about to get into here, what am I thinking about? Oh, man—a mixed marriage in the South? In the Alabama Black Belt? I got to be crazy. Maybe somewhere else, but not here, not in Macon County, not yet. A thousand years maybe—but not now. I just don't need that kind of trouble."

At last, one chill autumn sundown, Ford bolted—pitched a few belongings in his car and, without a word to Tas, plunged on out of Tuskegee, heading back for the impersonal anonymous refuges of the North again, this time Chicago. "I called his office the next morning," Tas recounted, "and they told me he had quit, was already gone. It was hard for me to understand why he hadn't even said goodbye." But as Ford later explained, "It was pure simple flight. It had just gotten to be too much, I was running away from all of it, everything. That was the longest drive I've ever made, though, I can tell you that. I drove right on through the night, like I was afraid to stop until I got there or it'd catch up with me and I'd never make it—hitting those cold rains and sleets above Kentucky along about two or three in the morning, with that song playing over and over again on the radio, you know, 'By the Time I Get to Phoenix,' where the dude has cut out on his woman just the same way and he's thinking how she's gonna feel when she wakes up and he's gone. All the way my eyes keep filling up with tears, I'm holding on tight to that steering wheel and that song's playing on the radio and the tears are rolling down my face."

After only a few days in Chicago, he took to the road again, winding up once more in New York. But finally, after a fitful week there of pitching about between motel rooms and the apartments of friends, for the second time in his life Ford made the long journey back down into the wide mild countrysides, the old red earth and windless woodsmoke hazes of that region which had birthed him and which, only two weeks earlier, he thought he had forsaken forever, freed himself from at last. Back in Tuskegee, on a mellow October evening, he phoned Tas and said simply, "I want us to be married."

The next day, after separate blood-tests, Ford notified a local black minister to meet him that afternoon in the office of a school principal to perform a wedding service. Ford arrived before Tas, and the minister, glancing over the marriage license, suddenly gaped, and looked up at Ford: "Oh, my Lord, they gave you the wrong thing here—it says here she's white."

"She is," Ford said.

The minister's eyes glazed. When Tas appeared, he lurched on through the ceremony with his hands still trembling, his voice wobbling.

*　　*　　*

"What brought me back was just that old deep-down yearn-ing to want to be home," Ford later recounted. "I just realized that this was where my destiny lay for better or worse, and there was no point in trying to escape it. It happened to be both Tas and the South, Tuskegee—all of them together, however hard that was gonna be to work out. So I said to hell with being mayor if it comes to that, to hell with the criticism and whatever physical danger there might be, the personal life is more important than all that, we're gonna do what we want to do as two human beings. This is our country, these are our folks, and we were just gonna have to make it work here."

Tas recollected, "Sure, we told each other we could go someplace like New York or Chicago and just forget about all the special difficulties we'd face down here. The reason we didn't, though, is that both of us like home so much. . . ." After a pause, she added, "And there was the question of our children. Tuskegee has always meant so much to the black man, you see, and they would have a much surer and stronger sense of iden-tity growing up here than in some place like New York or Los Angeles."

Tas' mother, when phoned the news, was stricken and aghast. Communication with her was scanty for the first few months. "But", said Tas, "after talking to Johnny a little more, getting to know him as a human being and not just an abstraction, it was easy—she came to love him like her own son." Despite that profession by Tas, it remained a gingerly conciliation which never proceeded beyond the detached medium of telephone calls. Yet, Tas declared. "Just before she died, she learned we were going to have a baby, and she seemed very happy, very excited. That's the way it is, I think—most people down here just haven't allowed themselves to think about this one issue except in terms of dogma. When you're dealing with any situa-tion through dogma, you have to have some truly compelling personal need to overcome that dogma—and for my mother, that need was her love for me. It finally moved her out of all the old structures of prejudice in which she had lived almost all her life. She began to discover, almost at the last moment, the larger truths and feelings about people."

But acceptance by Ford's parents, as it turned out, was a

more difficult, grudging, protracted process. "I was aware his father was scared to death when he heard about it," Tas acknowledged, and Ford said, "They just couldn't quite bring themselves to believe it." Even three years afterward, there still lingered between Tas and Ford's family a certain elusive unspoken discomfort, a formal distance. Often, when they stopped by the general store kept by the elder Fords, Tas remained sitting in the car parked outside in the pebbled shadeless yard while Johnny took John-John in through the clapping screen door to see Ford's mother. A slight, wiry, puckered woman reposing in a cane-bottom chair back among the dim shelves of sardine tins and cornmeal sacks and snuff cans, she would instantly sweep up her grandson with a fierce cackling affection, snatching down a box of animal crackers for him. "Ain't you a fine-looking young man now! What you want now, John-John, you want that bag of tater chips? Here you are, hon, here you go. . . ."

Though none of their more dire expectations materialized, for all the quiet and almost mundane sedateness of their marriage, both of them still seemed to be dwelling together inside some enduring glass bell of apartness, always a faint distance removed from the common daily play of life around them. One afternoon, Ford was riding around town with his black councilmen in a Cadillac that belonged to one of them, the leading undertaker in Tuskegee. One councilman sitting up front by the window—a jaunty and cricketlike man with a dapper little flick of a mustache, his head barely bobbing above the seat—maintained a constant chirruping banter while waggling a panetela in the air: ". . . and something else, how come you reckon all our black women still wanna act so proper and high-and-mighty and what-all? White women now, they all liberated these days—yessir, they gotten out of all those hang-ups, man, they all wanna *swing* now, know what I mean? Yeah! White women these days, they ready to *play*! But Godamighty, our black women still think they gotta keep those knees tight together just like their mommas taught them to be nice ladies. . . ." Ford twisted a little uncomfortably in the backseat and merely gazed out the window with a vague grin, nervously fingering the knob of the door latch, while the councilman obliviously burbled on.

Sitting in his living room with Tas one evening, Ford professed, "Neither one of us has ever liked going out much. We'd usually just rather stay at home with each other." Every now and then, they were visited by former sorority friends of Tas', who with their husbands would present themselves with a certain bright glint of sheer curiosity in their glad-eyed greetings —these polite evenings passed in a rather strenuously casual cheerfulness, ending usually at a sensible early hour. Among the comments in Union Springs that were relayed to Tas was the sprightly pronouncement of one white dowager, "Well, there's really nothing new about it. It's just Romeo and Juliet all over again, only in black and white instead of Montague and Capulet." But Tas was given to understand that most of the townsfolk of her parents' generation had simply effaced her from their communal memory, abjuring any mention of her name.

Among the few occasions the two of them did venture out was to watch Tuskegee's football games. At one Saturday-night game in nearby Columbus, Georgia, Tas—surrounded in the stands by black faces—sat very still and composed, watching the field with a diligent concentration, seemingly impervious to the turning and tilting heads up and down the rows around her, the swift bemused glances. With a yellow Tuskegee-rooter fedora tucked a bit hastily and askew on her head, she produced at appropriate points through the game, along with everyone else, eager yelling cheers, but there was a slightly thin quality to her festiveness. When she left once to go to the concession stand, Ford, after only a few minutes, began glancing around for her uneasily, craning his neck to peer toward the booth.

Afterward, on the slow hour's drive back to Tuskegee, Tas took occasional small sips from a drink in a plastic tumbler, and confided now in the comfortable enclosed darkness of the car, "People watch you, stare at you, of course—but we hold our heads up high. You just get to the point where you don't notice. You can't afford to notice. We've got our life to live. Johnny said from the beginning, 'If somebody has a hang-up about us, that's their problem. If we start worrying about it, that's going to be our problem.' So that's become the way we are. Now, when people come up to me and say, 'You mean, *you're* Mrs. Ford?' what I think to myself is that it's probably because Johnny's so well thought of."

Ford had begun campaigning at full pitch for mayor only a few months after their marriage. "It was sort of a thunderbolt around here, I guess, and there were some folks who wanted to make Tas an issue. I didn't run away from it, because I knew we'd get eaten up alive if we tried to keep it under cover." As he anticipated, the backfire was particularly spirited from students at Tuskegee. "They on that pride kick, you know," Ford said, "which is fine and refreshing—I can sure relate to that. But I told them, 'Here we are, living in a city where folks are still hungry and without jobs and living in shacks, children suffering from malnutrition, and all you worrying about is the light shade of my wife's skin—and you trying to tell me what mean, bad revolutionaries yawl are?"

In the end, though, Ford had to run a statement in the local newspaper, in which he proclaimed with a rather novel directness to the community at large, "I wouldn't marry a black woman. I wouldn't marry a white woman. Instead, I would only marry the *Woman I Love*. . . . You might as well face it, people, that white folk ain't better than black folk, and black folk ain't better than white folk. We are all God's children— human beings. There ain't nothing wrong with racial pride, but racism is wrong whether it be by blacks or whites. . . . I am not married to a 'white woman.' I am married to Frances Baldwin Rainer Ford, who is intelligent, who is professional, who is sincere and who is a human being whose skin just happens to be white. To me, she is as lovable as any other lady on the face of this earth; and she is no worse or no better than any other person. What makes her special to me is that I love her, and she is the mother of our son, and she loves us."

Eventually, Tas herself set out on some door-to-door campaigning in the black community, and one black matron later enthused to Ford, "You know what? That was the first lady *ever* come around asking for the votes of us womenfolks." During his own rounds one morning, Ford paused before the long front walk leading across elegantly gardened grounds to the white-columned porch of one of the more majestic mansions on the outskirts of Tuskegee. "That was about the toughest little stroll I ever had to make," he recalled, "up there to knock on that door." It was opened by a finely frilled, rigidly erect grand duchess of a lady, and Ford, after hastily introducing himself and his candidacy, was turning to leave when, stunned, he suddenly realized she had invited him inside. They passed a genial half hour sitting in the front drawing room, discussing his campaign over a delicate tinkling of coffee cups.

Ford's opponent, the white incumbent, C. M. Keever—a tall bespectacled man with the punctiliously officious demeanor of a Presbyterian church usher—was the same mayor who, six years earlier, had sportingly faltered through "We Shall Overcome" while standing in the pelting rain on the front steps of city hall. Ford defeated him, but only barely—by a mere 124 votes. Somewhat less sportingly, Keever then promptly closed down his business and moved to another town.

But Ford's first year in office did not unfold altogether mellifluously. That spring and summer, three aging white women were slain in seemingly random and purposeless executions. When one of the two blacks arrested as suspects escaped from the local jail, Ford spectacularly affronted the black county sheriff who had custody by demanding that city policemen move in to guard the second suspect around the clock. (Ford also distributed a wanted poster in which he additionally noted, "We are asking for calm and cooperation from all citizens of Tuskegee, and please don't take the law into your own hands. . . . We shall continue to provide surveillance and protection of *all* our communities. . . . May God help us in this endeavor and soon bring peace and harmony to our community.") At the same time, with blacks now having largely inherited city hall and the courthouse, Ford wound up in the thick of an energetic intramural political fray between city and county parties over trivial powers and priorities. The black director of one of the county's antipoverty programs filed bribery charges against Ford, after Ford allegedly agreed to fire him as the federal government had requested in exchange for an increase in program funds. Ford denied the allegation and had the black director charged with trespassing, on the premise that he was illicitly occupying his office. With that, the circuit court clerk, a compatriot of the poverty-program director, loudly bruited it about that Ford "ought to step down. I believe he's sick. I feel sorry for the dude." All this unseemly disarray encouraged a lively gloating from some unregenerate segregationists, with one Alabama newspaper citing as a precedent the solemnly burlesque free-for-alls in *Amos 'n' Andy*. But as one veteran Southern journalist observed, "It's really a kind of left-handed compliment—it's like everybody's astonished to find that, after all the elevated saintliness of the Movement, now that blacks have moved out some of the old white courthouse gangs and taken over, dawggone if they ain't acting exactly like the white folks always did. They're turning out to be just as ambitious, just as contentious, just as human as everybody else."

But there also seemed to be a promise of gentle but significant differences in black proprietorships over small Southern towns like Tuskegee. There was only one white councilman left in Tuskegee by 1972—the last surviving relic of that original intrepid company which, through the Fifties and Sixties, had directed the town's dogged and unavailing legalistic trench struggles against the advance of full citizenship for its blacks. A short, elderly, somewhat papery man with a soft white patina of hair over his worn face, the white councilman was usually the last to appear at council meetings, wandering in late with a slow, faintly laboring shuffle as if moving against some opposing gravity, or in a different field of time. At one council session, immediately on taking his seat, he proceeded to smoke cigarettes with the same slow deliberation, an air of vague suffering, one eye squinting, totally abstaining from the commentary and discussion around, only grunting once to a query from a black colleague, "Naw. Yawl know more 'bout that than I do." Then, to a white visitor in the room, he quickly transmitted a furtive, wan wink.

The discussion around him, as it happened, concerned the proposed construction of a civic complex with a new city hall and community cultural center. One possible location was the town square, owned now by the local chapter of the United Daughters of the Confederacy; such construction would entail moving the square's Confederate monument to the cemetery. Ford had explained earlier that morning to a deputation of developers from Atlanta, "We do feel we have an unusually deep Southern heritage represented here—both as a mecca of black history with Tuskegee Institute, and also an exceptional heritage in antebellum white history, with so many of those fine old homes still standing. We are unusually rich in the culture of the South here, you see, so whatever we do with this center has got to be meaningful, we don't want it to be a Mickey Mouse thing with hot-dog stands and a merry-go-round. . . ." Ford now advised his council that the ladies in the UDC had passed on to him the somewhat poignant assurance that "they wouldn't stand in the way of anything if we felt it meant progress." The white councilman, slouched low in his seat, listened to all this drowsily, as if it were tiny meaningless sounds coming to him from some far planet. But a hulking black councilman beside him heaved forward, clasping his massive hands together and clumping them on the table as he rumbled, "No, no. We don't wanna mess with their soldier stickin' up there. We wanna just leave that alone—"

"How come we don't wanna?" shrilled the cricketlike councilman with the debonair little wisp of a mustache, tapping his panetela over an ashtray. "Cemetery out there be a better place for him anyway—"

"Naw, listen to me now. Let's just think about lettin' the fella stick on up there, and then if folks decide they wanna move him, we can go ahead. But we don't wanna get into that kind of business, you dealing with a special institutionalized thing belongin' to folks. You just got to realize how they feel about that thing. . . ."

Owing to approximately the same pragmatic computations that prompted him to support Nixon against McGovern in 1972, Ford during his first year as mayor managed to strike a particularly intimate entente with, improbably, George Wallace. In fact, many submitted that the South's bemazing metamorphosis over the past ten years, for which Tuskegee and the Fords served as a consummate metaphor, at the same time told of a private, obscure, but no lesss singular metamorphosis that had quietly taken place with Wallace.

"I don't know if he's really changed the way they're all saying he has," Ford offered, "but we've sure arrived at a good rapport. I just seem to get along with him. I think I understand him, and he understands me. Whatever, it's been a very lucrative relationship as far as Tuskegee is concerned. We've had about nine million dollars in industry steered in here so far. 'Course, associating with him like I have has cost me in terms of criticism, but it's been worth it. My hopes for building up this town are a hell of a lot more important to me than any amount of carping." When he was asked if he and Tas had as yet received an invitation to actually visit the mansion, Ford paused and then admitted, "No . . . no, I don't believe we have." Then, with a slow smile, he added, "But you gotta understand, any journey of a thousand miles—or a thousand years—starts with just one step."

Nevertheless, among all those spectacles in the South then with that air of historical hallucination, none were more stupefying than those involving Wallace—his affable appearance at a Fourth of July barbecue shivaree in north Alabama on a flag-festooned platform with an equally affable Senator Edward Kennedy; his midfield crowning of a black homecoming queen at the University of Alabama ten years after his doorway stand there; and then his exuberant presence at a convocation of black mayors at Tuskegee, eagerly grabbing hands with convivial grins and cozy little winks. At that gathering, Wallace chatted with Tas for a while about their origins in neighboring Black Belt counties, their respective kinfolks—reminiscing about Tas' father. Ford then introduced Wallace to John-John. Wallace, leaning forward in his wheelchair, gave John-John a quick tight little hug, and Ford said, "C'mon, John-John, give the governor some skin," and Wallace and John-John exchanged light soul-spanks with their palms. It was only an idle happening; but in such nuances—trivial, fleeting gestures in the air—are the rise and wane of whole social orders registered, the passing of ages and immense gear-shiftings of history affirmed.

Not long afterward, a multitude from all over Alabama converged into Montgomery for the Christmas wedding of Wallace's daughter—florid, loud princes of the state's country-club aristocracy, gowned debutantes pale as tallow candles, raw-hided political touts in rusty black suits from outlying courthouses—milling out of a cold blue twilight into the governor's mansion, their whoops and laughter ringing in its high grave rooms. And among those presenting their invitation cards at the white-columned portico and joining the assembly that evening were Tas and Johnny Ford.

Ford, reelected in 1976, continues as mayor of Tuskegee, with two whites on the city council. He and Tas have since had a second child—another son.

THE SOUTH
DOMESTICATED

AT A FIRELIT dinner gathering one black and icy winter evening on an Iowa campus during the mid-Sixties, a humanities professor inquired of a student from Georgia, with a faint wince of irritation over his brandy snifter, "But why is it all you Southerners like to cherish yourselves as a people somehow set apart from the rest of the country? Why is it all of you are always so obsessed with history, with the past? Don't any of you down there ever get tired of living your life in a museum?"

After a moment, the Southern student replied, "You know, I don't think we really do much anymore. I think all that is actually about over with."

Indeed, for many moons—from *Uncle Tom's Cabin* to the Montgomery bus boycott, from Stephen Foster to William Faulkner, from Gershwin lullabies to Harvard sociology seminars—the South provided the national fancy with a kind of running theater of the dreamy and fantastic: an alien summer latitude of flamboyant sentiment and sudden savage violences, hung always half adaze in the past.

But that was yesterday. For the last two or three decades, the South has been mightily laboring to re-create itself into a tinfoil-twinkling simulation of Southern California, and in the process has unwittingly worked on itself a species of spiritual impoverishment. It has been an inexorable scenario, of course: none are so abjectly giddy for the shimmery barbarities of progress as the provincially innocent. But in the almost touching lust of its chambers of commerce for new chemical plants, glassy-mazed office parks, and instant subdivisions, the South is becoming etherized in all those ways a people are subtly rendered pastless, memoryless, blank of identity, by assimilation into chrome and asphalt and plastic.

The downtowns of Charlotte and Columbia and Jackson have now become perfect mirror-tower reflections of Everycity, and out beyond their perimeter expressways, barbecue patios and automatic lawn sprinklers have pushed out the mules and moonshine shanties in a combustion everywhere of suburbs indistinguishable from those of Seattle or Minneapolis, an endless proliferation of neat dollhouses, suggesting the rampant and delirious vision of some motel architect, mostly populated by a transient race of middle-level executives for computer and chemical conglomerates who speak in regionless electronic tones. Below Atlanta, in the mythic landscapes of *Gone with the Wind*, one drives now through a Santa Barbara gallery of pizza cottages and pennant-flickering trailer lots, a "Tara Shopping Center" abruptly glittering with the mica brilliance of a mirage out of empty fields of broomsage and jack pine, the countryside beyond it barnacled with auto junkyards sunk in softly overwhelming kudzu. There is still a scattering of old pre-expressway motels with little wooden cottages nestled back in oak groves; one vacancy sign submits in tiny waggling letters,

Uor God s Still
Aliv
? How Abot Yurs ??

But the interstates now have razed their way on out into the last aboriginal outbacks of the South, and in all the Fox's Dens and Bali-Hai Lounges of the motels that have accumulated along their length, townsmen from the peanut gins and feed mills of nearby scruffy little communities—great-grandsons of Jackson's fance skirmishers and Jubal Early's mounted raiders, who were accustomed until recently only to the beercan-popping hoot and stomp of local pine-planked honky-tonks—gather on a Saturday night to roost, in khakis and clay-clotted brogans, in a windowless grottolike clandestine gloom lascivious with dim glows and quilted leather and a sweet whiskey-tinged must of the urbanely illicit, fingering damp paper napkins imprinted with raffish cartoons as they brood over their bourbon-

and-ginger-ales at the waitresses bobbling back and forth in
Bo Peep thigh ruffles and net stockings, all the while mulling
the savory intimations of secret abandoned sheet-thrashings in
the rooms along the rear parking lot, until inevitably one of
them, after a waitress' leggy passage by him, jumps atop a
table with a loud obscene yawp of supplication, and then, as he
is being herded toward the door by the manager, snatches up a
chair and sends it skidding calamitously down the length of the
bar with a parting bawl of outrage and longing—this, a hundred years later, about all that is left of those legendary heedless charges with wild gleeful yodels up the slopes of Cemetery
Ridge and Malvern Hill.

Over the South now, the holocaustic battlefields of that great
folk cataclysm have mostly been preened and mown into suburban golf courses and apartment terraces. There still gutter
intermittent ceremonies to remember: fiberglass-boat dealers
and air-conditioner salesmen costuming themselves over their
Hush Puppies in what resemble paper-doll cutouts of the uniforms of their Confederate ancestors to perform mummeries of
the primeval dreadful battles, with now and then those old
ferocities, as if fleetingly invoked by their miming, briefly and
bloodily intruding into the commemoration—a hand blown off
by an exploding rifle, an eye lost to an enthusiastically flourished bayonet. For the most part, though, the memory exists
only in perpetual reruns of *Gone with the Wind* in far-flung
suburban mini-cinemas.

A loss of provincialism is not necessarily a circumstance to
be celebrated. In the South's case, at least, it's turned out to be
more like a cultural lobotomy. The passing of a sensibility is an
event perhaps too nebulous to precisely gauge, but it is no less
seismic for that in its effect on the inner lives, the *geist* of a
people.

For instance, certain psychic diminishments have befallen
the South's progenital, grandly baleful Calvinism with its almost Aeschylean vision of humankind's lot as an immitigable
sentence of struggle and guilt and judgment and suffering on
this earth. Those cadaverous, chigger-bitten, malarial tabernacle evangelists who once presided over the South's religious
dramaturgies—in which the things at issue were such guttural

matters as whoring, drinking, blasphemy, doom, and brimstone, with the sweat and sawdust and glory of terrific, shuddering, gas-lit contritions—have mostly receded now into a tiny canned crackle of radio gospelteering at odd hours of the night. In their place, dapper and coiffured young men in horn-rim glasses who could pass for bank managers or department-store floorwalkers deliver each week, in briskly air-conditioned sanctuaries with walls painted in pastel tints of rose and blue, Dale Carnegie devotionals and toneless litanies of upcoming family softball games and waffle suppers. What the old fierce tragic theologies have dwindled to, in short, is the bumper-sticker sentiment seen on one station wagon in one outer suburb of Atlanta: PEOPLE OF DISTINCTION PREFER JESUS.

Indeed, what one hears tolling over the South now is a clinking of dullness. Massively and uncomplainingly, the whole land is being trivialized. With its passage into the ordinary urban ennuis of the rest of the country, its old racial derangements may have subsided somewhat, but most probably those lurid violences have only been sublimated into the inconclusive grumpiness of everywhere else. The South may seem more sensible now, less outrageous and troublesome to the rest of the nation; the difficulty, though, is that life, when it is most full and real, also comes most prodigally and dangerously mixed. In the process of its domestication, then, the South's old, fugal range of possibilities of life—both gentle and barbarous, lyric and brutish, good and evil—has contracted to the comfortably monotone note of middle C.

One young Atlantan finally evacuated his family from that city's outer suburbs back to one of those mellow little towns in the South's interior which, he assumed, would be one of those few last pockets in time where the past and the memory still lingered. But he found there the same eager, hectic clutter of pancake houses and shopping centers, merely a duplicate in microcosm of what he had fled. He shortly retreated, dispirited, back to Atlanta. "Hell, you talk about *Gone with the Wind*," he said. "Sherman and the Civil War were only an illusion, for all the smoke and roar. This time, without anybody even noticing it, it's really happening. The South is vanishing quietly as a passing of summer light—and this time, for good."

*　　*　　*

And yet: there remains, even with all this, a last and admittedly evanescent possibility that the South still holds at least potentially, within its past and its folk character, its own native answer to what has lately been happening to it—a possibility posed, for one, by the career of a solitary Southern gospel irregular named Will Campbell, as we shall see later on.

A Question of Plastics in Beaufort County

IN THE SOUTH, the land of Canaan came to consist of a horizon of smokestacks. Industrialization—the devout acquisition of factories—became a kind of second religion there: the secular fundamentalism. Faulkner's Flem Snopes was more than a literary invention: he was a historical cultural species in the South, and his heirs were those eager, sharp-eyed, checker-coated, rawly barbered, ruthlessly enthusiastic young men in the Jaycee chapters of all the dowdy little Southern towns, with sniffs of wilt along their quiet streets, that pursued with a poignant indefatigability their own factory as a sort of golden fleece, a Holy Grail, a deus-ex-machina deliverance from impending exhausation and extinction. In this desperation, they seemed willing to suffer the loss of any elegancy. When a paper mill was constructed in a little Alabama town some twenty miles from Montgomery, it tinged even the capitol's corridors, on especially muggy mornings, with a vague reek: Wallace, who was then governor, would note on such mornings, "Yeah, that's the smell of prosperity. Sho' does smell sweet, don't it?"

Probably no other Southern state was quite so evangelistic about industrialization as South Carolina. One reason might have been that it was a state which was more or less one large company town anyway, operated by an informal consortium of predominantly textile business interests with the fierce orderly privacy of a mill village—all civic irregularities and crises briskly attended to in a tidy prudent corporate manner, as matters of personnel relations. Probably as a result, South Carolina, throughout most of the decade of the Black Awakening in the South, never had the dark glamour of Mississippi or even

Harper's, May, 1970

the hot hasty dingy meanness of Alabama. It seemed merely to lack the vitality for any serious viciousness. It was as if its defense were a colossal torpor. Along with occasional visitations by Billy Graham and fracases over blue laws, the central obsession had been, in the words of one Columbia legislator, "our program of industrial solicitation. We've brought in a half billion in new industry each year since about 1959. But we haven't reached the point where we can relax this effort. No-siree."

The conventional celebration, then, was orchestrated—the governor, the local legislative delegation, assorted chambers of commerce, newspapers like the Columbia *State*—when a German chemical empire, Badische Anilin- & Soda-Fabrik, announced in 1969 it was establishing a formidable outpost along the South Carolina coastline: a $200 million facility for the production of dyes and plastics which would be the third-bulkiest industrial presence in the state. The site was a sprawl of eighteen hundred acres along Victoria Bluff in Beaufort County—property consisting then of little more than a few scattered thin dirt roads passing like tunnels through long grievings of moss, ending at the wide expanse of the Colleton River, into which, BASF projected, two and a half million gallons of treated waste would be discharged daily, emptying finally into Port Royal Sound. Eventually, it was also mentioned, a railroad spur would be laid to the site, docks constructed, and, with federal designation of the area as a free-trade zone and grant of an oil-import quota, a channel dredged for two-hundred-foot-long tankers bringing in forty thousand barrels of naphtha a day.

There were instant assurances that the complex would comply with the state's pollution regulations—which, along with its corporate tax exactions, happened to be among the most indulgent in the nation, devised as they were in the Fifties when the avidness for industry was at a high heat. These assurances were particularly facilitated by the industrious attentiveness of the Columbia *State*, whose headlong enthusiasm seemed to startle somewhat even BASF's officials. "We had a reporter from the *State* simply walk into our office in New York and tell us, 'Now, show me how you aren't going to pollute,' " cheerfully reported the company's American overseer, Dr. Hans Lautenschlager. "It's very unusual to have that sort of attitude in a newsman, you know."

But there were also, from the first, certain uneasy murmurs in Beaufort County itself.

The South Carolina coastline around Port Royal Sound was an uncertain and capricious play between land and water, still arrested at that moment in the history of the earth when the sea was just beginning, reluctantly and tentatively, to relinquish the land, a slight release and hesitation and change of mind still enacted there every day. Grassy marshes yawned off level and limitless, past solitary marooned islands of palm and pine, into low red sunsets—one of those plots on the planet where man was still incidental to nature, instead of nature being incidental to man, a condition which seems to work some subtle mystic dislocation in the species. Specifically, its tidal creeks—a myriad and ceaseless discreet ebbing, with the occasional tiny slow flapping of a seabird across bright open roofless glittering spaces—was one of the few untainted estuarine landscapes left along the Southeastern coast. But it's not so much nature as man's commerce which abhors a vacuum: Dr. Lautenschlager, a badgerlike and altogether genial man with prickly close-clipped hair and horn-rim glasses, agreeably explained, "We always felt that the U.S. as compared to Germany was somewhat underdeveloped—excuse me that expression—in the use of plastics. Because you wouldn't believe it, but from, I would say, Philadelphia to Miami, there is nothing. Really—no plastics plant."

The fact was, Beaufort County was underdeveloped not only in plastics, but in almost all other respects. Altogether, the county was probably one of the most abject and squalid crannies of the country, with perhaps up to 40 percent of the twenty thousand Negroes there—who made up about half the total county population—illiterate. Some nine hundred families were eligible for food stamps. South Carolina's Senator Fritz Hollings—a tall, glossy, tanned, silvered figure who spoke with the organ-tone rhetoric of the old summertime palm-fan South, but who was eccentrically given to certain liberal humors—took a stroll about the county once, peering in the doors of Negro shacks, and came away eloquently aghast.

Some six thousand jobs of the eleven thousand in the county—about half of this total employing Negroes—were involved with fishing and tourism, enterprises largely focused on one of the county's offshore islands, Hilton Head. The resort developments there were largely sanctuaries for retired executives and industrialists who had fled lands they had laid waste behind them in the North, along with retired military officers with ruddy tomato-faces and frosty mustaches, who would gather in madras jackets at dusk at the club bars. Autumn was an enchanted weather of winy dawns and musing warm days and chill sundowns, fine for bicycle riding. At Sea Pines Plantation, on the furthermost tip of the island, Rolls-Royces and Mercedes-Benzes glimmered leisurely along the quiet private roads through groves of high pines and palms and live oaks with moss like downstreaming smoke—beyond which, there were glimpses of fairways, as sleek as the flank of a fawn, on which golfers occasionally appeared, distant, miniature, trivial, and soundless, walking and stooping and then moving on, figures materializing briefly out of nothing and then, after a moment, vanishing idly and tracelessly back into nothing.

On the whole, confessed a local political manager, "We got a few very, very rich, and then we got a lot of very, very poor, and there's hardly anything in between there." The first euphoria after BASF announced its intentions was that the plant would pass a magic wand over the economy of the area, but more reflective souls recognized that most of the sparkle would fall on the fortunes of real estate brokers, insurance agents, and town merchants, without really sifting on down appreciably into the lower zones of destitution in the county.

Before long, though, it was more or less tacitly acknowledged all around that BASF would only be the inception, the genesis, of a vaster industrial center in the area. However, to the north of Beaufort County was North Charleston, and to the south was Savannah, both of them with doomsday manufacturing wastelands of smudged bleary skies, slag heaps, rank winds, and vile waters. With these unnerving apparitions on both sides, Dr. Lautenschlager was a bit delicate about projecting visions of Beaufort County as an industrial complex, but he still admitted privately, "Of course, we will expect that new industries will come in, mostly in the polymers field. Plastics lend themselves to the creation of other plants, and we will encourage these along." One young local politician frankly declared, "This is gonna be a disaster area if we don't turn it around. What BASF will mean ultimately is that we won't be a sleepy village any longer, with a lot of open spaces and untromped-on places. This just has to be. Change is inevitable, you know."

Perhaps, but for the matter of only months, that would have been the case.

More and more Americans had come to experience by now those small interior bites of despair at abruptly discovering jaunty new jiffy curb markets or jumbo variety stores, glad and glittering with pennants, along a roadside where the last time there had only been an empty cleanness of earth and sky. But suddenly, it seemed, all those random moments of dim private distress were gathering into a massive popular outrage, a new popular conscience and consciousness that accosted the old profound American ethic of progress; in the bright jubilant proliferation of prosperity and convenience—ground clearings, ribbon cuttings, plant dedications, drive-in openings—a certain barbarism was now being sensed.

At a meeting of the Beaufort County Retirees' Association, one man arose and began in a voice like a slow rattling of paper, his fingertips faintly fluttering on the back of his chair, "I've been hearing all my life, since I was a young man, I guess—you get industry in, and life's gonna improve, life's gonna be brighter. Well, I've never seen it yet. All my life, I waited for it to happen, but I never saw it. Oh, there might be a lot more money, but it seemed things just got messier at the same time. Now they're saying bring this big industry in here too, everything's gonna be brighter. What I want to know is— when's it supposed to happen?"

What soon appeared on Hilton Head was the kind of spontaneous eclectic popular resistance, a makeshift hasty collaboration of the most disparate interests. BASF found improbably ranged against it, pressing an offensive of lawsuits and petitions and demonstrations, a miscellaneous assortment of housewives, professional men, retirees of both opulent and modest circumstances, black fishermen, rumpled young field commandos from the Audubon Society and Friends of the Earth, and certain local nabobs, including Charles Fraser, the brisk cherubic young developer of Sea Pines, and Fred Hack, an older and somewhat more weatherworn squire who owned much of the island, and who, with his Port Royal Plantation, had been doggedly battling to keep pace with Fraser.

A long and gawky figure with stray tufts of graying hair, Hack had remained fairly homespun in manner and conversation—given to that immemorial feint of his slow sly kind, "I'm just an ole country boy"—since he had arrived as the island's first developer twenty years before, coming over on a barge with his family to set up a timber operation. "I finally got a bridge built," he droned, "and then Charlie Fraser came over it." He still had a certain feudal sense of proprietorship about the island and its affairs, and lived in the aged house in the interior of the island where he had originally settled with his family, a white wooden edifice with mammoth fireplaces and long polished halls and a huge iron cooking range in the kitchen. In his generous living room one evening, he dismounted from a ladder where he had been hanging new curtains (he had forgotten to open the chimney vents in the fireplace several nights before after starting a booming fire for a party) and sat to talk with a pair of visitors regarding the advent of BASF six miles up from his island, gulping occasionally from a kitchen glass filled with Sprite and vodka. "That plant's not comin' in," he peacefully allowed, with an almost childlike simplicity in his voice. "Nothin' like this can happen to *me*—I just know that. I survived diphtheria when I was five years old, so I can sho survive this thing."

On another evening, a large number of islanders gathered at Fraser's Hilton Head Inn after their suppers, a freshly showered, tanned assembly in citrus-colored golfing sweaters and canvas shoes, sitting in a powder-blue chamber with potted plants, where they were to be addressed by a young state legislator from Columbia named Alex Sanders. An ample, panda-like thirty-one-year-old attorney with shaggy hair and a relish for the droll aspects of life, Sanders was a premature occurrence in South Carolina of the phenomenon of the New Populism, and had come to be regarded a bit askance, as a faintly dangerous aberration, by most of his colleagues in the house. He had once introduced a resolution—and passed it—that provided that at no time would the total membership of all legislative committees studying agriculture in the state exceed the number of farmers in the state—offering this after briefly contemplating another measure which would have stipulated that at no time would the membership of any state subversives-control board exceed the total number of subversives, including Communists, in the state. One bone-cold February night in Columbia, at a parlor gathering of state political brokers swishing tumblers of bourbon before a quietly muttering fireplace, Sanders was dismissed as "too inclined to take on these—uh—*quixotic* kind of causes, and just a little too *amused* by the serious business of politics." In the context of that evening, it was an endearing dismissal.

Sitting now in the audience at Hilton Head Inn before he spoke, Sanders grunted, after a glance around, "Lot of pretty people here tonight, ain't there?" A moment later, taking the lectern, he announced, "I wish I could tell you I have come to save you from this noxious threat to your well-bein' and peace of mind. But the candor of the hour requires me to tell you I am not concerned with you assembled here tonight." An uncertain hush settled over the floor. "I have looked beyond your beautiful homes and unpolluted golf courses. It's possible to replace those—but it's not possible to replace this beautiful Port Royal Sound and the fragile life-balance of these estuaries." At this, there was a relaxing release of rich approving applause. "The reason I bring you this message," Sanders continued, "is not to insult you. It's just that this issue won't be decided on preserving these homes and golf courses, but on a larger national scale . . . and in the course of this fight, you are likely to come into contact with those beyond your normal personal relationships."

For that matter, a number of those directing the front against BASF, like the people in the room that evening, were not particularly accustomed to having been on the sunny side of any recent national issue, and they seemed not quite able to trust the fact that, at least in terms of the national press and the liberal respectability, the conventional conscience of the country, they had somehow landed now on the side of righteousness. They thus proceeded with a certain awkwardness, with much the same instinctive conspiratorial furtiveness of their long rearguard wilderness action against all the massive marches of history since, for some of them, Roosevelt. When a young painter on the island began to assemble demonstrations at the plant site, it was suggested by a few residents that such a dramatic exercise might be "undignified." Other parties sought to engage in some of the more customary ploys and private arrangements of the old system, and one young conservation activist emerged from a session with this faction and snapped, "I feel like I ought to take a bath." But the resistance promised to survive such uneasy associations. Demonstrations continued through March of 1970 at the plant site and the BASF suite of offices on the island—mixed, ecumenical processions of Junior League matrons and black fishermen, long-maned college students and retired colonels in long-billed mesh fishing caps and khaki trousers. As one of these marches was breaking up, a young mother with a sign was asked if she had ever done anything like that before, and she sang, "Why, Lord, *no!*"

But the black fishermen, who after five years of struggle had finally begun operating successfully as a cooperative, were caught in special complications. As Tom Barnwell, the executive secretary of the co-op, explained it, "How the hell am I gonna be able to get out there picketing against BASF without also picketing against the welfare system and the political system and all the other pollution like that in this county?" However, they regarded themselves as menaced by the plant more critically and immediately than anyone else, and they finally sued for a moratorium on the plant's construction until extensive laboratory tests could confirm it posed no danger. But BASF—sensing now intimations of disaster should it be temporarily stalled—became particularly adamant on that point. "A moratorium is completely out of the question," snapped Lautenschlager. "We reject it. And everybody else rejects it. . . . The governor has said it is un-American and unjustified, and there is no legal possibility for it as far as I know."

But the confrontation at Hilton Head happened to be taking shape in a new, uncertain moral twilight-zone. John Gadsen was a young black who directed a job-placement center for the black community around Beaufort, and as he coldly eyed the issue, "BASF isn't going to mean that much to my people around here, I know that. It's the industry they'll bring in after them which will transform the whole economy of this area. That's the choice we've got to make—are we going to industrialize, or do we stay this quiet little peaceful area. It can't be both ways. These waters are going to be polluted, no doubt about that. And the people against it are saying now, if BASF doesn't come in, they'll open up other jobs without pollution. Well, one of our girls we sent out the other day on a waitress job was offered twenty-two cents an hour plus tips—if that's the kind of thing they're talking about, forget it. No, when it comes to a choice between the people I know who have to make it here on food stamps, who're still living like they've been living for the past hundred years, or whether we're gonna keep all these pure waterways and beautiful marshes and wildlife, all this wonderful scenery—I got to go with the people. If I got to put the oyster beds up against people, the oyster beds have got to go."

It was a rather forlorn set of alternatives. But other black leaders on the island regarded the advent of the plant with a special foreboding. South Carolina was a society whose politics had always been precipitously susceptible to the influence of the business estate, and the enormous presence of a firm like BASF had unsettling implications. Tom Barnwell of the co-op said flatly, with an angry brightness in his eyes, "We've just begun to work up a little bit in the politics of this county and this state, but this deal—the power you talkin' about here— will put us right back into slavery."

All the clamor caused considerable dismay among the country's establishment; as one of its spokesmen philosophized, "We just want all this damn fuss to die down." The executive director of the county development commission, Eddie Boyer, a man of slightly dusty and crumpled appearance with an expression of drowsy agreeableness, lamented, "Old ladies come into my office cryin', I tell you—chins quiverin'—and commence to tell me, 'Eddie Boyer, I'm gonna take up a collection in this town and erect a statue to you as the man who ruined Beaufort County.' I been here for thirty years, and have tried my best never to make an enemy, to get along with everybody —wasn't any home in this county I didn't feel I couldn't go into and be welcome. But now, people don't like me. I been in the hospital three times over this thing."

In the face of this unaccountable popular ambush, all the conventional rationales and enthusiasms were being energetically invoked. The director of the local Office of Economic Opportunity, a white, fortyish, chipper erstwhile Baptist preacher with a face tanned like a dye tint and a small cherry bulb of a nose, attired in a snappy black-and-white-check sport coat, drove a visitor along on a road on the outskirts of Beaufort lined with hamburger drive-ins and trailer parks and billboards and power lines under tatterings of moss: "Wasn't anything out here before, and now we got a nice new li'l shoppin' center along here, it's grown up real nice out here. I don't understand all this hollerin' about BASF. Why, I've seen estimates it'll mean probably one thousand more automobiles in the county alone. . . . I've said from my pulpit a million times, Beaufort is the virgin territory between Miami and New York." One Beaufort booster burbled, "They talk about alterin' the *look* of the place, the environment. If you want to know the truth, lot of plant grounds you see now are actually prettier than country-club grounds."

To counter this particular perspective, the melancholy case of the Tenneco plant was often offered—a similar facility established some years before along a tidal creek on nearby Dafuskie Island with the most fulsome and unequivocal assurances that there would be no contamination. Not quite two years later, a landowner with property along the creek noted that the marsh grass was withering away, and when he called in two scientists to investigate, it was discovered that vast concentrations of acid had been flushed into the waters there, corroding oyster shells and exterminating all mussels in the stream. Somehow, then, the breezy assurances that were being produced to answer the alarm tended to be not enormously reassuring. "Tenneco?" asserted the OEO director. "They say that the area over there at Tenneco is ruined? That ain't ruined—there's green grass growin' up to twenty-five yards of where they say the ruin is."

BASF officials also cited their scrupulous compliance with the antipollution standards in New Jersey, which did not spectacularly comfort the refugees from New Jersey in the area, nor others who had simply made the drive from the Newark airport into New York through one of the most obscene landscapes on the face of the earth. At the same time, BASF declared natural unindustrialized zones would be left along both the riverfront of its property and the road front; but when a local political apologist promised one civic meeting, "I'm sure that what goes on two or three miles back there from the highway will be virtually unknown and unobservable," it only deepened the frowns, narrowed the squints of those in the audience.

At a hearing finally before a legislative committee in Columbia, local proponents of the plant unwittingly added extra resonances to all the misgivings. The president of the county's chamber of commerce, a rangy and bony man who stood rigidly straight with his hands shoved deep in his pockets, clipped, "You fiddlin' with an opportunity that may be gone forevermore. . . . As far as this pollution is concerned, we've gotten assurances from the governor on down there won't be any pollution. . . ." At this, there was a tide of laughter from the galleries that even spilled over the floor, and the fellow plunged on back to his seat. He was followed presently by a modishly groomed, resolutely casual chap who introduced himself as the next mayor of Beaufort and proceeded to smilingly dismiss the issue of pollution as a matter of any real gravity: "Why, some of the best bass fishin' you'll find down there is right at the mouth of the Savannah River, which is the most polluted river in the state. . . ."

For that matter, virtually the whole political structure of South Carolina—from the impending mayor of Beaufort all the way up to the governor, Robert McNair—was committed to the plant and the immutable doctrine of "industrial solicitation." Senator Hollings, one figure of some heft who might have been expected to intervene at least on behalf of a construction moratorium, was somewhat seriously compromised by the fact that "industrial solicitation" was never a more feverish obsession than during his own term as governor. At a meeting of retirees in the Beaufort area, held in a country club with mint-green cement-block walls, one young local legislator proposed, "The concern over pollution now, it's certainly the sensible thing, and certainly now the *popular* thing, and the thing that's in the headlines. . . . But we have laws to protect us on this, and have had them on the books since the nineteen-fifties." When he was finished, a tall crew-cut man lunged to his feet and fairly blared, "Yes, and just a few years ago we had the same assurances on the Tenneco dye plant. They said they absolutely would *not* pollute the area. It was crammed down our throats, and they built their multimillion-dollar dye plant. So what happened?" The young legislator wanly submitted, "Well, you can't say absolutely-positively nothing's gonna happen. . . . I mean, you can't get out here and drive to Columbia and say absolutely-positively an accident's not gonna happen. . . ."

While BASF had assumed by now a high piety probably unprecedented in anti-pollution projections by industry, Dr. Lautenschlager himself still acknowledged, "We can't guarantee against accidental spillage from our plant. We can't guarantee against accidental spillage from tankers, because we are not in control of them." That was precisely the anxiety of a number of people in Beaufort County and over the state, including Representative Sanders—whether an accident could actually be afforded. Speaking to a state house committee after introducing a bill calling for a moratorium on the plant's construction, Sanders proclaimed, "Gentlemen, there are four estuaries in South Carolina—bodies of water uniquely constituted on this planet, with a sensitive balance of life there crucial in the biological chain of existence. Two of those estuaries have already been destroyed now by pollution. Port Royal Sound is one of the two left. No one knows without the facts at hand what the results of the location of that plant will be. But it is a matter of historical fact that when the process of industrialization devolves itself upon the underdeveloped people of this earth, those people lacking the sophistication of urban societies can be depended on to become so enamored of the shiny machines and the gold and silver it promises as to ignore sophisticated concepts of an undisturbed ecology. The Southern European peasant with a newly acquired automobile will stand in the street and fondle his machine while goats defecate in his house. And make no mistake about it, as compared to the highly industrialized society of Western Germany—the fatherland of BASF—the coast of South Carolina with its poverty and great expanse of virgin land is viewed by many as nothing more than another emerging nation whose people are for exploitation and—more important—for sale. But gentlemen, you and I know South Carolina is different. We have steadfastly demonstrated that our birthright is not for sale for a mess of pottage. We are not Southern Europe." Despite that last distinction, the word was spread by the plant's advocates back in Beaufort that Sanders had testified their county was populated by peasants who stroked their cars while livestock leisurely puddled their front parlors.

As it happened, with all the unanticipated high attentiveness to the affair, some members of Beaufort County's local legislative delegation found themselves caught in certain positions of rather specific intimacy with the plant—quiet arrangements which, in the past, had been more or less a matter of course in the customary discreet incest between the state's political and business interests. A member of the state house, W. Brantley Harvey, Jr.—a lean young attorney with a taut jaw and curly ashen hair and a quality of faintly mournful deliberateness about him—had, it turned out, been acting as counsel for BASF, clearing the way legally for its arrival in his district, the fee for which would amount to something like $25,000 in the first year of his service. (He also had as clients the South Carolina Gas and Electric Company and Tenneco Chemicals.) Another member of the house, Representative Wilton Graves, a reedy man with thinning hair who often holed up in his motel on Hilton Head, twice renewed an option he enjoyed on one-third of the property adjacent to the plant site, and then, after BASF made its decision to locate there, exercised the option.

Not long after BASF declared it would locate in Beaufort County, there was a deer hunt on the property site, the party including Dr. Herbert Ende, who would be the plant's manager, and the district's state senator, James M. Waddell, whose occupation in addition to legislation was selling insurance. Before they set out one frosty morning, Waddell, already a bit radiant and effusive despite the early hour, turned to Ende, draped his arms around his neck, and trumpeted, "Herbie, I love yuh! I just love yuh!"

As for the Germans themselves, they seemed, more than anything else, utterly befuddled by the outbreak of popular opposition. They had proceeded in all innocence on the natural assumption that the old theology of industrialization still prevailed, the old combinations were still viable. All the proprieties and mechanics had been attended to. "I was led to believe everyone had accepted the idea," said Dr. Lautenschlager. "I don't understand this. It was completely under control." According to one of the firm's public-relations deputies, a strapping blond apple-cheeked Berliner named Dietrich Rogala, it was all simply a question of "Facts! If everybody would just keep to the facts, there would be no trouble. Facts. But all this emotion—my God!"

They had installed themselves in a corner suite of offices in a newly erected one-story building near the island's main shopping area. A visitor there one morning found Dietrich and his colleague, an older, darker, and somewhat quieter man in a gray tweed suit named Fred Jacobson, and their secretary, the three of them rather awesomely alone in large rooms furnished with only a few desks and chairs, the wide walls around them blank and still smelling wetly of plaster. Looking a trifle alien and stranded, they nevertheless maintained a lively doughtiness. "Why is all this trouble, hunh?" demanded Deitrich pleasantly. "Do you think maybe it is we are foreigners? A little bit of that, hunh?" While Jacobson smiled thinly and politely from behind a desk, Dietrich rumbled, "In Germany, we welcome foreign investment with open arms. So why should there be all this here? We maybe finally take this up between Bonn and Washington, hunh? The American companies there, the bases—they will have to go back home. Hunh?" It was as if a Teutonic bunker psychology were already beginning to set in. "Nothing matters, we *will* build our plant," Dietrich boomed.

Later that afternoon, they drove out with the visitor to the plant site, confessing, "We haven't seen it ourselves, actually." (Earlier, when Dietrich had driven over to the island from Beaufort, he had been stopped for speeding by a highway patrolman, and as he reported with considerable gusto afterward, "I showed him my license—what is this, he says, *Berlin, Germany*? With—what? Badi—Badische—what? I told him, perhaps you can work for BASF, hunh? I left him very friendly, but I was something quite new for him, I am sure.") As the car pulled off the highway down a dirt aisle beneath phantomlike taperings of moss, Dietrich breathed, "Fantastic! Unbelievable! Jacobson, I believe I like our property we have bought." When the car reached a cable strung across the road, Dietrich heaved out and began struggling to wrench up a post to which it was fastened, and Jacobson, watching him still with his quiet flat little smile on his face, mused, "He is from Berlin. He is very enthusiastic, no?" The road ended at the far shimmering sprawl of the Colleton River, at a bluff of gaunt dead trees from which there drooped rags of moss, under a cold sky uneasy with a low steady vast flight of sunless clouds, a solitary hawk hanging in taut weightless suspension overhead. After standing at the edge of the bluff in the sharp wind for a few minutes, during which the apple-stain in his cheeks paled a bit, Dietrich—shuddering, his hands deep in his pockets—abruptly declared, "Well, gentlemen, it all looks wonderful. Excuse me, I believe we will go back to the car now." Returning to the highway, Jacobson eased the car with small deft turns of the wheel through low bogs in the road left by a recent rain, and Dietrich lunged forward from the back seat to remark, "Jacobson, the way you are handling that wheel—I think you must have driven a tank, no?" Jacobson, with only a barely perceptible tension in his jaw, replied quietly, "No. Oh, no. I merely did a lot of walking. I only did ride one once," and Dietrich happily thundered, "Yes, they called those Panzers, did they not? Panzers, yes?" Jacobson, his head only slightly thrown back, his mouth open, uttered a light soft laugh, more like coughing, and kept his eyes on the road. His knuckles merely whitened briefly on the rim of the wheel. . . .

The truth was, as their company now undertook to steer its plant through the larger bogs of unexpected and still brooding rains of protest, knuckles were whitening on wheels all the way up to New York, their American headquarters. They soon decided to jump up initial construction, and by March there could already be heard a distant clank and whining of bulldozers deep in the pines of their property.

Meanwhile the resistance in Beaufort County was encountering the central complication of the lack of any palpable demonology, the element of a recognizable personal villainy. The effects, the multilations and outrages, were plain enough, but trying to confront those responsible and answerable for it—corporations, county zoning boards, bureaucracies, all with their nimble pieties and postures of sympathy—was somewhat like trying to engage a vaguely malign fog. The question was whether the theatrical dynamics of the issue—which are essential to any popular issue—could survive this diffusion of the identity of the guilty. If it should, that would have also promised, by extension, a possible general perceptiveness eventually beyond *all* glib dissembling, all medicine-man rhetoric—that syntactic game which was the refuge of a whole legion of interests in our society, including officialdom and corporate apologists and the Pentagon and Madison Avenue alike, those recommending titanic excitements over such cretinous trivia as toothpaste ("Daddy! The dentist said I had no cavities!"), underarm sprays, laundry soaps, soda pops ("You've got a lot to live! And this one's got a lot to give!"), all those interests only able to survive in a nihilistic void between word and reality. (The danger was that they would draw us all into that void.) In a way, perhaps the pollution, the devastation of the language was also ultimately involved.

At the least, in the effort against pollution at Hilton Head, parties were getting together who had never been elbow to elbow before: a peculiar, erratic, still-faltering communalism between citizens up to then hopelessly alienated from each other—radical activists and establishment Brahmins, students and the aged, all of whom would now at least have a new understanding of each other's nerves, languages, since they had, on the issue of ecology, worked on common terms with a common urgency. One Hilton Head resort dweller in his middle years phoned an Audubon Society activist in Florida and ventured, "Uh—listen, are there any more outside agitators down there that you suppose you could bring up here to help us with this thing?" Also, implicit in the issue were certain final questions about our entire system, our habits of managing ourselves. In the crisis, not only in Beaufort County but over the new South and the rest of the nation, citizens were encountering a number of ghosts from the nation's origins—in particular, citizens began to sense the portion of simple sweating greed and rapacity that had actually been at play in the romance of the frontier, the expansion into the West.

But in Beaufort County, it boded to be not the least of the ecological issue's gifts if, in the Noah's Ark gathering of all those disparate elements who wished to survive the perils of development, certain illusions and suspicions about each other would be dispelled. And, supposing that Americans on the whole were still incorrigibly people of good will, in that familiarity and fellowship could lie the inception, both in the South and the nation, of a new community of vision and compassion necessary for the true civilizing of the land.

As it happened, only a few weeks after Representative Sanders introduced his bill for a moratorium on the plant's construction, there took place a sudden evacuation of BASF personnel from Beaufort County. "We just woke up one morning," says a South Carolina official, "and found they had all checked out of their motels down there." A short time later, BASF announced that its project had been "indefinitely post-

poned." Nothing has been heard from them since, and the state has reclaimed the property along the Colleton River.

The prospect of industrial estuarine contamination, though, has subsequently been replaced by a spreading pollution of oyster beds from the bright trumpery of tourist facilities now barnacling Hilton Head Island.

Tracking Sin
in the New South

AT THAT SMOKY HOUR of summer sundown out in the weedy
south fringes of Atlanta, he seemed from a distance no more
than a young man in a knit golf shirt lingering outside a small
auto-parts office, chatting with someone in a powder-blue station wagon. He was standing by the car in an easy slouch,
lightly tossing something—keys or a lighter—in one hand,
while late-afternoon traffic whisked windily past on the highway and the empty sky waned toward night beyond the power
lines and tin-sheeted warehouses, neon signs presently stammering on at a nearby shopping center.

In an olive-brown Impala parked off alone in a far corner of
that shopping center, a small thin man in blue jeans muttered,
"Yeah, that's him." He lowered his binoculars for a moment,
glanced around, and then lifted them delicately again for another long peer. "That's our boy. Sho is. I can tell just by how
he stands—I know him by the way he holds his body. And
that's her station wagon, too, by God. That's her in there for
sure. . . ." Slumped low behind the steering wheel, appearing
somehow to be huddling behind the binoculars, he went on in
the rapid, eager whisper of someone smuggling out a dramatic
confidence, "They definitely having some sort of confab. Notice
those backlights—something's not settled, the way her foot's on
that brake. No doubt about it, they deep into that screwing
syndrome—she wants to get laid tonight, but he's telling her he
can't, something's come up, and she's not a bit happy about it.
It's heavy, man. 'Course, true love's always heavy." He suddenly dropped the binoculars to the seat and scuffled forward
to snick on his car's ignition as, in the distance, the station
wagon now began backing to turn into the highway. "Yes in-

Esquire, December 1975

deed, never so heavy as when it's got that extra tang of the illicit."

Few there are among us who have not at least fleetingly imagined that we might—*God, what if!*—be under such scrutinies. Larry Hicks (an alias, he asking that his and all other names in this story be disguised), at thirty-five a slight man, quick and wiry as a squirrel, with rather the look, in a lumpy cap and with a two-day soot of beard, of an aging urchin from that delinquents' fantasyland in *Pinocchio*, happened to be the phantom goblin, in reality, of all those chill and wayward little hauntings. He was, in fact, the man we've feared was watching us.

These moments of dim unease are, quite probably, about all that is left now of that old archaic dread, in another stauncher age and in our own lost Sunday-school childhoods, about the vigilant and unblinking gaze of the Lord, when not a sparrow fell without His notice, the very hairs of our heads were numbered, all our deeds were implacably inked into the Big Ledger for a final accounting on the Day of Judgment. As one of Graham Greene's capsized clerics somewhere ponders, "There were no detectives in the Age of Faith. . . . God used to be the only detective when people believed in Him." But Larry Hicks and all his many obscure colleagues, all the plumbers, political or personal, had become something like the inheritors, by default, of that old omniscient Eye on high: the anonymous bookkeepers of the inner heart's most furtive secrets, the unseen recording angels now of sin and guilt and retribution.

For sixteen years, Hicks himself, like some attendant sprite of the illicit, had been the witness unawares, the secret sharer of countless assignations and mischiefs in south-Florida motels, Memphis warehouses at midnight, even once a leprous resort along the lost wild cliff-coasts of Mexico. ("Runaway Junior League housewife that one was, run away about as far as it's possible to get from all that. Found her barefooted, in beads, playing a flute among the flies.") Compared to the conventional dramatic pop image of his kind—such ponderously jaded knight-errants as, say, Gene Hackman in *Night Moves*—Hicks suggested more some vagrant jockey. Or, in the black wool-knit dockworker's cap which he was especially fond of affecting along with dark glasses, a slightly dissolute leprechaun. A wispily boyish figure—bowlegged, with an elfin energy in the

eager scamper of his moves and banter—he was disposed to
snug short-sleeved alligator shirts, pipe-stem denim trousers,
straggle-laced tennis shoes, togs reminiscent in all of a
grammar-school playground. In fact, he had about him the
slightly frayed innocence, the discreetly damaged freshness of
a choirboy gone truant—his quick, glittering eyes only a little
elusive and murky now and then in the early glare of morning,
his hand only faintly trembling when he lighted his cigarette,
lifted his cup of coffee. He happened, though, to possess a
singularly canny and articulate insight into his particular place
in the times.

Snuggling on his dark glasses, he swung out into the traffic a
few cars behind the station wagon that lilac late afternoon in
Atlanta, while he offered, "It's nothing but paranoia that keeps
me and nine-tenths of all other detectives in business these
days—a mixed blessing, in a way, because it's gotten a lot
harder to work cases, since whoever you're following is also
thinking along those lines. Everybody's seeing double now—in
fact, quadruple. It's like a fuddled television picture picked up
from a station a long way away, with all kinds of wavery ghosts
around the figures—nobody knows which of the ghosts is the
actual image. The thing is, we just about been turned by the
megacorporations into one big coast-to-coast suburban office
park and shopping center, it's all gonna be Los Angeles soon.
And what that's brought us is a general case of the Los Angeles
dreads. Nobody's able to relate to anybody else any longer.
God's not around anymore, and nobody knows what's actually
happening to 'em now, or who anybody else really is. Everybody's living in their own little sealed cellophane bag."

In this collective winter of alienation, then, it was as if the
only intimacies left were the meager dingy fevers of suspicion
and voyeurism and secret surveillances. Paranoia had become
something like the lust of the age. Hicks pronounced, "Just as
sure as there was an Age of Faith and an Age of Reason, what
we into now, buddy, is the Age of Paranoia. I mean, goddam,
everybody's fantasizing—I'll get a call from some guy who
wants to pay me twenty-five dollars to watch his wife working
one night at the car wash. Or a lady comes to me who met her
husband while they were both married to somebody else and
now six years later, she's convinced he's running around again
with somebody. I ask why, and she says, 'Because suddenly
he's started acting just like he used to act when he was seeing

me. He's happy all the time.' Christ. People call you all the
time just crazy to give you leads—got to where I was spending
half the day on the phone listening to these panting leads from
the private hallucinations of strangers."

So epidemic an avidity had it become, said Hicks, that he
finally had to resort for a while to removing his name from the
yellow-page listings. "What I am, see, is that extra third eye
they all want. They want me to give 'em that secret second
sight on what's actually happening to them with their wives
and business partners and their own children even—if they're
really loved, if they being made a fool of." He was once retained, Hicks recalled, by a baronial young landowner in south
Georgia whose wife had confessed to a brief dalliance with the
local Oldsmobile dealer—"She swore to him it had only happened twice, it had been a year ago, and it'd never happened
again, but he had me trail that woman day and night for almost
two months. She was completely clean, she was being totally
straight with him. I finally had to tell him I just couldn't be
wasting his money any longer, there just wasn't anything there.
But somehow he still couldn't find it in his heart to believe her.
And damn if he didn't wind up divorcing her anyway about six
months later." What Hicks most often found was that "they
don't want innocence. I mean, they just don't want to know it if
it ain't what they wanted to know when they hired you. They
want me to bring 'em guilt. They get downright mad sometimes if I come back and tell them there's nothing to their
fantasies—almost want to fight."

On the whole, from what Hicks had beheld of us all in his
clandestine surveillances over the years, he had wound up with
his own special vision of what the human species amounted
to—and it was hardly the stuff of high literature. Rather, by his
epiphanies, we were all made up mostly of the pulp-novel
truths of a Fanny Hurst soap opera, or at best, one of John
O'Hara's lesser suburban melodramas. "The so-called universal
human experience," he sniffed, "ain't nothing but a B movie."
Moreover, he had come to derive some fanatical purgative exaltation from watching, every Monday evening, the antic gro-
tesqueries of human nature on *Let's Make a Deal*. "Hell, now,
that speaks to me," he fondly reported. "It's better than *Hamlet*."

Even so, in his unending perusal of the shadow side of
humankind, Hicks regularly reached such a dreariness of spirit

that, as he reported, he was everlastingly poised on the verge of "just going to Australia and raising sheep and vegetables." Asked what had kept him at it then for so long, he would give a shrug. "Hell, *I* don't know exactly—it's hard to explain. I guess one thing is you're still as free as you were when you were a little boy playing alone in the backyard—you know, just you alone with your own wits and imagination in your own world. It may be a little bit what it's like for somebody writing stories and novels. I like to see a case I'm working on change and develop, especially one that's tricky where somebody's trying hard to throw me off. It gives you sort of a feeling of being in complete control—it's a bit of an ego trip, I admit." In this gratification, he also conceded, there was probably no slight prickling of the voyeur's vaguely luxurious sensation of power: as he confided about one subject, "I did play around with him a little bit this morning, but he still don't have any idea I'm on him." And mixed obscurely in all this was simply a magpie-like impulse for an endless and indiscriminate collecting of odd little tokens and articles; once driving past a fallen limb beside the road while he was closely tailing a car, Hicks noted eagerly to himself, "Traffic clears up, I'm gonna pick me up that piece of firewood too, sho am."

He was, in a sense, an ultimate collector. And over the long course of his trackings, Hicks had come by a sizable attic's accumulation of eclectic and incidental wisdoms about the vagaries of the race. "Like, the two rush seasons in this business when you really run your ass off are around January and then May to June. January because that's when folks turn loose with all those parties, get drunk and hung over, and then take another look at their lives and decide they want something else, their secretary or their best friend's husband or the paper boy, whatever. In spring, it's just the weather warming up— the sap starts to rise again, you know."

More than anything else, though, what energized and impelled Hicks was a sheer compulsive curiosity—the voracious curiosity of a four-year-old which, in his case, seemed simply to have never left him. In short, Hicks' obsession was working human crossword puzzles. And in this, one soon realized, what Hicks was really in ceaseless pursuit of was the hidden shorthand coda that could, in each case, contain and reduce to a simple equation all the dark and bewildering chaos of human character.

"Human nature ain't nothing but a matter of patterns, you can depend on that. Like on a case like this, where I been called to watch a wife somebody's wondering about, I've gotten to where I can usually tell about the second day whether I'm gonna find anything or not. She'll take on certain patterns —she'll circle the guy's business seven or eight times a day, then cruise his home at night even if it's only been a half hour since she left him. It's total concentration, man, when you in an affair, with everything you do from waking to sleeping focused right on it, and there's a complete abandon about consequences —kind of a berserkness, really. All of which, of course, only makes them more vulnerable—delivers 'em right into my sights. A woman'll plunge into something like that usually only once in her life, but men are more sentimental in a way—might happen to them three or four times. But the more passionate it is, the more strictly it's all going to be programmed. Meeting the exact same time of the day, the same days every week—I don't know, maybe there's something about the regularity itself that turns 'em on, that systematic anticipation, sin on a schedule where they can just sort of deliciously give themselves up to a ritual and a beat that's larger and beyond them, like fate. What it all comes to, though, is patterns. That's all human beings are about."

The particular crossword puzzle that had Hicks now trailing the station wagon through this summer dusk—a puzzle first posed to him, as usual, in a call from an attorney—seemed conventional enough: a young husband, suddenly and unexpectedly sued for divorce by his wife, with rather clobbering demands in alimony and child support, who was shortly given to grim speculations about some unknown Lothario poised just offstage. Hicks had, earlier that afternoon, stopped by the attorney's office in downtown Atlanta, emerging after a minute with a blank white envelope from which, once back in his car, he gently ruffled out several colored snapshots taken at idle and cozy moments back in the couple's oblivious simple days of wine-and-pizza happiness—one glimpse of the two of them cuddled together in a capacious black Naugahyde lounger in a yellow-paneled den, the young husband gazing at the camera flash with a vaguely startled grin which, considered now from the front seat of Hicks' car, seemed to hint already some dull uneasiness. She—perched in his lap, now Hicks' unsuspecting quarry—smiled musingly, some doelike haziness about her, with the fresh dewy lambent face of numberless other super-market madonnas of outer suburbia. "Her name's Judy," Hicks said. "Sweet-looking little gal, actually. But I've found it's those quiet, nice, demure little Karen-Valentine types who'll throw themselves into the real hell-for-leather affairs. . . ."

Trailing several cars behind her now, Hicks remarked, "Couldn't tell you how many station wagons I've followed over the years in this work—station wagons and Mercedeses, thou-sands of 'em. Always seems to be one or the other, for some reason." Ahead of him, she turned into a road, with Hicks turn-ing after her, that led down into one of those instant mazed subdivisions of the New South's self-transformation into one vast San Fernando Valley—a fathomless curlicuing of cul-de-sacs with Disneyland-tidy toy houses imitating Spanish villas and Aspen chalets ranked in endless and fiercely geometric reduplication across a moonscape of razed gullied red clay and scanty jack oaks, all bare to a blank unblinking sky: a neigh-borhood that seemed finally some zone beyond all time and place, without past or memory, part of that single monolithic anonymous American suburbia where all the little family scenes in the television commercials take place. "Yeah, what I figured, she's heading back to her house," Hicks said, "and this is the limbo, man, out here where she lives. Whole new class of people we invented, living out in these subdivisions—been manufactured out of thin air by the real-estate developers and the savings-and-loan folks. Hell, ten years ago, these guys out here were just good ole boys driving bread trucks and running filling stations, living in little frame houses with geraniums growing in those half-tires in their front yards. Now, they living almost like the doctors and bankers—they got them split-levels with charcoal grills on the patio and automatic garage-door openers. . . ."

Pausing at a stop sign, Hicks lit a cigarette. "And the cases I get out of these suburbs now has increased out of sight. It's not the folks suddenly going haywire when they start approaching middle-age crisis, like you might think—it's the young marrieds, people in their middle thirties living out in places like this, just beginning to achieve some stability in their businesses, got a family and a purty little house. What it is, is boredom. Like that song of Peggy Lee's sometime back, 'Is That All There Is?' It's what I call the station-wagon years in a woman's life. This little girl here, she's just a bored housewife in a deadend circle. It's boredom, plus mobility. Can you imagine back, say, in the days of the frontier, the problems you'd have carrying on an affair like this Judy's doing now? But no more. We in the TV-dinner age of affairs—instant and disposable."

. . . It had been on a preliminary cruise through the neighborhood the Saturday before that Hicks, scanning the geography and checking addresses after the attorney's call, happened to fall in behind Judy's station wagon as she was pulling out of her driveway, and followed her on to a nearby warren of apartments where "damn if I didn't hop right on top of 'em." To his surprised delight, she parked before one of the apartments and disappeared inside—and only a few minutes passed before a yellow Plymouth Charger with black racing stripes pulled up beside her station wagon, and a youngish man clad in a maroon jump suit climbed out and went in after her. "That just don't happen often, you make a strike like that the very first time out," Hicks later recounted jubilantly. "The guy didn't come back out until around nine-thirty that night, and she came out a few minutes later and drove back to her house. That was their hole. You ever find their hole, then you got 'em, you got it licked—they gonna be in that hole whenever they're together, 'cause that's the only place they feel safe. All it is, is fox hunting."

Returning the next afternoon, Sunday, Hicks had found her station wagon again parked in front of the apartment, backed to the curb. "That's so nobody can see her license plate, I guess," he had snorted. "All this is a few steps below Edgar Allan Poe, ain't it?" Then, as he was easing past for a closer squint, she had suddenly emerged out of the door with her two small children—no more, for that instant, than ten feet from Hicks, he merely emitting at this abrupt startling ambush of immediacy a low suppressed, "Umh. Um-hummh. . . ." She seemed to pause a moment on the steps—a tall and liltingly tapered figure with long loose black hair, in pale jeans and a lime terry-cloth sweater, regarding the slow passage of Hicks' car with a calm inscrutable flat gaze of dark glasses as she stood silent and composed and somehow briefly exposed, defenseless, in the afternoon's brilliant white glare.

"She sure got a look," Hicks had muttered as he turned at the far end of the parking lot. "I'm not too crazy about that. Don't like for that to happen more'n once or twice." He then parked his Impala around the corner of another apartment unit— "Let's just set here a few minutes. Wouldn't do for her to spot us cruising right back by." Snatching down the bill of his train engineer's cap and settling back in the seat, his elbow slung out the window, he then fell to ruminating, "Damn pleasant-looking lady. Makes you wonder what happened. I did find out who the guy is—fella name of Bobby Ray Telfair, owns him a little auto-parts store. Just happens to turn out ole Bobby Ray's in the middle of getting himself a divorce, too. Seems the two of them first met about two years ago in a Sunday-school class for young marrieds at the Baptist church. No way of telling yet how long this thing's been going on, but that would have meant she was pregnant when they first eyed each other. But of course, a lot of these things happen right soon after a woman's had a baby—you know, the first fella who comes along and pays her a lot of attention and makes her feel she's desirable again just as a woman, before you know it she's seeing him in a motel room at the Ramada Inn every Monday and Thursday afternoon. Hell . . ." He fastidiously spat a small speck of something from his front tooth out the window.

"But my people don't really want to take this thing to court," he had continued. "They just want some cards to play when the lawyers sit down to talk. Nothing but one big continuous poker game I'm involved in with this work. All it is. It makes these cases a lot easier, too, since you don't need that hard-core evidence any longer, just circumstantial enough for reasonable presumption of sinning. So all we really after on this one are some negotiables, know what I mean."

Pulling out finally to take another leisurely pass by the apartment, Hicks added, "But still, I sort of wonder what happened—to the marriage, I mean. 'Course her husband, he wasn't too impressive to me when I met him the other day. But then, the husbands never are. Not when they coming to you at this kind of moment in their life. I sure would like to know the whole story, though. You can bet there's some *Days of Our Lives* plot submerged in all this."

Hicks had now reached the entrance to the main road, and he suddenly ceased talking, then mumbled furiously, "Look-ahere, lookahere . . ." as, directly in front of his car, a yellow Charger with black racing stripes turned into the apartment drive and swept by him, the face behind the steering wheel heavy and blunt and sun-singed, with fine ink-black coiffured hair, the eyes rheumy with some blur of pool chlorine or whiskey, giving Hicks in that instant a quick glance in which there may have been the briefest cold glint of wariness. "Godamightydamn," Hicks murmured, "we bumping into 'em ever which direction here. This is like getting caught in the middle of a billiard game. . . ." He pulled on out into the road and drove a distance to the first side street, then hastily backed around and headed toward the apartments again. But, approaching the entrance, he found the station wagon and Charger both leaving, turning in separate directions. "That's funny," he said, his voice a bit thin and light. "They seem to be acting sort of restless all of a sudden. Can't believe they've made me. Well, shit, we already way ahead of the game, I don't want to press 'em too close. I'll just leave and let it float loose for another night. . . ."

So now this Monday dusk, the third day of his surveillance, Hicks tagged after Judy's station wagon as it wound on through the whorled streets of her neighborhood, past empty sidewalks scattered with tricycles and foot scooters, living-room windows already dimly tinted with the blue gloom of television suppers inside. "You know, it looks like she's just driving around here aimlessly," Hicks said after a while. "It's like she'll do anything to avoid having to go back to that house in that cul-de-sac. That house is a setting of her past." Then he said, "You know, she doesn't have those children with her tonight, which is strange. Hell, could it be she's not actually going back to her house at all?" Presently, the station wagon swung into a corner hamburger drive-in. On Hicks' second pass by, it was swinging back out. And after following her through a few more turns, Hicks suddenly barked, "Be damn. Know what? She's heading straight back for those apartments now. Sure as hell." With an eager little shuffle in his seat, he cocked his head back at a tilt of tight alertness, and softly chattered as he accelerated on after her, "All right. All right. I think we gonna be getting us some of those negotiables this evening, by God. This is turning out to be a dream, like I figured—like stealing candy, it's so easy. By God, I *knew* I had this thing pegged as a pattern case. . . ."

Hicks once admitted that he was leading the rather precarious existence of a body collector in the midst of a medieval plague. "Paranoia, friend, is a condition as contagious as smallpox. You around it only a little while, you gonna start catching some of it. And it happens to be the staple I traffic in for a living. You almost need to be a celibate recluse, some kind of eunuch, to be safe from it all."

Hicks himself dwelled with his second wife, Brenda, and their two small children, in a shady sedate Norman Rockwell neighborhood nestled just off Atlanta's fabled Peachtree Street. Theirs was a simple and inconspicuous frame house, painted moss green, with a sparsely furnished front room usually dim through the day with drawn curtains. Through a door to the right was Hicks' own small spare office, paneled in orange-lacquered pine. He and Brenda—a lithe girl with sunny hair and a pleasant freckled prettiness, quiet and measured of word, whom he had found at a quarter-horse show in Indiana— seldom ventured out for any social gatherings. Through the long months of spring and summer, if he wasn't on the road, Hicks would pass the blue cool of the evenings alone in his fenced backyard, diligently tending his patch of a vegetable garden—tomatoes, squash, collard greens. In fact, his neighbors for the most part were not quite certain what he did. "It makes 'em wonder when they see me coming out of the house in the middle of the morning to get the mail. People get a little uneasy these days with any unknown quantity in their midst." Actually, Hicks found this vagueness in the community about his precise fix not all that uncongenial. As he had remarked once about his negotiations with principals in a case, "They still a little confused about exactly who I am and how I fit into all this, which is the perfect situation—exactly how I like it." It was as if this had also become his instinct now in his personal life; to a degree, he even lived undercover in his own neighborhood. "Truth is, damn if you don't start pulling double-agentries on your own self, you don't watch out."

He did have one consuming extracurricular enthusiasm— turtles. Sitting alone in his dark car along country roads on long watches through moonlit summer nights, he would obsessively collect any he spied moseying over the pavement or bumbling along the weedy edges of ditches—bringing them back to his house, where, at times, he would have a whole congregation of them (individually named for the parties in the case he was on when he found them), shuffling and bumping in washtubs around his yard. He seemed to have found some special synergy with them—patient and impassive creatures, solitary, moving with a careful deliberation in their own self-contained enclosures, as old as Eden and the Fall. "When I was a little boy," Hicks reported one evening as he was driving to a stakeout, "I used to watch 'em all night long out my backroom window, moving around out there in the backyard. May not think it, but a turtle's got a personality, you sit there watching them long enough. And they so fuckin' tough. You can find one all mangled on the side of the road, been hit by a tractor and missing three-fourths its parts, but by God after a little while you see that mutha starting to move again across the pavement—they just keep on truckin'. But nobody yet really knows anything about 'em. All you can find is just a paragraph or two in these faded ole books. They still a goddam enigma, common as they are."

Occasionally, in the cavernous green glooms of Atlanta twilights, Hicks and Brenda would have a few friends over for bourbon and steaks on the cement patio just outside their basement recreation room. Most of these visitors tended to have a touch of the worn and fugitive about them: a stalled writer somewhat sour and moldering with angst, a derelict young architect who arrived usually wallopingly drunk and then commenced playing the piano with a galactic splendor. Toward the end of one such evening, Hicks—reposing, well sloshed himself, in a plastic-mesh lawn lounger and contemplating the drifts of summer stars above his backyard pines while his two dogs snuffled after the bones flipped in the grass—presently began to discourse: "Naw, not too many people last long in this business. It can be hell on a marriage, and psychologically the mortality rate's pretty high. The fourteen years I been in it is an awfully long life span. You got to have a kind of perverse love for it to last any while—got to be goddam *called*, in a way. Want to know what separates the artists from the hacks? The good ones, you can throw him on a rock and he can scramble—something he was just born with, like a cat. It takes real delicacy sometimes. You working these things with-

out any vested authority at all—just those primal damn instincts when you out there on that far brink with people. You
can't just slam 'em up on the side of the head. If you do, you a
cop. Ex-policemen and FBI agents who try this business, they
just not worth a damn usually. They gotten so conditioned to
bullying things out of people with their authority, they don't
know how to operate outside of that. Working any case is
really 90 percent a matter of just patiently letting somebody's
character develop before you. It's all a game of chasing glim-
mers. You hang, waiting for that one quick little accidental
glimmer in a situation, and suddenly there it is, and you dive
into it, and it opens up the whole picture pattern."

In truth, Hicks' craft was not without its own intuitive and
existential graces, and by all indications, Hicks himself was one
of the virtuosos of the medium—in possession of those extra
wizardries which, in any game, make the difference between
adequacy and genius. "I'm a goddam moving kind of investiga-
tor," he allowed. "I don't believe in sitting still. You can get out
of the natural pitch and rhythm of real life like that." He also
had a discomfort with the elaborate mechanical equipage
employed by many other investigators, confining himself instead to such minimal props as a pair of binoculars, a Nikon, a
vintage 8mm movie camera. "You start relying on all that technology and gadgetry, it'll dull your instincts. You can lose your
art in a hurry like that."

In a sense, Hicks was to his art peculiarly born and nurtured.
His own father, who now desultorily occupied himself with a
general store in a musty little Georgia junction near Atlanta,
happened in fact to be a professional gambler through most of
his son's boyhood—prone to week-long marathons of poker in
Memphis, Charlotte, Birmingham. To Hicks growing up, his
father was a seldom-seen, mythic figure, and Hicks still insisted, "I'd rather be around professional gamblers than anybody else I know. They exist totally out there on that windy
edge, man."

Nevertheless, Hicks' mother finally removed herself and her
children to Atlanta, and there Hicks wound up, during his
teens, working four hours on the night shift at the Greyhound
Bus Terminal—no inappropriate novitiate, for that matter, in
the old elemental musks of the human condition. Hicks, still
not much more than a boy, small and nimble and alert, flickered among it all, fetching baggage, answering phones, sweep-

ing the tile floors. "Best job I ever had," he fondly reminisced. "Damn place has never had its doors closed once since it was built, and something was always happening. It was like being in a carnival that just went on forever."

It was while he was in college that Hicks, more or less as a petty-cash expedient, sidled sideways into a few casual investigative chores for Retail Credit. "It was strictly Class-D ball, but I knew the minute I was into it that I was home. I was there." He was then only twenty. From that, he paced through the next six years as an agent for such interests as Mutual of Omaha, at last peeling off from a large private-investigative firm in Atlanta and, with an elder from that firm, a still sporadically ambulatory seventy-four-year-old detective named Hamner Mullins, opened up his own shop: Mullins & Hicks. "I was ready to fly, man."

Back then, Hicks would later recall, "I was totally and surgically detached on a case. I wasn't much more than a hunting machine." Indeed, photographs of Hicks from those years were like barely recognizable glimpses of him in some distant alien incarnation—plainly snipped and barbered, taut and prim as a paper clip, ruthlessly sober in horn-rim glasses and neat dark blazers and collegiate-stripe ties. "I could of gone straight, without a blink, on into the FBI or CIA." But then in the late Sixties, with a sudden swarm of commissions to track down runaways in the dislocations of those years, Hicks began moving more and more into the inner rainbowed regions of the counterculture—and, as it turned out, never emerged again. In his tarryings among communes of gentle young vagabonds in San Francisco basements and out on New Mexico mesas, he underwent an aurora-borealis, Zen-like dawning of consciousness himself which worked on him an almost corporal alteration, as if he had wound up permanently assuming not only the interior vision but even the guise of those he was pursuing.

"I felt like Lazarus waking up," he remembered. But he soon found that his amplified perspectives had placed him in a certain uncomfortable disjunction with his customary patrons. In particular, it became his suspicion that the corporate estate, which he was continuing to serve as an agent for personnel and credit investigations, quite likely composed the superstructure of a new, American-style totalitarianism. Such enlightenments left Hicks now like an imperfect changeling, hung in some arrested stage of transition between two profoundly different natures.

He was constantly engaged in a private skirmishing of conscience now about the dubiousness of his craft. Assigned by one national firm to pursue "signs of instability" in one of its young branch managers who had just gotten a divorce, Hicks watched him late one Friday afternoon, from the sidelot of a filling station, as the man emerged from an apartment building with a small boy. "That would be his son he's picking up for the weekend," Hicks said, and following him as far as the expressway, Hicks there released him into the wide free spaces of the sunset, with the chipper benediction, "Okay, fine, he seems like a right upstanding young man to me, picks up his little boy every Friday afternoon. See, in a way, all this has been a service to him too. It's not gonna hurt him at all, it's gonna reassure his employers."

On another sundown, on his way to try coaxing a suspect in a large warehouse-theft operation into turning prosecution witness, Hicks explained as he drove, "This is just a good ole country boy who was mostly used by the others. He's never had it that easy, not all that bright, served time in the state pen. I'm just trying to spare him the sort of humiliation and bullying from the police that throws his kind completely out of control. But goddam if you ever know where those kind are gonna be coming from—what he was in the pen for, by the way, was manslaughter. . . ." Heaped heavily in a vinyl rocker in his house trailer, his supper just finished and his shoes off, he was a beefy youth named Wayman with larruped tar-black hair, wearing a rose-red shirt and maroon slacks and pink socks, and he listened to Hicks' somewhat gingerly delivered suggestions with an expression of wary sullenness on his chubby sunburnt face, mopily wiping his finger back and forth under his nose. Hicks allowed as to how he might be able to arrange immunity in exchange for his testimony, and Wayman submitted in a soft voice vaporing almost to a whisper, "I just don't want to go back to that penitentiary. You know I'm a two-time loser, and if they come out here to get me this time, they goan have to chase my ass through that briar patch out yonder, I promise you that. Way I been worrying, I tell you something, it's got to where my wife's seeing me cry in the middle of the night over this thing. I go to jail, and my wife and kids will be

on welfare, we'd lose everything of the little we got here. . . ."
He nodded sulkily at the interior of the trailer around him, the
television set in its glossy caramel cabinet, a suspended wire
cage containing a torpid chalky parakeet, a fringed satin
tapestry of a cinnamon stag against a violet sunset that was
hanging over the nubby sofa where Hicks was lounging, his
legs crossed, with a kind of neighborly easiness. "I know,
Wayman," he gently proposed, "I know, and it's not you my
folks are after, it's the other three. Look, man, you got to quit
worrying about them, it's your family that counts now. If you
help us on this thing, just go down there with me tomorrow
morning and give a statement, I promise you ain't any police
gonna be coming out here after you." Wayman grumped,
"Well, hell, I got no choice, looks like. I don't like it, but I
will."

But afterward, as Hicks drove back home through the warm
plummy deeps of an Atlanta April night, he kept up a fretful
monologue. "Hell, I ain't any better than they are. Me and
Wayman, we were both just a couple of cabbage-town boys
sitting in that trailer. Only difference is, this thing's dead serious to him and his hillbilly wife, while I'm kind of abstract
about it—I can sit there coverin' what I tell 'em with all this
walnut-flavored bullshit. . . ." He could not seem to cease muttering over it. "Hell, I'm the whore in all this, I know that. I'm
just the hired hand. But I can deal from where I am—I know
who I am, and if you lose that, then where are you?"

Nevertheless, it had become Hicks' lot to live in an abiding
disquiet about the implicit indecency of what he was doing. "I
mean, really," he would grumble periodically, "why the hell
should I be watching and reporting on some poor lonely housewife who's just trying to get some pleasure in her life that she's
probably got every right to want?" Another awkwardness,
Hicks had found since his cultural mutation in the late Sixties,
was that most of the clients who came to him tended to be the
sort who now dismally appalled him: "To tell the truth, I
really don't have much use for the kind of folks who hire me.
They just aren't the line of people I especially like to be
around. Most of 'em are these reactionary conservative semi-
Birchers with damaged infantile-omnipotence complexes." It
was like a variation of Groucho Marx's sentiment: *Any country
club that would have me as a member, I wouldn't want to
belong to.*

At the same time, though, Hicks remained extravagantly testy to the faintest suggestion, from anyone else, of the same sort of distaste. After returning from a morning's conference with one woman considering contracting his services, Hicks snapped, "No, it didn't work out, and I'm glad of it. I didn't like her attitude at all toward me. I was just a little disreputable to her, you know, the whole scene with us sitting there was a little disgusting to her. To hell with the bitch, I don't need that from anybody." In fact, one reason he and Brenda rarely ranged beyond the comfortable seclusions of their life at home may have been that, almost always at any party or large soirée, Hicks had learned he could depend on someone finally accosting him with the demand, "I wonder, how can you really live with yourself doing what you do, rummaging into other people's privacy?" To which Hicks, a small muscle flickering along his jaw, would briskly inquire, "And who do you work for, you work for a bank or law firm here?—oh yeah, them, they called me just a couple weeks ago to check out one of their people."

All of this had led to what could be considered the climactic complication for Hicks in his calling: "It's gotten now to where I'll wind up identifying more with who I'm following than who hired me to follow them. That ain't too good in this business. But on about every case, I pass in and out of schizophrenia about four times. In the beginning, I never felt any connection at all. But over the last several years, I've begun to find there's just no way to spend a week shadowing somebody, copying every single move in their life, without there growing this strange kind of intimacy between me and them. They don't even know I'm there, but I get to know them probably better than anybody else ever has—including themselves." To a degree, in fact, through such a sustained, daily, single-focused absorption in the peronality of a principal and that moment in his life, Hicks acknowledged he would even *become* who he was following—become something like that person's doppelgänger.

While this facility for being a psychic chameleon was much of Hicks' art, it also became a special disquiet for him. "The main thing in any role or pretext is to feel completely at home in it," he said. "There's no disguise better than that. But I can have me an alias—another identity—on a case which gets to be so natural, I think if somebody jumped up and started hitting me over the head with a stick, I'd blurt out that name before my own." One evening, as Hicks was questioning a woman on her screened side porch who was marginally involved in an embezzlement case, she suddenly interrupted him, "Haven't I see you before? Weren't you in that bar at the motel the other night, sitting by yourself over there in the corner watching us?" And Hicks froze for a moment, a light blank smile on his face and that tiny muscle rippling along his jaw, as if he had just received a small quick blow to the pit of his stomach. . . . But later as he was driving back home, he speculated, "Well, I wouldn't want to be completely invisible, I guess. I ought to be glad for that. You worry about that sometimes—being *too* invisible."

But the world in which Hicks dwelled, finally, was largely one of mirages. He operated in a kind of free-float out on the edge of the void, in a vertigo of illusion and reality, innocence and guilt, a twilight of endless possibilities. In the late lost hours of one Wednesday night, Hicks sat blearily hunched over his fifth bourbon and water in the narrow dank cave of a bar miles away from Atlanta and home—one of those Shangri-La lounges in the patent-brand motels that have clamorously collected along the length of the interstates blazed out into the South's interior in headlong oblivious continuation from Minneapolis and Cincinnati and Pittsburgh. With sun-toasted ole boys from nearby dusty little towns roosting gawkily about him in cranberry blazers and diamond-patterned dress shirts, and a swoon of liquid electric guitars swimming from the jukebox, Hicks confessed, "It's all a bedlam, man. Half the time, the realities turn out to be more byzantine than the paranoias— some woman comes to me absolutely convinced her husband is seeing another gal, so I check it out, and it's a totally ridiculous notion, nothing like that at all. He's running around with another man. Damn right, it's Chinatown. Also, most of the time when I get into a case, pretty soon I realize the wrong person's being followed—it ought to have been the person who hired me. Hell, it's like living in a maze of trick mirrors."

Every few months, he would simply flee it all with Brenda— flee that anarchy of possibilities and appearances, innocence and guilt—to Las Vegas, for rapt forty-eight-hour communions at the crap tables. There at least, on calm green surfaces of felt pooled in quiet hooded glows, it was all reduced and contained in the sacramental design and ceremonies of a game, a formalized metaphor abstracted out of the furies and heat—

pure pattern. "When I'm over those crap tables," he declared, "I've never known such peace. It's like paradise."

On his way that Monday for his last evening's surveillance of the young housewife in south Atlanta, Hicks maintained, "Once a year, maybe, you'll get one that actually interests you. Big criminal case or missing person, something like that—the kind that'll give you those blood-rushes. They'll make you over again. But after that, I just run on automatic pilot. Naw, it just don't happen in petty domestic junk like this. This is the kind of thing that just keeps the shoes on the baby." Even so—as he headed south again, in another of those low red smoldering sundowns over expressway wastescapes when the hunting usually starts for Hicks—there was an unmistakable rising exhilaration in the car. Leaving the expressway finally, drawing near those outer suburban barrens where he would resume his tracking that evening, Hicks suddenly pulled off the road beside a vacant stretch of pines and broomsage, mumbling, "Damn, my adrenalin's flowing, I gotta take a leak here. . . ."

And it was about an hour later—after staking out the auto-parts shop where she had been talking with the young man in the golf shirt, and then trailing her station wagon on through her neighborhood—that he had picked her up again as she wheeled out of the hamburger drive-in: "All right. She's heading straight back for those apartments now. We gonna get it all in focus tonight."

From several cars behind, he watched her station wagon now curving down the hill toward the apartment entrance— and then, startlingly, sweep right on past it. Hicks blinked. He was silent for a long minute as he tagged along after her in abrupt empty bafflement again. "Weird," he pronounced at last. "She's just not going to cooperate, is she?" He began shuffling hurriedly through the deck of possibilities. "I don't know, it could be a totally different case now, 'cause we informed the client this morning what was happening. You never know what they'll do once you let 'em in on the story, they can mess the whole thing up good. . . . 'Course, you'd think these two'd naturally be a little spooky in their situation, but then the thing to remember, for anybody, if you involved in this sort of thing, you think nothing's ever gonna happen to you. They could have actually made me, though. Sho could. There was just a little bit too much of that brushing past each other in that apartment lot yesterday. *Doubt* it, but they could have. 'Course, one thing about them making you, they never know how long you actually been on 'em, and lots of times they just give up right there. Still, I don't think . . ."

Ahead of Hicks, the station wagon now slowed and pulled into a curb market. "God *damn*," Hicks whined. He floated on past her, around a curve, then slung back around in the parking lot of a bank branch. "That's the thing about them stopping on you like that, every time you gotta go through your setups again. And it's still just a little too bright and clear—summer's the worst for these kind of surveillances, with those long afternoons going on till nine o'clock. I like that overcast winter weather."

From the parking lot then of a shopping center across the road from the curb market, Hicks stood alone under the aluminum-slat awning of a television showroom, watching with a blank gaze of dark glasses. Her station wagon backed out again, swerved around and then headed down the road toward the apartments. Scurrying back behind the wheel, Hicks murmured, "I'm almost afraid to say anything," and he pulled swiftly out into the road after her. Then, drifting on down the hill three cars behind her, Hicks suddenly breathed, "There she goes—she's turning. She's in the hole. She's in the hole. I got her. You just have to wait long enough, see. He's probably already in there waiting for her. This is the way I like it, now."

Driving a short distance past the apartment entrance, Hicks looped back and then turned in after her—but the station wagon had somehow, inexplicably, vanished, as if taken into the very air. Hicks grunted. "Strange optical slip there . . . I could have sworn . . . damn, I can't believe she's made me. But that was awfully foxy, turning in there and then right back out again. Unless she was checking to see if he . . ." He paused. "That's what it was. Bet you. That's a pattern too, cruising by when you can't actually be with 'em. But what the hell, we got the other end of the stick if he's still back there at his auto-parts store."

On the way there, suddenly, at no more than an instant's blur of a car passing in the other direction, Hicks snapped, "There he is, there he is, and that's her in there with him."

Slewing around in a vast fuming of dust in the dirt yard of a small brick church, Hicks crooned, "That's what this game's all about, buddy—you notice I don't happen on many of 'em from the back." Surging on after them, he leaned back luxuriously with one arm stretched out straight against the wheel, with his other hand deftly lighting a cigarette with a snick of his Zippo. "Yessir. It's not only patience, it's that sixth sense of thinking like they're thinking—*feeling like they feeling*. You're just gonna happen to be at the right place at the right time. . . . And there they go, by God, they turning down that road to the apartments." Hicks, turning after them, then slowed. "We'll just hang back here a little bit, give 'em a chance to get settled in without our booming right in there behind them."

But again, when Hicks eased into the entrance drive, bumping gently over the speed breakers, the curb in front of the apartment was blank. It was as if they had simply disappeared like swallows into the nightfall. "I tell you, I'm getting a stink off this case," Hicks announced. "Breaking patterns like that is hardly ever done unless you're trying to shake somebody. But it's usually the older ones who're cool like that, because they aren't obsessive, it's not their whole life—they can be tough as a snake. But these two, they just too young to be pros."

He drove then back to her neighborhood, where he found her house's driveway empty, but with all the rooms brightly lit in the gathering dark. "This is getting awfully strange. It looks more occupied now than it ever has. Hell, I'm gonna check his place—nobody's been there for the past two days, but it's just down the road." Moving slowly up that street past a repetition of meager clipped lawns, he found Bobby Ray's house this time also illuminated inside, with the yellow Charger parked in the driveway. "Sonuvabitch. Know what? I bet that wasn't Judy at all in his car—it was his wife. That's what the whole problem was between them tonight—he couldn't see her 'cause he had to come back here with his wife for that last little ritual of divvying up the spoils before the divorce." Then, coasting back down past the house, he considered again, "Or, of course, he could be having second thoughts about the whole thing. I can see this thing from several sides of the prism. This little arrangement could of actually been going on for a long time now, and I could be coming in just as it's playing out. It may

have all already happened, and now that it's down to the
crunch, he might have started thinking about trying it over
again with his wife. That's the pattern a lot of times too. . . ."

Then, taking another pass by Judy's house, he found it now
lightless, hulking darkly under the moon. "What the hell's
going on?" He quickly drove back to Bobby Ray's house—it
too was now dark, deserted, the driveway empty. "Goddam,"
Hicks said, "I almost get the feeling I'm being played with
here." Heading back once more to the apartments, he began
increasingly to fret. "Damn, all I'm seeing on the road now is
blue station wagons and Dodge Chargers, seems like. This ain't
no work of art, that's for damn sure. I *knew* it was coming
together too quick and neat." The curb in front of the apartment was still vacant, the windows black and blindly mirroring
the brief flare and fade of Hicks' headlights as he turned
around. "Well, the hell with it. My people have already got
their ace—they know about her staying in there with him the
other night for four hours. When the lawyers sit down to talk
at the conference tomorrow morning, it'll be like a game of
seven-card stud—they can raise on that ace showing, and if the
other side ain't holding one too, they won it."

Nevertheless, at ten o'clock—the point when he had been
instructed to turn it loose if nothing had developed by then—
Hicks was still making swoops past Judy's house, Bobby Ray's,
the apartment, the auto-parts shop. "Just say I'm off the clock
now. I'm just curious what the hell's actually going on out
here." Plunging now back and forth in the night as if hoping to
find again somewhere in the darkness some trace, some edge of
the pattern he had lost, Hicks presently proposed, "I tell you,
most goddam irrational folks—you just have to keep that always in your head, you dealing with totally irrational people.
Do every kind of goddam devious thing in the world on you. . . ."

It wasn't until after midnight that he at last gave it up. On
the way back into the city, he stopped off at a lounge in a motel
just off the expressway, plopping himself in a lantern-lit booth
with a short scrub of his jeans on the maroon velveteen nap,
and then proceeded to bolt down rapid successive bourbons.
He fumed now, "Well, fuck 'em, they'll both probably be married to somebody else in six months anyway. Or maybe shoot
each other in a couple of weeks. You think I really empathize
with any of 'em on these cases? No more than a dog does a
rabbit. You think I'll actually be talking about this dinky situa-

tion even a week from now? I couldn't give less of a shit what happens to those people. You won't ever know, and you can drive yourself crazy if you let yourself get involved like that. Hell, I just hit my lick and move on to the next one. No other way you can make it in this business. You got to keep on moving."

The next morning, after a call from the attorney who had hired him, all Hicks was left with was the somewhat amorphous denouement of the lawyers' negotiations, which he reported as, "Well, we played our ace, and they must not've been holding any of their own, 'cause they folded right there: no alimony, not even two-thirds the child support she was demanding. But I still wouldn't mind knowing what the story really is down there. It began to get damn strange there with ole Bobby Ray's wife in it suddenly, all that running around, those lights going on and off. Christ, who knows, it could have been that—but you never gonna know."

And that night, Hicks flew with Brenda back out to Las Vegas.

A month or two later, Hicks quit Atlanta altogether, and withdrew to a farm high in the fastness of the North Carolina mountains. From there, he takes on only a few sporadic investigative assignments now.

The Technician
from Plains

ONE OF THE more notable aspects of the South's assimilation into America's corporate civilization has been the vanishing of all those splendidly gargoylish, uproarious old razorback demagogues of the South's age of tribal politics—the Vardemanns, the Longs, the Tillmans, the Ross Barnetts. That long pageantry of country Cyclopses has been succeeded by a generation of tidily circumspect young political stockbrokers, earnestly sensible sorts who nevertheless possess about all the garlicky smacks and hoohawing hair-raising voltages of Methodist summer-camp directors. Somewhat Styrofoam figures, they are, all of them, eminently inoffensive men. Like the South itself in its assumption into the suburban void over the rest of the country, they afford considerably less distress to the national decency. But yet one elusively senses that some vital, reckless, dark energy of life has somehow been lost in the improvement. The taste of respectability unhappily tends toward vanilla custard.

Among this new order of polite young Southern political worthies was, of course, Governor Jimmy Carter of Georgia. And in him, the South's whole incorporation at last into America Proper was to arrive at its grand consummation.

For most of the country, the event of Jimmy Carter's installation as President of the United States was not unlike waking up one morning to discover oneself suddenly married to a stranger. There was a certain stir of faint unease in the sensational novelty of it all. It had been barely a year since he had first presented himself forth, with his wide officious half-moon

New Times, February 20, 1976
The New York Review of Books, May 18, 1978

grin, out of the farthest outskirts of the nation's life—a trim, subdued, mannerly onetime provincial governor, a genial Georgian who was to all appearances absolutely serious about this undertaking of his, but who was utterly and forlornly marginal to the national political estate.

Astoundingly, he passed the miracle. Among other things, it afforded a considerably unnerving start to other governments over the world: unthinkable that someone could materialize out of nowhere, out of the dusty obscurities of south Georgia and the relative innocuousness of one term as governor of that backyard state, to suddenly preside over the destiny of the mightiest nation on the planet; that so much—the leadership, really, of the Western world—could be entrusted to so capricious a process. But it was an even more phantasmagorical happening given the aery improbability, in the end, of the figure himself who had brought it all off.

Even back in Georgia, he was remembered from his previous incarnation as governor as merely a decent and diligent but otherwise unarresting steward of the state's affairs. In all, he seemed to carry none of those burly hefts and brawns in his presence that are usually found in the truly heavy-gauge political personalities, those egos big and furious and redoubtable enough to make it all the way up the brawling salmon run of national power. For all his commendable earnestness, there still lingered about him some sense of a final innate slightness —a quality of balsa wood. It may have been the light, zitherlike lilt and wisping of his voice—in that voice, with its muted fogs of a drawl, some flimsy sound of thin grasses—or in the fine and almost mincingly polite demeanor he maintained, an unrelenting niceness and diffidence that often made it appear he was offering himself for President on the premise simply of an ingratiating friendliness.

All through his campaign Carter was scrupulous to explain how his aspiration for the Presidency—a stage of ambition at which one passes into a kind of infinity of presumption—nevertheless "prompted in him as much humility as pride." But such insistent self-effacing professions, his air of an abashed and unassuming ordinariness, began to give off, after a while, certain disquiets of their own. As much as one should beware, as Nietzsche observed, of those in whom the instinct to punish is strong, perhaps also one should be on a special alert with those in whom recitations of their humility begin to seem unusually persistent. There are probably no compressions of ego more forbidding than the pent impulsions of an unremitting modesty in men of large eagerness and self-purpose.

Despite all these misgivings, though, on election night as Jimmy Carter's impossible fantasy became an actuality, somehow one was curiously elated. His nomination acceptance speech at the Democratic convention three months earlier had turned out to be one of the doughtiest Populist testimonials— that old unrealized political dream from the time before Huey Long, before William Jennings Bryan—ever put forward by a Presidential nominee. He seemed fresh, winningly unpretentious, bracingly spontaneous and generous of instincts, intense, not without a tentative flair of the romantic in his spirit. He had made it to that moment, after all, as a freebooting irregular, totally outside the conventional magistries of authority in the land. And it seemed anything could happen now, all possibilities had suddenly been thrown open—one sensed, in the late hours of that night of his election, that the nation might be about to embark on one of the most exhilarating adventures in its recent history.

But watching him then on the day of his inauguration striding hatless and brisk with his jack-o'-lantern grin on down Constitution Avenue to establish himself in the White House, there returned that vague queasiness of uncertainty at so abruptly finding our future irrevocably attached to this amicable but still slightly dubious stranger. That uncertainty, over the ensuing months, was hardly dispelled. If anything, he became even more a bafflement. There remained about him some inconclusiveness of nature that made it particularly difficult for journalistic commentaries and profiles to arrive at a true fix on him: it was like an equivalent, with his personality and his policies, of the infernal difficulty editorial cartoonists had encountered with the indeterminate countenance of Gerald Ford —a curiously indistinct and hesitant off-focus now in all the journalistic attempts to comprehend this neat soft-spoken martinet of conscientiousness, this odd man so suddenly at the center of our collective life.

At a dinner later for White House newsmen, Carter proposed of one reporter, who had recently given him grievance, that he had become "the Erica Jong of *The New York Times*." No one there precisely understood what he meant by this little waggery. Rather, it had the quality of an epigram laboriously, if not torturously, devised in solitary steepings of resentment. In fact, his utterances often came out strangely awry in nuance and aptness; there seemed in him peculiar misrhymings of moods, awkward asymmetries and dysjunctions. There was a suggestion of this even in his carriage as he had propelled himself through the rounds of his campaign, slumped slightly forward, his head thrust out resolutely with its shallow-lopped curve at the back, giving him rather the look of an unshelled terrapin; he swooped along corridors and down main-street sidewalks with something of a marionette's dangle and flop in his movements, some strange lightly hinged looseness of wrists and jostled discombobulation of joints as he resolutely loped on.

With this air of misalignments about him, certain fractions of grace missing, it was as if, in some elemental way, he were not really at home in nature. But then, an impression of some gawky disproportion of parts is often the case with such a totally self-wrought figure—those personages who have methodically and implacably fashioned themselves into so much from so little. Intimations enough of this were afforded by the man out of Whittier. What Carter began to present was a sobering manifestation, on the ultimate scale of President of the United States, of the singular liabilities inherent in the classic American mystique of the self-made man.

For a certain order of strong and proud men in this country, there is only one thing to be in the United States, and that's President of it. Most anticipations of personal greatness first arc in that direction: no neighborhood or schoolyard of Inner America turns up an exceptional youth—an eager and exultant Icarus among his fellows, charged with an extra fierce vitality and an air of self-possession—who is not instantly, to his family and his teachers and then to himself, a potential President. And decades later, even after all the others have forgotten, it lingers as the solitary sunset *tristesse* of unnumbered men in chairmen's suites and executive penthouses over the face of the land that it somehow never happened, they never made it. After the magnesium flare of their beginning, they have somehow wound up strayed in a long, vague, declining afternoon, their Promethean will and energies finally left unanswered.

But it's the sort of compulsion that, even more ferociously than nature, abhors a vacuum—which might have been why, in the emptiness left by the Democrats' disaster in 1972, there transpired such a profuse population in the field for 1976. They continued to multiply almost overnight like mice. It was something like a Malthusian political phenomenon: as if the more who entered, the more possible it seemed to others, the more appetites were engendered and enlarged, even while with each new entry—Carter, Bentsen, Shapp, Jackson, Shriver, Harris, Bayh, Udall—the possibilities for all of them were impoverished by another quotient. An extraordinary if not unnatural passion it seemed, indeed, that kept them all beating about glum little auditoriums with metal chairs, that lusted to spend itself among so much drab beaverboard and chewing-gum-gray tile floors and plastic cups. . . .

For all the commotion of that throng of candidates in 1976, though, there was a sense that the nation had come to an obscurely unsettling stasis in its experience. After passing through the grand struggles of the past two decades—civil rights, Vietnam, Watergate—we suddenly seemed to have emptied out into a limbo, some stale lassitude of spirit. It may have simply been that we had lapsed into one of those transitional hiatuses in history. But it was a dull weather in which it was hard for any single figure to emerge and take on dramatic definition and dimension—a monotone and middling time vacant of any great angers or passions or belief, made up of vague and meager presences, vague and meager matters having to do with little more than maintenance problems in the system.

Indeed, it was a season whose heroes offered themselves as heroes of efficiency. It was no surprise, then, that the 1976 campaign for President of the United States became for the most part a contest of technicians. For that matter, the very effort of running for President had become almost wholly an exercise—natural enough in an empty age—of the technique of appearances. For each candidate, the struggle for nomination and election was a matter of performing the same set repeated choreography of sentiments and style and personality in a vaudeville tour of one-hour stands across the country. It amounted, really, to an ordeal of showmanship—like those dance marathons of the Thirties, a trial of nimbleness and concentration apart from any actual connection with the audience. During one of his expeditions into Florida, Carter began chat-

ting with a gathering in a hotel suite: "It's good to be here in . . .
here . . . in Tampa. Yesterday I was in . . . was in . . ." and
after a wordless silence, an aide called from the side of the
room, *"Pensacola,"* and Carter went on, "Pensacola, and we had
a very good day there." At the contenders' scattered moments
of solely personal and individual encounters, their looks would
go glazed and flat, they were not really there behind their eyes.
The act itself, the endless recurrences of those few minutes of
performing their image, became the whole reality in which
they existed, were imprisoned. It was all, thus, an immense
gymnastic tournament, the American Olympics of appearances.

In all this, the campaign of Oklahoma Senator Fred Harris
took on, at times, the slightly daft and whistly eccentricity of
Peter the Hermit's crusade. Harris, proceeding outside all the
conventional sophistications, was a rather unlikely article in a
political age of executive managers. A hefty, swart boar of a
man with a pouchy face, a bit mussed in attire, with a certain
barging slam-bang urgency about him and a hot glare in his
anthracite eyes, Harris was, in fact, a singular evocation, some
forty years later, of Huey Long—not only with exactly the
same look of some rambunctious backroad drummer of pans,
cold medicines, novelties, but more importantly, in preach-
ment.

In his campaign Harris was engaged in a pentecostalism
uttered directly out of that vision which had haunted American politics for over a century like a distant, phantom glimmering of Beulahland—Populism, that popular combustion of
country-Jacobin radicalism after the Civil War, which constituted perhaps the only truly home-grown American revolutionary proposition since 1776, and which continued to gutter
through the decades, luridly flaring with Huey Long during
the Thirties, then with Wallace, a meaner and more pinched
version. And Harris now came barrelling out of the same
roisterous political energies—a memory, an apparition out of
that old lustier politics from the time of the House of Long,
ironically reappearing now in this same campaign with the
triumphant manifestation of the new species that had evolved
since then, Jimmy Carter.

With one thick paw stroking and strumming his tie and coat

lapel, Harris would bellow, "Corporations run this government, they run this country, don't fool yourselves about that. Too few people got all the money—and that translates directly into *political power*. So what we got? We got a foreign policy that mostly answers to the interests of the multinational corporations, and a domestic policy that mostly serves the interests of the super-rich and the corporations, the Exxons and the IBMs and the Gulf Oil companies. Well, look here now—*we got to change all that!*"

Briefly plucking at his nose as one would plunk at a jews-harp, Harris would peal on with a delivery in which there whunked the deep-gullied, tin-bucket Okie inflections of his origins. "Break up these monopolies like GM, and really give 'em a dose of the free-enterprise system. Prices would come down naturally and there'd be a heap more people *working* out there if we really had a competitive business system in this country. But we haven't had anything like that since, as the lawyers say, the memory of man runneth not to the contrary. We been miseducated in this country—bigness is not generally better, *bigness is generally worse*. It grinds people down. What I'm talking about is all deeply American, actually. It's almost primitive American. Too few people run it all, and it ought not to be like that. That's not what Thomas Jefferson had in mind. That's not what we thought we'd agreed to back there two hundred years ago. It's time we got our country *back!* And let me tell you something—you don't get it by beggin'. *You take it!*"

But the truth was, something about Harris' actual persona seemed curiously dissonant with his radical testament. He carried an ambience which afforded slight disconcertments to the finer sensibilities of his faithful. He spoke one evening to a drawing-room gathering in a manorial suburb of Detroit—a tweedy and ethereal assembly of dispossessed liberals left adrift since the McCarthy and McGovern crusades, all collected now in small auroras of scattered lamps among potted ferns and Persian rugs and Impressionist paintings. Into this salon of liberal aesthetes Harris improbably brought the burly, pig-eyed ferocity of some warty, back-county Oklahoma sheriff, the brutish heats of a red-dirt demagogue. His feet spraddled, with one hand plunged deep in the pocket of his wadded buttoned coat and his other hand heavily punching the air, his coarse oil-black hair stiffly askew now, he accosted them all a little uneasily; they were unaccustomed to attaching this sort of appearance and manner to what he was actually saying: "I'm talking about a diffusion of wealth and power, the sort of things we haven't been seriously talking about for fifty years. What Wallace has done is make the frustrations and discontent of the common folks into a race deal. It's not a race deal at all, it's a *class* deal. The issue is *privilege*." Then, raking his hair back with clumsy swipes of one blunt hand, between swallows from a glass mug of beer with a wild bullfrog glare over the rim, he took their questions. "Naw. We got to quit propping up every dictator around the globe who can afford a pair of sunglasses. Looks like we'd of learned that by now. . . ." Afterward, late in the night at the end of a long day, riding in the front passenger seat back to his motel with three aides, he presently bent over and, scuffling a moment, luxuriously removed his shoes, whereupon, after another moment, the car windows around him began to be stealthily rolled down a discreet inch or two.

On the whole, there was a faerie quaintness about the way Harris went about his pursuit of the Presidency. With negligible funds and organization, he conducted his campaign from pay phones in airline terminals, phone booths on the corners of grimy little New England towns late at night, huddling bulkily inside the closed glass door and mumbling on a shabby unlit cigar as he scrawled notes on the back of an envelope in the bleak shine of a streetlight overhead. Checking into a motel, he would rummage out of his wallet cash in advance for the room. It all seemed interstellar distances away from 1600 Pennsylvania Avenue—deposited by himself up front in the cabin of a lumbrous propeller plane parked at a stopover at some scrappy wind-sock airfield out in the lost expanses of Wisconsin, ruffling through an airline magazine in the long wind-buffeted silence outside and then dozing off. An hour later, met at his destination by two students, he toppled his suit bag and briefcase into the front trunk of their Volkswagen with an affable hoot, "Damn, somebody been haulin' stove-wood in here, looks like," and so set out for his next call, stuffed into the front seat of the Volkswagen as it slapped on across the wide empty Wisconsin plains. Geneva conferences, National Security Council sessions, State of the Union addresses, all seemed as remote as the emerald City of Oz.

One Democratic handicapper dismissed Harris' adventure, with a sniff, "There's a kind of whiskey lunacy to the thing. Sure, he's got the fire in his belly—but it's the great energy of hopelessness." In fact, Harris struck a number of parties more disagreeably than that. He also seemed to have about him a certain hurry and sweat of the opportunist's glitter-eyed hunger, something of the travelling horse trader about him, a riverboat Gildersleeve hustling mining bonds.

But as a neo-Populist apostle, Harris' origins were authentic enough. He was the son of a dust-bowl sharecropper and occasional migrant harvester, and was picking cotton by the time he was five. An old photograph from an FFA convention ceremony shows him later as a thin, whippy, dark, tomahawk-faced youth, already glistening with eagerness. But through those years of viciously laboring to hack and scrabble mere survival out of a worn, shabby, intractable earth, the local town bank came to seem to Harris a kind of temple, a mystic sanctuary holding the magics of deliverance out of desperation into a distant bourn of plenty, wealth, power, security, peace: paradise.

Accordingly, after bounding on into the state legislature at twenty-six and then at thirty-three being anointed to succeed to the unexpired term in the U.S. Senate of the late Oklahoma oil baron Robert Kerr, Harris during his first years in the Capitol dutifully answered to the customary solicitudes for oil, gas —that firmament of interests which he had fixed on almost religiously as his salvation for so long as a boy. He seemed then little more than a precocious and enterprising Senate hack, merely possessed of an unusually spry curiosity. But in his service on the Kerner Commission, investigating civil disorder in the nation's cities, Harris began to blunder through a succession of larger illuminations—about the chasmic divides of race and economic lot in American society, about the corporate galaxy which had been the star-faith of his youth, about the pathologies of privilege. He found himself, in his late thirties, unexpectedly pitched into a new consciousness. And in the process, it was as if he rediscovered his beginnings, his source —and so discovered himself. At one New York gathering of party liberals, it was posed to him, "Very frankly, your early record leaves a lot to be desired. What do you say to that?" Harris replied, "I grew up."

Indeed, his past was not unspeckled. Among other things, during the Presidential primary campaign a Gulf Oil lobbyist reported he had smuggled money to Harris' first solo run for the Senate. But somehow, however wayward his course to his belated political enlightenment, it was precisely because Harris had been so mixed a creature that he seemed now to carry some extra register of reality. He had that peculiar existential authenticity of the prodigal—of having known, in the sinks of his own heart, if not evil, then dull brackish eddies of baseness, cheapness, the monotonies of venality. He had, as the preachers say, grappled with sin, looked into the eye of the Devil, and had emerged with a smoky singe of fuller experience than most other men. With this quality of an earthy authenticity, though, it was simply his misfortune, much like Lyndon Johnson's, to appear as a gusty anachronism at a moment of almost Proustian fastidiousness in the political sensibilities of the nation, a time of patented polyester personalities.

One morning in Manhattan, addressing a small deputation of Democratic counts and duchesses sipping coffee in a sunlit drawing room of soft beiges and cocoa-browns and dove-grays —with languorously tapered women in long black ankle-length dresses settled like swans in the corners—Harris assumed, in this bower of privilege and power, a somewhat more muted and modulated manner, looking for once almost stately in a rich gray suit. But in the low browse of his voice over the room, there still reposed those whumping, burly chords of the American Interior: "The thing about McGovern now, there were just a lot of blue-collar people out there who never joined up with that campaign. McGovern kept talking about calling everybody to a higher ideal. Well, my daddy down there in Oklahoma working on a farm for a living, he wants you to say a word or two about him. Heppin' the folks like him in this country, that *is* the higher ideal."

Harris now with one heavy mitt began rummaging at the cigar tucked away in his coat's handkerchief pocket. His voice gathered some of its customary steams. A spiky strand of hair fell over his brow. "Now Wallace is absolutely unacceptable, we all agree on that, but having said that, you have to think about all those people who are attracted to him—what it is about him that speaks to them, and why. It's not really race, but privilege for the few. They're *right* in what they feel is wrong with the way this country's working."

He cuffed his scattered hair back from his forehead, then tugged thickly for a moment at the fingers of one hand, while several heads in front of him bent for small, careful sips from their cups. "You know—you know, they tell me at a lot of these elitist cocktail parties, 'Fred, we love what you say, but will *they* get it'—meaning, of course, the great unwashed. Well, I come from that 'they,' I come from those folks"—his black eyes were crackling now, his voice was at full surge—"I'm a member of the great unwashed. And let me tell you something—*they get it quickest. They get it quickest!*" In a chair immediately in front of Harris, a silver-haired gentleman quietly removed his glasses, the lenses fogged, and briefly cleared them with the end of his tie. . . .

Back in New Hampshire the next evening, surrounded by a small cluster of supporters in a dumpy little town hall, Harris humped forward wearily in a wooden folding chair with his cement-sack knees spraddled out, holding his inevitable cup of coffee in both hands, looking up once to call to a couple hesitating in the door, "C'mon in, we got some coffee and doughnuts left in here," and then went on simply chatting in a low, hoarse, gravelly voice, with a neglected and dilapidated stage in the shadows behind him, and no more than a dozen people listening to him now in this feebly lit room in some little New England town lost in the vast deeps of an American night: "I just wanted to stop by here and see some of you people again. I think we're doing awfully well, I never thought by this time we'd have come as far as we have. Seneca, you know, said something about the danger always in organizing of losing sight of your original purpose. But we've deliberately tried to stay away from a lot of structured organizing in this campaign. What we want it to be is a true citizens' movement, just to see if that can happen. And I think we're gonna do it. I've just got a feeling. . . ."

But of course, even then one knew in the quick of one's spirit that it was hopeless. It was no more than a night ride come snorting out of the old deep woods of the nation's past, a brief whinny and whirl on the far edges of America's glassy-towered corporate age now—a computered civilization made up of the technological metaphysic and the Madison-Avenue theology of appearances and market research. But if we were indeed entering almost unnoticingly into some new and as yet undefined electronic ice-age of the human spirit, Harris' campaign, however doomed, seemed at least one last windy whooping foray in our old long adventure and struggle to know who we were meant to be.

As a Presidential candidate Jimmy Carter as well could not have seemed a more vaporous proposition in the beginning—a peanut grower out of south Georgia's vacant, sun-musing flatlands, with an occasional fancy for Dylan Thomas and Reinhold Niebuhr. (One reporter with him for several days observed, "You know, it's like after all those years of tilling and ginning peanuts down there, communing with those peanuts, he gradually took on something of their quality, their texture. Damn if he doesn't look vaguely like a peanut hull himself now.") He had been regarded even in Georgia while governor as a passably pleasant if rather strikingly ravenous opportunist and was commonly referred to there as "little Jimmy Carter." Of course, any prophet is always without honor on his own turf. Carter, however, always had rather less of the prophet than the bookkeeper about him—this spare, slight figure of impeccable Sunday-morning-at-church neatness, hair the blanched glisten of beach sand fluffed atop a pink, splotchy, sun-chapped face, with a grin, wide as a watermelon rind, of an almost anguished conviviality, yet with a certain arctic manner about him, eyes pale-blue as sleet. But as one correspondent with him during the early days of his Presidential campaigning submitted afterward, "He reminds me of what Roosevelt once told an admiral who was having a lot of trouble with MacArthur—'Never underestimate a man who overestimates himself.' "

In a sense, it was George Wallace who had engendered him, by loosing into the atmosphere (as he also had for Harris) the possibilities of a new Populist dynamic outside all the appointed national processes of power. The popular potential of the discontents at work beyond race in Wallace's astonishing primary showings beyond the South had not precisely been lost on Carter. And it was also Wallace who, in sheer logistical terms, made that potential's full realization possible for him.

By posing himself early as an option to Wallace in the primaries in the South, particularly Florida, and thereby as a promise for dispatching that still unsettling poltergeist, he gained his first authentic, if still tentative, validity. Wallace lent Carter that critical initial fraction of importance that attracted the early strategic interest of others, most crucially Andrew Young. Carter was born, and prospered, out of Wallace's predecession.

In his 1978 biography *Dasher*, journalist James Wooten cites Carter's lingering quaintness anyway as a Presidential contender: "He drawled. 'Ahmuh fahmuh and ahmuh Suthnuh,' he would say, and somehow it just didn't sound quite right within the context of an American Presidential campaign." But in fact, Wallace had also broken for Carter that dialect barrier to a national pertinence, that disconcerting inappropriateness somehow of a Southern cachet to a Presidential candidate—it no longer seemed quite so bizarre. If anything, Carter was enhanced by any evocations of a similarity to Wallace, appearing out of the same clime, with those same saps and lints in his voice, but yet so novel a contrast in spirit, in manner.

It became, for that matter, one of the whimsies attending Carter's progress toward the Presidency that the newly regenerated South might have special gifts to lend to the life of the rest of the nation—light musics of civility and a style of easy warmth between people, those old simple graces lasting still in a culture that had continued to belong to the earth long after most of the nation had metastasized into factories and megapolises. But in truth, what Carter came more to suggest was the advent, out of the South's massive homogenization into America's corporate technological order, of a new variant on Faulkner's species of Southerners: a hybrid between the genteelly civilized Gavin Stevens and the remorseless avidity of the Snopeses.

Plains, the community of his boyhood, was a negligible clutter of flat brick buildings set out in the wide piney buzzard-floated emptiness of south Georgia—only a few miles up the road, as it happened, from the town of Americus. From the beginning he was a somewhat uncommon lad, consuming *War and Peace* when he was twelve. But then, there had always been at play in such far barren reaches of the South a feverish application to cultural fineries, Carter's own parents on their first date having sallied forth to Americus to witness a performance of *The Merchant of Venice*. Perhaps nowhere as in such bereft locales were the arts and erudition taken with such a religious, if not desperate, reverence. Early in high school, one of Jimmy's teachers presented him a marathon reading list, with the promise of a gold star for every ten books he dispatched. And as his mother would later report, "Jimmy was a gold-star boy."

More than that, such terrains as Plains' Sumter County, with their meager mumblings of life, holding in their dusts and level monotonous horizons intimations of some final void of meaninglessness, tended to produce, in those spirits of larger eagerness and energy growing up in them, a formidable and outsized restlessness. The doings going on in the world beyond those pockets of stillness took on aspects of the mythic and fabulous. But it was a restlessness—an impatience to escape— that would often last as an enduring instinct in itself: the very *sensation* of escape, escape just *to* something else—that sweet excitement would become a simple habit of heart.

As for Carter, for the rest of his life he would seem at peace, at home, only in stages of transition to yet fuller prospects for himself—as if he felt truly alive and complete only in the suspense of greater expectations, in approaches to yet braver horizons, an endless tentativeness that succeeded in eluding the confinement of having to arrive at any final arrested definition or resolution—that dull preemption of any further possibilities.

With the same industry with which he had invested himself with those gold stars, he systematically proceeded then to enlarge his situation. From Plains, it was first the remote glory of the sea, as a cadet at Annapolis, where he studied nuclear physics, and then a beginning as a naval officer. In the meantime, in much the same calibrated manner, he set about a courtship in Plains. It was while he was on leave from Annapolis that he had taken a closer look at a friend of his sister's, a resolutely chipper girl with a certain demure, gingham-simple prettiness who was named Rosalynn. "She was just an insignificant little girl," as he later told it. But what seemed to endear her to him finally was that, like himself, "she had goals and purposes." That proved enamorment enough. The way he eventually proposed to her was that curious mixture, which he was to employ years later in his effort for the Presidency, of greeting-card sentiment and careful calculation. According to Wooten, "he looked over at her and told her she was beautiful and told her he loved her and told her he wanted to marry her and asked if that seemed a good idea to her."

The large destiny he had plotted for himself in the Navy, though, was shortly precluded by the death of his father. With the responsibility now devolving on him for his family's spacious farm holdings in Sumter County, he became resigned, with some reluctance, to the different prospect of achieving himself as a prosperous young landed squire. But as soon as that was comfortably nearing realization, he relayed himself on to a seat in the Georgia state senate—an entirely new ambience of possibilities, one of which was the governorship itself, which in turn might offer its own vistas of yet larger possibilities.

After tarrying a short while in the Georgia senate, Carter in 1966 made a first, dashing, but failing strike for the governorship, casting himself as a temperately liberal young spirit. His civil perspectives on race he had largely acquired from his mother, Miz Lillian, herself a restless sprightly soul who regularly disconcerted the townfolk of Plains by, among other things, inviting the son of a local black bishop, a boy educated in the North, for chats in her front parlor. But such small Southern communities in those days abided eccentricity only up to a point, and Carter himself, throughout the years of the high moral drama of the Movement in the South, had exhibited a certain measured circumspection of conscience.

As one of the young worthies of Sumter County, a locale long famous for the special viciousness of its racial frays, Carter happened to be quite close to the hot front of crisis of those days—not only to Americus during that troubled summer of 1965 in which Warren Fortson wound up wrecked (Carter merely made an appearance with two other legislators at a county commission meeting to suggest that Fortson should not be dislodged as county attorney on the basis of a petition, and then rapidly departed), but also to the collective farm nearby called Koinonia, founded as an interracial Christian community by an uncle of Hamilton Jordan, which was recurrently firebombed through those mad-dog years of the late Fifties and early Sixties. But Carter passed through that time of travail mostly at a decorous detachment from such live crucibles of conscience. When Ham Jordan once asked him, "You know my uncle? My uncle Clarence?" Carter replied dryly, "I know who he is—I don't think I've ever met him."

In his eventual gaining of the Presidency, Carter was to become the triumphant heir of Martin Luther King's momentous handiwork in the South. There can be little doubt that, without King, there would have been no Carter—it could only have been out of the kind of redeemed and reborn South which King principally brought to pass that any serious Presidential aspirant could have emerged. But just as much as he proved King's beneficiary, Carter made himself also a direct legacee, as has been noted, of King's antipodal counterprotagonist in the saga of the Movement in the South—George Wallace.

At some point after his defeat in the 1966 governor's race, Carter, ever the pertinacious student, had managed to sense and appropriate for himself Wallace's peculiar genius for the true vital source of political life: that immediate personal communion, past financial coalitions and newspapers' approval and all the conventional mediators of power, with the common people. At the same time, as the 1970 governor's race approached, Carter determined to inherit Wallace's legions in Georgia left from the 1968 Presidential campaign.

Carter began studiously altering and crafting himself for his next effort according to the Wallace political dialectic—a rude, fractious Populism that was far more generic, really, to Wallace's own glandular nature. Affected by Carter, a man considerably more prim and heatless of deportment, presenting himself as "just a redneck farmer from south Georgia," it was a manner which inevitably had a quality of a premeditated vamping. He even assumed Wallace's political aesthetic of a dumpy drabness. At a supper of steaks and Scotch one evening in a river house below Americus, a guest happened to remark to Carter that his campaign billboards—rather bleary productions with a blowup of Carter's face, scrubby-looking and fish-eyed, gazing out forlornly—struck one as "awfully dowdy." Carter's eyes widened a bit, and he retorted in a low flat murmur, "I don't think they look dowdy at all. They are exactly what we want. People are turned off by all those slick professional-looking ads."

Carter's major competitor in the Democratic primary was a former governor named Carl Sanders, a dapper and decently moderate squire who inhabited now the high towers of Atlanta's enclave of New South Medicis. Carter accordingly mounted against him Wallace's sort of rowdy Populist railleries, hooting him as "Cufflinks Carl" and belaboring him for his consortings with "the Atlanta bigwigs"—in all, succeeding in rendering Sanders' suave sheens into mortal blights. Somewhat more unpleasantly, in what amounted to a variety of racist McCarthyism, Carter's campaign indulged, if it did not instigate, the anonymous distribution of copies of a photograph showing Sanders being splashed with champagne by celebrating black members of Atlanta's pro basketball team.

Indeed, Carter conducted this second offensive for the governorship with a predesigned seediness not only of style but of sentiments. After his 1966 disappointment, he had comprehended that even his tenuous liberalism then had been far astray of the actual humor of the state. Now in 1969, Carter composed his campaign out of such Wallace dogmas as "restoring local institutions to local control" and maintaining "the highest standards of quality in the public schools and colleges of Georgia, in spite of any obstacles brought about by integration, court rulings. . . ." He may have been merely a more sanitized, sublimated Wallace—a kind of Kool-Aid simulation of Wallace. But he began nonetheless putting in appearances at private segregationist academies over the state, and in case any implications were still lost, he finally struck an entente—in a quiet chat in the back seat of a car driving one brassy September morning around the hot little river city of Augusta—with a stubby, bald political tout named Roy Harris who happened to be one of the more squalid and raucous racists of that time. These were rather bizarre affinities, on the whole, in a man who, approached only a few years earlier by his fellow townsmen in Plains with an invitation to join them in the White Citizens Council, became the only white citizen of substance in the community to demur, even when they offered to pay his dues for him—in fact, refused with a knot-jawed face mottled white in a fury of revulsion.

After he had accomplished it, after he had won, several friends noted that he "seemed jittery, edgy." It was like a vague after-nausea left from a conscious debasement and self-debauchery he had felt obliged to enter into in order to smuggle himself on to that larger vantage point of promise which he had missed the first time. He confided to a number of people that he was "distraught" by the campaign he had run, and reportedly vowed to Rosalynn that he would "never go through such a campaign again."

So it had been merely a campaign of appearances, contrived prefab attitudinizing. And with his inaugural speech, he simply dismissed and obliterated, without a blink, all that had gone before, that elaborate mime he had enacted. "The test of a man is not how well he campaigns," he insisted; rather, "This is the time for truth and frankness." It was as if he were announcing: *Now* was coming who he truly was and what he truly meant— this was really it now. And he then delivered perhaps the most fateful phrase in all his political career of ever-becoming: "I say to you quite frankly that the time for racial discrimination is over."

With that, even before his governor's term had begun, he passed on through the star gate into a national magnitude, was translated onto the front page of *The New York Times,* onto the cover of *Time.* Not a little ironically, it had been through George Wallace's physics of political power that he now assumed the legacy of Martin Luther King. He had become, almost instantly, the personification of the Born-again South.

Carter's most notable undertakings as governor were actually something less than Homeric. His administration was mostly occupied with the rather passionless, odorless ardors of economy and efficiency and various engineering rearrangements in the state's departmental structures, while Carter himself maintained his demeanor of well-mannered conscientiousness. But if there prevailed a certain amiable insubstantiality to his tenure, a vision of a yet vaster scale had nevertheless already begun unfolding itself in his head. Some years later, Jody Powell would relate, "I mentioned running for the Presidency to him once about midway through his term as governor. I was a little embarrassed to even suggest it, you know. But I noticed that it didn't surprise him at all. I realized then that he'd already thought of it himself long before."

In this, he once again was operating according to Wallace's

political senses, in the same way Wallace had been enspirited to proclaim during his own campaigns, "I want to let yawl in on a little secret. These here big national politicians like Humphrey and Nixon, they don't hang their britches on the wall and then take a flyin' jump into 'em every morning, they put 'em on one britches leg at a time, just like you and me do." So it was Carter's genius now, undaunted by all the orthodox probabilities and the apparent outrageousness of his speculations, to begin quietly and raptly drawing a measure of himself —for someone of his fearsome ambitions, probably already a simple unthinking reflex—against the other Presidential hopefuls who happened to pass through Atlanta for an evening or two at the governor's mansion: "I couldn't help but study the material coming through there on visits that was being considered at the time as Presidential possibilities. I'd always thought of Presidents as historical figures, you know—they were really above human beings in my mind. Then, as governor, I met Humphrey, Jackson, McGovern, Ted Kennedy, the others when they came out and stayed with me." They little suspected —relaxing in those evenings, weary and a little unlaced, some of them getting a trifle sozzled—the ferocious and meticulous scrutiny that they were actually under from that pale gaze with its spacious hospitable hoecake grin. "After a while, I began to realize I knew more about most matters than they did. It sort of surprised me. There wasn't anything all that special about them at all." He was heartened, as it were, by their prosaicness, inspired by their mundaneness. It was their bad luck not to impress him sufficiently to dissuade him from his secret contemplations of contending against them.

At an early point in the primary campaigns, Mo Udall pondered, "Seems like everywhere I've been lately, they tell me Jimmy Carter was just through there a week or so ago. Everybody said when he started out that there's just no way you can get elected President the way he got elected governor in Georgia, shaking hands with everybody in the nation. But damn if he doesn't seem to be doing something like it. Incredible, he's even out there in Arizona, running around. The sonofabitch is as ubiquitous as the sunshine."

Indeed, Carter seemed to be managing, to an uncanny extent, a continental extension of his governor's campaign in Georgia. In a feat of sheer relentless diligence over all obvious likelihood, he began to prosper through a preternatural capacity for shaking hands from early dawn on sidewalks and at shopping centers with the steady, oblivious, tireless application of a sewing machine. He seemed as fatigueless as aluminum. It was a faintly forbidding fortitude (Carter liked to relate that, when he began running cross-country as a youth, "I used to cough blood, but I wouldn't stop") that carried him, with his unflagging neighborly grin, right on without falter through those flat coffee-haggard gullies of spirit of four o'clock in the afternoon, on up to midnight. "It's almost unholy," remarked one newsman. Waiting outside a factory gate for a shift change in the Florida panhandle, Carter himself proudly reported, "While ago in New Hampshire, I shook hands with forty-five hundred people before I had a bite of breakfast." Standing in the bleak sunlight of a cold afternoon with a wind like deep icewater ruffling his hair, he then began hastily grabbing handshakes and shuffling out his handbills as rills of workers lapped past him, murmuring with his intrepid grin, "Hi, I'm Jimmy Carter, I'm gonna be your next President, hi, I'm Jimmy Carter . . ." Once, after swooping swift and delicate as a swallow to open a mailbox for one kerchief-wrapped lady with a handful of letters who had tried to circle away from him, he commented to a newsman with an odd instant detachment, "They'll take that brochure home I've given 'em and read every word. All most of 'em get is the weekly newspaper and the Baptist magazine. And later on when they see you on TV, they'll tell their friends, 'I shook hands with that guy,' or, 'My cousin shook hands with that guy.' This is exactly the way I won in Georgia."

Devoid of any of the swaggers or machismo of a truly dramatic political presence though, Carter seemed to be presenting himself for the Presidency as little more than an excellent, enterprising clerk—his proposals for the nation amounting, for the most part, to merely a recycling of his gubernatorial preoccupations. He was running on the administrative passions, the managerial fervors of salvation through procedure and technique. With an urgency that was almost spiritual, he would proclaim, "We have a real need for uniform, predictable, well-structured, well-organized programs." But if he seemed to be aspiring to the Presidency largely as an earnest clerk, he managed to make himself into one of the most formidable clerks ever known. At the least, he prompted certain solemn second meditations on the beatitude "The meek shall inherit the earth." Through no more than a single-minded, unremitting assiduousness, it stunningly began to seem possible that he could actually bring it off—that he could inherit the White House.

For all his industry, Carter also seemed to move in a constant rainbow of political good luck—most notably, when he was blessed with the almost supernatural stroke of good fortune of having most of the other candidates agree, back when Carter still looked altogether irrelevant nationally, to refrain from Florida and leave the field there to him so he could attend to the special task of disposing of Wallace. As it happened, though, Wallace—that stumpy and dowdy gremlin who had been harrying the Democratic Party now over the past fourteen years—had become, since the sudden berserkness in that Maryland shopping center four years earlier, a blasted ghost of who he once was, merely imitating the furies and motions and sounds of his prior self. It became more and more evident that his campaign would flare more thinly and emptily than anyone had supposed, the last instant false glare of a light bulb before it goes out forever.

In Carter's increasingly jaunty sorties now into the furthermost reaches of Wallace's old tribal territories in Florida, he affected a kind of gleeful unintimidation, taking a moment aside as he was shaking hands outside a Pensacola cardboard plant to inform a reporter with a small smile, "We only about three and a half miles from the Alabama line here, you know. . . ." Swinging down the sidewalk of Pensacola's main street, Carter was directed by local aides—"Let's run 'im into Child's here"—into a cafe with barbershop-tile floors and a slightly tatty, glazed mummy of a tarpon mounted on one wall; Carter strode eagerly to a long table at the back full of businessmen taking their midmorning coffee, where he was notified, "This is Wallace country back here round this table, sorry." Carter's face colored, and then became almost all grin, as he burbled, "Okay, good deal, wouldn't want it to be unanimous."

Even though Florida had been more or less ceded to him in the beginning, Carter began buoyantly professing, "It always would have suited me if the rest of 'em came on in. I'm willing to beat 'em all." Indeed, in his pluckiness he was prone to over-strut now and then, to overadvertise his auspicious associations, happily announcing, "Golda Meir, Mr. Rabin, Mr. Allon—they're all close friends of mine." He began indicating he was being regularly advised by former Under Secretary of State George Ball, until Ball finally grumped to reporters he'd only chatted once, and that only momentarily, with Carter.

No matter. If simple motion were substance, Carter could have been Charlemagne. In Pensacola, out of a chill ashen-skied morning he abruptly appeared through the glass doors of the courthouse and, followed by a churning wake of report-ers and Secret Service agents, proceeded to course through its corridors and offices with the dispatch and thoroughness of a Roto Rooter, greeting its early-morning population of secre-taries and officials and citizens—"Hey, lemme shake your hand, I intend to be your next President. . . . Yawl gettin' any peanuts down here at all? . . . Oh, yeah, you from Georgia? Got any kinfolks up there?"—all the while, with each handshake, trans-lating with a deft magicianlike flicker into their palm one of his pine-green pamphlets, as he did giving a quick little curious possum-grin of shyness and abashment. Any open door along the way exerted on him an immediate gravitational check, tug-ging him in—"Hi, I'm Jimmy Carter, is it all right if I speak to you folks in here?" He glanced at a closed door in one office—"Is there somebody in there, too?"—and hesitated before it, strumming and ruffling his sheaf of pamphlets while someone behind him said, "Yes, but she's . . ." with a sudden muffled short grumble of water then sounding behind the door and a secretary emerging to discover, with a small start, almost bumping into him, Carter standing immediately before her, beaming. "You the first lady I've ever given a pamphlet to in the bathroom," he warbled, and impulsively dabbed her cheek with a slightly awkward little buss.

And so, off again, this subdued stampede moving after Car-ter in its own isolated pocket of urgency, forging up stairwells with sudden small scuffling collisions with idle downcoming traffic, a dull storming of feet down the hallways with Carter now and then glimpsing over his shoulder happily to check the entourage spilling after him. At one point, he charged on through closed double doors, and everyone after him, into what turned out to be the county criminal courtroom, its wooden pews holding a scatter of rather funereal faces awaiting the convening of that morning's session for the disposition of their assorted delinquencies and griefs and woes; Carter nevertheless proceeded to bustle among them, regarded with dull incredulous stares as he chirruped to them, "Hope you enjoy your day in court!" A few minutes later, at a bank across the street, he startled customers in glass cubicles in the midst of the tense privacies of applying for loans—and wound up once, in his swoopings about, briefly behind a teller's window, apparently unnoticing, greeting folks over the glass panel as they stepped up uncertainly, "Hi, I'm Jimmy Carter, I plan to be your next President. . . ."

As it turned out, his campaign was provided an unexpected galvanization by the sheer gap of agreeable surprise between the initial assumptions about his trivialness and his actual engaging, assured personal bearing. He traveled far out from obscurity on the mere dazzle of that difference: he became, spectacularly, what Saul Bellow terms a contrast-gainer. It was soon his own marveling, elated suspicion that the journalistic establishment, "especially *Time* and *The New York Times*, looks like they've sorta decided to adopt me."

Carter also happened to have, dimly, the look of some unknown, undiscovered country cousin of Jack Kennedy—the ghost of that look, however dwindled and dusty in Carter, not the least of his serendipitous political properties. If nothing else, JFK was a protean happening in American political life simply in his effect on the style of political theater here—forevermore altering it from a play of protagonists like Eisenhower and Taft and even Stevenson who suggested high school principals, spiriting the nation into an age of romantic politics, of matinee princes, of cavaliers. The following generation of politicians, in image and manner, were indeed all the children of Kennedy, with Nixon only an aberrational atavism in it all, as was his extension, Gerald Ford. The Kennedy political dramatic became pandemic—a national mythos of nostalgia, brought to its greatest utterance in Robert Kennedy, yet still so profound that it continued to resist all hopelessness in its pining after the last harried one of them left, despite his own reluctance and dubious fitness. It was by no means, then, one of Carter's inconsequential windfalls that he happened to provide to that terrific nostalgia a certain tantalizing illusion—and this faint *déjà vu* evocation he carried was not lost on him. Especially with assemblies of students, he would, before taking their questions, execute the ceremonial flourish of removing his coat after the manner of Bob Kennedy, slinging it over the back of a chair, and then, with an almost formal deliberation, fold up the sleeves of his shirt two precise laps, so standing then with feet spraddled and hands clamped on hips to engage their interrogatories, their challenges—responding to the blunter questions with a sporting, softly murmured "Aw right. Good deal. . . ."

Despite the furtive Kennedy ambiences of his campaign, though, Carter seemed to be proceeding in it as if he were teaching a Sunday-school class. It was as if he were pursuing the Presidency through a kind of politics of niceness—a gentle, bread-pudding didacticism, made up of sentiments having about the subtle flavor and complication of the Sunbeam Pledge. What he conducted, really, was a campaign of good intentions. Given his rather scanty experience, it may have actually been about all he had to offer to recommend himself. But after so protracted a national trauma of dislocation and disillusionment, Carter devised his campaign as an appeal for a national redemption and atonement after the shames and despairs of the recent past. And he went about this as if, by simply proposing it, all of that—Vietnam, Watergate with its accessory complex of scandals—could be expiated and abolished. At the end of almost all his appearances, he would quietly intone, "We need a government that can be"—a short breath of a pause,—"as decent, and honest, and truthful, and fair, and compassionate"—his eyes briefly glaring glassily wide in emphasis at the gently uttered rustle of each word—"can be as pure, and honest, and idealistic, and compassionate as the American people." It was like an incantation, as if by simply sounding those words in the air, *kind, and truthful, and decent,* their reality itself might, by some magic of mimesis, be conjured forth—or more, by his sheer insistent recital of those words, he might assume and become those qualities themselves.

It may have been something like the exhilarating moral romance of commitment and courage excited by Robert Kennedy that Carter had set out to reproduce, but with Carter, it turned out to be more a Disneyland soul he emoted, like those Coke commercial chorales, *I'd like to build the world a home and*

furnish it with love, grow apple trees and honey bees. . . .
Rather than ideology or any real political principles, Carter's
was an enterprise of a moral sentimentalism. It prompted some
cynics to begin suggesting after a while that Carter was not so
much sicklied over with the pale cast of thought as with a
potato wash of Parson Weems goodliness. But in fact, Carter
utterly, unblinkingly subscribed to all of his platitudes. "Social
workers are my favorite kind of people," he would frequently
enthuse. "When they went to college, before they got disillu-
sioned by the bureaucracies they wound up in, their hearts
were opened to help blind people, poor people, the handi-
capped, the afflicted. . . ." But it was a curious compound of the
managerial and altruistic that inspired him. To those on welfare, he would administer through government programs
"understanding, respect, and love." Citing one employment
program for the indigent in his home county, Carter related,
"To see the pride that exists now in those women who are
doing something useful . . . in God's sight"—and he hesitated, a
lapse of suspended breath while he rolled his eyes about him
gravely for a moment—"will bring tears to the eyes. Only ten
percent of those on welfare can actually work," he went on to
announce, standing very still as he presented this news. "The
other ninety percent"—and again he paused with that melodramatic breathlessness—"can't work," this last almost mumbled, a soft downbeat finish in the syncopation of his delivery
in these offhand little political devotionals. "What we oughtta
do with that ninety percent," he would sing, wait, and then
smile, "is love them," this uttered again with that low, wispy,
portentous, sinking finish and a faintly apologetic and pained
grin, his eyelashes batting softly as if in fleeting embarrassment
at the simple, obvious, overwhelming decency of these pro-
poundments. "The question is whether we can have a government"—another vapor-hang of hesitation, his grin then
stealing forth again—"that is right, and decent, and honest,"
tolling forth the words once more in awe, as if in some adolescent's stricken infatuation at his discovery of idealism and
nobility.

On the whole, Carter's main occupation in his campaign
seemed to be, with his squeezed grin of graciousness, to convey
the effect—in the phrase of the aging Texas ranch foreman in
Jane Kramer's *The Last Cowboy* when he cites what he most

admires in Western cinema heroes—of "expressin' right." His
conversion as a born-again Christian of the Southern Baptist
declension having transpired during the dispirited interlude
after his first governor's campaign, Carter posed himself for the
Presidency on more or less the same Calvinist ethic of rigorous
worthiness. He would entreat gatherings in the small sober
voice of his years of teaching a Baptist men's Bible class, his
hands held in a delicately spread cage of touching fingertips at
his buttoned coat waist, "I want to be tested in the most severe
type of way. I'll try to conduct myself as a candidate in a way
that'll make you proud. I'll never tell a lie, I'll never betray
your trust, and I'll never avoid a controversial question. Test
my character, my ability, my weaknesses—and if I don't measure up," he gamely proposed, "I don't *deserve* to be elected."

This campaign of gestures and attitudinizing may have been
somewhat more commendable than the variety he employed
in that second campaign for the governorship of Georgia. But
it was a fixation with the sententious and rectitudinous—for
"expressin' right"—that has always acted as a central vigor in
the American folk character, and that may, in fact, be one of
our more disquieting enthusiasms. While it has often accounted for the best in our past—the Abolitionists, Woodrow
Wilson, Robert Kennedy—much of the rest of the world has
also come to entertain a wariness of the mischief and mayhem
worked by that eager didactic simplicity in the American nature. But it was that national disposition which Carter had
come to sense, to understand, perhaps more fully than any
other politician of the time.

But Carter also happened to hold, beneath all the cotton and
caramel, closely precisioned machineries. Undertaking once to
lyricize on what returning back home to Plains meant to him,
Carter offered, "There's some sort of strength there for me. . . .
Maybe it's in the air or the water," and then went on to note,
"I've really made an effort to define what it is that happens to
me when I go home, because I think it's important to understand that process if I'm going to completely understand myself." Even in this melo-sentimentalism, he operated finally as
the technician, reducing the mystery of the call of home to a
"process" that "it's important to understand." In his self-
compelled magnification from Plains to the Presidency, Carter
proceeded as, more than anything else, the utter engineer, the

total programmer—of himself most of all. Not for nothing did he cite Admiral Hyman Rickover—that tight, raspy, taciturn, metallic autocrat of ruthlessly efficient performance—as the most consequential presence in his past. Ever since his brutally grueling days at Annapolis with Rickover, Carter had directed himself according to a scrupulous personal budgeting of his assets and options for maximum self-realization and effectiveness. Never especially graced when it came to making speeches, he applied himself to that particular inadequacy in himself, conscripting a local radio announcer to tutor him, with the same grim doggedness for self-improvement with which he addressed every other item he found insufficient in his life— with speed-reading courses, cultural sieges of museums and opera halls. In the matter of his oratory, the results never did turn out to be all that auspicious: his voice never lost that faint shrill of reedy strain and its odd off-tempos. It was as if, however far he was to range in eminence and self-certainty, his voice would still be left somewhere back around the point of his high school graduation.

But Carter's most imposing impediment throughout his political progression was the fact that he had never been particularly social of inclination. He had never really been a public personality. Perhaps for that reason, then, he would incessantly proclaim to the anonymous throngs at his rallies, "I feel very close to all of you"—essaying in that way to invoke, at least, a peculiar sort of mass, impersonal intimacy. If the end of all this sedulous self-enlargement was nevertheless the impression of a man of befuddlingly disparate parts, Carter protested once with the same considered purposefulness, "People say they don't know me. . . . I've tried, and I've tried hard. I've spent two years now trying to let people get to know me. I don't know what else to do."

So finally there always seemed some furtive tone of calculation to his folksy flourishes, his breezy "This Land Is Our Land" effusions, his advertised affinities for Dylan Thomas, Bob Dylan, the Allman Brothers, Reinhold Niebuhr—they somehow carried a tinniness of studiously acquired enthusiasms, a sense of a carefully designed soulfulness. This combination of effects—the sentimental with the deliberation of a mechanical engineer—moved some to aver that Carter was merely Nixon with cocoa and sympathy. He even programmed himself to imitate, to an extent, Jack Kennedy's rakish élan, flicking up the scarf of a receptionist to softly ruffle her hair in his fingers, letting his freckled hand linger on the back of another secretary's hair as he murmured, "Mighty purty girls in this office," snatching the hand of a blond and dimly pretty matron introduced to him and exclaiming, "I been lookin' forward to meetin' you, I sure have, and now I know why I have been," as he swung their nestled cuddle of hands back and forth between the two of them in the manner of schoolyard sweethearts. But it was a part of Carter's finely computered composure that he allowed himself no more than such momentary tantalizations with those wanton sirens beckoning in the enchantments of power. Once, after a radio talk show during which he had been called by a girl whom he had briefly dated as a teenager back in Plains, he indulged himself in the exquisite headiness of phoning her back, sitting behind a desk in a side office of the station with one cordovan wingtip shoe cocked up on the rim, flushing to a tea tinge as he mumbled, "Roxie Jo? Hi, this is Jimmy. . . . Yeah. . . . Well, fine. . . . Married? . . . What part of town you living in now? . . ." and then stammered with a strangled-looking grin, "You still as purty as you ever were? . . . Sure. . . . Sure. . . . Naw, naw, I couldn't do that," and his face, in a suffusion of crimson, melted almost completely into his grin.

But no more than that. Even as he moved through repeated public surfs of exuberance, he yet remained, under his own festiveness, somehow unfalteringly self-contained and deliberate, keeping his arms for the most part crossed in a neat tight tuck, pausing to stand with feet close together, his gestures spare and clipped. It was as if, for a creature of such precise gaugings, nothing could be trusted to the reckless vagaries of spontaneity. Later in the White House, before a special piano concert Carter would hail Vladimir Horowitz for his "fearless expression of emotions"; only someone of Carter's constricted disciplines would acclaim it as "fearless" to express emotions, and this peculiar accolade even lifted Horowitz's eyebrows in a brief startled wagging. Recalling one incident during the campaign when he became exasperated over a disarray in scheduling, Carter remarked that no one would have noticed his reaction "because I have complete control"—the only evidence of any irritation he ever betrayed being a faint splotchiness mottling his face. Though he was prone to dispense blandishments extravagantly—he would tell reporters, "We really feel honored and privileged that you're spending some time with us, really do"—he seemed to find it unbearably uncomfortable to have to entertain flatteries himself. He was made squirmish and taut of neck whenever he found himself captured in casual one-on-one banter, as if it offended his compulsion for absolute economy of expenditure—"I don't really like to waste time," he once conceded, "if it looks like somebody's just trying to contrive a conversation." It soon began to be proposed by observers that his celebrated inexhaustible industry in campaigning really owed to the sublimated tensions of such unrelentingly pent compressions in his manner.

In an aside to a relative during the campaign, Carter himself allowed, "I can will myself to sleep until ten-thirty and get my ass beat, or I can will myself to get up at six o'clock and become President of the United States." In the end, it all seemed to come to only a matter of that—of willing it. That was all it really took, as it had served all the new becomings of his self-levitation out of Plains, to transubstantiate himself now at last into the most important leader in the Western hemisphere. And he would assert again and again through the campaign, as if the repetition were a part of that effort of willing it, "I don't intend to lose." It was as if he meant somehow to simply insist it into actuality.

In a sense, as it turned out, he did.

At a reception of some 450 supporters at Tampa's convention hall before the Florida primary, Carter found himself most thoroughly among his own people, a definitive gathering of his variety of faithful. It was a tumultuously jubilant convocation ("You lookin' *good!*") of the New South's country-club Bourbons—junior bank executives and architects and attorneys with pale, pampered, faintly translucent faces and chestnut manes of fine-spun hair, wearing vest suits of large plaid prints, their wives otter-sleek and sun-burnished in pastel gowns, furiously vibrant, the new Scarlett O'Haras of the South's suburbs, faces shiny with a kind of bright-eyed, constant, hectic expectancy which seemed to have only begun wasting them discreetly, at their tight temples and cheekbones. Among them were older women with candied bouffant confections of hair and sweetly shattered faces, their husbands in Western-cut leisure suits of popsicle hues of yellow and orange with string ties, their cheeks a little whiskey-scorched. They were, if not precisely the beautiful people, the Glad People of the Brave New South.

Carter swam into them, in high elation. Many of them he recognized with delighted squeals, "Aw, I can't believe it! Lookahere who's here! . . . McRae! Great day in the mornin'!" He moved on through exchanges of whoops like some small-town high school homecoming, "You just keep that nice smile, Jimmy. . . . Jimmy, you gonna do great down here, I'm working all the Christians for you, now," on into a vast and dimly illuminated area like an airport hangar where the bar was in full boisterous swing. In that bleary blue light, a white frost of beard was just beginning to show on Carter's jowls and chin like a dusting of ground glass. "Jimmy, what in the world you doing running for President?" one old friend brayed to him, and Carter, taking a quick little chest-expanding breath of excited concurrence with the dizzy audacity of it all, cried, "Winnin' it, it looks like."

During the dinner later in the main convention hall, a chorus from a local high school—all neatly barbered, spankingly sanitary and radiant and unanimously grinning—serenaded the crowd, belting out "California Dreamin' " like thronging Easter bells. Finally, Carter could not resist arising from the head table on the rostrum and skipping down and strolling over to stand by himself at the foot of the low stage where they were ganged and singing, cozily beaming up at them while personally receiving their blessing, his arms snugly crossed and cuddled to his chest and his head shoved forward in that stubborn terrapin manner of his, a beatific grin of sheer transport on his uplifted face as they hymned to him,

> "*Oz never did give nothing to the Tin Man*
> *That he didn't, didn't already have. . . .*"

With his gaining of the White House, though, Carter's lifetime scenario of ever becoming something else arrived at a kind of magnificent blind end. For the first time, there was no larger estate which he might use his new circumstances to begin realizing. Aside from the possibility of inflating the office of the Presidency itself into an awesomely more titanic institution, the invigoration of any grander expectations was gone.

Now he had to come at last into some conclusive definition apart from his restlessness for higher prospects. Inescapably, he had to execute now.

With what ensued over the next few months—the ramifying dishevelment of the energy crisis, the Bert Lance debacle, his confoundment with Congress, the collapsing dollar and somersaulting inflation, the deepening bewilderment and consternation of allied governments, even proliferating speculations eventually about his competency—that vague, lingering sense about Carter during the campaign of some essential slightness rapidly became a sense of overwhelming slightness. It all came to suggest that those cherished American canons of industry, virtue, amiability, undiscouragability, grit, might not in some instances, such as the Presidency, quite be enough. While it had been Carter's persistent doughty assurance during his campaign that "I'll be good, you wait and see, I'll be damned good," what his administration began to bode was the vengeance on America at last of its venerable Dale Carnegie ethic of unsubduable confidence.

Carter seemed left with little else, before long, than ghosts of the poses and gestures of the campaign that had elected him. His means to power—that constituency which had responded to his campaign's prospects of a Populist national regeneration —had not transferred, when he reached the White House, into the power to achieve it, the power to govern. Instead the candidate who had proclaimed during the campaign, "I owe the special interests nothing!" had found now, once in office, that there was to be really nothing else there for the duration of his term but special interests. At the same time, as journalist Elizabeth Drew noted, while Carter may have gained the Presidency through a Populist-tempered crusade, it became his vulnerability once he had won—the immemorial vulnerability of the outsider—of being "too impressed by the importance of those institutions he had vowed to defy." Oddly, it became a kind of higher, Presidential replay of what had happened to Lester Maddox when he found himself stranded in the Georgia governorship right before Carter's own term. In the same way, Carter now wound up populating his Cabinet largely with regulars out of that conventional preserve of eminence which he had so energetically belabored.

The most conspicuous exception, of course, was Andrew Young. In terms of the promises and portents of Carter's campaign, Young was without doubt his truest appointment. The furors Young subsequently occasioned in Washington and other capitals owed principally to the fact that he was speaking not diplomacy but a kind of prophecy, an international extension of his pulpit apostleships during the years of the Movement. But those same rows and dislocations were also an eloquent indication of what would have happened had Carter actually undertaken to fully, or even appreciably, realize in his Presidency the mood and implications of his campaign.

But then, if anything should have become evident by now since the times of Tom Watson and William Jennings Bryan and Long and Wallace, it was that any Populist perspective had always proved notoriously resistant, if not impossible, to ever actually articulate into the active. It was as if it only existed in prospect. Carried on into the gravities of reality, somehow it always permuted or vanished. Instead, it had always been important only as a style of campaigning, as a means to and vision of power, rather than as a way of actually governing.

But still it endured, that peculiar mirage of a Peaceable Kingdom which had been glamoring now through the experience of the South and the political life of the nation for over a century—Carter but one more failed pretender, one more errant and lost prince of that old dream.

On the morning of his ascension to the Presidency, Carter had been invited to an early sunrise commemoration at the Lincoln Memorial where Martin Luther King's father was to preside at a prayer service. If Martin Luther King had left behind him the order of redeemed South which provided Carter the release and blessings out of which to make a campaign for President, Daddy King himself had lent no little nurturings to the fortunes of Carter's actual candidacy, with its promise of a sweet summer of humanity and righteousness in the life of the land. But already, the dissolution, the equivocations had begun to set in. "Although he had told the old man he would be there," as biographer James Wooten reports, "he had no intention of going and never had. . . . So he had said 'perhaps' to the old man, knowing all along the answer was really 'no.' " And on through the proceedings in that cold coral winter dawn in the capital, Martin Luther King, Sr.—all his years now of so many noble hopes ending in ambush, in blankness—found himself caught in the thrall of some strange sluggish desolation that had descended over him the instant he emerged from his car, and which did not pass through the rest of the brave pageantries of that day.

With his campaign's final collapse in the Massachusetts primary, Fred Harris removed himself out to a small spread in the high plains of New Mexico. He is now teaching a political science class at the state university in Albuquerque.

Travels with Brother Will

THE GRAINY LITTLE highland city of Nashville, Tennessee, has long served not only as the spangled Ilium of country-and-western music, but also as a kind of collective administrative Jerusalem for much of the Southern Protestant church, with the headquarters of a number of denominations, most notably the Southern Baptist Convention, ranging like monumental granite-and-glass fortifications over several downtown blocks. And every Sunday morning, with a calm scattered clanging of steeple bells over a sunnily empty Music Row, Nashville becomes for a short while virtually a city of congregations, collected in translucent-windowed sanctuaries in a hush of organ tones and offertories.

But on Easter Sunday in 1972, during that bright morning hour of doxologies in town, out on a twenty-one-acre hillside homestead several miles east of Nashville, the Reverend Will D. Campbell—an ordained Southern Baptist minister with a divinity degree from Yale—was occupied instead with hauling stovewood in his pickup truck, now and then depositing a precise spit of King Edward tobacco juice into an empty Coke bottle. Campbell had, in fact, already observed Easter. The night before, with a few friends assembled in his log-wall study set out in a stony windy field a short distance from his white farmhouse, he had thrummed a few country ballads on his Gibson guitar, the toes of his fancy-patterned cowboy boots pumping—*Hello, brother mother, friend of mine*—and then he had presided over a communion service like those he often conducted late at night in dwellings of black sharecroppers and Ku Klux Klansmen alike: "Everybody in this room, now, who believes that through the loving sacrifice of Jesus Christ we have all been reconciled to each other, everybody who knows

that, let 'em say, Hallelujah! and drink now to that victory"—
and those around him then took a long swallow from their
lifted glasses of bourbon and water.

If, the next morning after that communion service, there was
little sign on Campbell's place that it was Easter or even Sunday, that was because each day passes for him more or less as a
common informal Sabbath. A smallish and wholly unporten-
tous figure, with soft shy eyes peering behind black-rim glassses
from a mulish mulling face, and a long hang of William Jennings Bryan hair fringing a knuckle-bald pate usually covered
by a wide-brimmed black hat that lends him the look of some
strayed Amish elder, Campbell has long been engaged in a
curious sort of fundamentalist guerrilla ministry, deriving directly out of the South's old dour religious vision but improbably transposed by him into the living critical edge of his time.
In his clanky ketchup-red pickup, often carrying with him no
more than his guitar case, into which he has packed a single
change of underwear and socks along with a bottle of his
Tennessee mash "medicine," he moves about as a peripatetic ad
hoc Christian partisan among the unlovely and wrathful, not
only Klansmen but the dispossessed and despised all over the
back reaches and urban concrete desolations of the South. He
has always tended to scandalize more conventionally religious
sorts as a blasphemer, a heretic, an anarchist. At one campus
seminar, a professor of theology kept demanding, "But what's
your actual *business*, Reverend Campbell? I mean, what do
you actually believe in?" and finally Campbell barked, "Look, I
been trying to tell you, I believe in Jesus, dammit—*Jesus!*
That through the saving grace of his sacrifice on the cross,
we all been redeemed and made brothers to each other. So
if we accept this gift, we're free, there ain't no need to hate
anymore. Getting the word around about that is my business,
professor."

On his twenty-third wedding anniversary, leaving his wife at
home to observe the occasion with their four children, Campbell appeared at the home of a North Carolina Klansman to
pass the night with him before the Klansman's jailing the next
morning for refusing to divulge Klan data to the House Un-
American Activities Committee. With other Klansmen sitting
around him in the small linoleum-floored kitchen, Campbell
whunked out gospel hymns and hillbilly ballads in the vicious

brightness of an overhead bulb burning on through the long tunnel of the night—"Now, this song coming up, it's kind of powerful material. It's the whole New Testament boiled into one song, really. And its message is, black or white, it doesn't matter *what* we done, Jesus Christ loves us anyway. That's the miracle none of us deserves. . . ." When Campbell was asked once, in regard to his ministry to the Klan, "But how in the world do you manage to *communicate* with those brutes?" he replied, "By emptying the bedpans of their sick."

His church pulpitless, roofless, unpropertied, uncodified, Campbell's is a peculiarly eclectic and variegated ministry—or witness, as he prefers to term it. He can be found not only among the destitute, but equally in the company of the urbanized New South's merchant princes, among patrician Southern aesthetes patterning sibilantly around the poolside of a bamboo-screened courtyard in a perfume of gardenias, sipping bourbon with Walker Percy in his backyard or sitting in a chandeliered drawing room on Manhattan's East Side, whittling away by an Italian-tiled fireplace while in a spirited exchange with old friends like David Halberstam and Jules Feiffer and Robert Coles.

Indeed, as much as he ministers to the Klan and others in those sullen drifts of social slag left by the South's industrialization and corporate agglomeration, Campbell also makes regular appearances before convocations of establishment worthies—business executives, university dons. And to them he brings tidings that they are deeply implicated in a tragedy, confronting them with that mentality not only in the New South but in American society, pervasive and diffused and found in teak-paneled corporate boardrooms among sensible modulations of language and manners, which has accomplished incalculably more havoc, he maintains, than any Klan cow pastures lit with burning crosses. "Now, I know there's a lot of sickness and meanness and evil amongst the Klan," he explains, "but I'm saying it's a lie to make them the problem. They ain't the real enemy. The real enemy is what that thing is that's keeping the redneck a Kluxer and the black man, too, a nigger—that's keeping folks like them outside and poor and without hope, and makes for the emptiness in their lives and the violence that always comes out of emptiness. In the words of a famous ole country song, it's hard to find the blame, it's too smart to have a name; it ain't flesh and blood we fight with, it's powers and principalities. Let me give you an example: I was involved in civil-rights work back around 1960 when the sit-in movement started, and I heard one Southern mayor and business leader after another say, 'Look, we not arguing with you about the *morality* of this thing, it's just that we happen to be in business down here on the corner of Seventh and Broad, and you can't run a business or a town government either on anarchy and chaos.' You turn it all into a matter of maintaining a system, see—make it all a question of keeping the machinery running—and that way, the misery that functioning machinery might also happen to be incidentally causing in the lives of human beings, such little problems as that, that's not what's at issue. The system, the stability of the structure—that's what's at stake."

Propounding all this once to a seminar of Atlanta's mercantile and civic notables gathered into an auditorium at Georgia Tech, Campbell reflected as he whittled away on his usual stick of cedar kindling, "You know, I asked a Klansman a few years ago, 'Grover, what exactly does the Ku Klux Klan stand for, anyway?' and he said, 'It means peace, harmony, and brotherhood, preacher.' I said, 'Well, what means are yawl willing to use to achieve that peace and harmony?' He said, 'Any means we have to—shootin', burnin', blowin' things up, whatever it takes.' So I said, 'But Grover, how in the world can you get peace and harmony out of shootin' and blowin' things up?' and he said, 'Well, preacher, you tell me what you think we doing over there in Veet Nam if we ain't burnin' and blowin' things up—and it's supposed to be for freedom and peace and harmony, ain't it?' Now, around this same time, I also had occasion to talk with a dean at Harvard University during the Dow Chemical sit-ins up there, which of course were simply an effort to get this country to realize what it was actually doing with all that napalm in Vietnam, and this dean said to me, 'Believe me, I'm in such sympathy with these young people. But you just can't run a university on unrest and disorder.' What I'm saying is that institution, and this institution right here and respectable institutions like it all over the country, have contributed, unwittingly or not, to incomparably more bloodshed and misery, done more to maim and murder, than the whole lot of pore ole boys in sheets holding cross-burnings in rented meadows back there through the Sixties."

This was answered by a profound hush over the auditorium. "I 'spect some of yawl disagree with that right strongly. But I wonder if any of us really has an idea what crimes are committed in the name of order and progress." Campbell—with his black plowman's hat resting on the table at his elbow, looking like some turnipy hillbilly prophet with his scraggly scarf of hair hanging limp below his ears—briefly lifted his cedar stick for a few delicate sniffs of its winey tang. "Been noticing lately that they've even begun trying to get us affectionate about technology, trying to make technology cozy and friendly. But you know, I buried a man up in Chicago last Saturday who'd spent thirty years in coal mines—*thirty years*—and after all that, he literally didn't even have a shirt we could bury him in. We held this service, now, almost in the shadow of a statue up there to the famous railroad free-enterpriser, George Pullman. What I'm telling you gentlemen is, that man was *lynched*. He was lynched by the system in this country—the kind of system that'd keep a man toiling for thirty years in a coal mine to keep himself alive and then leave him without so much as a shirt to be buried in."

Campbell dusted some cedar shavings out of his lap, resumed his whittling, and went on, "You see, in a way it's the redneck who's been the special victim of the whole system. It took his head away. The system got about everything else from the black man—took his back, took a portion of his spirit maybe—but it never quite managed to get his head. All along, the black man's known more or less what's been going on. But the redneck—hell, he's never really known who the enemy was. If any of yawl remembered anything about the course of Populism, every time the poor white began getting together in natural alliance with the equally dispossessed black, he's been told by the reigning establishment of the day that it meant unrest and disorder, the blacks were gonna ravish his wimminfolks and the Bolsheviks were gonna invade the courthouse. He's never known how he's been had. . . ."

And here, Campbell wagged his cedar stick at what were by now the incredulous stares of his audience. "And it's been the *respectable* folks, mind you, the substantial and progressive elements of society, who really took that head, who blew out the light in that brain."

*   *   *

What is most singular about Campbell is that, after long years as a liberal activist in the civil-rights movement, he eventually came to repudiate all the conventional liberal instruments for creating a just society—legislation, politics, bureaus, programs. This disaffection of his offended a number of his compatriots then as not a little perverse, but it was born out of a larger, terminal disillusionment with the whole social firmament of institutions and institutional processes: no matter how benign their intents, Campbell came to sense, they merely magnified and codified the estrangements between people and ultimately worked to debase life. And from all this, Campbell emerged with a peculiar vision—an answer itself generically Southern, a passion for human community inherently part of the Southern experience—that would pose at least one prospect, however tenuous, for the South's surviving, after all, those progressive depredations of spirit that have come with its passage into the void of America's corporate technological massociety.

"The South," Campbell maintains, "still has a better chance of working out its problems than the more urbanized rest of the country, simply because more of us still know one another's names. Even a lot of these rednecks who hold cross-burnings out in nighttime fields, you find—once they take off their sheets —they have a truer sense of human community than you'd suspect." He took a visitor once to a tavern on the grimy outskirts of Nashville—a spot, Campbell explained, "which this black guy opened about fifteen years ago just to have a place where folks could duck into and relax and be themselves and drink a few beers without their wives hearing about it and raising hell. You'll find it just as full of rednecks as blacks now. It's *real* integration out there, man—that blessed community we all supposed to be after. And it didn't take no Justice Department decree or HEW directive to create it, either."

Called Dreamland, it was tucked far back from the highway at the end of a long gravelly dirt road winding through crowded pines, a low, rambling, ragamuffin building set in a clearing strewn with engine parts and bedsprings and doorless rusting refrigerators. Through its slapping screen door, its interior resembled nothing so much as a dim, neglected attic— mangy Victorian parlor chairs, blind-eyed hulls of vintage television sets, murky dresser mirrors—and the bar was lit in this gloom with an auroral rainbowed glow like that of an old nickelodeon. There, a burly, sunburnt white man, grinning like a stump-toothed Buddha, was listening in fascination, along with the tavern's owner and two other blacks, to a wolfishly gaunt white youth detailing his outrage over being accused by a friend one night recently of some nocturnal tusslings with the friend's wife. "It took me two damn days to figure it out. You know what it was? It'd been my own goddam twin brother— and the sonuvabitch was using me as *trapbait*. What he did, he switched clothes on me, and then he used my own truck and went out there and fucked that gal pretending he was me." The black owner chuckled, "Hell, that couldn't of been much fun, havin' to pretend he was you all the time." With guffaws whooping around him, the youth cried, "What the hell's so funny? How the hell would *you* feel, your own twin brother. Go ahead and laugh, but the next time I see that sonuvabitch, I'm gonna *kill* his tricky ass—swear to God I am. Gonna blow him to ninety-nine pieces."

Leaning over the bar, the black owner said quietly, "Yeah, well, but wait a minute now. How you thinking about it in your head now, that may not be exactly the way it happened. You know? You oughtta think about that a second too." The youth squealed, "Naw, shit, no, I *know* what happened, he went and—" "Naw," the black owner insisted, "you *think* he did. But maybe what happened, see, didn't necessarily happen the way you're *thinking* it did, what I'm tryin' to say." The youth grew quiet then, pondering this possibility, and finally grunted, "Yeah, well, lemme have another Pabst. . . ." Campbell turned to his visitor and murmured, "That's the kind of counseling, you understand, they take three years trying to teach you up there at the seminary at Yale. Or the mediators and diplomats been trying to bring off for twenty-five years in the United Nations."

Later, driving back to his place, Campbell observed, "Hell, that ole boy wasn't gonna kill anybody anyway. Any given Saturday night, you'd probably find him out Kluxing in a bed-sheet like all getout, and if you asked him what he was doing, he'd tell you he was fighting the goddam Communist hippies and the race-mixers in Washington. You ask him then what he was doing the other day out at Dreamland, why, hell, he was just drinking beer and talking to some fellows.

"Now all that might not be much to go on," Campbell continued, "but it's more than anybody else has got, I'd submit. One of my Klan friends, the last time I was up at his house, he took me out to Klan Hollow and showed me this grave right outside the door of Klan Hall—the grave of an elderly black man who'd lived there on this fellow's farm. My Klan friend had told me once about this black man, 'I pay Cliff a little more because he's'—and he couldn't quite bring himself to say foreman, boss, so he said, 'he's been here longer, he knows more about the work.' And at nights, this elderly black man used to come by my friend's house, was invited in, and he'd sit down, watch television, visit my friend's sick mother for a while, drink some coffee, and then get up and go home. I'd tell my friend, 'Man, you already got more integration right here than all these people you want to take your guns and kill are even asking for. You got open-occupancy housing, fair wages, you got social mixin'. . . .' He kind of rared up a bit at that, but I told him, 'Well, look, when your neighbor comes by in the cool of the evening and visits your sick folks and watches teevee for a spell and drinks some coffee with you, if that ain't social mixin', I don't know what is.' Whether my friend would ever acknowledge it put that away, I greatly doubt, but still, when this old black man died my friend had him buried right there beside Klan Hall, and had a twenty-foot cross burned at the head of his grave, which in this case was the greatest act of homage and honor my friend could think of.

"Of course, even in the South now, these kinds of personal relationships are beginning to disappear like they did a long time ago in the North. But they do still exist—people who at least know one another's name. At least, we ain't all Manhattan commuters yet, riding in the late afternoon through Harlem and wishin' that damn train would go just a little bit faster, get us on out to Westchester County. Those people on those trains don't even want to *look* at those people they're passing in those tenement buildings in the bloody sunset—let alone have any feeling for what's actually happening to them down there."

As it happens, Campbell—himself reared on a forty-acre cotton farm in lower Mississippi—is one of those few white Southerners who was intricately involved in the whole long unfolding of the civil-rights movement almost from its beginning, ranging about as a mediator and strategist for the National Council of Churches, escorting the first black children into Little Rock's desegregated schools in 1957, negotiating with white businessmen in Montgomery and Birmingham, on hand at the genesis of Martin Luther King's Southern Christian Leadership Conference. "But in all that work in race relations, I think I was really looking for a home," Campbell says now. "I had been educated out of the one I came from, so I was trying to find my home in black people—like a lot of other white liberals in those days. But then some of my black friends like Stokely Carmichael started telling me, 'Look man, you wanna help out in this race-relations thing? Well, we pretty much got things cool and together with *our* folks. So you wanna help so bad, why don't you go where the problem really is now—why don't you go to work on *your* people.' I said, 'Man, you happen to be talking about rednecks when you talking about my people. I can get *killed* by those folks.' And he said, 'That sort of means they the problem, don't it?' "

It was out of this illumination that Campbell, around 1962, began widely proposing, "The racist is perhaps the greatest challenge we face today in both the North and the South—the most unlovely and the most in need of love. We must not abandon him in an attempt to punish him to maturity." If that was not a particularly fashionable notion at the time, it was later to come into a certain political currency, with the recognition—primarily prompted by the startled alarm over Wallace's popular prosperity—of those brooding masses of whites who had long inhabited along with blacks the shabby outer precincts of the nation's promise, a discovery that eventually came to be styled, through the campaigns of Robert Kennedy and McGovern and Carter, the New Populism. But Campbell's approach to those alienations was in an entirely different vernacular.

"Look, all it's about is this," he would declare, scrimmaging for a moment through the voluminous litter on his desk until at last he found his Bible, his fingers then scuffling through its pages. "Here, listen to this now . . ." and he would begin reading from Second Corinthians, "For the love of Christ constraineth us, in that he died for all. . . . Because God was in Christ, reconciling the world unto himself, not imputing their trespasses unto them." Smacking his Bible shut and pitching it back on his desk, he would pronounce, "Sure, that's a hard idea to accept—our trespasses are not held against us, we are *already* forgiven—and that's why the gospel's far more drastic and important than a lot of folks have ever dreamed. Because nobody who truly accepts that is gonna use that pardon as a license to keep on abusing folks. It's gotta change his behavior. Don't you see how that liberates us all? Black, white, Kluxer, preacher, murderer, chairman of General Motors, head of the Ford Foundation—we are *all* bastards, but God loves us anyway."

It was a proposition, though, that frequently unsettled Campbell's liberal colleagues, and did sometimes seem to affront elemental humanitarian decencies. Shortly after the trial in Lowndes County, Alabama, in which middle-aged white deputy Tom Coleman had been acquitted by a jury of his fellow townsmen for the shotgun slaying of the young white seminarian named Jonathan Daniels who was working in local civil-rights demonstrations, Campbell propounded in the religious journal he edits, "Jonathan can never have died in vain, because he loved his killer—by his own last written words. And since he loved his murderer, his death is its own meaning. And what it means is that Tom Coleman is forgiven. If Jonathan forgives him, then it is not for me to cry for his blood, his execution. Any act on my part which is even akin to 'avenging' Jonathan's death is sacrilege." This commentary occasioned some spectacular instances of ideological apoplexy in liberal quarters. Says Campbell, "A whole lot of my civil-rights friends came to me and said, 'Good God, Campbell—you can't be going around saying things like that to those rednecks. You tell 'em stuff like that, "Why, we not holding your deeds against you, fellas, it's okay, you're forgiven"—man, that just gives 'em *license*.' But of course, that's not true, I told them. What that jury down there in Lowndes County told Tom Coleman was: You are foregiven and congratulated, go thou and kill again, if you want. But what the gospel, what Second Corinthians says, and what we are obliged to say is: your sins are already forgiven you, brother, go thou and kill no more. That's the difference. And that's all the difference in the world."

The truth is, comprehending Campbell requires a number of turns around some unfamiliar corners, and the only term that would seem to approximately describe him would be, perhaps, fundamentalist gospel existentialist—a rare genus, without doubt. His reversion to all the forbidding business of the Southern religious sensibility—his dark pessimisms about the congenital orneriness of the human species and the unalleviable adversity of man's lot, and his trust in all the mysterious supernatural machineries and alchemies of the Incarnation, the Blood Atonement—has given considerable pause to those who answer to the rationalist humanitarian ethic. Yet Campbell has somehow construed from his Southern fundamentalist vision, with all its dire metaphysical smokes, a liberation and grace to believe in the race that, curiously, would seem a quantum leap beyond the customary optimisms and sympathies of the standard liberal decency. It is a kind of ultimate hope and compassion: that the angry, the predatory, the corrupt, the base, the indifferent, can be redeemed, not through efforts of the law or governmental agencies to compel or scourge or regulate, but only through inducing in them the transforming realization that they are in fact one with all other men, including even those whom they abuse—that we are all finally of one nature and one flesh and one grief and one hope—and only with this recognition can any real contrition and compassion and regeneration come, and then it is immeasurably more overwhelming. In the end, Campbell proceeds on the persuasion that American society itself, the American neighborhood, will only be reordered and recreated into those more humane dimensions which his liberal colleagues have been struggling to effect, by revolutionizing and recreating, in this most radical Christian sense, the hearts of individuals.

Even so, as plentiful as the skeptics in the liberal estate are Campbell's critics in the formal church. In the words of one, "Absolutely nothing seems to be sacred to the guy." Rather, to Campbell there is simply no real distinction between the sacred and the secular. If the Incarnation meant anything, he believes, it was the accomplishment in Jesus of a final closing of any divide between the divine and the temporal, between the religious and the profane, between the church and the street—between heaven and earth: that in fact, the whole history of the faith from Abraham through Moses to Jesus has really amounted to a series of recognitions that God and the earth were always drawing closer together, with the final great moment of merging coming with the Incarnation. But it is also

Campbell's conviction that the institutionalized church has acted ever since to resist and subvert that cosmic event by reasserting the old dichotomy between the divine and the earthly. And this failure of comprehension and of belief constitutes, to Campbell, the original and still greatest betrayal of Jesus' meaning: when the sacred and the secular were resundered by the official church—when the gospel was reextracted out of the common daily dusty welter of humankind—that reopened divide then admitted all the monstrous mischiefs throughout the course of Christendom like the Crusades and the Inquisitions and the Hundred Years War.

"Every time a group of believers has moved from a catacomb or a brush arbor into a steepled sanctuary, they've lost something they once knew about Jesus," Campbell declares. "And they never seem to get it back. The result is that you have, all over this nation, these magnificent church steeples casting their grand shadows over people living in almost prehistoric hunger and misery, or in all Dante's circles of hell out in the pretty ghettoes of suburbia." Indeed, anyone spending any length of time with Campbell in his trackings over the country begins, before long, to wince at the appearance of any steeple in the distance, invariably provoking as it does another snort from Campbell, another fulmination—"Now that little stubby unpresumptuous steeple there on that little country tabernacle, that's all right, those kind can stay. But look at that one up yonder— that's a brave one, ain't it? Ain't that a proud tower? You realize, you could sell that thing, that splendid spire sticking up there, and buy a seeing-eye dog for every blind person in the whole state of Texas? And still have enough left over for half of Arkansas?"

Campbell was baptized when he was seven years old, on a hot summer Sunday morning, with the lumpish hands of an itinerant preacher tilting him backward into the sluggish current of an olive-brown creek while the congregation of the East Fork Baptist Church, gathered on the shade-mottled bank, sang together, "Oh, Happy Day." Mississippi's Amite County, back then during the Depression, was a countryside of ragged pine hills and gullied roads of pebbly pale-orange dirt trailing thinly up to isolate scrubby farmhouses perched atop bare ridges, a countryside with a communal past of numberless shotgun-and-wood-ax violences. Campbell remembers his father talking of how, as a boy, he had been taken by his own father early one morning in a mule-drawn wagon to the county seat to witness the hanging of a youth who had slaughtered his bride's aged parents, had found the village at noon filled with other wagon teams, buggies, saddled mules, and then the youth himself, after a last meal of fried chicken and biscuits and rice and milk gravy, had been dutifully hung with only a quick gurgle and a few small light kicks of his feet like an idle little gay soft-shoe in the air, transformed then startlingly into merely something sacked in clothes sagging at the end of a rope. "My daddy's daddy was a man who opposed violence in any form and for any reason," Campbell relates, "and it's likely he took my daddy and his other boys out there to let them know, to see and experience for themselves, the kind of society into which they had been born—to introduce them to its inevitable tragedy. It was like he was saying to them, 'Take a look, boys—this is the way your world is. Shouldn't be—but is.' "

Campbell grew up with both his grandfathers, "and one granddaddy taught me how to pray, and the other'n taught me how to cuss—both right useful facilities, I later came to find." In the casual and colloquial kind of racism of that community, no more real thought was given to the black people around them than to the roosters in their backyards or the rabbits in the fields. "But then one day, this old black man we knew, who'd just been released from the penitentiary for stealing a sack of roasting ears from his landlord, he came walking by the store where a bunch of us boys was hanging out. We all hollered out, 'Hey, ole nigger!' My praying granddaddy happened to be there, and he snatched me aside and said, 'Now, look here, hon—maybe nobody's explained this to you yet, but there ain't no niggers anymore. Not since the Civil War. There's nothing but colored people now. So let's don't be hollering that ugly old dead name to Turner no more, hunh?' My granddaddy was legally illiterate, see, but somehow he'd managed to figure out that the Civil War was over, being one of the few white citizens in the state of Mississippi at that time who had."

It may have been that Campbell's acute discomfort of later years with all the officious benevolences of bureaucratized liberalism had its inception with, he recalls, "this federal hookworm grant to our little school down there, which involved all the boys being called into the auditorium one morning, with all the girls waiting their turn outside, and this very alert chap in a bow tie distributing around what looked like tiny tin snuff cans. Then we all got a sheet of mimeographed instructions, and after we read it, the man asked if there were any questions. Somebody finally spoke up, 'Uh, this word here—*specimen*—what's that spose to be?' Five minutes later, when the man finished talking, we still didn't know. There was a long pause. Then one of the older boys slowly turned and looked at me unbelievingly, and declared loud enough for everybody to hear, 'I think he's telling us to go home and shit in a snuff can.' It took a long time for the howls and uproar to subside. But then when we stopped laughing, it began to occur to us: *Wait a minute, now. What the hell business is it, our own goddam personal specimen, of Washington, D.C.?*"

Even as a small boy, Campbell recounts, "I was the one marked out in the family to be a preacher, and thereby special. I'd already accepted that—I had in mind tendin' to the altar fires and tea parties under the steeple." Some nine summers after his creek baptism, he found himself mounting the pulpit of the East Fork Church, having earlier that Sunday morning drunk a can of pineapple juice to lubricate his larynx, and proceeded to preach his first sermon, which he had been practicing for weeks from a sheet of notes tacked to plow handles behind a mule. When he had finished it, he stood in the vestibule to receive congratulations, his spirit wheeling in high winds of euphoria. Shortly afterward, at seventeen, he was ordained, and even now, the only certification legitimizing his ministry—hanging on the thin-slatted walls of his farmhouse along with a print of Chagall's *The Rabbi* and a disembodied ceramic hand pointing to a duplicate of that ominous inscription which appeared on the wall of Nebuchadnezzar's banquet hall, *Thou art weighed in the balances, and found wanting*—is a framed document which "attests to the fact," says Campbell, "that in 1941 I'd had certain hands laid upon my head, and when they were removed, I was a Baptist preacher, and it's signed by my daddy, my uncle, and my cousin."

Campbell began then his long and haphazard pilgrimage of understanding. After serving in the Pacific during the last years of World War II, he wound up at Yale, and went from there to his first pastorate in a little mill town in Louisiana. "But I didn't get to stay there too long. For one thing, I did a little picket-line walking during a strike at the paper plant. More than that, though, the folks in the church began getting a little upset about the sort of music I was imposing on them. I'd been up there to Yale, see, where among other things I found out the kind of music they were used to down here was *undignified,* so I started furnishing them right away with dignified music, like Handel and Bach chorales, you know, cathedral music. Finally, a delegation came up to me one Sunday morning after the service, and kind of politely complained. So the next Sunday, by God, the first song I listed in the bulletin was 'Jesus Loves Me,' that sweet little ditty Sunday-school children sing. This, of course, they recognized as an insult, originating out of hopeless stupidity."

Before long, Campbell had moved on to Mississipppi as the campus chaplain at Ole Miss. "This was about 1954, and I lost that job when I was observed playing Ping-Pong with a local preacher friend of mine who happened to be black, and a few other little things like that. In a short while, it just appeared best to everybody that I sort of move on." He alighted then in the Southern office of the National Council of Churches —"and felt I was home at last."

But it was in his protracted passage over the following years through the grand struggles of the movement—Montgomery, Little Rock, Birmingham, the Mississippi Freedom Summer of 1964—that Campbell finally arrived at a total disenchantment with all political and institutional intercessions to improve man's behavior toward his own kind. "I grew up in the Roosevelt era, and I desperately believed in the validity of liberal politics," Campbell said at the time. "I think I can say I've traveled the whole liberal route. But the dream of reconciliation based on law and politics is gone. If one does not believe that, then let him go into a tavern in Alabama and hear the manager say, following the visit of a thirsty Negro, 'Yeah, we have to serve 'em, but we break every glass they drink out of. There ain't no law against that yet.' This may be a kind of justice, but it's empty. It's sure not reconciliation."

Striking out then on his own freebooting ministry, Campbell began preaching, "All institutions, and I mean *all* of 'em, are fundamentally inimical to what Christ was about on this earth." What was ultimately subversive about them, he contended, was their common reliance, however humanitarian their pupoises, on the mechanistic for deliverance: "It's the assumption that everything lies in technique. Everything, every issue or moral question, is made just a question of technique, of management, of programs. The ideology of the left and right draws strength from the same myth: that processes of law, social structures and systems, are all that is necessary—all that is *possible*—for ministering to any human crisis. Damn, technique defines it *all* for us—defines the menace and the hope, evil and salvation. There's nothing wrong with us, this mentality says, that political and social technique, legislation or revolution, can't overcome. And if that ain't a proposition that God is dead, what is it?"

Campbell recalls that "one time I was driving down through the Mississippi Delta, and I stopped in this little town to see a friend of mine, the son of a big plantation owner, who had wandered into the liberal revelation and was now a teacher of sociology. I found him in the front parlor of his daddy's house in a conference with a group of other sociologists and some foundation field workers, all of them busy working out the problems of the Mississippi Delta with census graphs, population surveys, demographic projections spread everywhere over the rug and chairs and tables. So while I waited for them to finish their deliberations, I rode with this boy's daddy out to one of his tenant houses, where he had to check up on somebody who hadn't shown up for work the past couple days. After a lot of loud rapping, this poor aged black woman came tottering to the door, wrapped in a scrappy quilt, and the old man yelled, 'How come you didn't show up for work again today? Whaddaya mean, you *sick*? You were sick yesterday, you said. Well, what's wrong with you? Whaddaya mean, you *hurt*? Where do you hurt? . . . ' Here while this guy was railing at one of his ill tenants in a way you don't often hear any human being talking to another, his enlightened son was huddling with his colleagues around card tables up there in that living room with their demographic charts and pencils and rulers and gum erasers, plottin' how they were gonna bring the kingdom into the Mississippi Delta."

More than that, Campbell came to conclude that "what institutions actually institute, in the end, is inhumanity, by advancing this illusion that form is substance, the means are the meaning, doing is being, procedure is redemption—and so they can only further dehumanize the relationships between those they were instituted to reconcile. In fact, what characterizes our brave new technological era is the capacity now of all its agencies and departments and bureaus, whether kindly or just regulatory, to complete the utter totalitarianization of mankind, by making all life just a matter of systems and management."

Back during those campaigns of the Sixties, says Campbell, "I would get this uncomfortable feeling that all those programs presumably designed to make us free nevertheless seemed, somehow, to be leaving us less free. What we were doing, unaware, was constructing ourselves right into an enormous bureaucratic and technological concentration camp." The proliferating possibilities for further tidying up life that technology arrayed before the institutions of the progressive conscience increasingly afforded Campbell unease, casting him at times into especially rude collisions with certain liberal respectabilities. He once dropped by a gathering in an expensive Memphis home of young urbane civic activists, all of them with a quality of immaculate niceness and goodwill, among them a businessman in this thirties who presently began enthusing to Campbell about a medical program being launched by the National Council of Churches in Southeast Asia "which will allow us to detect very early in pregnancy, like the first month, whether a fetus is deficient. It's really very, very exciting, very promising." Campbell, who had settled himself in a glossily elegant chair with his hands folded atop a walking cane and his black hat hung on his crossed knees, lapsed into silence for a few moments, staring rather morosely into a vacant varnished fireplace while the others went on talking. Suddenly he inquired in a small flat voice, "You know, I just been wondering. What's a deficient fetus, exactly? You talking about, like with no arms and legs? Or maybe mongoloid? I mean, I was just wonderin' how yawl gonna go about reachin' a conclusion on which ones are deficient and gotta go, and which ones you'll let be." The young businessman, sitting on an ottoman beside Campbell, gave an agreeable abashed grin, and began busily tugging up his socks and rubbing his ankles, "Yes, yes, I see what you're saying. Of course. I don't know, I'm not . . ." and Campbell asserted still in a low even voice, "No, now,

I'm not accusing you, understand. But it just seems this project you're talking about is another instance of that general arrogant liberal wisdom which would blandly propose it can act for God in determining those lives which are worthwhile, and those lives which are deficient and ought to be eliminated before they are born and become a burden on society. That serene arrogance, I'm always fascinated by just how it works." Leaving the house later that night, Campbell muttered from the back seat of the car, "That fellow back there is probably as decent and sincere and well-meaning a man as you could find in Memphis—he's good, a genuinely good man. But sometimes, from the goodness of folks like that, I get these strange whiffs of Buchenwald. God help us—*deficient fetuses!*"

After a minute or two, Campbell added, "You know, it's been right out of that progressive liberal vision that we've produced all these monolithic apartment-and-shopping-center complexes, like one I passed outside Chicago not long ago. The guy driving me proudly announced, 'Everything those people in there need is right in there with them—amusements, medical care, supermarkets, schools, even their own chapels. They never have to leave that complex once in their whole lives.' I thought, for the love of Jesus—you don't need barbed wire anymore, you don't need guard towers with machine guns, we're inventing concentration camps with comforts and total conveniences."

The next morning, Campbell set out on an expedition down into the Mississippi Delta, the car passing through the outskirts of Memphis along a narrow back road of plank shacks sitting under chinaberry trees, Campbell noting happily, "Awright, awright. Washing machines on the front porches. It ain't far away now. . . ." And presently, with the abruptness of a roller-coaster swoop, there was a tremendous rush outward of space and sky—a limitless yawn of land in the wide spring morning. After a time, passing along the endless level sprawl of rowed fields with the far hulks of abandoned tenant houses stranded, frail and solitary, long sun-tranced distances apart, Campbell remarked, "Twenty years ago, now, every one of those little houses out there would of had cotton growing right up to the front door and right up to the back door. But the people living in them just couldn't keep up with mechanization, and finally the sprays and chemicals and weedkillers just displaced them. So now, they all up there in Chicago and Rochester and Detroit City. Yeah, I used to drive along here and see those little houses empty, and I used to think that was progress. But dammit, you can't tell me that all those people wouldn't be better off out there on those places. I think if they were given just half a chance, half a hope, they'd start coming back down here in a stampede. Don't tell me they hadn't rather be back down here, sittin' out on those little bitty porches in the cool of the evening, sippin' water out of a dipper and watchin' their kids roll those ole tars around in those dirt yards. They'd be freer in every way. But oh, *freedom!*—how many times have people been screwed in thy name. . . ."

Campbell suddenly turned then in his seat and craned his neck to look back over his shoulder: "Damn. There was a tractor looked like nobody *atall* was driving it. Man, I think we about to turn that corner at last, we can see that light at the end of the tunnel, the millennium is about here. We finally 'bout got it fixed so we don't need *nobody*."

Campbell's antipathy to the institutional regalias of statistics, files, policies, and programs seems to owe to some deep instinct of his that all social systemizations necessarily constrict and impoverish human experience. "All I'm trying to do," he explains, "is just be faithful to that part of the gospel which would keep us from being turned altogether into automatons— the element of the gospel which would save that old portion of the human heart which needs, sometimes irrationally, to be free; which is also the contrary and troublesome part maybe, but is at least free, at least human, and also happens to be the only part of us that can love."

Because of that, Campbell entertains a special distaste for the institutionalized church. "I'm convinced that it's come to act as the single greatest barrier to the propagation of the gospel. Somebody once said that any church truly of Jesus would be an instrument literally and constantly being used up in his service—that is, service to those not even in it. But any institution, however altruistically it may have been conceived, sooner or later winds up serving primarily the interest of preserving and enlarging itself. It's just the nature of the beast. And like every other institution, the church—with all its budgets and four-year plans and accessory agencies—has come to serve

mainly the purpose of perpetuating itself, by the trick of identifying its own perpetuation with the advancement of the
gospel. That's the great blasphemy of it."

In his own religious quarterly, *Katallagete*, Campbell once
reported with some acerbity that the Southern Baptist Convention headquarters in Nashville had just adopted an office-
security program entailing not only Pinkerton guards but
emergency provisions for the use of tear gas, and not long
afterward, a Baptist official from that headquarters appeared at
Campbell's study late one afternoon for what he amiably proposed as "a little chat about your article." Seating himself among
the cabin's customary disorder of cardboard boxes and walking
canes and scattered hummocks of cedar shavings from Campbell's perpetual whittling, the official—a small neat gentleman
with a film of sandy hair, attired in a crisp pale-blue summer
suit—at length began to explain, with an air of scrupulous
pleasantness, that he knew, of course, that Campbell realized,
naturally, that his department really had a *duty*, unfortunately, to protect its premises. Campbell softly interposed,
"Protect it from who?" The official, crossing his legs then with
a certain preciseness, cleared his throat lightly behind his fist:
"Well. Of course, I'm aware you'd have no way of knowing
this, Reverend Campbell, but the fact is, we'd had a number of
people to report lately that they'd seen undesirables in the
building." Campbell's whittling knife paused: "Undesirables?
Undesirables? Can you tell me exactly who you think it is that
our Lord asked us to reach and to serve?" The official blinked
several times, and then submitted patiently, "Reverend Campbell, I don't think you understand what I'm trying to get across,
exactly—" and Campbell snapped, "Yessir, I think I *do* understand. Somehow we've wound up in the position, God help us,
where our Savior's church is forced to deal with those very
people it was commanded to rescue and minister to, to deal
with them as undesirables now and barricade itself against
them, and make sure they stay set apart even if it takes gas to
do it. *Gas*. When you all were discussing this security program,
wasn't there *anybody* in that room who jumped up and said,
'Whoa, hold on a minute here, brethren, what in the name of
our Lord Jesus Christ are we talking about here? *Gas!* What
are we saying?'" At that, the official—his face having taken on
a faint pink tinge—suggested with a slight brittleness, "Now, I
think we might be getting a little bit overzealous here," and

Campbell shook his head. "No, we ain't. We're *supposed* to be zealous on these points. But I'm not blaming you, understand that. If I were in your position, I'd have to feel exactly the same way you do. See, you *got* to protect all that stuff over there—if I had an office building I was in charge of, with all those files that some demonstratin' undesirable might pour ketchup into, all those elevators and wall safes and adding machines, yessir, I'd feel obliged to protect it too, I'd be worrying about some undesirable maybe dropping a pill into the air-conditioning ducts, too. But that's sort of my point, see. You enter into a contract with the devices and means and procedures of Caesar, then it's caught you, you got no choice, of course you have to act then according to Caesar's ways, Caesar's terms. . . . But those aren't exactly the terms of the gospel, are they?" The official simply peered at Campbell for several seconds, unmoving, and finally Campbell offered, "But it's hard to get, ain't it? It's hard to make it make sense, ain't it? And I can't say I understand it all myself. It's just the way Jesus said to act, that's all I know."

But precisely because of his antistructural approach, Campbell's own ministry tends to elude any hard assessments. It consists, for the most part, of small private incidents, haphazard and spontaneous—like the phone call he received late one night from an elderly black neighbor who asked Campbell to meet him as soon as possible out on a nearby dirt road. Campbell drove slowly along the road until his headlights found the man standing beside a ditch—and once in the car, the man simply began weeping. He told Campbell then that he had discovered a few hours before that his unmarried daughter, whom he'd sent off to college, had just borne a child. Campbell, chatting with him quietly, drove him on into a stately white neighborhood close by, and as they rode through the empty streets of lordly suburban manors towering silent and black-windowed at that late hour, Campbell began telling him, "Now those folks over there, Claude, they sent their daughter out West somewhere, and she left the baby in a home out there after it was born. . . . And in that big brick house up there, what they did was find themselves a doctor who performed an abortion for them, they took care of it that way. . . ." At last the man said, "I couldn't of ever done anything like that. But I just don't know what to do now, Will." Turning to drive his black neighbor back to his place, Campbell said,

"Hell, you already know what you gonna do, Claude. You gonna love your daughter, and go to her up there in that hospital where she's lying now and tell her just that—that you love her—and you're gonna comfort her. And then you gonna bring that baby back home. You gonna love your grandchild, and raise it up in the home of its own people."

Now and then, Campbell is called upon to perform more formal ministerial offices, like the funeral he conducted for a young mother who had died suddenly of an unsuspected disease: "Toward the close of that service, I felt moved for some reason to ask all those there who felt like it to just stand for a minute, in honor of who Jenny had been and all she had meant while she was among us, and to applaud whatever memories they had of her—for this life now ended that she had spent among us. I really wasn't too sure how they might take this—but they began standing up all over that auditorium, first her friends and then her family and then her husband, getting to their feet and starting to applaud louder and louder, a standing ovation that went on and on, looking at that casket with tears coming in their eyes and still clapping on and on. . . ."

In the end, Campbell seems simply to act out of some incapacity to detach himself from the pain or despair of anyone touching on his own life. One winter morning, a friend phoned to inform him that the Nashville Housing Authority had dispatched convicts to eject indigent black tenants, who had lapsed in their rent, from the wooden shanties the authority had purchased from them for a new expressway's right-of-way —that, in fact, two aged women and an old man were already, at that moment, standing out on the sidewalk amid the tumble of their belongings. Shortly thereafter, Campbell came flurrying through the office door of the authority director, his black Shaker hat clamped on his head, and while the director gaped at him, Campbell—his plain face glowing red as a pimiento pepper and light winking flatly off his glasses—recited the news he had just received, and then proceeded to pronounce, from a passage in Matthew, in a voice like a bleating pump organ, "Woe unto you, feller. The scribes and the Pharisees bind heavy burdens and lay them on men's shoulders, and will not move them with one little finger. Woe unto you, for ye devour widows' houses. *Woe!* unto you, for on that day—listen to me, feller, this ain't me talking, it's the Lord God Almighty talking"—the director had started to rise from his chair, but sank back down—"for on that day, the Lord God shall set the sheep on his right and the goats on his left, and he shall say to those on his left, 'I was hungry and you gave me no meat, thirsty and you gave me no drink, a stranger and you took me not in, naked and you clothed me not—in fact, you, feller, you threw me out of my pore little house on that cold winter morning back there in Nashville—so depart from me, you accursed, into the everlasting fire prepared for the devil and his angels'—" At this point, the Housing Authority director interrupted in a thin voice, "Stop. Please . . ." A balding middle-aged podgy man sitting behind a metal desk in his dowdy office, he swallowed. "Just please stop. Don't preach to me anymore. If you can do anything at all about that rent I have to collect, I'll help move them all back in myself. When do you want me down there?"

Made up of such extemporaneous moments, then, Campbell's ministry has largely been beyond capturing by flashbulbs and television screens, the registers of pop significance. But Campbell also cultivates this anonymity for its own sake, out of a suspicion that, like other commando clerics caught in the white blaze of the media reality, he might find himself soon appropriated into all the gallimaufry of pop relevance and isolated from his own first purposes. "More guys than one," he ruminates, "have stopped serving and all of a sudden gone to performing without ever realizing it's happened to them." Nevertheless, cults are always struggling to collect around Campbell, and their enthusiasms fill him with foreboding. "If I ever look around and find a bunch of folks following me, I'll fall to pieces. What I'm doing is just my interpretation of the Christian faith, and anybody following me is following a secondhand situation, which means they in a thirdhand situation. I don't want that responsibility. Anyway, there's hardly anything dramatic or messianic about just holding a man's hand whose brother has died, or singing a few songs to a fellow who's about to go to jail. But folks keep exaggerating and romanticizing the damn thing. I used to get these college students wanting to come down and do what I'm doing, and finally I got up a trick question—I'd say, 'You kind of want to be our *disciple*, is that right?' And they would say, 'Yeah, yeah, that's right. That's what I want to be.' Then I'd say, 'Well, that's too bad. I'm having a hard enough time as it is just trying to be a good disciple myself. The last thing I need is any disciples of my own. I'd be terrified of 'em.' "

Campbell, though, is sometimes oppressed by the consideration that "in all these years, I can't really point out one thing I've actually, substantively accomplished." Of course, that would largely be because he is operating almost exclusively beyond the statistical measurements of agencies or bureaucracies, on that interior front of the individual human heart— which, Campbell would maintain, is the only real and lasting one anyway. But it also makes any sequence of effect between his work and its results impossible to trace: rather, those effects would only brim forth back into life seemingly sourceless, like artesian wells. "Anyway, you really can't get concerned about what actual difference you're making in society. That's not for you to ask. All you know is just how you're supposed to be." Asked by one Atlanta churchman, "You think you're ever going to save the souls of the Ku Klux Klan?" Campbell replied, "Naw, this business of saving souls sometimes works in peculiar ways. Maybe they'll save my soul. At the least, I can always count on them asking me to play my guitar."

More than anything else, he simply visits with them, sometimes when they are stricken by loss, disaster, death, or just retiring with beers to a circle of aluminum lawn chairs in backyards on summer evenings after supper—quiet moments removed out of those occasional glaring nights of antic ferocity in dewy pastures where they are transmuted for an hour or two into hooded apparitions, all human particularity effaced, listening to an unhuman electronic whinny of fantastical rhetoric coming from the back of a flatbed truck while sparks billow upward across the moon from a flaming cross. Tarrying with them instead in a rocking chair on a screened back porch at twilight, with crickets resuming their myriad timeless chittering in the dark, Campbell will now and then begin casually strumming one of his own self-crafted ballads: *Yeah, that Mississippi madness, be Mississippi magic again. . . . 'Fore we was born we was all kin. . . . When we dead we'll all be kinfolks again. . . .* And one of his listeners will chortle, "Hell, maybe you will, preacher, but I ain't ever gonna be no kin to niggers, dead or alive." But he is abided. And with a nod, a sly smile, he will thrum on, *Hello, brother mother, friend of mine. . . . Ain't seen you in a long, long time. . . . But I know just where you been, 'cause it's all a case of skin. . . . So hello, brother mother, friend of mine. . . .* until someone else whines, "Aw, hell, c'mon, preacher—can't you git on something else?"

Perhaps the most that could be projected from a ministry like Campbell's is that such discipleships—modestly tending, in faithfulness to a universal ethic and concern, to the immediate neighborhood of one's own life—could ramify through multiplying personal impingements on through society. "If what Campbell is saying ever got through to people," the director of the American Civil Liberties Union in Atlanta once acknowledged, "we could close this office and dismantle every other agency in the whole liberal institutional complex." And in an essay speculating about the import of Campbell's simple improvisational gospel witness, historian Herbert Butterfield asserted, "It was by bringing society in general from the lower to the higher level of religious experience that the Church most promoted the cause of civilization itself, and most affected the character of the Western world. Those who preached the gospel for the sake of the gospel, leaving the further consequences of their action to Providence, have always served the world better than they knew."

But, says Campbell, "I can hardly afford to start fantasizing about all of that." For his part, Campbell confides, "Even though you got to proceed as if you can single-handedly solve all the woes that confront you, still you must know that there will be times when all your human efforts will fail, and only your understanding of the tragedy will remain—only your broken heart, and your ability to weep, because you can understand." He continues, then, to move about in an inconspicuous discipleship to his peculiar call—a compulsion arising out of his almost primitively Southern values of life—which, however imponderable its final promise of any effect, he realizes it would be spiritual suicide to deny. And all the toils of his long spiritual journey from the East Fork Baptist Church in Amite County on through Yale and then the Movement to his own ambulatory one-man ministry now, Campbell admits, could come in the end to no more than the benediction contained in the last refrain of one of his ballads: "*O yeah. They gonna love me when I'm dead. They gonna come in from miles around— the old Hartmann Funeral Home in McComb City—stand 'round my coffin all night. And they'll say, 'Ole Will was a good ole boy. He just had some crazy ideas.' . . ."*

Campbell labors on. He has most recently been absorbed in a witness against the reinstitution of the death penalty in America.

Acknowledgments

I READILY ALLOW that most of what I have felt to be my best work has really been a collaboration, somewhat in the way that any play performed is a collaboration between writer, producer, and director. I therefore wish to thank, first of all, the following publications in which the stories and material in this book initially appeared in varyingly amended form: *The New York Review of Books*, the *London Sunday Times*, *The Saturday Evening Post*, *Harper's*, *Mademoiselle*, *Newsweek*, *Life*, *New Times*, and *Esquire*. And I owe a special debt to the following for their contributions of craft and vision, as editors or counselors or both, over the course of doing these stories: Willie Morris and Midge Decter, Berry Stainback and Steve Gelman, Robert Silvers, Lee Eisenberg, and the editors on this volume, John Thornton and Gerald Howard. Of course, there has always been Joe Cumming, my bureau chief years ago at *Newsweek*, by whom I first came to understand the possibilities of a journalism employing the extra eye of the artist, and in whose spirit I suppose I have been working, to better or less effect, ever since.

I must also record my great appreciation, for similar and various other crucial services, to Robert Lescher, Nelson Neiman, Joseph D. C. Wilson III and Maria Stefanis, Larry Ledbetter, Michael and Mary Nations, and, most decidedly, Sterling Lord.